D0138592

JOHN N. PETROFF

CFPIM

HANDBOOK OF MRP II AND JIT

STRATEGIES FOR TOTAL MANUFACTURING CONTROL

PRENTICE HALL
Englewood Cliffs, New Jersey 07632

Prentice-Hall International (UK) Limited, *London*
Prentice-Hall of Australia Pty. Limited, *Sydney*
Prentice-Hall Canada, Inc., *Toronto*
Prentice-Hall Hispanoamericana, S.A., *Mexico*
Prentice-Hall of India Private Limited, *New Delhi*
Prentice-Hall of Japan, Inc., *Tokyo*
Simon & Schuster Asia Pte. Ltd., *Singapore*
Editora Prentice-Hall do Brasil, Ltda., *Rio de Janeiro*

© 1993 *by*

PRENTICE-HALL

Englewood Cliffs, NJ

10 9 8 7 6 5 4 3 2 1

Library of Congress Cataloging-in-Publication Data

Petroff, John N.
    Handbook of MRP II and JIT : strategies for total
manufacturing control / John N. Petroff.
        p.   cm.
    Includes index.
    ISBN 0-13-374158-3
    1. Manufacturing resource planning. 2. Just-in-time-
systems. 3. Production control. I. Title. II. Title:
Handbook of MRP 2 and JIT. III. Title: Handbook of
MRP Two and JIT.
TS176.P435 1993
658.5'03—dc20   93-16364
                                                    CIP

ISBN 0-13-374158-3

PRENTICE HALL
Career & Personal Development
Englewood Cliffs, NJ 07632

Simon & Schuster, A Paramount Communications Company

Printed in the United States of America

To my wife Joan
always encouraging, always helpful, always understanding—
through thick and thin

ABOUT THE AUTHOR

John N. Petroff, CFPIM, is founder and President of Raeker, Petroff & Associates, in Minneapolis, Minnesota, leading consultants in manufacturing and distribution resource planning and control. He has over 30 years of experience in management consulting, manufacturing resource management, data processing management, and distribution management. He has successfully implemented MRP II-based systems for a number of manufacturers in the U.S. and abroad. He has consulted on five continents.

An accomplished speaker and seminar leader, Mr. Petroff frequently makes presentations for APICS and other professional societies, at the international, national, regional, and local levels. He also has published a number of articles in professional journals.

An active member of APICS, Mr. Petroff is a Certified Fellow in Production and Inventory Management (CFPIM). He is a past president of the Twin Cities APICS chapter and was a founder of the Arabian Gulf Chapter. He holds a B.S. from the University of Minnesota, and an M.B.A. from New York University. He also holds the Certificate in Data Processing (CDP) and is a Certified Systems Professional (CSP).

WHAT THIS HANDBOOK
WILL DO FOR YOU

We are at the threshold of rejuvenating manufacturing in North America. To compete in today's market, we must manufacture at the world-class level. This book shows you how to do this with an MRP II/JIT-supported system.

A modern manufacturing system is not just a factory system. It is an integrated business system that touches almost all of your company's departments. You must achieve a high level of performance company-wide to be successful in the world market of today. Although this book is not a technical data processing or inventory control book, it will help you progress to a level of integrated excellence.

A formal, MRP II/JIT-based business system is likely to be the only major computerized business system in your company that has an impact on your entire enterprise. All of your other computerized systems distinctly follow departmental lines. Your company probably has an accounts payable system, a payroll system, a sales analysis system, a customer order processing system, and so on. All of these systems belong to one department. This is not so for formal manufacturing systems. Out of necessity, they cut across all departments from engineering, to sales, to accounting, to purchasing, to manufacturing, to personnel. A good business system is an integrating force.

This *handbook* recognizes that your MRP II/JIT-based system must be company-wide, and that the business management aspect is the real challenge in using them to their best advantage.

In the age of commercial software, you no longer need to waste precious time and energy designing and writing computer programs. Very good systems are available for just about every size of company, on just about any size or brand of computer, and using just about any operating system. In addition, commercial software is steadily getting better and more cost effective. At the small end, if your office is in more than one room, you already are big enough to afford an MRP II/JIT system and commercial software to support it. At the other end of the scale, there is no maximum size. If you have a computer with enough disk space, there is commercial software capable to handle your largest plant.

There are two main purposes for the *Handbook of MRP II and JIT*. First, this handbook helps leaders at all levels of your manufacturing company get the most out of their existing MRP II/JIT-based systems. Manufacturing is a complex activity, and the planning and control systems are also complex. These systems have been around in one form or another for about two decades. They have a reputation of not fulfilling their original promises for effectiveness and profitability. This handbook will help you understand why, and what you should do to get the most out of your system; to make it perform at its peak potential.

Second, this handbook helps companies who are thinking of implementing a modern MRP II/JIT system either from scratch or converting from an old, worn-out one.

This handbook offers many tips, techniques, and cautions on a wide range of business and technical issues, to help you understand the development, implementation, and profitable operation of your formal, company-wide, MRP II/JIT-based business system.

WHAT THIS HANDBOOK OFFERS

The *Handbook of MRP II and JIT* is organized to cover the main functional activities in a modern manufacturing company, as well as some of the more important tools and techniques that can lead to and support your success.

Chapter 1 gives you an overview of some of the main determinants of success in the global manufacturing arena—broad-based and integrated business systems, and a well-balanced management team bent on optimizing your company's total operation, not just that of one or another favored department.

Chapter 2 shows you how to manage customer orders with your formal business system; and how to integrate your company's strategic plan, marketing plan, financial plan, and sales plan into your manufacturing planning systems. It shows you five different ways to consume your forecast, and helps you decide which apply best to your product lines. This chapter also covers distribution requirements planning which is useful for your make-to-stock products.

Your company may need to support your customers with service parts. This aspect of the business is important both for profitability and for your reputation. If one of your machines is out of commission in your customer's factory, you need to help get it back into operation as fast as possible.

Chapter 3 building on the concepts of Chapter 2, shows you how to integrate your plans for purchasing and for production to satisfy your demands. This is known as supply planning. This chapter will show you all the main methods for planning supplies including older methods such as reorder point and safety stock, and the newer MRP II/JIT-based techniques of production planning, master scheduling, capacity planning, material requirements planning, and shop floor controls. This chapter also shows you several practical techniques for drastically reducing factory throughput time.

Chapter 4 brings you the accounting connection. Your manufacturing activity is very broad, and your accounting requirements must be firmly supported. This chapter shows you in detail how best to record and monitor the important activities of manufacturing within the accounting system. Some of the details covered include receiving, inventory ins and outs, work-in-process, accounts payable, and sales orders.

This chapter also provides you with extensive coverage of standard cost systems, with an emphasis on emerging techniques such as Activity-Based Costing (ABC) and new-age accounting methods and principles.

Chapter 5 helps you master the seven basic disciplines of manufacturing. These include master scheduling, item numbering ideals, the item masterfile, your bills of material, managing engineering change control, defining your work centers, and process and routings. You must have these basics under good control for your modern system to work well, and the details given here will show you how.

Chapter 6 shows you how to plan to implement a formal manufacturing system. This includes starting from scratch as well as upgrading of a worn out, old system. Implementing a world-class, MRP II/JIT-based business system in a manufacturing company is difficult and arduous. This chapter shows you how to organize a steering committee and a project team, as well as how to mobilize the entire company through a good project organization, wide involvement, education, and training.

Chapter 7 gives you details on how to execute a sound implementation. One of the major tools covered is how to develop and use a detailed time-phased implementation plan. If you don't plan it, you won't do it. This chapter also gives you details on how to find and select good commercial software.

It is widely acknowledged that education and training are key determinants in the success of a modern, formal business system. This chapter tells you how to fulfill this very important threshold requirement.

Chapter 8 tells you how to make your master schedule work. In a modern, MRP II/JIT-based system, the master schedule is the main driving force for all of your planning and execution activities. This chapter shows you how to take full advantage of the power of a good master scheduling system. Some of the important topics explained are capacity planning, the use of time fences, and the role of the master scheduler in the success of your planning activity.

Chapter 9 gives you many details on how to minimize inventory and still assure good coverage for components in the factory, for finished goods for your customers, and for service parts in the field. You will learn how to create a superior system that will actually improve inventory coverage while you cut inventories drastically. You will find separate details for purchased, semi-finished, work-in-process, and finished goods inventories. This chapter covers excess and obsolete inventory, and sets forth steps you can take to avoid them. It also gives you techniques for planning and managing stocking locations and shows how to implement a comprehensive cycle counting system. (You need to do cycle counting to eliminate your annual wall-to-wall physical inventory, if you still have one.)

Chapter 10 shows you how to take advantage of group technology, classification coding, and standardization. In this chapter you will learn how to use modern classification coding methods to depict the physical characteristics of your purchased, manufactured, and finished items. You will learn how to use this and other techniques to foster standardization in the design of your components and products.

Group technology, sometimes called continuous flow production, is the opposite of a job shop. Group technology lines up dissimilar machines in a work center to manufacture a family of similar items in a smooth, continuous flow. This chapter shows you how to analyze your factory to see where this concept can be applied, and where the disadvantages and pitfalls lie.

Chapter 11 gives you an extensive, detailed description of most of the Just-in-Time (JIT) ideas, even though many JIT techniques are found throughout the book. These ideas are grouped as they apply to material control, production control, engineering, and administration. You will learn the details of what each concept is and how you can apply each one profitably. This chapter also gives a frank explanation of changes you will need to make in your traditional administrative rules and managerial attitudes to make best use of these excellent ideas. It will also tell you of some common problems with JIT.

Chapter 12 gives you a blueprint for continuous improvement in your business organization. Resistance to change is almost a universal problem, and this chapter gives you a number of ideas for overcoming it.

In order to achieve world-class, you need world class performance measurements. This chapter tells you how to evaluate and select the right mix, and how to implement them into your environment. You also will learn how to identify and eliminate any of your current measurements that would be a roadblock to improvement and success.

This chapter also explains several techniques for making your quest for constant improvement a steady part of your environment. This will help you avoid the frequent problem of this idea becoming just another fad, to be abandoned a few weeks after the initial project is completed. This chapter also gives you details on how to incorporate the tools of MRP II/JIT into your constant improvement program.

Appendix I shows you how to calculate and use reorder points. Reorder points are used mainly for items not incorporated in your MRP II system, especially those having independent demand such as service parts. This appendix also details the two-bin variation of the reorder point method.

Appendix II gives you details on the major lot sizing rules. You will learn how they work, and how and where each is the most appropriate. You will also learn how to use modifiers, to keep the various rules from running out of bounds. Some lot sizing rules make for nervousness in your system, and here you will learn how to avoid that problem.

Appendix III gives you practical tips on how to use safety stock. Although using safety stock is not a popular technique within a good MRP II system, this technique does continue to have good application in certain areas. This appendix will show you how to identify appropriate applications, and to minimize the expense involved.

Appendix IV gives a detailed explanation of an ABC analysis, also called a Pareto analysis. This technique allows you to separate the important few from the trivial many. Used in an inventory control setting, it identifies your most important items, usually about 20 percent of the total, so you can apply more detailed and extensive planning and control techniques to them.

Appendix V explains many facets of forecasting. It helps you identify what you should forecast, and gives you an introduction to the many forecasting techniques available, so you can select the most appropriate ones. It also describes methods for measuring and monitoring forecast accuracy, and how to take advantage of these analyses.

INTERESTED IN CERTIFICATION?

The American Production and Inventory Control Society (APICS) administers two certification programs—the Certificate in Production and Inventory Management (CPIM) and the Certificate in Integrated Resource Management (CIRM). To the best of my ability I have kept the material in this book compliant with these two programs. The material included here is far broader than the CPIM program, but more closely fits the scope of the CIRM. Anything you learn from this book should get you a correct answer on these certification examinations. Other professional organizations also have certification programs, such as the American Society for Quality Control (ASQC) and the National Association for Purchasing Management (NAPM). I believe that the details in this book also are compliant with their respective bodies of knowledge.

John N. Petroff

ACKNOWLEDGMENTS

Thanks to Richard E. Kust, Lecturer, Department of Management, California State University, Fullerton, CA, for writing Chapter 8—How to Manage with Your Master Schedule.

Thanks to Charles J. Luman, Principal, Raeker, Petroff, & Associates, for writing Appendix V—Forecasting; for providing me with raw material and a critique on the How to Implement Activity-Based Costs section of Chapter 4; and for preparing a number of the graphics included throughout the book.

Table of Figures

TABLE OF CONTENTS

1

KEYS TO ACHIEVING WORLD CLASS MANUFACTURING MANAGEMENT

Manufacturing is becoming exciting again. After over 40 years of neglect, we have come to realize that manufacturing is dynamic, profitable, and a competitive tool. We are implementing some spectacular new ideas and techniques to make us competitive again in the world marketplace. Being able to thrive in the global marketplace is often called being *World Class.* Looking at this performance level from a manufacturing manager's point of view, there are several key elements to achieving and staying world class.

- Stay ahead of your competition.
- Really know what your competition is talking about.
- Implement total management. Being oriented around one department is doomed.
- Ask for what you want and measure it. Send the right signals.

HOW TO STAY AHEAD OF YOUR COMPETITION

The new manufacturing environment is proactive, not reactive. You have a number of tools and techniques in the manufacturing sphere which you can use.

Establishing Good Product Design

Although this may be mainly engineering-focused, manufacturing can give valuable assistance. Modern computer-assisted manufacturing, planning, and control systems are able to react fast. This is especially true in companies with small inventories, and fast throughput. This means that a new or modified design appears in the hands of your customer faster. We have heard of cases where Company A started on a product enhancement sooner than Company B. However, because of their enhanced systems, Company B got to market sooner, and captured a larger market share than they had before.

As you achieve world class excellence, you can make changes and improvements to your product line with speed, efficiency, and low cost. You can turn this into a competitive advantage, instead of having product enhancements be a major inconvenience.

Achieve Excellent Product Quality

The 1980s brought a new understanding of quality. Quality can be considered from two different viewpoints. One viewpoint is that of the customer, or company-external. The other viewpoint is that of employees or company-internal.

The external, customer view of your quality is often difficult to quantify. Your customer probably will be satisfied with your quality if it fulfills their expectation. Does your product do the job? Usually the customer's expectation is not very well documented. Consumer products are especially susceptible to the customer's vagaries of perceptions and expectations.

Looking at quality from the customer's aspect, my favorite definition is:

> Quality is selling a product that does not come back—to a customer who does.

However, most of us who work manufacturing products are too far away from the customer to be able to make changes and adjustments based on customer knowledge. This forces us to have design specifications, drawings, and all the other control and auditing mechanisms that accompany product design. You assume that if you conform to your specs, the resulting product will satisfy the customer. This is true for the most part, but notice that the quality measures that we adhere to in manufacturing are indirect ones. Somebody has interpreted the customer's perceptions of quality for internal use. This puts a great responsibility on those doing the conversion as well as on those who execute the designs.

Another powerful use made of internal-oriented quality activities is that of repeatability. With modern manufacturing and quality control techniques, we can repeat the manufacturing process over and over again, and be sure that all the items are alike.

The 1980s brought quality to the fore to such an extent that everyone expects your products to be flawless, and that of your competitors as well. This has converted quality from a competitive edge to a threshold requirement for most manufacturers.

Achieve Excellent Customer Service Quality

Unlike flawless product quality, which has become a survival issue, quality of service has not yet arrived. In this setting, service means order processing, shipping, invoicing, scheduling, tracing, and the hundreds of contacts and services you provide your customers. Automated telephone switchboards are a good example. Nobody I talk to thinks they represent excellent service, yet it seems that most companies of any size have one. They may be cheap, but they are not appreciated.

One supplier of desktop computers revamped their switchboard on their customer hotline. They discontinued the system that had the recordings and caller selections. Instead they have a competent technician answer the call directly in less than three rings. This is a competitive edge for them.

You can stay ahead of your competition by analyzing all possible customer contacts from the customer's viewpoint. I don't acknowledge the standard excuse of cost, at least until the cost has really been analyzed. In many cases, degraded service comes from batching incoming material, or by having a queue at clerical work places. Neither of those techniques reduce cost. It takes just as much time to process a customer's order whether it just came in this minute, or if it has been in your in-basket for a week. When analyzing work flows, be sure to understand that large batches and several days of queue do not improve efficiency.

Actually, they decrease efficiency. When you have any amount of delay, you will insist on a tracking system. When a customer calls to find out where his order is, you will want a method to find it. This adds cost while actually degrading your service. If you process the order the minute it is received, your acknowledgment will be on the way back to the customer before they think of tracing it.

Schedule Short Lead Times

In the factory we have made good progress in reducing lead times. These same techniques will work in administrative areas as well. This is part of good customer service. Short lead times become a better competitive tool as the idea is spread to activities that precede and succeed manufacturing. This idea is now emerging as the new competitive differentiator, and is called *Time Compression*. (Time Compression is covered more extensively in Chapter 11.)

Offer Fast Response

Combining good customer service and short lead times is part of fast response. The other aspect of fast response has to do with processing non-clerical jobs. A request for a special configuration of a standard product is a good example of this. In some companies, a configure-to-order goes into the main engineering department, and takes its turn getting the attention of an engineer to process it. Days or even weeks go by before the customer gets a response. This same response delay could apply to a totally new design. Another example might involve an inquiry about a spare part you don't usually stock.

Know Your Products' Costs

Cost Accounting is covered extensively in Chapter 12. But as a competitive topic, it is very important. A good MRP II-based system has two very good features regarding product cost. Your bill of material will deliver a very accurate material content for everything you make. Your route sheets will supply an equally accurate total for direct labor for everything you make. Purchased items are easily costed, except for overhead.

After computing material and labor, the last task is to allocate overhead. Many companies still do this as a percentage of direct labor. This is where the problem lies, because direct labor is no longer an adequate vehicle to use. Many companies find that products that the cost accounting system says are profitable are really losing money, while those that look unprofitable really are making a good profit.

You need accurate product costs in order to make corporate profit plans and to plot pricing strategy. Especially if you are in a competitive situation giving you price pressure, knowing your products' costs can become a survival issue. Knowing your costs will allow you to be price competitive where you have earned this ability, such as with MRP II and JIT. This knowledge also will help you de-emphasize products that are not delivering the gross margins you want.

If your marketing strategy is to be a "niche seller," knowing your costs is a necessity in helping you choose your niche and pursue it profitably.

Cut Costs Sensibly

Beware of the corporate restructuring mania. It may be tempting to cut out whole groups of white collar employees. But the process usually cuts activities that need to be done.

I know of a software company that had been successfully offering its users a steady stream of upgrades for an annual maintenance fee. One day they decided to merge all the regional groups who were administering this activity to their central headquarters. They made no elaborate conversion plans, resorting to an arbitrary cut-over date when the regional clerks were simply terminated. As a result, a number of contracts were lost, billings were missed, and the customers were furious.

Cutting costs sensibly means you should analyze what you are doing and why. You may find there are a variety of redundant, duplicate, and unnecessary jobs being done in your various offices. These should be trimmed, without regard for vested interests, organizational disputes, or empire building. However, be very cautious of large scale terminations. It may be better to allow the reductions to come from transfers and attrition. You will damage cooperation in implementing a cost-reduction program if it becomes a harbinger of terminations.

REALLY KNOW WHAT YOUR COMPETITION IS TALKING ABOUT

This seems almost like a truism. However, in our consulting practice we run across managers who have heard the buzz word at the country club or at a motivational seminar, and immediately vow to have one themselves. We often find managers who think you can buy JIT from your software vendor. They want to plug it in and play it just like a videotape.

World class companies know what these techniques are, and use them or ignore them according to their situation. This is based on a true understanding of what is involved. Some of the modern techniques we have seen lately are large and integrated, others can be applied selectively where useful.

In a manufacturing setting, some of the recent buzz word topics are:

- MRP, both I and II
- JIT
- CIM
- TQC
- SPC

- Self-Directed Work Groups
- Focused Factories
- Baldrige
- ISO 9000 ✓
- Time Compression

Defining Material Requirements Planning (MRP, I), and Manufacturing Resource Planning (MRPII)

MRP I means Material Requirements Planning, and is where the revolution started. Before MRP I, the main method of planning and scheduling the factory and purchasing was reorder point and safety stock for inventory items, and launch and expedite in the factory.

Reorder point and safety stock uses a minimum inventory balance as a trigger point for the next order. The reorder point is its average demand divided by lead time. In order to account for various kinds of upsets, you use a safety stock.

The launch and expedite method causes shop orders and purchase orders to be launched to their respective targets as soon as possible. Thereafter the orders are expedited according to the vagaries of customer orders and safety stock running out.

These early methods were based on looking back into history. MRP I is entirely different. It looks forward. The Master Production Schedule provides this look into the future. This is where your end items are scheduled. MRP I looks at your bills of material, on hand and on order balances, leadtimes, and lot sizes and plans orders into the future. When things work right, purchased and manufactured items arrive on schedule.

MRP II means Manufacturing Resource Planning. It takes MRP I and expands on it to cover the details of the manufacturing process, notably scheduling the shop floor. Related accounting activities also are integrated.

MRP II, when used properly, gives you good schedules and performance against them, notably end items going to your customers.

MRP II really shines whenever you have more complexity than you can carry around in your head or on the back of an envelope.

Describing Just-in-Time (JIT)

Unlike MRP II, JIT is not a closed-loop system. But when added to MRP II, JIT is certainly a tool to achieve world class. The main attraction of JIT is that it emphasizes excellent performance. MRP emphasizes excellent planning and scheduling.

Because JIT is not a closed-loop system, it does not have a great deal of internal interdependency. This means that largely you can pick and choose the techniques that are most important to you at the time.

MRP and JIT are the main themes of this book.

Describing Computer Integrated Manufacturing (CIM)

In order to understand this concept we should start by defining integrated. *Integrated* is a computer term that means that all related systems share one data base. When a piece of data is needed the program just goes to the spot where it's located and gets it. This means that all programs must include code that does this.

Next you should consider what are being integrated. The usual cycle is to integrate the following activities:

- Design Engineering
- Manufacturing and Industrial Engineering
- MRP II
- Purchasing
- The Factory's numerically-controlled machines and robots
- Cost Accounting

In most cases equipment such as Computer-Aided-Drafting (CAD) and numerically controlled machines come from different companies. Software products, such as MRP II and CAD also come from different companies. Writing the code to thoroughly integrate different hardware and software from diverse vendors is not really feasible with today's programming techniques.

Interfacing is another computer technique where transfer programs and techniques are inserted between systems. These interfaces allow the programs to share their data, and even to update each other's files, but indirectly. Where true integration is not available, interfacing is. Suppliers are working together to create interface programs to offer jointly to their customers, and there are software houses who supply other good products.

By wise and judicious selection of hardware and software interfaces, you can take advantage of much of what CIM has to offer.

Interfacing, however, has the reputation of being slower than integrated solutions, and uses more computer resources. When you are considering a CIM application, be sure to take response time and resource utilization into full account. This may take some digging, since the suppliers may not volunteer this information.

Establishing Total Quality Control (TQC)

Traditional quality control measures the parts to see if the batch is acceptable. This often is coupled with sorting out the bad parts and reworking them. Or, the batch is rejected, and returned to the supplier, based on an "acceptable quality level" usually a percentage. Zero defects, however, measure defects in parts per million, which means you must abandon the old mode and adopt the new.

The idea of Total Quality Control has been developing over the last 30 years, and was made world-famous by W. Edwards Deming, in his work in Japan and the United States. Deming's approach, now becoming the world class norm, is that you should control your processes and not allow a bad product to be made.

The main tool of Total Quality Control is Statistical Process Control (SPC), as described in the next section. Also many of the ideals of JIT reinforce this concept.

MRP II is a total quality tool, although not usually recognized as such. Basic MRP II logic does not allow for scrap fallout. Both the back scheduling logic and the production activity control schedules assume that the entire batch will be acceptable, on time, and ready for the next need. Modern MRP II-based software have features that allow you to add your own scrap allowances. But this is a deviation from the basic logic. This means that you can use your MRP II-based system to support the total quality control concepts of zero defects, as you get your processes under control.

Using Statistical Process Control (SPC)

SPC is your main method to achieve world class quality. We cover SPC extensively in Chapter 11. The main difference between SPC and traditional quality control, is that SPC helps you make sure that your machinery, equipment, and processes are under control and not manufacturing "un-quality". Some advanced companies are discontinuing the actual use of the control charts. They have proven themselves to be consistently within tolerances, and have installed self-checking devices to monitor tolerances. In this environment you can get defect-free production without the overhead of using the statistical approach.

Establishing Self-Directed Work Groups

The use of self-directed work groups is expanding rapidly. Its concepts are already challenging the conventional "chain of command" organization. Self-directed work groups operate without a supervisor.

Some companies are reporting strong success with this technique, which is a natural extension of the movement to empower workers. There are reports of dramatic increase in productivity, while quality problems disappear. The self-directed team's success comes from knowing intimately what needs to be done and having the authority to do it. These successes are making this new concept into another tool for achieving world class performance.

Using this approach can allow you to have fewer levels in your organization chart, which brings many advantages in communication and cost saving.

However, you cannot just proclaim that you will have self-directed work groups and start right in. You first must develop the company's supervisory culture to accept this radical approach. Next you must form the teams carefully, train them, and coach them through the initial stages, where the group starts out as a collection of individuals. Then you move through development stages as a real, working team.

The Quality Circle idea is a form of self-directed work group that has earned a bad reputation in the United States, mainly because they were not instituted properly. This lesson underscores the requirement for proper implementation.

Defining Focused Factories

A focused factory is a smallish one, usually under 1,000 people.

The focus is on a specific product or product line. The world class advantage is that by using a focused factory you become skilled at doing all the aspects of running a manufacturing company. The focused factory is a natural extension of Group Technology process flow factory layout.

To be a world class company means that you must do all of your business functions at the world class level. The focused factory is a very good world class tool.

The focused factory is covered in more detail in Chapter 11.

Applying for a Baldrige Award

The Malcolm Baldrige National Quality award has become very prestigious. While he was U.S. Secretary of Commerce, Mr. Baldrige and many others, became alarmed that the world-wide prominence of U.S. Manufacturing was eroding rapidly. Research by Department of Commerce and Congressional investigators concluded that much of the fault was with deteriorating quality of U.S.-manufactured products, or at least that perception by consumers.

To combat this slide, Congress commissioned the Malcolm Baldrige National Quality Award to give an incentive to manufacturers to achieve world class quality in all their efforts. Three awards are given each year to:

- Manufacturing Companies

- Service Companies

- Small Businesses

Two awards can be given in each category, and the winners agree to share information to help others achieve the same high quality.

The award is broken down into several categories, and a company earns points in each one. Figure 1.1 shows the categories and the 1991 and 1992 weights given to each and the average points earned by the winners of the 1991 award.

Figure 1.1 Average Scores of Past Winners of the Malcolm Baldrige National Quality Award

Category	Possible Points, 1991	Possible Points, 1992	Average for Winners
Leadership	100	100	80
Information and Analysis	70	60	45
Strategic Quality	60	90	65
Human Resource Utilization	150	150	115
Quality Assurance of Products and Services	140	150	125
Quality Results	180	150	140
Customer Satisfaction	300	300	250
Total	1000	1000	820

There are some fees involved, and only six awards can be given each year.

The great merit in this program, however, is not so much in getting this outstanding award. You can benefit from this program by using it as a diagnostic tool to help you identify places in your company where you are deficient. Following an analysis, you can concentrate on a few areas where you need the most improvement.

The award program also can help you set world class standards for yourself—standards that you can compare with other companies both in your industry and in general. (For further information, contact the U.S. Department of Commerce, Technology Administration, National Institute of Standards and Technology, Route 270 and Quince Orchard Road, Administration Building, Room A537, Gaithersburg, MD 20899.)

Meeting Requirements of the International Standards Organization (ISO 9000)

The International Standards Organization is primarily a European Common Market organization. They set some quality standards in 1987 that they consider necessary to make their common market work. ANSI (the American National Standards Institute) and ASQC (the American Society for Quality Control) are helping promulgate these standards in the United States. (For further information, contact the American National Standards Institute, 11 West 42 Street, New York, NY 10036.)

If you want to sell your products into the European Community, you should have ISO 9000 certification. You could still sell without certification, but your sales efforts will be severely hampered.

The standards are divided into four sections:

- ISO 9001. For use when the supplier assures the customer that they are conforming to certain standards that could include design and development, production, installation, and service.

- ISO 9002. For use when the supplier assures the customer that they are conforming to standards regarding production and installation.

- ISO 9003. For use when the supplier assures the customer that they have done a final inspection and test only.

- ISO 9004. Used by manufacturers to achieve a quality system.

There is a structured procedure to become certified, which includes an application, on-site assessment, development, and certification. The final certification is done by ISO-approved evaluators.

Using Time Compression

Many consultants and writers have identified time compression as the new competitive tool for the 1990s. Part of being world class is to constantly be improving. Time compression seems to be emerging strongly as one of those new ideas for incremental improvement that will help you maintain world class performance.

Time compression may very well be one of the important vehicles to carry U.S. manufacturers high up into the ranks of world class competitors.

Time compression takes some of the JIT ideas from the factory and applies them to administrative chores. The object will be to perform administrative tasks with a minimum of delays as they pass from hand to hand, from department to department. Time compression starts with analyzing and streamlining, and progresses to Tiger Teams who meet regularly to dispose instantly the processing now done in different departments. Finally, some see that the current top-down organization chart will be replaced by a horizontal, process-oriented organization. (This subject is covered more completely in Chapter 11.)

HOW TO IMPLEMENT TOTAL MANAGEMENT: BEING ORIENTED AROUND ONE DEPARTMENT IS DOOMED

The ideals of TQC must be applied to management in general.

In January, 1992, President Bush led a trade mission to Japan. In the aftermath, Yoshio Sakurauchi, Speaker of Parliament, accused American workers of being lazy. Naturally there was a big hue and cry on both sides of the Pacific, and Foreign Minister Michio Watanabe eventually apologized.

A couple of days later, Akio Morita and Shinaro Ishihara, the authors of an extensive white paper called *The Japan That Can Say "No"* said the problem is not with American workers who are as hard working and productive as anyone. The problem, they said, was with American management.

These authors went on to focus on the well-publicized fixation of American managers on quarterly profits. These, and other real and imaginary criticisms are well known.

But there is one managerial weakness that largely is being ignored. This problem is what I call "Johnny One Note" management. When we visit clients we frequently hear excuses for not being able to implement new ideas and systems. One popular excuse is that the company is being run by one or another function, or that the CEO is a graduate of that function. Have you heard such comments as, "We're marketing oriented"? Or, "Accounting runs this place"? Or, "We're an engineering company"? That's "Johnny One Note" management.

It may have been possible to run a manufacturing company in the past by favoring one or another. But this is not a world class condition. Top management must run the company to achieve teamwork among all departments and every individual. Every functional department must be blended and balanced; encouraged to contribute their best work and their best ideas. Perhaps this is another manifestation of worker empowerment.

You can easily survey your employees to find out if you have fallen into this trap. Curing the syndrome is fairly easy. A good JIT-modified, Class-A MRP II system goes a long way in achieving this teamwork because it is inherently a company-wide planning and control system.

HOW TO ASK FOR WHAT YOU WANT AND MEASURE IT—SEND THE RIGHT SIGNALS

Many people say that you get what you measure. I believe this and add another. You get what gets people their raises. What gets people their raises may be casual "attaboys" from their boss, or a very formal monthly performance rating incorporated in your salary administration system. Performance at all levels is measured by different departments. Accounting is preoccupied with budgets and variances. We traditionally have concentrated on monitoring direct labor in manufacturing.

The world class company has world class goals. These start with strategic goals, as we will cover in Chapter 2. Most other goals derive from those goals, and in Chapter 12 we will cover world class performance measures extensively.

In relation to achieving world class, measurements must support your new performance in the factory as well as in the white collar areas as you embrace Time Compression.

Many JIT concepts lend themselves to objective measurement. JIT also stresses group or team achievements, and less individual performance. Some companies award bonuses to teams instead of individuals.

One of the most important, and often overlooked requirements of a world class measurement system is to discontinue the ones that are contrary to our new ideals. In the factory, setup variance, machine utilization, and labor utilization are three common measures that go counter to JIT.

Without shutting off the wrong measures, you will send mixed and perhaps wrong signals to your employees, suppliers, and customers.

After you have recognized your demands, and made manufacturing plans to satisfy them, the difficult part starts. If we lived in a perfect world, there would be no problem in executing manufacturing plans. However, things are never perfect in the manufacturing world. You are lucky if there are no upsets or changes in today's schedule by the end of the day. Companies who try to freeze schedules for weeks or months ahead know that it cannot be done in our dynamic world. And marketplace demands are pressuring us to become even more dynamic.

HOW TO MANUFACTURE YOUR MASTER PRODUCTION SCHEDULE—EVERY DAY

In an MRP II/JIT-based system, one vital key to success is adherence to your Master Production Schedule. No matter how much you improve them, your leadtimes are always too long, and your time fences are too far out. You have upsets in the factory and so do your suppliers. Many factors contribute to the difficulty of staying on schedule in the factory.

However, no matter how difficult it may be, you must stick to your Master Production Schedule, or all of the schedules derived from it become unreliable, unstable, and unusable. Then expediting reappears as the real execution tool. By nature, expediting is uncoordinated, which causes you to miss more of your promises to your customers. This also causes you to have excessive inventories, while at the same time you experience an alarming amount of shortages and stockouts.

Here are a few simple tools to help you manage the execution of your Master Production Schedule.

Closing the Loop with Progress Reports

In an MRP II/JIT-based system, you have a great deal of computerized data available which can be made into management reports. Your management should have a few key reports to show how well you are executing your production plans.

Measuring Customer Order Fulfillment

Next to quality this is your most important performance measure. This includes warehouse replenishment orders if you make them to stock. There are two ways to measure customer order fulfillment—by order or by line item.

By order is the more stringent. In this case, if you cannot ship the entire order complete, your customer doesn't want any of it. This situation occurs if your customer needs everything to start one of their orders. If they don't have everything, their manufacturing order won't get started, so the items that are available would be excess until the shortage is corrected.

Other customers, however, do not have interdependent line items, and could be willing to take an occasional back order.

To measure your fulfillment performance you must base it either on the whole order or line items. Current standards call for customer service in the high 90s percent performance.

Measuring Final Assembly Scheduling Performance

Some companies are fortunate and can do final assembly from modules after receiving the customer order. This is an excellent way to keep inventories down, while offering custom-tailored end items. In this environment, lead times are often hours or days. Some companies promise next day shipment from final assembly, down from the weeks or months required when starting from scratch.

With such a short horizon, fewer things can go wrong, and you should be able to hit your Final Assembly Schedule in the high 90s.

Measuring Master Production Scheduling Performance

The Master Production Schedule "drives" the whole rest of your MRP II/JIT-based system. It causes all of the other schedules.

Most modern systems have daily-oriented schedules, with some advanced users beginning to explore finer scheduling by shift or even hour. For most companies, the Master Production Schedule is a daily one, often summarized into weekly columns on displays and reports.

This means that for your MRP II/JIT-based system to work at all well, you must complete your master schedule every day, not every week or every month. In order to keep your promises to your customers without expensive inventory buffers, you must adhere to your daily master schedule.

Scheduling Shop Order Completions

You must complete your shop orders for sub-assemblies and piece-parts on schedule in order to support your master schedule and final assembly schedule, especially in a job-shop with several levels in the bill of material and the related serpentine routings.

However, since these items frequently have a lot size that exceeds the next day's needs, you will often be producing for inventory. This makes it less critical to hit each day's schedule. However, as you take levels out of your bills, reduce lot sizes, and reduce queues, completing your shop orders on time becomes more and more important.

For this measure, you may not be able to identify a specific target. But in every case, you should insist on steady improvement. Start a base line early, and graph your performance.

Monitoring Production Rates

The process and repetitive environment often is not shop-order oriented. Process and repetitive production often is based on rates of production per hour, shift, or day. In this situation you would measure your output by production line in terms of actual production compared to planned production. Some companies watch their aggregate totals produced each hour as the day progresses.

It is easier to stay on schedule in process production than in a job shop. But because process production is usually capital-intensive, it remains important to monitor performance against schedule.

Evaluating Supplier Delivery Performance

Although it is appealing to rate suppliers against your due dates, this is not a good measurement until you achieve a stable schedule. In traditional companies, the best suppliers are responding to expediting phone calls, and original order due dates are ignored until all the expediting has been satisfied. But as soon as you have reliable, stable schedules with your suppliers, and especially as suppliers reduce their lead times, purchase order or release due dates do become a good basis for performance measuring.

In a very fast, JIT situation, where suppliers make daily or even hourly deliveries, measuring their daily performance becomes both possible and important.

As you approach JIT performance in your factory, you will not be able to tolerate much variation from your scheduled receipts.

HOW TO USE EXCEPTION REPORTS TO STAY ON SCHEDULE

An MRP II/JIT-based system usually has quite a variety of exception reports associated with it. Here are a few selected ones that focus on performance against schedule.

Monitoring Pick List Shortages

Modern systems, particularly those with a shop-order orientation, usually provide a pick list (material requisition) for each order. The pick list shows all of the components needed for the shop order. The extended quantity required for each component is shown, and often their locations. The pick list also shows the deliver-to work center and a pick completion date. If you have items that are in floor stock with automatic issue, they are tagged in some way so that the stock picker will ignore them.

In order to be able to complete shop orders on time, you must start them on time. And it is a good rule not to start shop orders short of parts. You can get a good measure on the execution performance of your system by monitoring how many pick lists can't be completed as scheduled. Your percentage performance should be about the same as shop order completions, and should be graphed in order to highlight the trend.

Because one of the main objectives of your MRP II/JIT-based system is to have components available to start shop orders on time, pick list shortages are a good gauge on how your system is performing.

Handling Capacity Overloads

One of the characteristics of an MRP II-based system, is that it loads against infinite capacity. You do resource planning and rough-cut capacity planning early in the planning cycle to make sure that enough capacity will be available when you execute your schedule. This means that the detailed, daily capacity requirements plan should only be needed for fine tuning, and should have few if any unreconcilable overloads.

At the detailed capacity requirements level, any unmanageable overload indicates a deficiency in planning and will impede execution. These can point to a pattern of problems that need to be investigated and eliminated.

The rule is that when the production planner and the work center supervisor can't resolve a capacity shortage, they must inform the master scheduler so he/she can alter the master schedule. The new master schedule in turn causes re-scheduling of related, dependent schedules.

These emergency changes to the master schedule should be made into a management report. The Master Production Schedule is crucial to the success of your system, and this means that having problems with the MPS is a management issue.

Using Reject and Rework Reports

MRP II-based systems assume flawless quality when computing dependent needs. This means that rejects and reworks can easily cause a delay in your schedules. As you move to the JIT ideals of low buffers and queues, these disturbances will be harder to take in stride. Depending on the nature of your manufacturing operation, you should develop some simple, appropriate reports to be used in monitoring rejects and reworks, focusing on how they affect master schedule fulfillment.

Regarding scrap and rework, you should be watching supplier performance as well as that of manufacturing.

Monitoring Exception Messages

Modern MRP II-based systems give the planners both action messages and exception messages. Exception messages always indicate that something is wrong. You should ask your information services department to develop a simple report to be used in monitoring the number of exception messages that relate to the execution of schedules. You can use these reports to help you point to the causes of execution problems so you can take steps to eradicate them.

SIX STEPS TO MAKE YOUR SYSTEM PERMANENT

More than one MRP II-based system has degraded after implementation. Your project team and your upper management must make sure that the new system takes hold, and the old system is discontinued. In addition, since your company probably is in a dynamic environment, your new system will need to be enhanced and improved steadily. There is no going back to the old days.

There are six steps to take to ensure that your system will be permanent. They are described in the following paragraphs:

1. Make Sure Management Participates

One of the key success elements in running a modern system is management's use. You should make sure that management at all levels use the system to its fullest advantage. This also means that everyone respects the rules and nobody is permitted to abuse them. Especially this means respecting the Master Production Schedule.

2. Publish Written Organization Charts, Written Policies, and Written Procedures

Your implementation probably will include some organization changes. Publishing them will cement them into your organization, and help publicize your new system. Written policies and procedures are needed to assure consistency throughout the company and repeatability over time.

3. Conduct Adequate Education and Training at All Levels

Copious education and training is needed to make sure that everyone feels comfortable with the new procedures and can use them to perform their jobs. Without a high level of comfort, they easily could revert to informal, manual methods which would impede or defeat your new system.

4. Establish and Promulgate New Goals

We covered goals earlier in this chapter. It is important to start using them with the advent of your new system, and to discontinue the counter-productive ones.

5. Shut Off the Old Systems

If your old systems are computer-based, it will be easy to shut them off—just stop using them. Manual systems, however are harder to extinguish. It still is necessary,

6. Use the System

Everyone now should be using the new system to help run their jobs. The more you use your new system the better it gets. Don't let budget pressures seduce you into corner-cutting in the essential areas such as bill of material maintenance, cycle counting, or the Master Production Schedule.

2

HOW TO PLAN
THE RIGHT THINGS
BY MANAGING
YOUR DEMANDS

A *demand* takes inventory away. A *supply* brings inventory in. When you are discussing the strategic aspect of planning, end items and perhaps service parts are involved. These are demands for product to sell to customers.

Within the company, you have demands for components and assemblies to support manufacturing. These are lower-level demands which must be planned to support manufacturing requirements.

Supplies are manufacturing and purchase orders needed to cover your various demands, no matter from what source, no matter at what level of the bill of material.

Planning supplies precisely and accurately to cover your demands is the trick. And MRP II/JIT has emerged as the best way so far to do this planning. Think of it as synchronization.

In this chapter we will discuss planning end items at several levels of detail.

You need to plan and manage your demands as every manufacturing company does. Manufacturing is a very complex activity and does not just happen. The better your demand planning

is the more efficient and effective your factory becomes in satisfying your demands.

I know an East Coast manufacturer who doesn't do this at
all. Their headquarters building is in Atlanta, and their factory
is in Massachusetts. They are a subsidiary of an Austrian company. Not only do they not have a planning system in place,
they don't even know one another. As a result, the production
control and manufacturing engineering departments at the factory location try to guess what's coming in the next year or so,
and try to take some actions to accommodate their guesses.

They try hard and do a surprisingly good job of containing
the chaos that constant surprises cause. But they are always
behind, always expediting. They are hard-pressed to provide any
kind of good customer service. And they are paying a heavy
price in excess inventories and excess capacities.

As a former colleague of mine always said, "if you can't plan
it, you can't do it".

In this chapter we will cover:

■ Strategic Product Planning

■ Marketing Planning

■ Sales Planning

Figure 2.1 shows the relation between these activities. The
strategic plan is passed on to the manufacturing planning activity. The manufacturing plan has more detail, but adds up to
fulfill the strategic plan. When completed and approved, it in
turn is passed downward for more detailed planning.

The manufacturing plan in turn is given to the sales planning
function for more detailed demand planning.

The strategic, marketing, and sales plans all are used by
those preparing the production plan. The production plan is
your first stage in planning your supplies. This is the topic of
Chapter 3.

GETTING STARTED WITH
A STRATEGIC PRODUCT PLAN

Strategic product planning is a subset of your company's
comprehensive strategic plan.

Figure 2.1 End-Item Demand Planning Cycle

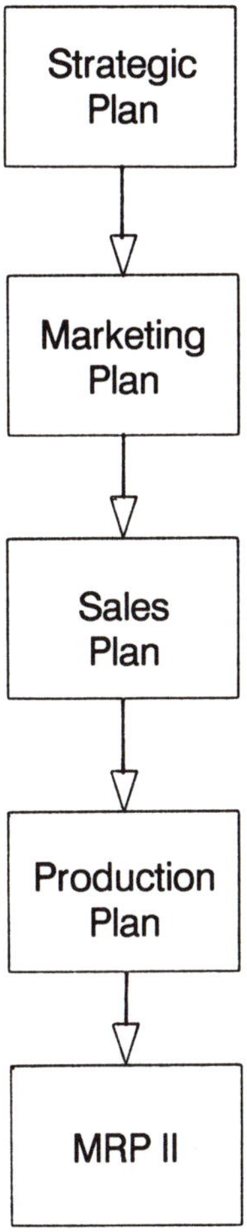

```
        ┌─────────────┐
        │  Strategic  │
        │    Plan     │
        └──────┬──────┘
               ▽
        ┌─────────────┐
        │  Marketing  │
        │    Plan     │
        └──────┬──────┘
               ▽
        ┌─────────────┐
        │    Sales    │
        │    Plan     │
        └──────┬──────┘
               ▽
        ┌─────────────┐
        │ Production  │
        │    Plan     │
        └──────┬──────┘
               ▽
        ┌─────────────┐
        │   MRP II    │
        │             │
        └─────────────┘
```

Every company has a strategic plan. Some companies have a periodic, formal planning system and cycle. Often this is done away from the company offices, away from disturbances and meetings. This kind of strategic planning often takes several days, and involves most of the top executives of the company.

Other companies don't bother with this, relying instead on a casual, informal approach. But if you don't have a formal, published strategic product plan, distributed to everyone who needs one, they will invent their own, individually. They do this because they must put their own plans into place in order to keep their own jobs running. When each person or work group guesses at what the future will bring, you will have a helter-skelter environment, conflict, and inevitable sub-optimization of the departments and the company as a whole.

I have had several clients who attempt to use their yearly budgeting exercise as their strategic plan. But since yearly budgeting rarely extends beyond the coming year, it can hardly be called strategic. It just doesn't go out far enough. Besides, this is backwards. The yearly budgeting process should be done after the strategies are in place, so those making up their detailed financial budgets know where the company is headed, and what they must be planning to do to support the strategy.

In order to be a world-class manufacturer, your many departments and functions must be able to shape their activities to support the same goals. Considering the thousands of decisions and actions taken every day, this shaping must be spontaneous and self-directing. While it may be possible for larger decisions to be developed in committee meetings or by staff studies, the everyday, minute-by-minute activities obviously cannot. I frequently hear complaints about politics or bureaucracy. To a large extent this reflects a disagreement on the basic strategies and goals of the company. What seems like a perfectly good action to one person is perceived as petty or foolish by another. Both people may be correct as they relate to their differing understanding of the company's long-range strategy.

I have discussed the strategic aspect of the planning cycle with managers and executives of over 200 companies. In the overwhelming number of cases, my clients are not satisfied with what their companies are doing. Since I do not consult directly in strategic planning, I was unable to pursue the exact reasons why. But there was a recurring theme that has led me to a conclusion. It seems to me that strategic planning is often just given lip service by the top executives, and often not done at all. This means that a large fraction of American manufacturers are facing their problems and trying to service their marketplace with flawed and ambiguous strategic direction from the executives whose main task is to provide just that leadership.

I believe that this area of strategic planning, and especially strategic product planning, represents a major unrecognized area in the manufacturing cycle that needs sharp improvement. In this light, you could view improving your strategic production planning as an area that can yield fast and large improvements in your business operations.

Figure 2.2 shows a simple strategic product plan for Intercontinental Wheel Goods. This plan is part of their overall strategic plan. There are several important characteristics of this plan, bearing on how it will eventually be converted into manufacturing activities.

Planning in Yearly Time Increments

The first thing you can notice is the time increments involved. This plan is shown in yearly steps of time. At the strategic level, this is the correct level of time detail. Your executives are accustomed to thinking about things in yearly bites.

The plan for Intercontinental goes out five years. In each succeeding year they drop the first year and add one more at the end.

Figure 2.2 International Wheel Goods
Strategic Product Plan
($000's)

	1993	1994	1995	1996	1997
Bicycles	16,500	19,000	25,000	28,000	31,500
Small-Wheeled	2,600	3,300	4,800	6,100	7,700
Infant	1,600	1,800	2,100	2,300	2,600
Health	350	1,300	3,000	5,000	8,000
Gardening			1,000	2,000	3,200
Total	21,050	25,400	35,700	46,400	53,000

Intercontinental has decided to expand strongly in Europe, beginning with 1993. As internal national barriers have fallen, their factory in Belgium will find it easier to sell and distribute all over the continent. They are planning a vigorous promotional campaign to prepare for 1995, and are planning for a strong increase in sales as a result. This is reflected in the plan for 1995 and beyond.

Your strategic product plan should extend far enough into the future to allow time to acquire (or eliminate) resources. Resources include plant and equipment, personnel, vendor development, warehouse capacity and location, and an efficient distribution system. Resources also include your sales and marketing organization and their locations, and the finances to support the entire effort. And finally a skilled work force is strategically important. Workers are decreasingly just "drones" monotonously tending an ever-cycling machine. Electronics and automation are pushing workers upward to technician status. In addition, one important JIT principle is to have each worker capable to perform many different tasks in the factory. This is the Multi Functional Worker.

Considering the product lines that Intercontinental has, five years is sufficient. An industry such as electrical generating needs a strategic planning horizon of 20 years or more. I have a client who manufactures novelties. For them two years is a sufficient preview for strategic purposes. I once had an engagement with a company that manufactures warships. One warship every two years is fast for them, and they have several contracts in backlog. Their strategic product plan is provided for them, in effect, by the U.S. Navy.

The rule is that the time horizon of the strategic product plan should go comfortably beyond the longest leadtime of any resource needed to support it.

Developing a Strategic Plan for Each Family of Products in Your Product Line

The next thing to notice in the sample plan of Intercontinental Wheel Goods, is what they have included. Their plans are made at a family level within their product line. Unless you have only a handful of end items, your strategic plan should be done at the family level.

Almost every company I have worked with has their end items grouped into families. Your company might have a wide variety of end items that should be grouped into just a few large families. Or your product line could require quite a few smaller groups.

Many companies have a huge number of end items, and deceptively so.

Several years ago I was Director of MIS for a medium-sized brewery. The casual observer might think a brewery has three or four products, the regular brand, the deluxe brand, the light brand, and the discount brand. However, a brewery manufactures hundreds of different products. We had cans, throw-away and returnable bottles, and three different keg sizes. Compounding that we had six-packs, 12-packs, and cases of 24. We multiplied that by promotional packaging, such as the 4th of July. We also had a multitude of individual state and local labeling laws, each resulting in different end items. But for strategic product planning, we would just show the four brands.

In the Intercontinental Wheel Goods example, the families were grouped according to manufacturing similarity. Intercontinental has a generous variety of bicycles, but they are grouped into families because they all are manufactured with similar processes and equipment, and share many common parts.

In our case a bicycle family also shares common warehouse space and needs, have generally the same customers, and are promoted and sold in a coordinated effort, often through the same channels.

Their small-wheeled family is made up of skateboards and scooters. Their manufacturing is fairly similar, and their bills of material much simpler. They have much the same customer base as bicycles, but promoted and marketed differently.

The infant category is baby buggies and strollers. They need different manufacturing processes, and their volumes are less. They also have an entirely different distribution chain.

Intercontinental is just getting into the wheelchair business and expects that this family will be augmented steadily with new models. They are planning on sharp increases in sales in 1995 and beyond. Intercontinental also recognizes the gradual aging of the populations in North America and in Europe, which means an expanding market for health products. Health products also need separate production facilities from their other product lines. Their marketplace is altogether different from the other families, and this product line even has a separate sales force.

The company plans to add an entirely new line of gardening products beginning in 1993. Current plans are to acquire a certain manufacturer in Europe, to take advantage of the unity of the common market. They plan to supply their worldwide needs for gardening products from this acquired factory. They are in the final stages of negotiation with this company and local bankers. This accounts for the large increases planned for 1996 and beyond.

I worked with a company in Europe making tire fabric. They have decided that the market is moving from fibre fabric to metal fabric. Accordingly, their strategic plan includes gradually diminishing production in the fibre tire cord factory, and increasing production at the metal fabric facility. This includes a significant plant expansion.

We seem to be in an era where the life cycle of products is becoming very short. Your car radio looked just about the same during the 1950s and 1960s. Today, a state-of-the-art car radio is quadraphonic and changes the vehicle into one giant speaker. The compact disc suddenly has replaced the phonograph record, which had been around for generations.

The strategic product plan is more important than ever in managing the introduction and elimination of products from your product line. It starts the process of communication to every nook and cranny of your company of what's happening and what to do about it. It is the start of the "same script" that you want everyone to be reading.

The rule here is to delineate your product families on your strategic product plan to support the further planning needs not only of manufacturing, but for all the other departments such as engineering, finance, and marketing who need to make their plans from the same strategy.

Using Dollars For Your Unit of Measure

Another characteristic of the strategic product plan is its unit of measure. In the example, the numbers are in dollars. (This could just as well have been pounds, marks, rubles, or yen.) At this level it is far preferable to use monetary terms rather than physical units. Monetary units represent the common denominator across all functions of the business and across geographic boundaries.

Using monetary units makes it much easier to make comparisons between families, and allows totaling across product lines. This allows plans to be made and conflicts to be resolved. There are always more demands for finances than are available, and expressing the various ideas in monetary terms helps support evaluation and decision.

From a manufacturing standpoint, however, this does create a problem. The conversion from monetary units to production units is an important part of production planning and master production scheduling, which take place later in the planning cycle, and are covered fully in Chapters 3 and 4.

In an international company such as Intercontinental Wheel Goods, they use dollars at this point and convert to local currency later, as detailed plans unfold.

Using dollars as the unit of measure of this plan also gives you a start on your yearly revenue plan for the horizon period you use.

Showing Geographic Locations

Another important characteristic of the strategic product plan has to do with their geographic locations if you have several manufacturing facilities. Many manufacturers do have multiple factory locations, and they have to be planned for properly.

World-class manufacturing implies an international scope. Some companies will manufacture in one place and distribute widely. Many larger companies have factories spread all over the globe. Sometimes each producing location has its own dedicated marketing zone. This would occur when the factories produce the same or similar products. Other companies have a diverse number of factories, but each makes different products. In such cases marketing zones would not be strictly delineated. Since the end items are different, they have little problem with overlap. But in any case, you must organize your strategic product plan to recognize your circumstances.

Another variation on the multiplant theme is the situation where one plant feeds another. And you could build the picture of a number of plants feeding one another back and forth, but with each plant having its own outside customers as well.

To compound the complexity, I have worked with companies with multiple factory locations, feeding one another, with outside customers as well, but with central engineering and purchasing. Central purchasing confines itself to products and commodities common to several locations, where each facility buys its own peculiar items. In addition, these companies with centralized tendencies often try to have central accounting and engineering. Some even go so far as having a central sales force and central sales order entry.

The strategic product plan is one of the early tools for keeping these complexities, severe or mild, under control. If your several plants each make a different product line, then the strategic marketing plan, organized by product family, automatically represents the plan for each factory. However, when your different locations make the same or similar product, you should make a provision for this in your strategic product plan.

This is a strategic issue because this plan will govern the pace of activity at each location as well as their detailed planning.

It could be that you want to taper off producing at a high-cost factory, and build up a low cost one. If you decide to close a plant entirely, or build a new one, these strategies must show on your strategic product plan.

For example, I worked with a company a few years ago when they were going from three plants to two, discontinuing one product line, and introducing a new one. Of their existing three facilities, they closed two and built one new one. They also refurbished the remaining old plant. Concurrently, they also implemented a new MRPII system and its software on new computer facilities. One of their many planning and implementation challenges was to create a strategic product plan that was synchronized to match the whole project. They did survive and prosper.

One Just-in-Time principle is small factories of around 500 people, total. In such companies, multiple factories are a matter of course.

I worked with another company that converted one huge factory into several smaller ones. Instead of abandoning their one large building and constructing a number of small ones, they merely painted lines on the floor and hung banners from the ceiling to identify each entity. This created factories within a factory. In this case, each new "factory" makes a unique line of products. They created a business organization to match the new delineation. Now the employees use the old, common parking lot and cafeteria, but both physically and mentally, they identify with their independent business units.

Several of these small "factories" have since achieved impressive Just-in-Time gains. One in particular, making a consumer electronics product, has reduced factory lead time from seven weeks to four days. They are working on cutting this still further.

In these complex examples, the detailed plans of all of the many operating departments will be derived from the strategic product plan, in unfolding detail, delineated as needed. In this area of detailed planning and execution, good computer systems are necessary. Such systems are commercially available and can be counted on to help you keep your complexity under control, however great or small.

Show enough geographic delineation in your strategic production plan to support your cascading planning needs as they proceed at successively increasing levels of detail.

How to Get Acceptance and Approval for the Strategic Plan

The last characteristic of the strategic production plan is its acceptance and approval. You have to make this a working document. To be effective, your top management must have accepted it and agreed to it. Top management includes the CEO, and all of his/her functional managers, plus other major executives who will take part in the fulfillment of the plan. It would be best if all parties agreed enthusiastically. But different personalities with different perspectives can be expected to have different opinions and desires. The strategic planning process should be designed to give all these parties a fair and rational hearing, where opinions and arguments are freely exchanged.

However, at the end of the process, the strategic production plan must be published to guide the rest of the company, and it must be fully supported by all employees. This includes those top managers who lost their arguments in the planning sessions. It is very important that all managers support the strategic production plan, even when they see flaws. Unswerving support of the plan is one way to develop smooth teamwork and execution throughout the whole organization. This also will sharply reduce the "politicking" and irrationality that employees often complain of.

HOW TO GUIDE PRODUCT STRATEGY BY DEVELOPING A MARKETING PLAN

A well-known company manufactured a consumer product. They had some very good advertising and their products had excellent acceptance and loyalty among their customers.

But, as it sometimes happens, they began losing ground. At first, they were just slipping in market share. Then sales began to fade, finally at a rate of 10 percent a year.

By this time, the marketing department had fallen prey to their own propaganda, and confidently predicted a turn around each year. But each succeeding year showed another 10 percent drop. When January closed behind plan, they pronounced that the sales shortfall would be made up in February. This fiction was repeated every month far into the year before they finally began to make other excuses.

Then they decided that introducing a new product line would be the salvation of the company. So they diverted a good chunk of the advertising budget to the new product and most of the sales force. Sadly, the new product didn't take hold and was abandoned. They even had negative sales in one month because retailers exercised their privilege to return a portion of the merchandise that had been loaded on them.

Outside the marketing department, nobody believed that "this year is the year of the great turnaround." Nor were they convinced by the hype surrounding the new product.

As a result, each department made its own guesses as to what the year would bring, and made their own individual plans. None was exactly alike, and their diversity was large. The result was disorganization, and what I call departmental nationalism. Each department tried to optimize itself, with almost no attention to company-wide coordination.

The company was finally sold off to a competitor who wanted the factory. All of the nonfactory employees lost their jobs.

A realistic marketing plan would have brought focus and urgency to the company's underlying problems. These basic problems could have been taken care of in time, and that company could have been thriving and prospering today. But their acceptance of a fictitious marketing plan for each year obscured the problems and did nothing to mobilize all departments to rectifying them.

World-class company performance requires world-class performance from every function within the company.

The managers in your marketing function take the strategic production plan and use it to develop their marketing plans. In many companies the marketing plan is prepared by a forecasting and planning group in the marketing department. Other companies have adopted a product or brand manager approach. In these cases a product manager is made responsible for many aspects of managing his/her product families. In these companies the product manager is an active advocate for the welfare of his/her products, including design changes and manufacturing schedules. When the product manager organization is in place the product manager prepares the marketing plan.

The marketing plan is a refinement of the strategic product plan, presented in more detail, to support further planning activities. The marketing plan has several characteristics, similar to the strategic production plan:

- ■ It includes time spans and horizons.

- ■ It identifies what to include.

- ■ It identifies what unit of measure to use.

- ■ It includes geographic detail.

Establishing Time Spans and Horizons

The most common time span for the marketing plan is still yearly increments, much like the strategic plan. However, in some circumstances you could plan by quarter for the coming year.

The marketing plan also should look forward far enough to allow supporting plans enough lead time. Especially with product introduction or phase out, and to support shifting geographical emphasis, the marketing plan should go out into the future far enough to allow these activities enough time for orderly development.

In our Intercontinental Wheel Goods example, in Figure 2.3, we show yearly plans for the coming four years.

Deciding What to Include

The marketing plan usually includes families of products, not individual end items, unless you have a very narrow product line. When the product line is quite narrow, you can prepare this plan showing end items.

The families shown often are at a more extensive level of detail than you have on the strategic production plan. For example, the strategic production plan for Intercontinental Wheel Goods, shown in Figure 2.2, shows bicycles as one line item. Their marketing plan, shown in Figure 2.3, breaks out bicycles into two families, heavy duty and light weight. The break-out could have been more detailed, if that would have been useful. The degree of refinement at this point depends on the product line, how extensive it is, and how they are marketed. This is a marketing-oriented plan, and the details are meant to support and assist the marketing effort for the families.

Selecting What Unit of Measure to Use

We still are at a planning level where monetary units are the most common, although some companies may find it useful to show both dollars and units. The example in Figure 2.3 is stated in thousands of dollars.

Figure 2.3 International Wheel Goods
Marketing Plan
Heavy Duty
($000's)

	1993	1994	1995	1996	1997
US & Canada	5,500	6,000	6,500	7,200	8,400
Central & S. Am	1,800	1,800	1,800	1,900	2,000
Europe	3,200	3,700	6,700	6,700	19,000
Total	10,500	11,500	15,000	16,500	19,000

Including Geographic Detail

The marketing plan is a good place to show a geographic breakdown. The geographic areas shown here are marketing areas, unlike the strategic production plan, which would show manufacturing locations as its geographic detail.

Our example of International Wheel Goods, Figure 2.3, shows detail for U.S. and Canada, Central and South America, and Europe. If the markets within each of these large zones have wide variations in marketing considerations, a further refinement could be useful.

Using Forecasting Tools

There are a number of forecasting tools that the marketing planners can use to help them in their work. Some of the more common ones are:

- Polling the Field
- Statistical Evaluation of History
- Market Research
- Test Marketing
- Econometric Forecasts

Polling the Field

Many companies have built planning techniques where their regional offices prepare their own forecasts and plans and submit them to the central office for consolidation. This works especially well when regional distribution centers are used. Some people call this "pulling," where the regional locations pull their needs from the central factories. In a complex environment you could find several regions each pulling from several factories. This would be somewhat further complicated when some locations are in different countries.

In other cases, the regional plans call for shipment from one central point. In most cases, however, the planners at the consolidation point will evaluate the individual plans and make adjustments. This is especially true when the aggregate plans add up to a total either much higher or much lower than is reasonable or expected at the home office. People with a marketing view of the world tend to have an optimistic bias, whereas those with an inventory management standpoint tend to be conservative.

Using Statistical Methods to Evaluate History

If you have three to five years of sales history, there are a number of good mathematical techniques to assist in forecasting. We are in the computer age, and we now find that there are good commercial software products on the market that can compute these forecasts for you, and many of them run on desktop computers.

Appendix V gives an overview of statistical forecasting and describes six methods for analyzing the data you have available and 13 methods that can be used to forecast from them.

In using these statistical methods, however, there are a couple of factors to observed. The first is that these methods assume that the future will be very much like the past. This means that they have difficulty predicting a dramatic change in the economy, such as a serious recession or the subsequent turn-around. Some wags describe using these forecasting systems as being like steering a ship by watching its wake. This may be useful in continuing a straight course, but not good at all when the ship needs to make a turn. There may be some merit in this quip.

Another factor regards your data. Are they complete and reasonably error-free? Many companies have a difficult time with data integrity. One source of the problem is the difference between the date the customer asked for, versus the date you promised, versus the date shipped. It frequently occurs that the actual customer request has not been recorded. This means that any forecast based on this data base will not correctly show the customers' true desires, and could simply and mindlessly perpetuate poor performance.

Product identification is another problem. You must have in place a product coding system that will allow you to group them into the families as you want them constituted. Especially with consumer products, a minor variation often is given another product code. This becomes especially problematic when these historical data are used to forecast individual items.

One good way to maintain flexibility in assigning products to families is to use a separate field on the product's masterfile. This field is used to designate the family to which the item is currently assigned. Then it is easy to adjust the alignment of products and families, merely by editing this field. This will allow you to keep using your historical data even when the families are realigned. Using a separate field allows you to avoid the mistake of burying the parent's identification into the item number of the product.

Using Market Research

Market research has evolved over the years. Personal interviews were once the mainstay of this practice. Nowadays, market research is usually done over the telephone, which brings in many more responses and can be done in a fairly short amount of time. But since the interviewers are more clerks than professionals, the subjects covered must be kept quite simple. Another observed danger in market research is sometimes called The Edsel Syndrome. It is said that sometimes the facts are assembled, and then analyzed and reported on according to what the boss wants, rather than on pure scientific analysis.

Using Test Marketing

Particularly with consumer products test marketing frequently is used to confirm a new product's appeal. This technique has the merit of being quite accurate, but is time consuming and expensive. Test marketing a product can give manufacturing some difficult problems, particularly if the product is different enough to require new or different machinery, tooling, and equipment. The quantities needed for the test are but a small fraction of expected quantities after a full roll-out. It is too risky to buy the high-volume equipment because the acceptance of the product is still in doubt. Purchasing runs into the same problem with commodities and piece parts. Some companies go into full production acknowledging that if the product does not achieve a minimum success, it will be withdrawn. This could result in obsolete inventory and useless plant capacity. These potential costs should not be ignored when contemplating this approach to a new product roll-out.

Using Econometric Forecasts

An econometric forecast is a very complicated mathematical algorithm that takes a wide number of economic facts, analyzes them, and attempts to predict the future. Many of these models have been developed over many years, and offer a supplement to statistical forecasting. The econometric forecast tries to predict economic swings, while statistical forecasting says next year will be like former years. Used together, econometric and statistical forecasting can supplement each other.

There are many such forecasts, many are industry oriented. Some of these models treat inventory improperly, which may make a difference in which one you choose, should you decide to choose one. Traditionally, inventory has been considered an indicator and factored into the equations accordingly. But, beginning with MRP, and now especially with JIT, inventory is performing quite differently from the past. More and more companies have instituted new methods that allow them to increase their output with much less inventory build-up than formerly was needed. These techniques now have become widespread enough to affect the national economy. Some econometric forecasting models have taken account of this basic alteration, others have not.

If you decide to use an econometric forecast to help you craft your marketing plan, be sure it treats inventory properly.

HOW TO USE THE SALES PLAN TO ACCOMMODATE THE PRESENT PRODUCTION SCHEDULE

Managing the sales plan involves monitoring your actual sales against your forecasts, product by product, or family by family. In the case of Intercontinental Wheel Goods, we will monitor specific models, but lumping all the colors to make a sub-family.

As the year progresses, actual customer orders will not exactly equal their sales forecast. This requires that the actual orders be used to replace the forecast in the near term. But looking farther out over the future months, your customers' orders have not yet all come in. So you will need to rely more on the forecast.

Another problem that frequently occurs is that as the season progresses, it becomes apparent that the sales forecast has become obsolete; it no longer is a good predictor of actual customer orders. But at what point do you make whole new forecast?

Five Ways to Consume Your Forecast

How you consume your sales forecast will depend on whether you are in the make-to-stock market or the make-to-order market, or a combination.

Consuming the sales forecast is entering incoming customer orders into your system and removing the appropriate quantity from the sales forecast. Usually this is on a one-for-one basis, but unusual events, such as an unexpected, large order, can alter this rule of thumb.

There are five rules for relieving the sales forecast, namely:

- Rule 1: Manufacture the Forecast

- Rule 2: Manufacture to Order

- Rule 3: Use a Time Fence

- Rule 4: Establish a Finite Capacity Inside of a Time Fence

- Rule 5: Use the Higher of Forecast or Actual Customer Order

Rule 1: Manufacture the Forecast

Figure 2.4 shows us how Consumption Rule 1 works. This rule simply states that we want to manufacture our Sales Forecast, with no regard to the presence or lack of actual customer orders. In this example we see our sales forecast for 26" Boys' Dirt Bikes, for the periods January through June. We also see our actual customer orders for the same months.

Our rule is to manufacture our sales forecast, so our bottom line, Demand to Master Production Schedule, simply shows the forecast. The actual customer orders are shown, but not used in the calculation. These figures could be useful in case there were some very unusual actual customer orders that should be accommodated, as an exception to the routine scheduling rule.

The Demand to Master Production Schedule line will be transferred to the Master Production Schedule for analysis and conversion into actual manufacturing orders and purchase orders, using conventional Manufacturing Resource Planning, covered in Chapter 3.

Figure 2.4 Consumption Rule 1
Manufacture the Forecast
26" Boys' Dirt Bikes

	Jan	Feb	Mar	Apr	May	Jun
Sales Forecast	1,000	1,100	1,100	1,300	1,400	1,500
Actual Customer Orders	1,050	1,200	1,000	900	800	300
Demand to Master Production Schedule	1,000	1,100	1,100	1,300	1,400	1,500

This rule is most useful for a company building to finished goods inventory, the classic "Make to Stock" situation. The make to stock environment has customer orders serviced from a finished goods warehouse, or a network of them, while the factory simply replenishes the distribution system.

Rule 2: Manufacture to Order

Figure 2.5 shows how the plan works, where we only build according to customer orders. In this example, the forecast is shown but not used, and only the actual customer orders drop down to the Master Schedule line.

Figure 2.5 Consumption Rule 2
Manufacture to Order
26" Boys' Dirt Bikes

	Jan	Feb	Mar	Apr	May	Jun
Sales Forecast	1,000	1,100	1,100	1,300	1,400	1,500
Actual Customer Orders	1,050	1,200	1,000	900	800	300
Demand to Master Production Schedule	1,050	1,200	1,000	900	800	300

As you can see, the demands transferred to the Master Schedule begin to taper off in April. This is simply because customer orders have not arrived yet, not because the company is going out of business. Because only actual orders will continue to flow into these time periods, the quantities will be raised as the months progress. The problem in this environment always is your ability to react to these increases, especially at the purchasing and first fabrication stages.

I have worked with only one client who could wait to buy raw materials until after the customer order arrived. They manufacture very high-quality and high-precision injection-molded plastic parts. The resins for each job are custom-tailored to the job. They purchase resin only in the quantity needed for the job, and only after the order is in the house.

Rule 2 has only limited applicability.

Rule 3: Use a Time Fence

Figure 2.6 shows how a time fence can be used to combine rules one and two. Under this rule, actual customer orders are sent to the Master Production Schedule inside of the Time Fence, while the Sales Forecast governs outside of it.

Figure 2.6 Consumption Rule 3
Using a Time Fence
26" Boys' Dirt Bikes

	Jan	Feb	Mar	Time Fence	Apr	May	Jun
Sales Forecast	1,000	1,100	1,100	¦	1,300	1,400	1,500
Actual Customer Orders	1,050	1,200	1,000	¦	900	800	300
Demand to Master Production Schedule	1,000	1,100	1,100	¦	1,300	1,400	1,500

In our example, we have a three-month time fence, which falls between March and April. The rule is that we will master schedule actual customer orders in January, February, and March, and switch over to our forecast for April and beyond. This is where the numbers shown on the Demand to Master Production Schedule line come from.

Most make-to-order companies live with the Lead Time Inversion. In this environment, you promise a delivery lead time to your customers shorter than your total manufacturing lead time. This means that you must begin to purchase and fabricate longer lead time items before your customers actually send you their orders.

One potential problem with this rule has to do with product mix. The forecasted quantities outside of leadtime "stand in" for the actual customer orders until they actually arrive. The forecasts are actually used for master scheduling and consequent purchase and manufacture of raw materials and components. If the mix of the eventual customer orders differ widely from the forecast, you still could be short of some items.

The other common problem with this rule is when actual orders exceed the forecast, more than can be accommodated in whatever buffering you have included in your system.

Both problems would result in expediting and could result in delaying some customer orders.

The lead time inversion forces you to start buying and manufacturing on speculation. By using the sales forecast beyond your time fence, you can use the powerful tools of Manufacturing Resource Planning to coordinate these orders. Then when actual customer orders arrive, they are substituted for the forecast, and MRP adjusts itself.

One way to reduce your lead time inversion problem is to reduce your lead times, both in manufacturing and purchasing. Many Just-in-Time ideas can be used to shorten lead times. In a job shop factory, organized by machine function, reducing queue time offers great potential. Reduced setup and smaller lot sizes also reduce your factory throughput time. And converting away from the classic functional work center organization to group technology manufacturing cells reduces leadtime drastically.

Purchasing leadtimes also can be reduced by single sourcing, blanket ordering, electronic data interchange (EDI) for sending out schedules, frequent deliveries, and no receiving inspection. These concepts and techniques are all discussed throughout this book.

Rule 4: Establish a Finite Capacity Inside of a Time Fence

Many factories try to firm their schedules, for a future period of time, particularly those with capacity limitations. Figure 2.7 shows such a situation, where we have firmed our capacities inside of leadtime. Under this rule, we master schedule only up to the finite limit represented by our sales forecast. Any overage, or shortage, is carried forward to the next period.

In our example, Figure 2.7, the 50 units of excess demand in January is carried over to February. But February also has excess demand, so 100 units from February, plus the 50 shortage from January, are carried over to March. The result is that March is also overwhelmed, so the remaining 50 are sent forward to April.

In our case, April falls on the other side of our time fence, so we will schedule the sales forecast. However, if the resulting carry-forward, plus actual customer orders were ever greater than our forecast, we would pass the larger quantity down to the Demand for Master Production Schedule line.

This rule helps to provide a measure of stability to the plans being sent to manufacturing, and avoids one of the sources of "nervousness" that MRP systems can be troubled with. This consumption rule is most useful for companies which have difficulty altering production rates in the short term.

Figure 2.7 Consumption Rule 4
Firmed Capacity Inside of Time Fence
26" Boys' Dirt Bikes

	Jan	Feb	Mar	Time Fence	Apr	May	Jun
Sales Forecast	1,000	1,100	1,100	⦙	1,300	1,400	1,500
Actual Customer Orders	1,050	1,200	1,000	⦙	900	800	300
Overage from Last Month		50	150	⦙	50		
Total Demand	1,050	1,250	1,150	⦙	950	800	300
Demand to Master Production Schedule	1,000	1,100	1,100	⦙	1,300	1,400	1,500

Rule 5: Use the Higher of Forecast or Actual Customer Order

This is a straightforward rule. We will schedule either total customer orders or the sales forecast, for each month, using the higher of the two.

This rule is illustrated in Figure 2.8. Here we see the forecast governing in March and beyond, while actual customer orders are used in January and February.

This rule works well when the forecast is very accurate. It assumes that a shortfall in actual orders in any month will be made up in that month. This rule also assumes that if customer orders are heavy in one month, they will not detract from the following month. If you look at the actual orders in February and March, you could guess that an order for 100 in February really should have appeared in March, violating this rule. The extra 50 in January, however appear to be a genuinely expanded demand.

How to Use the Tracking Signal to Tell When You Need to Reforecast

There is a fairly simple mathematical method for watching to see if your forecast becomes unrealistic. This is the concept of the tracking signal. The tracking signal compares your recent deviation of actual sales against forecast, compares it against your recent pattern of swings, and gives you a flag when actual sales drift far enough away from your forecast to require a new forecast.

Figure 2.8 Consumption Rule 5
Manufacture the Higher of Forecast or Actual
Customer Orders
26" Boys' Dirt Bikes

	Jan	Feb	Mar	Apr	May	Jun
Sales Forecast	1,000	1,100	1,100	1,300	1,400	1,500
Actual Customer Orders	1,050	1,200	1,000	900	800	300
Demand to Master Production Schedule	1,050	1,200	1,100	1,300	1,400	1,500

The first thing to do is to figure your recent pattern of forecast inaccuracy. This is done with a simple mathematical tool called Mean Absolute Deviation (MAD). This is an easy substitute for the standard deviation you learn in statistics class.

(Mean absolute deviation was invented by Robert G. Brown as a substitute for standard deviation before the days of electronic calculators. Standard deviation requires the calculation of a square root, while MAD only requires simple division. This was more easily handled by the clerks of that era.)

Figure 2.9 shows how to do this calculation. In our example, we have a forecast of 5,000 units per week, and actual sales as shown. The last column shows the absolute deviation, which ignores whether the difference is over or under. The total absolute deviation for this 10-week period is 1,600, which gives us an average of 160, which is our Mean Absolute Deviation (MAD). This tells us that on the average our actual sales are within 160 units of our forecast.

The next step is to figure the tracking signal. Figure 2.10 shows how this is done. We take the previous example and add a column for actual deviation, taking pluses and minuses into account, and in the last column, show a running sum of these errors. At the end we have a negative 800. When we divide this running sum of 800 by the MAD of 160, we have a tracking signal of five.

Figure 2.9 Calculating Mean Absolute Deviation (MAD)

	Forecast	Sales	Absolute Deviation
Week 1	5,000	4,900	100
Week 2	5,000	5,000	0
Week 3	5,000	5,100	100
Week 4	5,000	5,400	400
Week 5	5,000	5,300	300
Week 6	5,000	4,800	200
Week 7	5,000	5,200	200
Week 8	5,000	5,000	0
Week 9	5,000	4,900	100
Week 10	5,000	5,200	200
Total	50,000	50,800	1,600

$$\text{MAD} = \frac{\text{Sum of absolute deviations}}{\text{Number of occurrences}}$$

$$\text{MAD} = \frac{1600}{10}$$

$$\text{MAD} = 160$$

Figure 2.10 Calculating Tracking Signal

	Forecast	Sales	Absolute Deviation	Forecast Error	Running Sum Fcst. Error
Week 1	5,000	4,900	100	100	100
Week 2	5,000	5,000	0	0	100
Week 3	5,000	5,100	100	-100	0
Week 4	5,000	5,400	400	-400	-400
Week 5	5,000	5,300	300	-300	-700
Week 6	5,000	4,800	200	200	-500
Week 7	5,000	5,200	200	-200	-700
Week 8	5,000	5,000	0	0	-700
Week 9	5,000	4,900	100	100	-600
Week 10	5,000	5,200	200	-200	-800
Total	50,000	50,800	1,600		-800

$$MAD = \frac{\text{Sum of absolute deviations}}{\text{Number of occurrences}}$$

$$MAD = \frac{1600}{10}$$

$$MAD = 160$$

$$\text{Tracking Signal} = \frac{\text{Running Sum of Forecast Error}}{MAD}$$

$$\text{Tracking Signal} = \frac{800}{160}$$

$$\text{Tracking Signal} = 5$$

The general rule is that a tracking signal of 4 or higher represents a forecast that is obsolete and should be redone. Using a tracking signal of four is fairly liberal. You could tighten up your forecasting by using a smaller limit. How strict you want to be depends on how much you are dependent on good forecasting and how flexible your manufacturing operations is.

HOW TO USE DISTRIBUTION REQUIREMENTS PLANNING TO MANAGE FINISHED GOODS INVENTORY

Make to stock companies often have more than one distribution point where inventory must be maintained. Companies in this environment usually offer to ship customer orders within a very short lead time, often the same day. Many of these companies regularly ship nearly 100 percent of their orders within the promised response period.

In order to achieve good customer service and still keep inventory costs to a minimum, this environment needs a good planning system to communicate demands back to the factory or central stocking point. The several techniques and tools used in this area are known as "Distribution Requirements Planning" or "DRP".

The basic tool of distribution requirements planning is a time-phased plan, with data and logic very similar to Material Requirements Planning.

Figure 2.11 shows a simple situation where a company has two distribution warehouses which are served by one factory.

Both warehouses have a lot size of 100 and a lead time of one week, for the product involved. This is transportation lead-time only, and does not include leadtime needed in the factory.

In Warehouse 1, we start out with 100 on hand which we plan to consume in week two, where we will be 10 short. In order to cover this shortage, we plan to send an order to the factory in week one for a lot size of 100, which we will receive in week two. This will leave us with 90 on hand, available in week three when we plan to sell 70. At the end of week three we should have 20 on hand, which will leave us with a shortage of 40 in week four. This means we should send the factory another order for 100 in week three, which we will receive in week four. This will cover our needs and leave 60 to carry forward to week five.

Our plan for week five is to sell 40, which will leave us with 20 for week six. But our plan to sell 40 in week six would leave us 20 short, so we plan another routine, replenishment order. As a result we will have 80 to carry over to week seven which is adequate to cover week seven's forecast. We will run out again in week eight, which causes us to plan to place another replenishment order on the factory for them to ship in week seven, and we exit the example with 90 on hand.

Figure 2.11 Distribution Requirements Planning 1 (DRP)

Warehouse 1

Lot Size = 100
Lead Time = 1 week

Week	1	2	3	4	5	6	7	8
Forecast	50	60	70	60	40	40	50	40
Projected 100 on-Hand	50	10/90	20	-40/60	20	-20/80	30	90
Planned Order Receipt		100		100		100		100
Planned Order Release	100		100		100		100	

Warehouse 2

Lot Size = 100
Lead Time = 1 Week

Week	1	2	3	4	5	6	7	8
Forecast	70	80	100	80	20	50	60	40
Projected 50 On-Hand	-20/80	0	-100/0	-80/20	0	-50/50	-10/90	50
Planned Order Receipt	100		100	100		100	100	
Planned Order Release		100	100		100	100		

Factory

Week	1	2	3	4	5	6	7	8
Forecast	100	100	200	0	200	100	100	

Warehouse 2 has a similar situation. But in this example, we project a zero inventory in weeks two and five. Notice that we do not plan to receive another order in these weeks, because we will not have gone negative. Under this time-phased method, it is acceptable to have zero on hand. If that is to risky, you can build in some safety stock. If we were to have mandated a safety stock in warehouse 2, then we would have planned orders to boost inventory in weeks two and five.

See Appendix II for a full description on how to calculate safety stock correctly.

Our two warehouses now have planned their demands on the factory, which must make its plans to have this product ready to ship when needed. Each of the two warehouses have planned four orders of 100 each, and we show the aggregate of these demands as a forecast at the factory. The planners at the factory now blend these demands into their master production schedule and coordinate production to meet these needs.

As each week passes, we should recognize the quantities actually ordered by our customers, and make adjustments accordingly. This will help prevent both stockouts and excess inventory.

Figure 2.12 shows what could have happened by the end of the eighth week. Our actual orders were only somewhat different from our forecast. Although the orders and our on hand balances were different from our original plan, the resulting orders to the factory remained unchanged. If, however, the actual demands had been steadily stronger than forecast, we could have run short, because the factory might not have been able to increase our orders on short notice. Safety stock is the traditional answer to this danger.

Figure 2.12 Distribution Requirements Planning 2

Warehouse 1
Actual Orders

Lot Size = 100
Lead Time = 1 week

Week	1	2	3	4	5	6	7	8
Actual Orders	54	59	75	61	42	39	30	62
On-Hand 100	46	-13/ 87	12	-49/ 51	9	-30/ 70	40	-22 78
Planned Order Receipt		100		100		100		100
Planned Order Release	100		100		100		100	

But more recently, one JIT concept is to take drastic steps in the factory to reduce its leadtime. The faster the factory can react to fluctuating demands, the less safety stock we need to carry in our field distribution warehouses as a buffer.

Another JIT idea is to reduce lot sizes. In our example, if we had weekly lot sizes, coupled with very short factory leadtimes, we could have the situation where the factory would replenish next week the quantities we sell this week. Or, better yet, operate on a daily cycle, with replenishment shipments coming in every day.

HOW TO USE THE TIME-PHASED ORDER POINT TO MANAGE SERVICE PARTS

The time phased order point technique blends the traditional reorder point and safety stock (ROP), into material requirements planning logic. Instead of waiting until we reach a reorder point to start an order, we predict when the reorder point will be crossed, and thereby we can predict when we will send orders for service parts to the factory for inclusion in their planning routines.

Figure 2.13 contains a simple illustration. In this example, we are given a lot size of 1,000, safety stock of 500, an order point of 900, and a leadtime of two weeks.

In this example the forecast and the leadtime are hypothetical. However, both safety stock and order point are calculated. Safety stock is calculated according to the procedures covered in Appendix II. Reorder point is defined as the demand during leadtime plus safety stock. In our lawn mower blade example, our leadtime of two weeks gives us a quantity of 400, plus safety stock of 500, yielding the 900 figure used for reorder point.

Referring to our example in Figure 2.13, we see the forecast from our service department, a straight 200 per week. We have an open order for 1,000 due in week two. This 1,000, plus our beginning balance of 600, is planned to be steadily consumed. In week five, our balance falls to 800, which is below our 900 order point. This causes us to plan to send an order for 1,000 to the factory in week five, to arrive in week seven. In week seven, we would have to dip into safety stock, but our order for 1,000 will arrive in time, and we will have 1,400 to pass on to week eight. If the order due in week seven is delayed, we would have enough to cover both weeks seven and eight, with some left over for week nine.

Using safety stock in this situation buffers us both against unreliable shipments from the factory and sales higher than forecast.

Figure 2.13 Time-Phased Order Point

Part 4711
Lawnmower Blades

Lot Size = 1000
Safety Stock = 500
Order Point = 1000
Lead Time = 2 Weeks

Week	1	2	3	4	5	6	7	8
Forecast	200	200	200	200	200	200	200	200
Projected On-Hand 800	600	1,400	1,200	1,000	800 *	600	400 **	1,200
Planned Order Receipt		1,000					1,000	
Planned Order Release					1,000			

* Reorder Point Encountered
** Safety Stock Breached

CONCLUSION

Manufacturing is a very complex activity and does not just happen. In this chapter we have covered how to manage demands, specifically demands from customers for finished goods and service parts. A demand is an order that will take the product out of inventory. (Demands for parts and assemblies in the factory are covered in Chapter 3.)

Here are some guidelines for managing demands:

- Develop a strategic product plan:

  - Plan in yearly time increments.

  - Extend the plan into the future far enough to allow for major changes in the company.

  - Plan by family group.

  - Express the plan in monetary terms (dollars in our examples).

  - Break the plan down by geographic locations, especially if there are several factories involved.

       – Obtain approval and acceptance by all levels within the company.

- Develop a marketing plan:
  - Refine the strategic plan.
  - Phase out old products and introduce new ones.
  - Plan in yearly increments.
  - Look far enough into the future to support changing equipment, shifting geographical emphasis, prospecting for new sources, and developing new markets.
  - Express the plan in families, sometimes the same ones as before, but often at a more refined level of detail.
  - Show greater geographic detail, especially where companies market across national boundaries and where a series of shipping points is used.

- Use forecasting tools:
  - Poll the field organization, and add up their results. (Be careful of overoptimistic responses and edit before using.)
  - Use statistical forecasting based on past history.
  - Use market research, especially when planning for new products.
  - Use test marketing where necessary; it may cause a delay and expense in introducing a new product.
  - Use econometric forecasting; it can help predict sharp alterations in the marketplace.

- Make a sales plan:
  - Show specific end items in monthly time periods.
  - Follow five rules to consume the sales plan:
  - Manufacture the forecast.
  - Manufacture to order.
  - Use a time fence.
  - Establish a finite capacity inside of a time fence.
  - Use the higher of forecast or actual customer order.

- Monitor the accuracy of the forecast:

    - Use the Mean Absolute Deviation to analyze the quality of past forecasts.
    - Use the Tracking Signal to see if recent actual sales are deviating from past experience.
    - Do a reforecast when necessary.
    - Use distribution requirements planning if you have multiple stocking points for shipments to customers.

- Manage the demand for service parts:

    - Use the Time-Phased Order Point method.

3

HOW TO MAKE THE RIGHT THINGS BY MANAGING SUPPLIES

A supply brings inventory in. A supply order is either a manufacturing order or a purchase order. You create supply orders for raw materials, fabricated items, sub-assemblies, and end items. You can make them or buy them, sometimes both at the same time for the same item. Your MRP system doesn't much care as long as their delivery dates and quantities are correctly synchronized, just in time for their intended use. And the intended use can be for fabricating a low-level component, for immediate final assembly and shipping against a customer order, or anywhere in between.

Your ability to synchronize purchasing and manufacturing to exactly support what you have promised your customers is one of the more powerful advantages you require from your MRP system.

Its easy to get mixed up between a supply order and a demand order. A demand is something that will draw inventory out. Your customer's order is a demand, for example. But the confusion occurs with manufacturing orders. A manufacturing order is a supply order, because it will bring inventory in. But every manufacturing order must have components issued to it. So the needs for components to support each manufacturing order are demands on those components. This means that a manufacturing order, a supply order, at the same time is also a demand order for its components. These component demands are said to be pegged to the manufacturing order, often called the parent.

Synchronization means that the components, as pegged, need to be on hand before the manufacturing order can be started, preferably just barely ahead of their need. How is that done? Your MRP system creates supply orders for the components with their due dates exactly lined up to the start date of the parent order. Then, just before manufacturing is to begin, the system creates a requisition, or "pick list, which is sent to the stock room.

The pick list is based on the bill of materials for the parent being manufactured, extended by the designated quantity for each component. Figure 3.1 shows a typical pick list. Most of the fields are self-explanatory, but some deserve some extra thought. Locations are in numerical order to make picking more efficient. The rear wheel, part number 48291, is found in two locations, shown in first-in, first-out sequence. Under issue type, "MAN" means manual; to be individually issued from stock. "AUTO" means automatic issue. These components are delivered to the floor in the bulk, and stock status is decreased as the order is completed. Until recently, automatic issue was used for parts with trivial value. But Just-in-Time ideals suggest that many items should be traced this way.

With an MRP system in place, supply orders, starting at the end-item level, create demands for their components. These, in turn, signal your MRP system to plan supply orders to cover, creating more demands. And the cycle cascades from the top of the bill of material to the bottom.

The arithmetic is not difficult, just the sheer volume. Many manufacturers have hundreds of end items and thousands of components. Moreover, MRP moved us from monthly plans to weekly ones. And now the JIT influence is making us strive for daily or even hourly schedules. You can't cope with planning and replanning thousands of items every day with manual/clerical methods.

Without a computer, the only way to manage your inventory ins and outs; your purchases, and your manufacturing is with classic Reorder Point and Safety Stock / Launch and Expedite (ROP) techniques. Sometimes you see the reorder point and safety stock portion of this classic referred to as Aggregate Inventory Management.

Figure 3.1 Pick List

INTERNATIONAL WHEEL GOODS
PICK LIST
MANUFACTURING ORDER 7558

ITEM NUMBER	ITEM DESCRIPTION	U/M	ON ORDER	PICK DATE	START DATE	DUE DATE	WORK CENTER FINAL ASSEMBLY	PLANNER
4716	DIRT BIKE BOY'S HEAVY DUTY	EA	500	01/15	01/18	01/26	FINAL ASSEMBLY	11

ITEM NUMBER	ITEM DESCRIPTION	U/M	REQUIRED QUANTITY	ENG REV	ISSUE TYPE	ISSUE QUANT	PICK DATE	PICKED QUANTITY	WORK CENTER	PLANNER
48208	FORK, HEAVY DUTY LOCATION: 2607	EA	500 / 8000 OH	01	MANUAL	500	01/15			11
48593	GOOSE NECK LOCATION: 2844	EA	500 / 2000 OH		MANUAL	500	01/15			11
48852	HANDLE BAR LOCATION: 2992	EA	500 / 3525 OH		MANUAL	500	01/15			11
48054	FRONT WHEEL ASSY LOCATION: 3085	EA	500 / 3000 OH		MANUAL	500	01/15			06
48291	REAR WHEEL ASSY LOCATION: 3182	EA	500 / 100 OH		MANUAL	500	01/05			06
. . .										
48438	GREASE LOCATION: 9239	OZ	750 / 100000 OH		AUTO	750	01/15		AUTO	03
48623	FRONT WHEEL NUT LOCATION: 3271	EA	1000 / 60000 OH		AUTO	1000	01/15		AUTO	09
48379	REAR WHEEL NUT LOCATION: 3387	EA	1000 / 55000 OH		AUTO	1000	01/15		AUTO	09
48909	LOCK WASHER LOCATION: 3417	EA	2000 / 22500 OH		AUTO	2000	01/15		AUTO	09

You should note that ROP is an entirely different way to accomplish production and inventory control. ROP and MRP are antagonistic. You could use both in your factory at the same time, but usually not on the same item. It is universally acknowledged that MRP is a far better planning system for dependent demand items than ROP.

HOW TO USE THE REORDER POINT AND SAFETY STOCK SYSTEM

To be complete, however, you do need to understand the basics of ROP. The reorder point and safety stock half of this system deals with when to order and how much to order. The launch and expedite half of this method is concerned with issuing purchasing and manufacturing orders and then managing their due dates. Since the manufacturing environment is always dynamic, managing due dates is important and difficult.

Calculating the Reorder Point

In an ROP system, you identify all of the items possible that have some common or recurring usage, those items that are not peculiar to one or another end item.

Then for these selected items, you determine historical usage per day or week. Next you look up the lead time of each item. Then the reorder point is simply the demand you expect during the lead time period. (See Appendix I for a full description of calculating reorder point.)

Now your clerks simply monitor the inventory record of each item, and launch a purchase or a manufacturing order whenever an item hits its reorder point.

The quantity to be purchased or manufactured is called its lot size. There are many methods for calculating lot size, many of which attempt to balance setup or ordering cost against inventory carrying cost. For a full description of the common lot sizing techniques, see Appendix II.

Actual usage, however, always is different from the average. When the rate is lower than average, inventory piles up. If usage is faster than average, you run out. A basic rule of ROP is that it is good to have a generous amount of inventory, and running out is the worst thing that could happen to an inventory planner.

How Safety Stock Affects Your System

In order to guard against running out, planners put an extra pad in the reorder point. After gaining respectability, this pad was named safety stock.

The ROP method makes ample provision for safety stock. Now if the actual use of an item is faster than your average, there is a buffer to keep you from running out. Or if the factory or the vendor falls behind schedule, safety stock is there to protect you from this tardiness. Keeping enough safety stock on hand to cover the quality rejection of an entire lot, is a big problem with heavy implications regarding inventory investment.

Gradually graduate students at the business schools began writing papers about safety stock, and some worthwhile methods of calculating them have emerged. Appendix III gives a detailed explanation of the more usable methods.

Considering the emphasis on not running out, and the conventional attitude that inventory is good, it is easy to understand how inventories become bloated.

Here's a classic example: There was a stock-out of goosenecks for one of the bicycles, which resulted in shutting down that assembly line for two days. George, the planner was called into the plant manager's office. Mary, the plant manager, scolded George something fierce, making veiled and not so veiled predictions about George's continuity with the company. After this trauma, George resolved never to run out of goosenecks again. Or any other part either. George went back to his desk and adjusted his triggers accordingly, beefing up lot sizes, safety stocks, and leadtimes across the board. After telling his peers at the lunch table about his session with Mary, all the other planners did likewise. Repeated periodically over a period of years steadily, this episode reinforces the bias in favor of too much too soon, which is the opposite of Just-in-Time.

Figure 3.2 shows a graph of how this technique works. Here we see inventory gradually being used. When the count hits reorder point, the planner launches a replenishment order. Sometime later, one lead time, the replenishment quantity comes in and inventory zooms up to its maximum. If usage and leadtime are both normal, the replenishment arrives just before you must dip into safety stock. This saw-tooth pattern repeats itself over and over. Sometimes usage is a little less than average, and the replenishment comes in before the safety stock level is reached. Other times, usage is faster than average, and you dip into safety stock, which is why it is there.

Figure 3.2 Reorder Point and Safety Stock Model

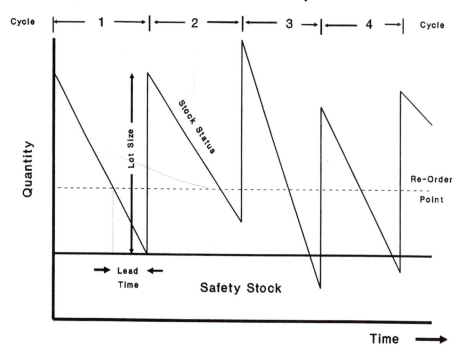

This graph also shows very clearly, that under ROP, average inventory is one-half of a lot size, plus safety stock. This is just the opposite of the Just-in-Time principle of zero inventory.

ROP is most applicable to items having independent demand, which usually are end items you build to stock, or service parts. Dependent demand items, items used in manufacturing, are better managed with MRP.

HOW TO USE THE LAUNCH AND EXPEDITE SYSTEM

The second half of the ROP method is concerned with creating purchase and manufacturing orders and managing their due dates. In an ROP system this is called Launch and Expedite. When reorder point is reached, the inventory planner writes up a requisition and sends it either to purchasing or to manufacturing. There are three main methods of creating requisitions, individual, traveling, and 2-bin.

For nonrecurring items, the planner fills out a requisition form, showing the required details, and sends it to the buyer or manufacturing planner. A traveling requisition is just a ledger card, with running historical data on it, that is used over and over. This saves writing up a separate piece of paper for every recurrence.

The two-bin system is a way to manage reordering with almost no recordkeeping. With this technique the quantity represented by the reorder point is put into a bin inside the main quantity. The smaller bin contains a traveling requisition. The stock room picks from the main bin until it is empty. Then they resort to the small bin, find the traveling requisition, and send it to the buyer or manufacturing planner. A refinement of this technique is yet a third bin containing the safety stock quantity and an expedite tag. If a stock picker ever has to dip into the safety stock bin, the expedite tag is forwarded for action.

Purchasing or manufacturing then convert the "req" into an order, which they launch to the vendor or into the shop. Orders include due dates.

As time moves forward, schedules change. When you want to make something sooner, some components likely will be short. These shortages are turned over to the expeditor who works with shop supervisors and the buyers to bring in the parts sooner. In ROP companies, about 70 percent of each buyer's time is spent expediting vendor deliveries. In the factory, shop supervisors usually spend more than half of their time chasing parts, and in the legendary, morning supervisors' meeting.

Because so much time is spent expediting, there is never any time left over to figure out which orders aren't needed as soon as originally planned. This would be called de-expediting if it ever occurred. Considering how much expediting goes on with no corresponding de-expediting, you can quickly understand why the original due dates on all those purchase and manufacturing orders are altogether unreliable.

How Kitting Affects Production

In trying to recognize shortages before it is too late, many companies resort to "staging" or "kitting" before manufacturing begins. In this classic, you have the stock room pull all the parts needed for a month's planned production, and set them aside in a segregated area. The kitting is done well in advance of the start of the month. Many companies kit four, five, or even six weeks ahead of the start of the month. Now you have plenty of time to expedite shortages.

Kitting never works very well. What always happens is the shortage for one job is tied up in the kit for another, and few kits have all their components. Then at the beginning of the month, when the factory needs work, the expediters get busy robbing one kit to complete another one, sometimes keeping track of what they are doing, usually not. This makes for a rather chaotic situation that feeds on itself, getting worse by the day as the month cranks forward.

I once visited the staging area in an electronics assembly plant. There, lined up in neat rows just inside the door of the stock room were tote pans containing components for pending manufacturing jobs. Neatly on display on the front of each tote pan was a list of shortages. The idea was that as the missing parts were expedited into stock, it would be easy to slip the short parts into the pan, and cross it off the short list. Of course, the short part just put in the pan could easily be on another hot list somewhere else. Expediters found it very convenient to go shopping for shortages in the staging area, where new arrivals were easy to spot, having just been crossed off one of the shortage lists. And the sought-after item was usually on top of the pile in the pan, ready for the taking. The resulting chaos is standard for this method.

Frequently the situation becomes so bad that the stockroom experiences a form of gridlock. They have tons of inventory stacked up in the kitting area, with a hair-raising dollar value, but can't seem to start any manufacturing orders with their full complement of components. When the situation gets this bad the only thing to do is shut down the factory for a few days, put everything back into the main stock room, update the records, and start over. This is called de-staging.

Reorder point practice does allow some items to be managed individually.

Using the ABC Method

In order to keep things from getting completely out of hand, experienced practitioners turned to the ABC approach. Under this technique, they analyzed their items, selecting the top 20 percent, which always accounted for 80 percent of the value of all parts. Then the planner calculates the needs for A-items, based on the sales forecast. The planner then makes requisitions with deliveries timed to fit the month's schedule, not by a historical reorder point. The ABC theory says that we should pay close attention to the important few, and use more casual methods on the trivial many. This helped. (See Appendix IV for a detailed explanation on the ABC method for analysis.)

Because the planner does this on a monthly cycle, the due dates aren't very accurate to start with, and get worse as constant expediting warps the plan still further. However, this is better than trying to set order points for the items involved and represents a primitive form of MRP.

Five Disadvantages of the Reorder Point and Safety Stock/Launch and Expedite Methods

Although the Reorder Point and Safety Stock/Launch and Expedite method of production and inventory control has worked historically and does continue to work in some applications, it does have some conspicuous drawbacks.

1. ROP is backward-looking. This system tries to plan for the future by looking at past experience. When the future is just like the past, this can work, but this cannot predict changes in demand. ROP is like trying to steer the ship by watching the wake.

2. Due dates are meaningless. Extensive expediting and no de-expediting sees to that.

3. Inventory is always excessive. If an ROP system were ever to work according to the ideal, total on hand inventory would be one-half of your aggregate lot size plus aggregate safety stock. And since ROP systems never work exactly according to the model, inventory is always higher than that. Having a generous amount of everything on hand at all times is just exactly opposite from Just-in-Time!

4. Service is poor. This starts with service to your customer, but includes service to the factory.

5. Expenses are higher. You have a large inventory to finance. And inventory carrying cost is at least 36 percent a year, or 2 percent a month. Incessant expediting is costly beyond

just the payroll of the expediters. Jerking factory schedules around on a moment's notice degrades efficiency. Unnecessary overtime at the end of the month is prevalent. Overtime and premium transportation from vendors is a tangible out-of-pocket extra expense.

These techniques, now called Aggregate Inventory management, can successfully be applied to items with independent demand. However for items with dependent demand, MRP techniques are far better.

HOW TO ESTABLISH YOUR PRODUCTION PLAN FOR WHAT YOU WANT TO MANUFACTURE

Strategic plans, marketing plans, and sales forecasts represent end-item demands, as we discussed in Chapter 2. The production plan is your first strategic step in the planning process to produce these end items to satisfying your marketplace. Your production plan is your top level, first supply plan.

Production planning is an upper management activity. It represents a foundation upon which lower level plans are built, notably the master production schedule and the capacity requirements plan.

The production plan has several important aspects. They are:

- Scope

- Multiple Plants

- Planning Horizon

- Production Rate

- Product Introduction

- Replanning Frequency

Figure 3.3 (page 64) shows a sample production plan.

Defining the Scope of the Production Plan

What do we include in the production plan? What is its scope? This is the first characteristic of your production plan. Unless your product line is very narrow, you will want to group your end items into families. You designate your family groups according to similarity of manufacture. Family members should have many common or similar components, and should be manufactured the same way, perhaps in the same facility or work centers. The choice of family groupings could be the same as shown on the marketing plan, but not necessarily. Grouping by manufacturing similarity also supports group technology practices, which is covered later in this book.

Figure 3.3 shows Intercontinental Wheel Goods' production plan for two years, grouped by family designation. They have three families of bicycles, one each for scooters, skateboards, baby buggies, strollers, and wheel chairs. Each of these families have a varying number of actual end items. The specific end items will be planned through the master production schedule and the final assembly schedule.

How to Accommodate Multiple Plants in Preparing Production Plans

Another aspect of scope comes to play if you have multiple manufacturing sites. Most companies with multiple plants have them making separate product lines. A more complicated situation is where plants feed other plants, and treat each other as customer-supplier. In both of these cases you should prepare a separate production plan for each plant. In a company with centralized corporate functions such as marketing and engineering, the production plan is best managed at the corporate level. In those companies that have truly independent plants, with their own sales, marketing, and engineering functions, the production plan is more appropriately done at each plant.

The most complicated multiple plant environment is where the separate plants are considered work centers within the final assembly plant. This is very difficult to manage you should avoid treating supplying plants as work centers.

Defining Your Planning Horizon

How far ahead should your production plan look? Your production plan should extend into the future as far as the marketing plan, and should look forward far enough to allow for capital, material sourcing, and personnel staffing plans to be made. Usually, buying new equipment has the longest leadtime. Another aspect of timing in the production plan is its time increments. Most production plans have monthly time periods, often called buckets.

Figure 3.3 Intercontinental Wheel Goods Production Plan

		Jan	Feb	Mar	Apr	May	Jun	Jul	Aug	Sep	Oct	Nov	Dec	Total
Dirt Bikes	1993	5000	5000	4500	8000	3500	4500	5500	2500	4000	3000	4500	5500	55500
	1994	5500	5500	5000	10000	4500	5500	6000	3000	5000	4500	5500	6500	66500
Racing Bikes	1993	6000	6500	5500	5000	4500	4500	5500	3000	4000	4000	6000	6500	61000
	1994	7000	7500	7500	7000	6000	6000	6500	4000	5500	5000	6500	7000	75500
Mountain Bikes	1993	10000	4000	3500	3000	3000	4000	4500	1500	3000	4000	4500	5500	50500
	1994	10000	4000	3500	3000	3000	4000	4500	1500	3000	4000	4500	5500	50500
Scooters	1993	1000	1500	1500	1800	5000	4000	3000	1500	2500	3000	3000	3500	31300
	1994	3500	3500	4000	4000	9000	6000	5000	2000	3500	3500	3500	4000	51500
Skate Boards	1993	6000	6500	6000	7000	7200	7500	7000	1000	6000	4000	8500	6000	72700
	1994	6500	6500	7000	7000	7500	7800	7500	3000	7000	5000	9500	7000	81300
Baby Buggies	1993	150	150	150	150	150	150	150	0	100	100	150	150	1550
	1994	150	150	150	150	150	150	150	0	100	100	150	150	1550
Strollers	1993	2000	2100	2100	2000	1800	1600	1700	500	1200	1300	1000	1200	18500
	1994	2500	2500	2500	2200	2000	1800	2000	700	1500	1500	1200	1500	21900
Wheel Chairs	1993	0	0	50	100	100	100	150	50	150	200	250	250	1400
	1994	300	300	350	350	400	400	500	200	500	600	600	650	5150
Training Wheels		4000	3000	2000	2000	1000	1000							17000

The production plan for Intercontinental Wheel Goods, Figure 3.3, has a two-year horizon, January 1993 through December 1994, by month. This horizon together with the monthly quantities supports long range planning and budgeting.

Establishing Your Production Rate

The next characteristic of the production plan is production rate. In our example of International Wheel Goods, we see a production rate for each of the eight families for each month. The rate for both Augusts is considerably smaller, because that's vacation month for the factory. There is no such attenuation in December, because the company has eliminated the year-end physical inventory in favor of daily cycle counting.

They also are planning a big promotion of dirt bikes in May of each year, and the needed production is reflected in April's numbers. Similarly, Intercontinental has a standing order from a large retailer in Brazil for 6000 mountain bikes to be shipped in January of each year, and this bulge can be seen in January's plans.

Planning for Product Introduction

Introducing new products and phasing out old ones is another function of production planning. We seem to have entered an age where old products fade much sooner than in the past, and new products are being introduced much more often.

There is a California company that manufactures a small line of electronic devices used in hospitals for diagnosis. Their equipment also uses video displays. They have competition in this field, and semi-conductor and video technology is advancing at a breath-taking pace. They have to completely redesign their entire product line on a two-year cycle. Given the complexity of the product, and how long it takes to do the new designs, by the time they get each generation out into the marketplace, it is nearly obsolete. This may be an extreme example, but not uncommon.

Formal manufacturing systems have many powerful tools to assist in new product introduction, starting with the production plan. The production plan should show the quantities per month, usually starting with a small number, and gradually increasing, in phase with the marketing plan.

International Wheel Goods has a plan to go into the wheel chair business in April, 1993. Accordingly, they are planning to start by manufacturing 50 in March, 1993, gradually increasing production, month by month, to 650 in December, 1994.

International Wheel Goods introduced their line of scooters in 1992, and are planning increased demand over the next two years. Their rate of production is planned to go up from 1000 in January, 1993 to 4000 in December, 1994.

The production plan also is used to phase out aging or obsolete product lines. International Wheel Goods is phasing out its line of training wheels, and will quit producing them just before vacation, in July, 1993.

Establishing Your Replanning Frequency

Replanning frequency is another important aspect of production planning. Manufacturing is a dynamic activity in a dynamic world. Manufacturing people like to talk about freezing the schedule months in advance. But practical considerations dictate otherwise. If you are like most companies, you are lucky if your schedule stays the same for more than a few days. This is why your production plan should be revised and updated monthly.

This requires a regular, formal procedure for dropping last month from the schedule, adding a corresponding new month on the end, and for reviewing any of the months in between as circumstances suggest.

Considering the general nature of the production plan, more often than monthly usually is not necessary, but less often than monthly obstructs the kind of flexibility that world-class, Just-in-Time demand.

But just how extensive should we permit this monthly revision to be? The marketplace is demanding flexibility and change but manufacturing can cope better when schedules remain stable.

You should develop a company policy to cover how much flexibility you need and want. This policy should be tailored for each of the families of products used in the production plan. In all cases, there is more flexibility farther into the future, less close in. Your policy should be tailored for each product family used in the production plan. It should simply state how much of an increase or decrease you will accept for each succeeding month in the schedule, by family. Your tolerance for decreases will be greater than for increases. Your tolerance range will be narrow for the first month, and become successively wider into the future.

This sets a standard framework for your planners and dictates what can be done routinely versus what needs special approval from management.

HOW TO MANAGE THE PRODUCTION PLAN

Being dynamic, the production plan must be managed responsibly. This is an upper management duty.

How the Planning Board Functions

Whether decentralized to the plant level, or centralized at a corporate or group level, managing the production plan should be done by a formally constituted group, the planning board. The planning board is made up of the top executive of the business unit involved, plus all functional managers reporting to him/her. In a decentralized planning environment this would be the plant manager and the head of manufacturing, sales/marketing, engineering, materials, purchasing, quality, and any other executives who contribute to the success of manufacturing and marketing.

In a centralized, corporate planning environment the members' titles vary greatly, but it is important that the executives in charge of those vital functions attend.

This is the ideal. But I often find that these managers do not report to a common boss. This is especially true in larger companies. I have had clients where manufacturing operations, and production and inventory control were in one location, sales and marketing somewhere else, and design engineering still elsewhere. And the organization chart reflected it. We often find several plants dealing with central corporate purchasing.

Companies with such exploded functions always have a harder time in creating a production plan. However, this does not reduce the need, and therefore the necessity of making a production plan. You still must have participation and concurrence from these functional executives, no matter what the organization chart looks like. Without this you will degrade your system and lapse into sub-optimal planning, an appearance of arbitrariness, and intensify politics.

Developing the Production Plan

Developing the Production Plan can be divided into five steps. They are:

■ Preparation

■ Review

■ Negotiation

■ Approval

■ Implementation

1. Preparing the Plan

Preparing the production plan is an important chore. A well-run manufacturing company will have a strong master scheduling function. This is a good place to draft the master production plan. The master schedulers use the marketing plan, any sales forecasts that are available, the volume and pace of incoming customer orders, finished goods levels and activities, and any other factors that have an impact on what to manufacture.

Using all available information, and calling on their skill and experience they develop the monthly production schedule, extending out two years, typically, by family. After approval, this will become the raw material for your detailed master scheduling. Crafting the production plan is partly a technical operation, but it is also a creative activity, requiring experience, skill and judgement. Your planners must know your company and its products intimately, as well as your customers and marketplace. When done, the production plan is distributed to upper management.

2. Reviewing the Plan

The new plan has been prepared based on all sorts of information, including last month's performance. The first thing your planning committee does is review all significant schedule deviations, either shortfalls or overages. Their purpose is to decide on the causes for these deviations and decide how to eradicate them. In order for the benefits of a formal system to happen, you must provide the wherewithal to manufacture your plans routinely and regularly.

3. Negotiating the Plan

The production plan is distributed to upper management several days before the regularly-scheduled monthly production planning meeting.

The monthly planning meeting is a strategic activity, demanding the attention of the business unit's upper management. This is not a trivial committee meeting. Even given its importance, it should not take longer than one hour. Even the marketing executive should be able to work that into his/her schedule.

For most families, the production rates will not vary much from last month's, and require little discussion. Occasionally, however, something unusual is occurring, needing upper management attention and strategy. Gaining or losing a big customer is such an occasion. A pending strike in your plant or a vendor's could be another. A new federal regulation could easily affect production. Rising or falling tariff walls around the world certainly should be recognized in the production plan.

A frequent discussion point is the introduction of a new product line. For example, the VP of Marketing turns to the VP of manufacturing and asks, "When are you finally going to get into production on the Batman® Bike?" At this the VP of manufacturing turns to the VP of engineering and asks, "When are you going to get the bills of material to us?" Now the VP of engineering turns to the VP of Marketing and says, "When are you going to firm up the specs?" And 'round it goes. After considerable discussion, perhaps even argument, they agree on an introduction timetable, probably one that taxes all departments. Then they are able to put into the production plan the introductory quantities, increasing over the months to support the forecasts being made.

4. *Approving the Plan*

When all is said and done, these executives must approve the production plan, thereby certifying it as the official plan of the company. Everybody won't be completely satisfied, but if the CEO has given everybody a fair hearing, the decisions can be rational, and not arbitrary which could easily happen if this planning forum were not in place.

5. *Implementing the Plan*

Now you turn over the certified production plan to the master production scheduling department to be fulfilled. In this regard it represents a direct instruction to the rest of the company what they are expected to accomplish in the coming months. This included all levels in the organization chart and all locations. Indirectly, this also influences your vendors in the same way. Now the direct use of the production plan is to prepare the master production schedules for each end item for each plant.

HOW THE MASTER PRODUCTION SCHEDULE TELLS WHAT TO MAKE, WHERE, AND WHEN

The master production schedule is the most important single schedule in your formal manufacturing (MRP/JIT) system. It fulfills the monthly production plan, and schedules each end item exactly. The master production schedule is then used by the MRP software to calculate precisely all of the raw materials, parts, and sub-assemblies needed, their quantities and due dates. This applies equally to purchased and manufactured items.

Where your production plan is a family schedule of supply, the master production schedule is your supply plan for each end item.

The master production schedule has several important aspects:

- It must be honest.

- It must be detailed.

- It must be maintained.

- It must have a planning period.

- It must be reiterative.

- The master production scheduler should have corporate responsibility.

Adhering to an Honest Schedule

The master production schedule must be honest. You must be able to manufacture it every week at first. Then if you want to achieve world-class, JIT performance, you must manufacture your master schedule every day.

Because it is derived primarily from the monthly production plan, endorsed by management, it is an instruction to everybody in manufacturing and its support departments on exactly what to produce and when.

The master schedule is not a wish list. Bills of material must be in place; no fictitious products. Manufacturing facilities must be adequate. Your plant and your vendors must have the capacity to make the volumes involved. It must be reasonably producible in the week (or day) scheduled.

Honesty also prohibits overloading or front-end loading. Front-end loading does not provide incentive to produce more. It only causes confusion and false schedules. Many is the master schedule that has five weeks' worth of work past due, the next few weeks overloaded, the work tapering off after that, to a vanishing work load in 10 weeks.

Another part of being honest is to recognize and respect time fences, which are covered in Chapter 8. The worst abuses I see in the use of MRP systems occur in master production scheduling. Overloading and changing quantities within leadtime are the worst offenders. This is known as "jerking the master schedule" and always results in a great deal of confusion, expediting, and low morale. This bad practice can ruin an MRP system and propel the company back to informal, reaction-oriented hot list/expedite procedures. It is incumbent on management to see to it that the master production schedule is respected.

The temptation to jerk the master schedule around is great, especially for executives who have no direct involvement in manufacturing.

I worked for a military subcontractor in the 1950s. Being at the end of the supply chain meant that the planning and execution problems of our customers were amplified as they were dumped on us. I was production control manager. When a customer called with an order to be expedited, we made an honest attempt to give a realistic ship date. Our ship date was seldom soon enough. All of our major customers knew that when they wanted an earlier promise, all they had to do was call the general manager, who would promise anything to anybody. Then he would come to us with the good, old college football coach act and tell us that he was counting on us to fulfill this new promise. He acted as if we could do it by sheer dedication and college try effort.

He chose to ignore vendor lead times and our own capacities. Each new promise went into the hopper, where we pulled new work according to the last expedite phone call. The result was that we were delinquent on 75 percent of our promised dates and had a terrible performance reputation with the very customers who, together with our general manager, were causing the problem. However, we were blamed for our poor performance.

In my experience, irrational management of the master production schedule is by far the worst abuse of MRP II systems worldwide. In order for your system to achieve excellence, the master production schedule must be managed correctly, rationally, and realistically.

How to Assure the Schedule Is Detailed

The second aspect your master production schedule is its level of detail. The master production schedule almost always shows shippable end items. This is an important refinement of the production plan which usually shows families. You can expand on the end item rule in some applications with planning bills or modular bills, which I will cover later in this chapter.

Each item shown on the master schedule must be identified with its unique item number which must have a corresponding bill of material. It is your bills of material at this and successively lower levels that will allow the computer to calculate all needs for all components. I will cover Bills of material extensively in Chapter 5.

Since the master production schedule covers shippable end items, it is necessarily organized by factory. This is the way the centralized production plan is apportioned to each specific factory. If your company makes each end item only in one designated factory, the apportionment is already done. But if your company makes the same end item in more than one plant, the master production schedule becomes the vehicle to apportion work, and achieve whatever balancing of capacities at the producing locations is needed.

How to Be Sure the Schedule Is Maintained

The master schedule must also be maintained. This means that it is open to review at least weekly, perhaps more often. This is needed to accommodate changes occurring in the real world.

One source of change comes from manufacturing and purchasing. Since the schedules for components and subassemblies derive from the master schedule, you must adhere closely to these schedules or you won't be able to fulfill your master production schedule. This is where expediting still has use. Manufacturing and purchasing must try their best to get on schedule and stay there. If circumstances stand in the way of doing this, the problems must be eliminated. The schedule is very important.

Meeting schedule gets even more important as you move to Just-in-Time performance. Under JIT you will have smaller lots and much more frequent deliveries. Quite a few companies now have daily deliveries from vendors and upstream work centers, and many are even talking about "shiftly" or even hourly deliveries. In such an environment, even a slight delay could cause a line shutdown and a domino effect of cascading missed schedules.

However, when a schedule really is impossible to meet, and the master schedule is imperiled, it must be changed to honestly reflect the new reality. The alteration of the master schedule at this point is crucially important, because it then reschedules and resynchronizes all its other dependent components. This often involves rescheduling dozens if not hundreds of components. If we are not going to be able to build an end item until later, we certainly don't need its components until later. One of the very powerful features of an MRP system is its ability to de-expedite as easily as it expedites. This constant replanning activity, occurring at electronic speed in the computer, can be looked on in terms of synchronization. All components are kept in constant synchronization as to their real needs.

Establishing a Planning Period

Another aspect of the master production schedule is that it is a daily or a weekly schedule. When first introduced, MRP systems mostly were organized by week, commonly called weekly bucketed. With weekly planning periods, there was a problem on what to do first thing Monday morning and what to do last thing Friday afternoon. This problem (probably more of a symptom) was solved with a rich array of priority rules. These rules took account of scheduled end date, today's date, number of operations remaining, number of setup and run hours left to do, and so on.

As companies began to understood the theories involved, and got better at using these new systems, they gradually began to move toward daily time increments, to a daily bucketed system. Especially with proprietary software, teamed up with cheap disk drives, daily schedules are almost universal, and it's difficult to find a weekly bucketed system nowadays.

A daily time-phased master production schedule will cause a daily time-phased material plan and support many JIT principles. JIT advocates are now even beginning to suggest scheduling by shift or even by hour.

How to Be Sure the Schedule Is Reiterative

Life in manufacturing is very dynamic. Lots is going on in the factory, and your vendors are experiencing the same. Your customers, and especially your sales force, are constantly asking for changes to schedules and quantities. This means that the master schedule process must be repeated at frequent intervals.

In order for a change to the master schedule to become effective, it is necessary to run the whole MRP calculation. Until recently this was considered to be too time consuming to be done except on the weekend. But within the last few years computer programs have been made more time-efficient, computers have gotten a lot faster, and disk storage capacity much larger. Now it is possible to run "full bore MRP" every night.

The result of this increased functionality is that the master schedule can be fine tuned on a daily basis. This means that all schedules are reviewed every night and resynchronized for the start of the next day. This makes your schedules more timely and precise, and better supports the JIT idea of daily lot sizes.

On the negative side, this new functionality offers five times the opportunity to jerk the schedule. When you step forward to daily MRP, you must have very firm policies and procedures regarding time fence zones and the degree of flexibility you can tolerate within each zone. This topic is covered in detail in Chapter 8.

Assigning Corporate Responsibility to the Master Production Scheduler

Because of its importance to the whole system, the master production schedule must be carefully and skillfully developed. This is why the master production scheduling activity should be a separate organizational unit, a separate box on the organization chart. It should be on a par with the production control, inventory control, and purchasing departments. The manager of master production scheduling should be a person of stature, not a senior Kardex™ clerk.

The master production scheduler has an obligation to promulgate the production plan, as issued by upper management each month. In order to do the job right, the scheduler recognizes and works with an array of information. Certainly the most important one is the production plan. This monthly plan by family must be converted to a daily plan by end item. The master scheduler also must recognize resource limitations both in the factory and among vendors. Such nonroutine things such as weather or potential strikes enter in as do vacation and holiday schedules. The master scheduler also knows the mix and volume of customer and/or warehouse orders. He/she also knows lead times and lot sizes of the end items going on the schedule.

Even more than with the production plan, the master production scheduler blends routine technology with wisdom, judgment, product knowledge, and a profound understanding of the factory.

The most contentious duty that the master scheduler performs is to turn down incoming requests that do not make sense. It frequently happens that one salesperson requests something special that will ruin the schedule for another salesperson's customer. Since the master schedule must be a truthful and accurate statement of what will be manufactured, the idea of somehow muddling through and doing both is no longer acceptable. The master scheduler must say no to many worthy requests. And management must keep its hands off. Or, if management decides to intercede on behalf of one customer, you must understand and accept that another customer's order will be delayed.

It is management's rightful prerogative to take liberties with routine policies and procedures when circumstances dictate. What is not permitted, however, is the oft-heard directive, "put both into the schedule, or I'll get someone who will." This kind of irrational and arbitrary behavior will ruin the integrity of your schedules and prevent your system from functioning. This attitude also will drive out your competent schedulers, which will further degrade the performance of your system.

The most important single thing that management can and must do to achieve excellence is to preserve the integrity of the master production schedule. The master production schedule is a daily or weekly statement of what will be manufactured.

HOW TO USE THE ROUGH-CUT CAPACITY PLAN TO MANAGE YOUR VENDOR AND MANUFACTURING RESOURCES

Over the years, MRP has been criticized for ignoring capacity constraints; for scheduling against infinite capacity. The problem has long since been overcome, but the critics persist. In a modern MRP II system, capacities are carefully planned and managed at two different levels, rough-cut and detailed.

Rough-cut capacity planning has evolved into a method of simulating the relation between availability and need of selected resources, based on top level plans. This simulation identifies shortages far enough in advance to remove them or to change the plan. No more muddling through. The modern MRP II system knows well in advance the capacity loads on its key resources, and management has enough time and information to keep them properly balanced.

Rough-cut capacity planning was one of the later techniques to be incorporated into MRP, and is becoming more important as JIT methods drastically reduce manufacturing throughput time. JIT factories are organized differently and move so fast, that many of the traditional capacity constraints are disappearing.

Rough-cut capacity planning occurs either at the production plan, master production scheduling level, or both. Rough-cut planning is based on capacity bills. These are mini-bills of material, separate from the product bills. Rough-cut capacity bills are developed and maintained separately, and contain not only traditional manufacturing resources but any other resources that can be linked to an end item or end item family. Examples of traditional manufacturing resources include bottleneck work centers, scarce skills, inspection capacity, preventive maintenance schedules, etc.

Capacity bills often include availability from critical vendors and overseas procurement constraints. But unlike product bills, capacity bills often include nontraditional resources such as floor loading, storage capacity, engineering time, regulatory agency approval, and so on. In some advanced companies, their accounting departments are using rough-cut capacity planning to simulate their monthly financial statements. This simulation is tied to the actual plans in each month, not to an historical extrapolation, and provides a much more accurate and realistic financial forecast.

Examples of Rough-Cut Capacity Planning

Figures 3.1 through 3.9 show examples of rough-cut capacity planning. Figure 3.4 shows the production plan for Intercontinental Wheel Goods for their dirt bikes. This is the same production plan we saw in Figure 3.3 above, just for January through June, with each month's planned quantities.

Figure 3.5 shows the rough-cut capacity bill for dirt bikes. I have selected the final assembly department, the frame vendor, standard cost, and selling price to use in this example. Notice that I am including an outside vendor, and two planning items from accounting. The two from accounting will show us how nontraditional resources can be served with this tool. From the capacity bill we see that it takes 0.2 hours to finally assemble a dirt bike. They also need one frame per bike.

Figure 3.4 Intercontinental Wheel Goods
Partial Production Plan
for Rough-Capacity Planning

Dirt Bikes

Month	Quantity
Jan	5000
Feb	5000
Mar	4500
Apr	8000
May	3500
Jun	4500
Jul	5500
Aug	2500
Sep	4000
Oct	3000

Figure 3.5 Intercontinental Wheel Goods
Rough-Cut Capacity Bill of Load Units

```
                                              DATE: 11/23
ITEM NUMBER     ITEM DESCRIPTION
    4711        DIRT BIKES

    LOAD        LOAD CENTER           LOAD
 CENTER ID      DESCRIPTION           UNITS    U/M

    FAS         FINAL ASSEMBLY          .2     HRS
    FRAM        FRAME VENDOR             1     EA
    COST        STANDARD COST        57.90     DLR
    SELL        SELLING PRICE        96.50     DLR
```

The accounting department has determined that the average standard cost of goods sold for the family of dirt bikes is $57.90, and the selling price is $96.50.

Figure 3.6 shows the resulting load on the final assembly department, given the production plan and the rough-cut capacity bill. In this example we see the scheduled load versus the capacity for each month and cumulative. We see this information both in terms of hours and as a percentage. And to make the report more usable, we see a simple graph at the right, showing the percentage load for each month, corresponding to the percentage in the period load % column.

In the heading, we find that the supervisor of the final assembly department plans to have a capacity of 1000 per month starting in January. The capacity will be raised to 1,500 just for April, so that they can build up for their May promotion. Then the capacity will go back down to 800 per month for the rest of the planning horizon on the report.

It looks like the final assembly department is fairly well balanced in the aggregate. If we look at June, July, and August, we can see that the monthly overload for June and July looks bad, but the year-to-date load is much more level. Based on year-to-date capacity, July is only going to be 4 percent short, and we can assume that this promotional lump has been adequately planned for.

Intercontinental's frame vendor is portrayed in Figure 3.7. It looks like this vendor also has planned for the May promotion. Even though the monthly overloads look a little cyclical, the aggregate, year-to-date look very well balanced, with April just 2 percent short. The vendor, responding the surge in planned demand has planned their capacities for 5,000 per month from January through March, raising it to 7,000 for April and May, and dropping back down to 5,000 from June on.

Accounting has made revenue and expense plans to match the production plan, represented in Figure 3.8. They have targeted standard cost to run at $200,000 per month between January and March, upping it to $450,000 for April, then back to $200,000 from May onward.

Because this use is just a little nonstandard you must use a little care in reading the numbers. In this case, an overage means that the target costs are higher than what will be loaded, whereas a shortage means that costs likely will run over target. In our example, it looks like Intercontinental will consistently have higher expenses than targeted, although not serious except in July where the aggregate cost overage is 10 percent. Perhaps management will want to look into the causes for this situation.

Figure 3.6 Intercontinental Wheel Goods
Rough-Cut Capacity Load
Final Assembly Department

DATE: 11/23

LOAD CENTER ID	LOAD CENTER DESCRIPTION	LOAD U/M	CAPACITY 1 DATE	CAPACITY 1 UNITS	CAPACITY 2 DATE	CAPACITY 2 UNITS	CAPACITY 3 DATE	CAPACITY 3 UNITS	DAPACITY 4 DATE	DAPACITY 4 UNITS
FAS	FINAL ASSEMBLY	HRS	JAN	1000	APR	1500	MAY	800		

	/---------------PERIOD		--------------\		/--TO-DATE LOAD--\		/-----% OF PERIOD CAPACITY LOADED------\
MONTH	LOAD	CAPACITY	OVER/SHORT	LOAD %	OVER/SHORT	%	--------50--------100--------150--------200
JAN	1000	1000	0	100	0	100	********************
FEB	1000	1000	0	100	0	100	********************
MAR	900	1000	+100	90	+100	97	*******************
APR	1600	1500	-100	107	0	100	********************
MAY	700	800	+100	88	+100	98	******************
JUN	900	800	-100	113	0	100	***********************
JUL	1100	800	-300	138	-300	104	***************************
AUG	500	800	+300	63	0	100	*************
SEP	800	800	0	100	0	100	********************
OCT	600	800	+200	75	+200	98	***************

Figure 3.7 Intercontinental Wheel Goods
Rough-Cut Capacity Load
Frame Vendor

DATE: 11/23

LOAD CENTER ID	LOAD CENTER DESCRIPTION	LOAD U/M	CAPACITY 1 DATE	CAPACITY 1 UNITS	CAPACITY 2 DATE	CAPACITY 2 UNITS	CAPACITY 3 DATE	CAPACITY 3 UNITS	DAPACITY 4 DATE	DAPACITY 4 UNITS
FRAM	FRAME VENDOR	EA	JAN	5000	APR	7000	MAY	5000	AUG	3000

	/---------------PERIOD--------------\				/--TO-DATE LOAD--\		/-----% OF PERIOD CAPACITY LOADED------\
MONTH	LOAD	CAPACITY	OVER/SHORT	LOAD %	OVER/SHORT	%	--------50-------100-------150-------200
JAN	5000	5000	0	100	0	100	********************
FEB	5000	5000	0	100	0	100	********************
MAR	4500	5000	+500	90	+500	97	*******************
APR	8000	7000	-1000	107	-500	102	********************
MAY	3500	5000	+1500	70	+1000	96	**************
JUN	4500	5000	+500	90	+1500	95	******************
JUL	5500	5000	-500	110	+1000	97	**********************
AUG	2500	3000	+500	83	+1500	96	*****************
SEP	4000	3000	-1000	133	500	99	***************************
OCT	3000	3000	0	100	+500	99	********************

Figure 3.8 Intercontinental Wheel Goods
Rough-Cut Capacity Load
Standard Cost

DATE: 11/23

LOAD CENTER ID	LOAD CENTER DESCRIPTION	COST STANDARD COST	LOAD U/M DLR	CAPACITY 1 DATE JAN UNITS 280000	CAPACITY 2 DATE APR UNITS 450000	CAPACITY 3 DATE MAY UNITS 200000	DAPACITY 4 DATE UNITS

MONTH	LOAD	CAPACITY	PERIOD OVER/SHORT	LOAD %	TO-DATE LOAD OVER/SHORT	%	% OF PERIOD CAPACITY LOADED 50----100----150----200
JAN	289500	280000	-9500	103	-9500	103	********************
FEB	289500	280000	-9500	103	-19000	103	********************
MAR	260550	280000	+19450	93	+450	100	******************
APR	463200	450000	-13200	103	-12750	101	********************
MAY	202650	200000	-2650	101	-15400	101	********************
JUN	260550	200000	-60550	130	-75950	104	**************************
JUL	318450	200000	-118450	159	-194400	110	********************************
AUG	144750	200000	+55250	72	-139150	107	**************
SEP	231600	200000	-31600	116	-170750	107	***********************
OCT	173700	200000	+26300	87	-144450	106	*****************

81

Accounting also wants to have a preview of coming revenues from the dirt bike family. (See Figure 3.9.) They have set up their target revenues for dirt bikes at $480,000 between January and March, raising it to $775,000 for the April build-up. Then its business as usual, with a target of $400,000 for May through July, and $300,000 from August and beyond.

Because this is revenue and not cost, we analyze the variances opposite of the sheet for costs. On this plan, a shortage means that they will have revenue less than their target, and an overage means that revenue will exceed plan. Their monthly figures look quite good, with a marked overage in July. The aggregate figures are very level, and at the end of this planning period, they are only 2 percent less than their target.

In the case of Intercontinental Wheel Goods, they would have a similar set of plans for the other product families, and a total for the company. In a real-world situation you could have a more extensive rough-cut capacity bill. In a good system, several different capacity bills can be in existence at the same time, serving different departments.

With an on-line, real-time system in place, it is fairly easy to change your rough-cut capacity bills, and to request a simulation rerun. Results come back quickly, because the computer's processing is not extensive. By altering your assumptions and re-calculating, you can make very effective adjustments to your plans far in advance. You can repeat this as much as needed, making you proactive instead of reactive.

Even if you don't have a full-fledged computer system, you still can do rough-cut capacity planning. This segment of a formal system stands somewhat alone. It is not hard to do an effective job of rough cut capacity planning with an ordinary spread-sheet program on a micro computer.

The main use, however for a rough-cut capacity plan is to make sure that all resources are in place to support the production plan. It is very important that you do rough-cut capacity planning regularly, and solve shortage problems.

When a resource will be short, you have two choices. The first course of action, the preferred one, is to remove the shortage. Hire more labor. Get more machines. Help the vendor expand. If this is not possible, the second course of action cannot be avoided. That is to change the schedule. Better to change the timing or the mix on the production plan. But if necessary, reduce quantities. It is of primary importance to have a realistic,

Figure 3.9 Intercontinental Wheel Goods
Rough-Cut Capacity Load
Selling Price

DATE: 11/23

LOAD CENTER ID	LOAD CENTER DESCRIPTION	LOAD U/M	CAPACITY 1 DATE	CAPACITY 1 UNITS	CAPACITY 2 DATE	CAPACITY 2 UNITS	CAPACITY 3 DATE	CAPACITY 3 UNITS	DAPACITY 4 DATE	DAPACITY 4 UNITS
COST	SELLING PRICE	DLR	JAN	480000	APR	775000	MAY	400000	AUG	300000

	/----------------PERIOD		--------------	-\	/--TO-DATE LOAD--\		/-----% OF PERIOD CAPACITY LOADED------\
MONTH	LOAD	CAPACITY	OVER/SHORT	LOAD %	OVER/SHORT	%	--------50--------100--------150--------200
JAN	482500	480000	-2500	101	-2500	101	********************
FEB	482500	480000	-2500	103	-5000	101	********************
MAR	434250	480000	+45750	90	+40750	97	******************
APR	772000	775000	+3000	100	+43750	98	********************
MAY	337750	400000	+62250	84	+106000	97	*****************
JUN	434250	400000	-34250	109	+71750	99	**********************
JUL	530750	400000	-130750	133	-59000	103	***************************
AUG	241250	300000	+58750	80	-250	101	****************
SEP	386000	300000	-86000	129	-86250	103	**************************
OCT	289500	300000	+10500	97	-75550	103	********************

a "doable" production plan. An overloaded or front-end loaded schedule is a sure way to destroy an MRP system. And this destruction occurs quickly, because as the schedule falls behind, all derived plans are in error, and the old, informal systems reappear.

HOW TO USE YOUR MATERIAL REQUIREMENTS PLAN TO SYNCHRONIZE BUYING AND MANUFACTURING

This is where it all started, as material requirements planning, which focused on materials. Later, when we included factory operations, accounting, order entry, and accounts payable in our planning, we changed the name to manufacturing resource planning. Usually this popular method is simply called MRP or MRP II, and can be broad or narrow, depending on your company and the computer software you use.

MRP is a complete system that integrates all of the main planning activities dealing with materials and manufacturing resources. When first developed in the 1950s, it was a radical departure from reorder point and safety stock methods that were almost universally in use up to that time. There are three major concepts that MRP uses that are very different from their counterparts in the now-obsolete Reorder Point, Safety stock methods.

Three new concepts are:

- Independent versus dependent demand

- Requiring accurate records

- Computing future needs of dependent components

Defining Independent Versus Dependent Demand

The first major new concept in the MRP approach is the distinction between dependent and independent demand items. While this distinction could have been made before, it made no difference to reorder point and safety stock techniques. And ROP was overwhelmingly the conventional method.

Orlicky was an early advocate of MRP, beginning around 1965. He gives us useful definitions. "Demand for a given inventory item is termed independent when such demand is unrelated to demand for other items. Conversely, demand is defined as dependent when it is directly related to, or derives from, the demand for another inventory item or product."[1]

Figure 3.10 illustrates independent and dependent demand items. Here we see a flashlight. The finished flashlight falls into the independent demand category because its demand is not derived from anyplace else. Demand for the finished flashlight comes from incoming customer orders, warehouse replenishment orders, sales forecasts, or any combination of these. In an MRP system, end items almost always are independent demand items, and are put into the master production schedule by that MPS scheduler, as covered earlier in this chapter.

All of the other items in this illustration have dependent demand. You can easily recognize that if we want to manufacture 100 flashlights in a certain week, we will need 100 of every component shown, both purchased and manufactured ones. The master scheduler enters a manufacturing order for 100 flashlights in the proper week, and MRP processing logic takes over.

It makes plans to have all the other components, purchased or manufactured, available. The planned orders have their quantities adjusted for the lot size rule you designated for each. Every planned order is given a due date that is synchronized to the start date of its parent. This process continues for each parent, up the line, from the lowest purchased item to the start of the manufacturing order the end item as designated on the master production schedule. Components often have common use in many assemblies or end items, especially in companies with a standardization program in their design engineering department. MRP automatically takes multiple uses into account, and is fully supportive of standardization, all at electronic speed.

MRP does this by accumulating the needs for each dependent demand item, across all needs, before calculating the needs for lower level items.

Manufacturing companies often have hundreds or thousands of dependent-demand components, but only a small number of independent-demand items, usually end items. This is very important. Under MRP planners concentrate on the relatively few independent-demand end items, allowing MRP to compute the schedules for the mass of dependent demand items. In a dynamic world, you want to be able to adjust your production schedules.

---

[1]Joseph Orlicky, *Material Requirements Planning* (New York, N.Y.: McGraw-Hill Book Company, 1975), p. 22.

Figure 3.10 Independent vs. Dependent Demand

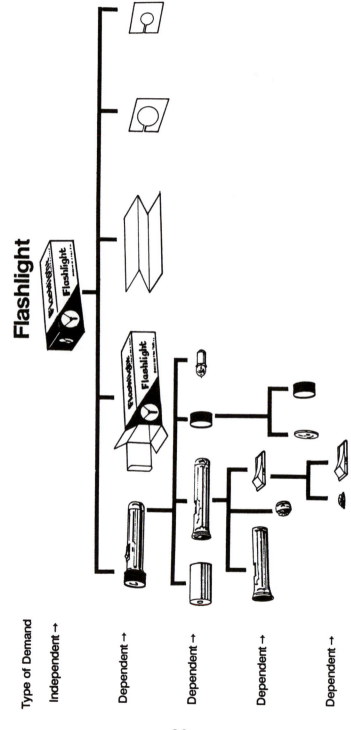

To do this you change the master schedule. Then MRP replans all affected items in its next run, usually overnight, taking advantage of the speed and data-handling capacity of modern computers.

Keeping Accurate Records

In order to make accurate plans, MRP needs a fair amount of accurate data. This is in sharp contrast to reorder point techniques that were able to function with poor records. It was during these days that manufacturing departments got into the habit of keeping poor records, and presents problems when first implementing MRP.

The now-classic, standard records where MRP I (Material Requirements Planning) requires very high accuracy are:

- Bills of material

- Stock status

- Open order status

Each of these topics is covered in later chapters.

Computing Future Needs

One big advantage of MRP is that it analyzes and plans your future needs for all dependent demand items. If an item is not needed, you don't plan for any more. This is in sharp contrast to reorder point and safety stock techniques which analyze past usage and tries to have some of everything on hand at all times. MRP also has the desirable characteristic of trying to consume any overages or residual inventory you may have before planning for any more. And with smart use of lot sizing rules, MRP will drive your inventory to zero, one of the main JIT ideals.

MRP processing logic is very straightforward, and requires only simple arithmetic. Figure 3.11 illustrates this logic for one item. I have chosen a flashlight for this example, which is an end item. It starts at the master production schedule level with its independent demand. The logic is the same for items with dependent demand, which I will illustrate later in this chapter.

Using Gross to Net Logic

In this example we see that the master production scheduler has planned for 100 flashlights to be available for shipment in periods three, five, and seven. The size of the period can be anything, with weeks being the most common. We start the example with 50 on hand. With no demand in weeks one and two, the 50 carry forward. Then in week three, we need 100, and have only 50 on hand to cover this need, giving us a net requirement of 50. This means that we must plan to manufacture more, so we look at the lot size rule which calls for 150. We therefore plan a manufacturing order, for 150, due into stock during the third week. We plan to start this order in week one, because the flashlight has been given a lead time of two weeks.

Figure 3.11 MRP Planning Logic

Item: 4711
Lot Size: 150
Lead Time: 2

	Period							
	1	2	3	4	5	6	7	8
Gross Requirement			100		100		100	
Projected 50 On-Hand	50	50	100	100	0	0	50	50
Net Requirement			50				100	
Planned Order Receipt			150				150	
Planned Order Start	150				150			

We will receive the first 150 in week three, which added to the 50 already in stock, gives us 200 coming into inventory in week three. We will ship 100 out to customers in the same week, leaving us 100 on hand at the end of this planning period. The 100 on hand carry through week four, and are consumed in week five, leaving us with zero inventory at the end of planning periods five and six.

Period seven contains another demand for 100, and we have none in stock to cover. This gives us a net requirement of 100. We must plan another manufacturing order, to finish a lot of 150 in that week. We will start this manufacturing order two

weeks earlier, in week five. So, in week seven, we get 150 in
and ship 100 out, leaving us with a projected on-hand of 50.

Using Multilevel Planning

This planning logic is continued through the whole bill of
material, level by level. In Figure 3.12 we see a simple, three-level
bill of material. A is a parent, with B and C as components. B
is also a parent with D and E as components. Finally, D has
two components, F and G. To keep the example easy, we assume
that component usage is one per parent.

Figure 3.13 is an example of MRP's multilevel planning. In
this example, the master production scheduler has recognized
requirements for the end item, A, in weeks three, five, seven,
and eight, with quantities of 60, 110, 50, and 40, respectively.
Using the method of calculation from our earlier example, we
plan to start a manufacturing order for 100 in periods four and
six. In order to start this order, we must have B and C available
for issue, which converts into the gross requirements shown for
each of them.

Figure 3.12   Simple Bill of Material

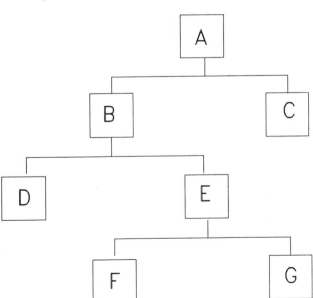

Figure 3.13 Full Planning for Item A, Gross Requirements for Items B and C

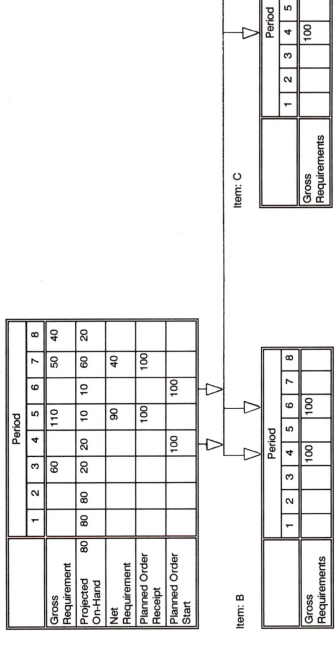

MRP now plans how to cover the needs for B and C (Figure 3.14). In the case of B, it's on hand of 10 cannot cover the requirement of 100 in week four, so MRP plans a manufacturing order to cover. In B's case, it has a lot-for-lot sizing rule, which means we plan only to cover its net requirement of 90. Notice that under lot-for-lot sizing, inventory falls to zero and stays there. This is the preferred lot size rule for Just-in-Time (zero inventory) operation.

MRP also plans coverage for C, but it has quite a large lot size, 155. No matter how small the net requirement may be, this rule will cause 155 to be put on order. This occurs in period six, where a net requirement of only 20 is covered with a lot of 155. Notice in C's case that a considerable inventory can be on hand. This occurs especially in weeks six and beyond. This is the opposite of zero inventory.

Because B requires components D and E, we see how the planned orders for B, starting in weeks three and five, precipitate gross requirements, due in those weeks, on D and E, for 90 and 100, respectively. MRP plans D's requirements conventionally, but E has a peculiar characteristic (Figure 3.15). It is packed 48 to a carton, and must be ordered in multiples. This explains why, in period three, the net requirement of 70 is covered by a planned order of 96, and in period five, 74 also is covered by 96.

Going to the lowest level, D's planned order starts of 150 each in periods two and four, drop a gross requirement onto its components F and G due in periods two and four. In Figure 3.16, for F, MRP's plans cause inventory to be entirely consumed and to fall to zero. This happens because F's lot size is consistently smaller than its net requirement. In G's case, however the situation is just the opposite. Its generous lot size of 800 has caused 600 to be in inventory at the start of the example, This amply covers the needs across the horizon and still leaves us 300 at the end. This is not a zero inventory situation!

In our example, we took just one end item through three levels, with a component usage of one in each parent. In a real situation, bills often are deeper and have multiple usage per parent. Another big difference between our example and real life is that there are hundreds or even thousands of bills of material in effect at the time of processing. And in every company, many components are used in different places, especially since computerized bills of material can be used for standardization. MRP

Figure 3.14 Full Planning for Items B and C, Gross Requirements for Items D and E

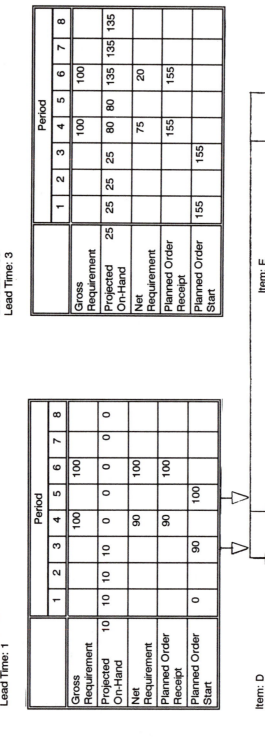

Item: B
Lot Size: Lot-for-Lot
Lead Time: 1

Item: B		Period							
		1	2	3	4	5	6	7	8
Gross Requirement					100		100		
Projected On-Hand	10	10	10	10	0	0	0	0	0
Net Requirement					90		100		
Planned Order Receipt					90		100		
Planned Order Start		0		90		100			

Item: C
Lot Size: 155
Lead Time: 3

Item: C		Period							
		1	2	3	4	5	6	7	8
Gross Requirement					100		100		
Projected On-Hand	25	25	25	25	80	80	135	135	135
Net Requirement					75		20		
Planned Order Receipt					155		155		
Planned Order Start		155	155	155					

Item: D

Item: D	Period							
	1	2	3	4	5	6	7	8
Gross Requirements			90		100			

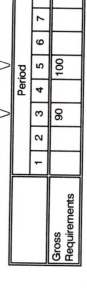

Item: E

Item: E	Period							
	1	2	3	4	5	6	7	8
Gross Requirements			90		100			

Figure 3.15 Full Planning for Items D and E, Gross Requirements for Items F and G

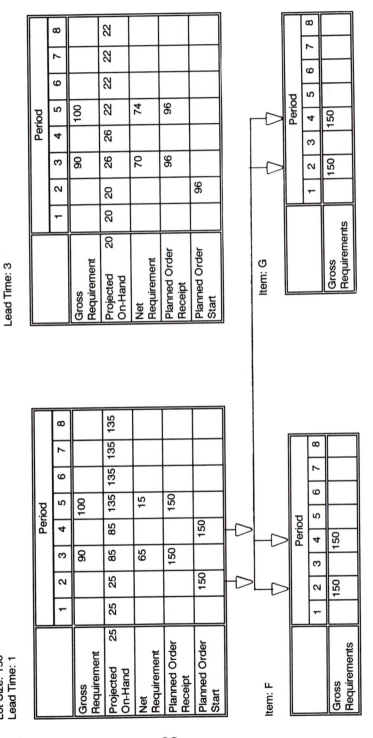

Item: D
Lot Size: 150
Lead Time: 1

		Period							
		1	2	3	4	5	6	7	8
Gross Requirement				90		100			
Projected On-Hand	25	25	25		85	135	135	135	135
Net Requirement				65		15			
Planned Order Receipt				150		150			
Planned Order Start			150		150				

Item: E
Lot Size: 48x
Lead Time: 3

		Period							
		1	2	3	4	5	6	7	8
Gross Requirement				90		100			
Projected On-Hand	20	20	20	26	26	22	22	22	22
Net Requirement				70		74			
Planned Order Receipt				96		96			
Planned Order Start			96						

Item: F

	Period							
	1	2	3	4	5	6	7	8
Gross Requirements		150		150				

Item: G

	Period							
	1	2	3	4	5	6	7	8
Gross Requirements		150		150				

Figure 3.16 Full Planning for Items F and G

Item: F
Lot Size: 100
Lead Time: 1

		Period							
		1	2	3	4	5	6	7	8
Gross Requirement			150		150				
Projected On-Hand	100	100	50	50	0	0	0	0	0
Net Requirement			50		100				
Planned Order Receipt			100		100				
Planned Order Start		100		100					

Item: G
Lot Size: 800
Lead Time: 6

		Period							
		1	2	3	4	5	6	7	8
Gross Requirement			150	150					
Projected On-Hand	600	600	450	300	300	300	300	300	300
Net Requirement									
Planned Order Receipt									
Planned Order Start									

keeps multiple uses over many bills of material straight, and correctly plans order starts and completions without error, and at computer speed. Even though its processing logic is very straightforward, the huge volume of processing means that MRP cannot be done by hand except perhaps in a one-person factory. Orlicky, in one his pioneering book on MRP, covers MRP processing logic in excellent detail.[2]

HOW TO USE A FINAL ASSEMBLY SCHEDULE TO SHIP THE RIGHT THINGS

For many product lines, a building block, or modular approach to design and manufacturing is the best way to plan. In these situations, major sub-assemblies are planned and inventoried.

Consumer electronics is a classic example of this planning approach. Many years ago my parents wanted a home entertainment center. They went to the store and bought an AM-FM phonograph combination, all wired together in a furniture-grade cabinet. Nowadays, when you want such an apparatus, you go to the electronics store and buy a tape player, a compact disc player, a radio receiver, an amplifier, speakers, and an optional and bewildering array of other components.

This same approach is very useful when your product line can be designed to support this approach.

Then when customer orders arrive, these building blocks are retrieved from inventory, assembled, and shipped. This increases manufacturing flexibility dramatically, while keeping inventory at reasonable levels.

Figure 3.17 shows a winch, with some of its major components. This illustration shows how the modular, building block approach can be put to advantage. In this example, the user can select one each of the needed assemblies. They can choose from four drum assemblies, six different motors, three gear boxes and three pendants.

If the manufacturer were to try to forecast all of the available combinations and keep them in stock, there would be 216 end items (4 × 6 × 3 × 3). This would be totally outlandish, since many of these combinations will never be bought by anybody,

---

[2]Joseph Orlicky, *Material Requirements Planning* (New York, N.Y.: McGraw-Hill Book Company, 1975), pp. 65-97.

Figure 3.17 Winch with Modular Building Blocks

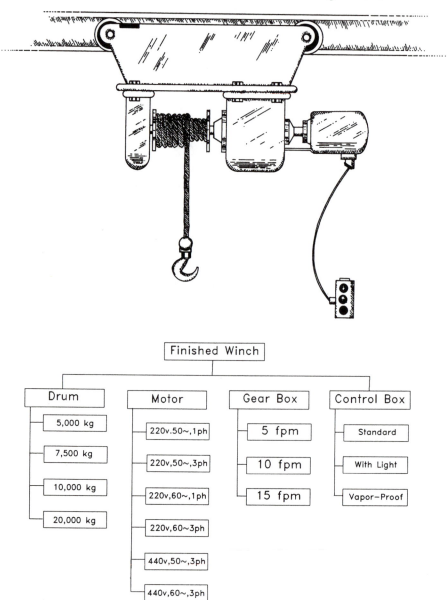

and many others very infrequently and unpredictably. I wouldn't want to be the one asking the sales department to make such a forecast.

But planning at the modular level means having 16 items available. This makes the planner's job much easier, and represents a reasonable task for forecasting.

When you use the building block approach, your master production scheduler plans components that are one level down from the end item on the bills of material. The quantities and due dates are governed by forecasting and by the rate and mix of incoming customer orders.

The entry of the customer order into the system presents a special problem, since the exact configuration may not have been sold before. In complex products, an engineer must define the components, and the routing. With simpler products, an order entry clerk can specify these details. In both cases, a manufacturing order must be developed with its unique bill of material and routing, and entered into the system. This final assembly manufacturing order functions almost exactly as any other manufacturing order in the plant, with two notable exceptions.

The first peculiarity is that since this manufacturing order is new to the system, its consumption of machine and worker time has not been included in detailed capacity planning. In order to have capacity available, the final assembly work centers will have to have their capacity plans made on the basis of forecast. Some seasoned users are able to simulate final assembly shop load with dummy or planning orders, which are removed from the system as real customer orders arrive.

The second peculiarity is that the final assembly manufacturing order does not have an established bill of material. The material needed to cover these orders must be available when the order is started. These are the building blocks I referred to above, and will have been provided for by the master production schedule. The computer system being used should be able to create a temporary bill of material and a material requisition (pick list), based on the specification created when the customer order was entered.

With the pick list and routing now available, the manufacturing order is dispatched to the final assembly work center, where it is completed and shipped in a short time. In a well-organized factory, final assembly could take as little as a few hours or a day. This is a great step toward JIT. Being in the final assembly mode allows you to offer next day shipment for most of your products.

In Chapter 5, I will give details on how to structure bills of material to support this approach.

HOW TO FINE TUNE WITH THE DETAILED CAPACITY PLAN

The detailed capacity plan occurs toward the end of the planning cycle. When MRP has finished its plans, it has planned all manufacturing orders needed to cover your master production schedule. During this processing the computer examines the due date for each planned order, and back schedules each according to its routing. To do detailed capacity planning, the computer examines the work content of each manufacturing order for each work center. It also records the day(s) during which this work is to occur. With much arithmetic, the computer develops a complete list of demands on each work center for each day, extending into the future as far as the master schedule goes. Because this part of the computer run is time consuming, most users limit the horizon of the detailed capacity plan to six or eight weeks.

The main use of the detailed capacity plan is for fine tuning. There should be no big surprises, and surely no unreconcilable problems. If you have done a good job of rough-cut capacity planning, there will be no surprises at the detailed level. Figure 3.18 gives an example of a detailed capacity plan.

We see the automatic screw machine department's capacity plan in this example. In the heading area we see some facts about this work center. It has 11 machines and can turn out 88 hours of production in the one shift currently scheduled.

The dates shown in this example are in shop date format. This format numbers the working days in a year in sequence, with the year as a prefix. This allows anyone to do simple arithmetic on the shop date when adjusting schedules. Some companies prefer this format, others the more conventional mm-dd-yy, or the European dd-mm-yy formats. Scheduling departments and work center supervisors tend to prefer the shop date format, and any software you use should be able to show any desired format.

In the body of our example, we see that each line represents five working days, making this a weekly-oriented report. The

Figure 3.18 Intercontinental Wheel Goods Detailed Capacity Plan

SHOP DAY 144

FROM DAY 145 TO DAY 184

WORK CENTER	WORK CENTER DESCRIPTION	TOTAL MACHINES	TOTAL SHIFTS	CREW SIZE	CAPACITY (HOURS)	PERIOD SIZE
ASCRW	AUTOMATIC SCREW MACHINE	11	1	6	88	5

CAPACITY 1   DATE
CAPACITY 2   DATE
CAPACITY 3   DATE

PERIOD END	/------LOAD------\ PLANNED	FIRMED	RELEASED	/----CURRENT----\ LOAD	CAPY	OVER/ SHORT	%	/----- % OF PERIOD CAPACITY LOADED------\ ------50------100------150------200
149	0	0	497	497	440	57-	113	RRRRRRRRRRRRRRRRRRRRRRR
154	0	256	111	367	440	73	83	FFFFFRRRRRRRRRRRRR
159	0	430	0	430	440	10	98	FFFFFFFFFFFFFFFFFFFF
164	0	459	0	459	440	19-	104	FFFFFFFFFFFFFFFFFFFFFF
169	0	498	0	498	440	58-	111	FFFFFFFFFFFFFFFFFFFFFFF
174	0	410	0	410	440	30	93	FFFFFFFFFFFFFFFFFFF
179	105	306	0	411	440	29	93	FFFFFFFFFFFFFFPPPP
184	310	0	0	310	440	130	70	PPPPPPPPPPPPPP

99

eight lines shown represent the coming eight weeks. Notice that this is a considerably shorter time span than the master production schedule would allow. The detailed capacity plan usually is limited to such a short horizon because it is meant for fine-tuning. Eight weeks is long enough to allow the production planner and the shop supervisor to make their last-minute adjustments.

The three load columns represent the work content of the three classes of manufacturing orders.

The current load column is an important one. It is the total of the loads from planned, firmed, and released orders. In manual systems, capacity plans often only showed released orders, which gave a false preview of the future. In these older, sometimes manual systems, you often find a large amount of past due work, plenty of released orders in the next few weeks, which taper off to nothing after about eight weeks. This is part of the same problem of queue reduction. In a traditional factory, as soon as queue starts to go down, the workers slow down, because they associate this condition with an impending layoff.

But, since the MRP system carries planned orders in its files, they can be included in the detailed load. Now the true capacity demands can be shown, making them realistic and usable. With this kind of tool, you can better be able to correct your schedules so there is no past due shown. Also with a realistic capacity plan, you can more easily begin to reduce factory queues.

The current capacity column, showing 440, is derived by taking the 88 hours of daily capacity, multiplied by the five day time increment being used in this report. The current over column shows if there is over- or under-capacity during the week, and the percent column states the situation as a percentage. The Gantt chart at the right gives a graphic representation of the data. An interesting detail is showing released, firmed, and planned orders by their respective initials.

Planned orders are designated with P's. They are the farthest out, and have not yet been firmed by the production planner. Planned orders will be moved around automatically during each time you rerun MRP, according to latest developments. Firmed orders are designated by F's. They have been accepted by the production planner with respect to both dates and quantities, and can be changed only by manual intervention by the planner. Firmed orders, however have not been issued to the factory, and their components have not been picked. They still are in an administrative status.

A released order, shown with R's has actually been sent to the factory, together with its materials. A released order is work in process and should not have its due date nor its quantity adjusted except in very unusual cases.

The production planner and the supervisor of the automatic screw machine work center use this report to fine tune its capacity in the coming weeks. In our example, it seems that we are slightly overloaded in the first week, by 13 percent, and the rest of the weeks appear to be well planned. Some overtime in the week ending on 149, or possibly shifting a little work to the following week would solve the problem.

You should prepare a detailed capacity for each work center each week. If the master production schedule is not being abused in the near term, and upstream work centers are finishing their jobs on time, there should be very little difference in the load from week to week, especially in the first two or three weeks.

If the work center supervisor and the production planner are confronted with a large discrepancy between actual load and available capacity which cannot be overcome, the planner must take steps to change the plan. Delaying some orders to a slack period could be the answer, but only provided that the following work centers can accommodate the change. But because of the complexity of manufacturing planning, such a problem might have to be resolved by changing the master production schedule. Especially as companies move more to the Just-in-Time ideas of small queues and flat bills of material, there is less and less opportunity to make up delays at later stages in production.

HOW TO FULFILL THE PLAN BY METERING OUT THE WORK

When MRP practices first were being developed, this activity was called shop floor control. Then later the name was changed to production activity control. Then still later, Just-in-Time practices came on the scene, which began to question the whole approach. This is the area where there remains the most discussion, perhaps even conflict, and many different practices now are being tried, many with great success.

The best procedure for you depends on your industry, your product line, volume, how your factory is laid out, and how far you may have progressed along the JIT trail.

Let's discuss the conventional factory. It is laid out with machines grouped together according to similarity. The punch presses here, the lathes there, the grinders together in their own locale. In this classic situation, bills of material are crafted with breaks to reflect the factory's layout. Manufacturing orders are given to each work center, together with needed components. At the end of production, the work center sends the completed item to intermediate storage, ready to be issued to a manufacturing order at the next higher level in the bill. Manufacturing orders tend to have generous lot sizes, and each work center has a generous incoming queue. Manufacturing time in a conventional factory tends to be long, owing to the large lot sizes, intermediate storage, and generous work center queues.

HOW TO USE INPUT-OUTPUT CONTROL

One useful tool to manage all this activity is input-output control. This is a simple and effective tool, often done manually, and is easily adaptable to a spread sheet on a personal computer.

The production planner prepares an input-output chart for each work center. This chart consists of three parts, input, output, and queue. Each section is divided into planned, actual, and deviation. These sections extend over the coming periods. Most planners use weekly periods, and usually plan six to eight weeks ahead, and use it in conjunction with their detailed capacity plan. Figure 3.19 is an example of an input-output chart for our automatic screw machine work center.

We are in week five now. Our inputs, planned and actual have been coming in reasonably close to plan, especially when we look at the deviation at the end of last week, week 4. We are just one hour over our input target so far in our four week plan. We are even doing better on the output side, with zero deviation coming our of week four.

We were also planning to reduce our queues by a third during the eight weeks. In this area we also are very close, having 23 hours less in the queue than planned. This could be considered a favorable variance, because everybody should have a bias in favor of smaller queues.

Figure 3.19 Input/Output Control

Work Center ASCR
Automatic Screw Machine

Input Hours

	Period							
	149	154	159	164	169	174	179	184
Planned	497	367	430	459	490	410	411	310
Actual	475	390	425	460				
Deviation	-22	+23	-5	+1				

Output Hours

	Period							
	149	154	159	164	169	174	179	184
Planned	440	440	440	440	440	440	440	440
Actual	465	440	435	440				
Deviation	+25	0	-5	0				

Queue Hours

	Period							
	149	154	159	164	169	174	179	184
Planned	152	79	69	88	138	108	79	89
Actual 95	105	55	45	65				
Deviation	+47	-24	-24	-23				

Plossl[3] gives an excellent description of this technique.

How to Use a Dispatch List

The work center dispatch list lends itself better to a fully computerized system. Essentially, the dispatch list tells every work center what to do next; what job to take out of the queue. The computer knows all of the schedules for all of your manufacturing orders, planned, firmed, and released. The computer

_____

[3]George W. Plossl, *Production and Inventory Control* (Englewood Cliffs, N.J.: Prentice-Hall, Inc.), pp. 284-91.

also knows all of the leadtime factors that apply, namely move, queue, setup, and run hours. Using these facts, it synchronizes all of the work centers such that their outputs are available just in time for the next happening. This could be a further assembly, a major sub-assembly, or final assembly.

Figure 3.20 shows a typical dispatch list. The supervisor can see the next five shop orders to be done in the work center, as well as the previous and the next work centers for every one.

The dispatch list supports de-expediting. De-expediting is absolutely necessary in order to keep schedules accurate, and is impossible to do manually. What's de-expediting? Let's take an assembly that needs three components. Each is fabricated in different work centers. One of the feeding work centers has a problem, and can't recover. It will be late with one of the three components. This means that the other two components suddenly aren't needed until later. When MRP is informed of the delay by the planner in the troubled work center, all other components are reviewed and rescheduled as needed. In our example, the other two components are rescheduled later, hence the term de-expedite. This operation re-synchronizes all of the activities in all work centers in the entire factory, at computer speed and without clerical error.

In such a dynamic environment, the dispatch list is re-computed every night, and a new one is on each work center supervisor's computer terminal at the start of each day. Or, lacking a fully on-line system, the dispatch list could be a printed version.

If this sounds like a confusing environment for the work center, it could be. If the factory is producing reasonably according to schedules, and if the master production schedule is reasonably stable in the near term, then today's dispatch list looks very much like yesterday's. However, sometimes those are big ifs. In a factory where the master schedule is being changed too often (jerked around) or where work center foremen don't follow the schedule, or if quality is iffy, the dispatch list isn't very useful nor is the whole system.

It is crucial that your master schedule is realistic and stable, and your work centers must live up to their schedules. If you fail here, the penalty is inflated inventories, frantic expediting, and poor adherence to promises to customers. In other words, a conventional environment!

Figure 3.20 Intercontinental Wheel Goods
Work Center Dispatch List

DATE: NOV 12

WORK CENTER DESCRIPTION	TOTAL MACH	SHIFTS	CREW SIZE	CAPACITY	SCHED DAYS
ASCRW AUTOMATIC SCREW MACHINE	11	1	6	440	5

ORDER NUMBER ITEM NUMBER	OPERATION DESCRIPTION ITEM DESCRIPTION	OPN PLNR	PREV OPN NEXT OPN	REQUIRED READY	COMPLETE SENT	/REMAINING HRS\ SETUP RUN	START DATE COMP DATE
4820 69094	TURN PER SPEC INNER BEARING RACE	010 03	– 020	100 0	0 0	.75 2.11	11/10 11/22
4840 68853	TURN PER SPEC FRONT BRAKE POST	030 04	020 040	100 0	0 0	.25 2.11	11/22 11/24
4891 62501	TURN PER SPEC STD 1/4X1-1/2 BOLT	020 04	010 030	500 0	0 0	.35 2.63	11/24 11/24
4857 58627	TURN PER SPEC HANDLE BAR BOLT	010 03	– 030	500 0	0 0	.20 1.05	11/25 11/25
4823 61294	TURN PER SPEC BOLT FOR B.G. SEATS	010 03	– 020	550 0	0 0	.40 2.95	11/25 11/26

In the well-run system depicted here, the supervisor dispatches the work to the workers in the sequence shown on the list, and watches to see that the work gets done as scheduled. To make the operation smoother, the dispatch list shows the sending work center and the next work center, so supervisors and planners can coordinate among themselves during the day. Here is where good, old-fashioned expediting still has a valuable place in a modern factory. Stay on schedule! Get back on schedule!

Regarding implementing a new system having a dispatch list— a word of warning. When I was director of materials for a printing company, I casually mentioned to a group of foremen at the lunch table that I was developing a dispatch list, and they would soon not be able to choose their own work. Their reaction was instantaneous and almost violent. It seems that their performance was measured in part on the basis of setup variance. Under this system, when a foreman could fish a job out of the queue that had a similar setup to the job just being completed, the worker could set up the new job in less time than planned, giving the foreman a favorable variance. At the end of the month he got a pat on the back, and a raise at the end of the year.

Now I was going to destroy this neat arrangement with a computerized dispatch list and they wouldn't have anything to do with it.

There are two lessons to be learned from this episode. The first one has to do with education and training on any new system. It really is imperative to get concurrence from almost everybody, in advance.

The second lesson has to do with performance measurements. If you ever want to have success with a formal manufacturing system, especially one incorporating JIT principles, you must review and renovate *all* performance measurements, particularly those that influence raises!

HOW TO REDUCE THROUGHPUT TIME—
THE FAST FACTORY

Because the computer recognizes all of the planning factors, including lead times, it is easy to use your system to reduce factory throughput time. The classic situation is where queue is 90 percent of factory time. When you are ready to attack factory throughput time, you could perhaps start with queue. By systematically reducing the queue times assigned to work centers in the plant, throughput will be reduced proportionately. Since the various leadtime factors are incorporated in your MRP system, merely changing values on a master file will cause your MRP system to act accordingly in its next run. If you can reduce queue and move times to nearly zero, you will have a close-coupled, or fast factory.

A fast factory is part of Just-In-Time. When you couple this with flat bills of material, and perhaps group technology, a number of conventional system requirements fade away. When queue is removed, many items can be finished the same day they are started. In such a case, your need to track manufacturing orders across their several operations can cease. If you need it today, start it today and finish it today. This idea is being applied to fabrication, assemblies, and to final assembly.

A close-coupled or fast factory has many advantages in reduced inventory, more flexibility in scheduling, and better customer service. But when a shortage does occur, or a machine does break down, lack of buffer stock makes this much more serious, and could result in line or even plant shutdown. Just-in-Time principles demand world class performance throughout.

4

HOW TO INTEGRATE ACCOUNTING INTO YOUR NEW SYSTEM

Before the advent of MRP II-based systems, Manufacturing could not be relied on to keep very good records. Planning and control systems were not oriented toward accurate recordkeeping, but rather toward macro-level planning, and brute force techniques.

This meant that accounting could not trust whatever records manufacturing had, and were forced to go their own way. Over the years, accountants developed elaborate methods to keep track of what was going on in manufacturing. The legendary year end physical inventory made a starting point for them. Then during the year they tried to track inventory, and other events, with a number of different forms. Purchase orders, receiving reports, issue tickets, move tickets, customer orders, reject notices, and return vouchers, are just a few relating to inventory. On the labor side, we often saw an elaborate web of labor tickets with space to clock on and off jobs, as well as on and off a wide variety of overhead activities.

After receiving these various forms, accounting tried to put a dollar value on each and enter them into the books appropriately. At the end of the year, a massive reconciliation took place, and some nasty inventory write-downs frequently occurred, much to the dismay of all. More than one controller was fired because manufacturing couldn't keep good records.

With the advent of MRP II-based systems, that require a lot of good data, accounting now can rely on manufacturing's recordkeeping, and dispense with most of the old systems.

When you are running an MRP II-based system, accounting should rely on MRP's transactions for all data it can supply. A good MRP II-based system will include data that accounting needs as part of the appropriate transaction records. You should be able to refrain from rekeying the same data. For example, don't have your accounting system call for receiving tickets or pick lists to be rekeyed. The resulting parallel files are always in disagreement; it is just a matter of how badly. Discontinuing rekeying and the resultant parallel files means that you will eliminate all the reconciliation that goes on now between them, and the work groups that do them. Coupled with cycle counting, covered in Chapter 9, one file or integrated set of files should be made to serve all functions with no duplications and redundancies.

HOW TO RECORD RECEIPTS

Traditional MRP II expects you to record all of your receipts at the receiving dock. The rule that many companies follow is to clear the dock every day. Don't allow a backlog there, because it increases confusion and degrades the system. MRP thinks the shipment is still owing, while it really is in the building. From an accounting standpoint, receiving dock backlog represents an unrecognized accounts payable liability. Modern data entry technology, notably bar coding, has made the receiving transaction faster, easier, and more accurate.

If you have good MRP software, each receiving transaction will have enough data associated with it to satisfy accounting. Date, item number, purchase order number, and quantity come from the receiving report. The item's master record will deliver the proper account number, item description, standard cost, and most other details that accounting might need to support their systems. Using these data allows you to book the accounts payable and inventory transactions simultaneously.

JIT enhancements to traditional MRP, may bypass the receiving dock entirely. Vendors are now delivering directly to the production line, where the item will be used. Some companies are discontinuing the receiving transaction entirely. With JIT vendors, some companies are assuming the material arrived, and book the accounts payable and inventory accordingly, based on date.

Another technique is to have the supplier's delivery person perform the receiving transaction. This is especially feasible with bar coding.

Other companies, who measure their manufacturing throughput time in minutes or hours, record only completions. If material comes in every day and gets used that day, with no timing or quality errors, you should be able to use the completion transaction to trigger the correct transactions. Making transactions at the end of production is called, variously, Backflushing, Automatic Issue, or Post Deduct. Regarding the receiving transaction, your accounting system could call on MRP for the same transaction as MRP's inventory system uses to control inventory balances, for their transaction. In this situation, finishing production would cause the computer to calculate the components needed to make that quantity. Item number, shop order number, quantity, and date are included in the transaction, while the item's master record supplies the rest. For accounting, the backflush would cause the accounts payable record to be entered. Inventory dollars could be booked directly to cost of goods sold. Or, you could book the dollars in and out of inventory, and into cost of goods sold simultaneously.

Keeping Track of Material Movements

Some accounting systems like to record every minute detail. In the old days of slow, lumbering manufacturing operations this could have made sense. However, given today's emphasis on fast throughput and elimination of waste, over sensitivity to material movements is a good target for elimination.

I suggest a general rule of thumb. The needs of manufacturing for keeping track of all their pockets of inventory is more pressing than accounting's needs for General Ledger entries. If your accounting system wants to keep track of certain material movements, confine it to tapping into manufacturing's inventory transactions. Chances are good that if manufacturing isn't keeping track of it, neither should accounting.

There is one category of material that accounting should pay special attention to. Manufacturing often finds inventory items to be questionable, and not available for manufacturing. Before they dispose of these questionable items, they reside in inventory at their full standard cost, even though they may end up being scrapped. Accounting should evaluate these inventories, and perhaps set up a reserve account for them on a quarterly or annual basis.

How to Issue Materials

There are two ways that manufacturing issues materials—direct and automatic.

Direct issue uses an issue voucher, often called a pick list. The pick list is prepared by the MRP system using the bill of material to identify the items needed, and the shop order for quantity. This enables the system to make an extended pick list, showing items and their quantities.

The stock room gets the pick list, fills it, and has the material delivered to the first work center. As the material leaves the stock room an issue transaction is recorded for every item being issued. Back orders and partial issues are accommodated. For your accounting system, the item number, shop order number, date, and quantity are in the transaction. The item's master record supplies the static data, such as description, standard cost, and account number. The shop order may also provide useful data for accounting.

Automatic issue is often called backflushing, or post-deduct. Items designated for automatic issue often are stored next to their place of use, but not necessarily so. Automatic issue can apply to stock room items as well. When production is finished, the completion transaction triggers the issue transaction. Whatever should have been used for the quantity of the item involved is backflushed. The details of the transaction coming back to MRP are the same as for direct issue, and can serve accounting just as well.

Backflushing is especially useful in process flow work centers. If you don't use shop orders, you can book the values against the work center, by shift or by day.

There is one problem with automatic issue having to do with timing. During the time of manufacture, components have already been taken into work in process, but not yet recorded. If your factory throughput time is short enough, this probably won't matter. Automatic issue begins to lose its appeal for items that take days or weeks to get through your factory.

A variation of automatic issue is frontflushing, or prededuct. Under this technique, the components on the pick list are automatically deducted from inventory at the start of production. Although a labor and time saving technique, frontflushing does not allow for back orders or partials.

How to Record Work in Process and Value Added

Recording value added during manufacturing is often a contentious topic. With the shortening of factory throughput times, it is less and less important to keep track of value added (actual time) by various operations during manufacturing.

If manufacturing records movement of a shop order from operation to operation, accounting's needs should be met from that transaction. The shop order transaction includes item number, quantity, shop order number, work center, and clock-on and clock-off time. The work center master file will contain labor grade, account number, perhaps an overhead rate, and any other static data needed to support the accounting transactions.

Fast factory throughput is making it undesirable for manufacturing to record progress through every operation. Some have enhanced their systems to designate milestone operations. Planning and scheduling can continue to be done at the individual operation level, but progress reporting is expected only for the milestone operations. The accounting implication is that the actual time for each operation is calculated, proportionally for all operations, based on the same data as before.

Taking the milestone approach to the extreme, some companies are just recording starts and completions of shop orders, and intermediate operations all are prorated.

These techniques supply the actual labor by shop order. The routing supplies the standard time. Accounting can compute variances based on this, if necessary, although this performance measurement is not popular in JIT settings.

In process flow operations, where there may not be shop orders, the booking is done against the work center, usually by shift or day.

How to Record Transfers to Finished Goods or Customer Orders

Finished goods inventory often is under the control of marketing, and in any case vanishes from MRP II's view when manufacturing is completed.

The accounting transaction comes from the completion of the shop order for the finished item. The transaction will include date, quantity, item number, and shop order number. The item's master record flags end items destined for finished goods inventory, and also gives description and standard cost. The item master also has the account number of the item, so when the shop order is finished, the accounting system will automatically be able to book the result into finished goods inventory. If you have several stocking locations, your finished goods stock locator will provide that detail.

Moving finished goods from the end of production directly to shipping and the customer totally avoids finished goods inventory. In an MRP setting, the accounting transaction is the completion transaction for the shop order. However, in addition to the data needed to record finished goods, the shop order usually designates the customer order number. Your accounting system now is supported to make its transactions as needed.

In a process flow environment, completion transactions are done by shift or day for each work center. As part of this transaction, you can designate which customer order received a quantity of product, and how much was sent to finished goods.

HOW THE THREE-WAY MATCH HAS BECOME OBSOLETE

Ever since companies had their books audited by outsiders, the "three-way match" was taken as a given. The three-way match works like this. You take each incoming invoice, match it to the purchase order for price and to the receiving report for quantity. If they match, your most junior clerk is authorized to process the invoice for payment.

MRP II, JIT, and EDI (Electronic Data Interchange), are eliminating these documents. Before JIT set in, suppliers delivered once or twice a month, and invoiced for each shipment. Now, in JIT factories, suppliers deliver every day or oftener. The sheer workload of the three-way match in Accounts Payable, will make this practice impractical.

JIT-style Purchasing has long term contracts and periodic releasing by inventory planners. Often this is done by EDI, and is paperless. Direct delivery to the line and automatic issue means that you might not even have receiving transactions.

There are a noticeable number of leading edge companies who "backflush" supplier payments. If you make little red wagons, and made 1,000 per day, you pay your supplier for 20,000 wheels at the end of the week. Your systems can handle this automatically as part of the backflushing inventory transaction, and pay the vendor's bank directly from your bank using EDI. This compresses time to almost zero, is paperless, and eliminates many administrative activities entirely.

The way things are progressing with world class manufacturing, the three-way match is doomed to extinction. Accounting professionals now are faced with the task of a substitute auditing tool.

RECOGNIZING WHEN TRADITIONAL ACCOUNTING ORTHODOXIES ARE BEING CHALLENGED

Every company has an accounting system. It's just a question of how elaborate. Until recently, we didn't question the accountants. Also, until the advent of cheap mainframe computers, terminal networks, and desktop computers, most functional departments had a hard time dealing with numbers in any quantity, nor accurately.

In the last few years, however, business persons across the continent have become critical and dissatisfied with orthodox accounting. Too complex and too late is one lament. The confusion between precision and accuracy, and poor quality standard costs are two more. It is now acceptable to argue with the accountants, and that profession is now scurrying to match their conventions to the modern world, especially as applies to manufacturing.

In their landmark book, *Relevance Lost*, written in 1987, H. Thomas Johnson and Robert S. Kaplan forcefully pointed out how accountants have gradually wandered away from their true mission since the Industrial Revolution. One major theme in their book is the distinction between financial reporting to the outside world versus management and responsibility accounting.

Safeguarding Financial Reporting to Outsiders

Depending on where your stock is traded, your company has responsibilities for supplying quarterly and yearly financial statements to entities outside your company. The Internal Revenue Service is one major responsibility. IRS rules govern in great detail how you account for everything. They are interested in maximizing their taxes, and don't concern themselves about whether the figures they require from you help you run your business or not.

Securities exchange rules also impose certain obligations for quarterly reporting. Your bank will certainly demand financial reports.

These and other external requirements must be met, using standard accounting rules. Some of these demands have the force of law.

Even when critically analyzing the role of accounting in a world class manufacturing company, we can't lose sight of these requirements.

Reconstructing Your Management and Responsibility Accounting

These outside reporting requirements, necessary as they are, are not particularly difficult to develop and provide.

One important lesson from the Peterson and Kaplan book is that we now realize that *all* other accounting activities are open to question. And in a JIT world, preoccupied with the elimination of waste, conventional accounting needs improvement.

One major area for improvement or outright elimination is in monthly management and responsibility accounting. Most accounting systems are replete with standards and budgets, to be compared with actual costs during the period, whereupon a never-ending series of variances can be calculated. The variances then are presented to the manager in charge, 15 days after the close of the month. He is asked to explain in detail and in writing to the controller every variance over 20 percent. The data upon which these variance reports are based are between 15 and 45 days old.

Moreover, since accounting systems only can deal with dollars, all events must be forcibly converted into dollars.

It doesn't take long before many of these management and responsibility reports lose their value, and the monthly reconciliation becomes a charade.

I worked for a company once that had the most amazing budgeting/variance system I have ever seen. Being a department manager, I made a monthly budget each year. Then I developed a planned variance to the monthly budget. During the year, accounting kept the records, and each month I was presented with a variance report analyzing the budget, actual variance to the budget, the planned variance, and the variance to the planned variance. Then I had to explain any variances over 20 percent. The exercise was a confusing farce, but contributed to overhead, nonetheless.

To make your MRP II/JIT system work really well, you should evaluate the applicable reports coming from accounting and justify each one. Does each support MRP II-JIT goals or not? If not, the reporting should be discontinued.

You should only retain those measures that help you run the business better.

HOW TO IMPLEMENT ACTIVITY-BASED COSTS (ABC)

Product cost is made up of material, labor, and manufacturing overhead. When you are running a good, MRP II-based system, your bills of material provide the material portion of your costs, while your routings provide the labor content. If your MRP system is running at all well, these two files will be complete and accurate, more than adequate for cost development and monitoring. The problem is in how manufacturing overhead is allocated.

You need good costs in order to make budgets and to set product line and pricing strategies. If you have bad costs, you can't really make good financial plans. Without good costs, pricing is really random. Some products that are making money are classed as losers, while other products that are too costly to make are pronounced winners.

Activity-based costing is emerging as the favorite alternative method for applying manufacturing overhead. Most cost accounting systems apply manufacturing overhead as a percentage of direct labor or machine time. This method is known as volume-based. When direct labor was the largest part of cost of goods sold, and overhead activities were few, applying overhead to labor was acceptable. In the early days, 10-20 percent on top of direct labor gave us adequate information. Today, however, most companies have direct labor less than 20% of cost of goods sold, and many are under 10 percent. As a result of the steady reduction of the labor content of our products, coupled with an equally steady rise in overhead activities, overhead rates usually are over 100 percent, and sometimes are in the thousands.

Any method of applying manufacturing overhead is an estimation at best, so applying these very high ratios magnifies the basic inaccuracy. The magnification is so great, that the result is a cost application that is far from accurate, and often results in standard costs that are grotesquely false. I have a number of clients who consciously ignore their standard costs when making decisions about product lines and pricing, because they don't want to have their decision-making process contaminated. Some companies are resorting to just looking at direct labor and material, ignoring overhead altogether. This is unwise insofar as the overhead activity is critical to the support of manufacturing operations, e.g., engineering, and data processing.

Volume-based allocation tends to overburden high volume products and subsidize low-volume ones. Volume-based costing also tends to subsidize high-tech products at the expense of low-tech ones.

For example the Ace Manufacturing Company has two products that are very similar, one old, one new. The old product sells at the rate of 10,000 per month. The new product is just getting established, and is selling 1,000 per month. Each product has one hour of direct labor.

The new product, however is experiencing growing pains and is plagued with engineering changes. The old product has long since settled into a comfortable routine, and has almost no engineering changes.

During the month there were 50 engineering changes, 49 of which applied to the new product. Estimating the cost of doing an engineering change at $50, Ace has $2,500 of ECO overhead to spread.

Divided by the 11,000 direct labor hours used during the month, gives an overhead application of $.227 per hour. When we apply this rate, the old product absorbs $2,270 overhead and the new product $230.

At a cost of $50 each, the true allocation should have been $2,450 to the new product and a mere $50 to the old one.

Activity-based costing is an emerging technique to assign manufacturing overhead costs based on actual consumption of each activity. In the example above, assigning $2,450 for engineering changes to the new item and $50 to the old one, is a simple example of an activity-based cost allocation.

There are four steps in implementing activity-based costing:

- Streamline Your Present Operations.

- Reduce the Manufacturing Overhead Pool by Converting Charges from Indirect to Direct Where Possible.

- Identify and Value Cost Drivers.

- Repeat, Improve, and Update.

Streamlining Your Present Operations

Historically, we have paid much more attention to monitoring direct labor usage than to indirect labor and our offices are full of white-collar workers. Indirect labor and many white collar workers all go into manufacturing overhead for eventual allocation.

The first step in implementing activity-based costing is to examine all administrative procedures, to see which ones can be eliminated or curtailed. This must be done with care and caution. You must first eliminate an activity before you make the personnel change.

Reducing the Manufacturing Overhead Pool by Converting Charges from Indirect to Direct Wherever Possible

Factory supervisors for years have been redesignating direct labor as indirect labor, because that has given them favorable direct labor performance. In-line inspection, and some material handling are two examples. Your industrial engineers should evaluate all indirect labor use, and try to put as many as possible on the routing. The routing is the vehicle for applying direct labor to your products, so any time accounted for in the resulting shop order goes directly to the cost of the product, and stays out of the overhead pool. In this context, your system should permit both direct and indirect labor, with time standards, to be incorporated in your routings and shop orders.

Before computerized bills of material became widely available, low-cost parts frequently were left off the bills in order to save administrative effort. Modern, MRP II-based systems are easy to use, including their bill of material processors. You should now put everything possible on the bills of material. This includes nuts, screws, and bolts. This also includes packaging materials. These frequently are left off the bills and flow into overhead for allocation. Although the unit cost of each may be small, in the aggregate, these indirect materials can be a big dollar value.

Depreciation should also be converted to a direct cost. You can also do this through the routings. Each machine in the factory can be assigned a depreciation cost per machine stroke. Then, as products use machines, they are charged depreciation directly.

Setup should also be routed so this expense can be charged directly.

Identifying and Valuing Cost Drivers

Identifying and valuing cost drivers is the central activity in converting to activity-based costing. A cost driver is an activity that creates cost and which can be attributed directly to a specific product or product line. A cost driver can occur entirely in one department or work center, or can cut across organizational lines. An engineering change order (ECO) is a good example of a cost driver. A purchase order, a receiving report, and a shop order are three more examples.

Your implementation team will analyze and identify all of the major cost drivers present in your company. They will try to consolidate a number of activities into major cost drivers. For example, can you include the cost of the receiving activity in the cost of a purchase order?

After the implementation team has identified all your major cost drivers, they will analyze the costs to support each. They will use work measurements, interviews, and perhaps the work flowcharts that they developed as part of the streamlining phase.

The purpose is to determine the personnel and related costs that can be ascribed to each activity. It is fairly easy to determine personnel time spent directly on the selected activities in each department. But how to allocate the indirect departmental charges, such as that for supervision and occupancy costs, is more of a problem. Through interviews, the team should be able to allocate departmental overhead personnel proportionally according to how they spend their time.

Sales expense, the executive suite, and corporate general and administrative expenses traditionally have not been included in manufacturing overhead. They largely will continue to be treated separately on the profit and loss statement.

Regarding sales expense, however, there is some discussion now about identifying some of these activities as cost drivers. Sales commissions, for example, could be allocated to the product or product family involved.

Repeating, Improving, and Updating

In order to get to world class and stay there, of necessity you will have a dynamic organization. The JIT fixation on eliminating waste also will cause you to change your organization and its procedures from time to time.

When you finish developing your cost drivers, you should adopt a continuous improvement routine. You should include a regular review of the costs for each of the drivers. Implementing activity-based costing will be a learning experience, especially at first. This means that you will be able to make solid improvements after implementation.

You should be sure that your activity-based costing system has a strong, user-friendly way to make updates to the system in order to reflect improvements and changes. Otherwise the system will soon go out of date and its strategic usefulness will be impaired. The costs assigned to each driver should be dynamic in order to keep the system accurate and useful.

How to Get Implemented

Since activity-based costing is quite new, there probably is not a great deal of good commercial software available to support it directly. However, if you have good, commercial MRP II software, you already have much of the data you will need readily at hand.

You can implement in stages. First, you will capture actual monthly activities. Once you have defined an activity, you can implement its use immediately. For example, let's assume you selected engineering changes as your first activity to implement. Your MRP II system's transaction history files should be able to give you a count of all the engineering change transactions during the month, and the item number(s) that it affected.

Next, you take the dollars involved in the month's ECO's out of the general factory overhead pool, and allocate them directly to the item number(s) involved. The remaining overhead pool continues to be applied conventionally. As you continue your activity-based costing implementation, you can implement each new one as it is ready.

This approach will allow you to go as far as seems useful in developing new activities to be costed, because overhead not included in the new activities will be accounted for and allocated according to your traditional practice.

You will want to use these new costs to help set next year's standards. With some analysis, your cost accountants should be able to project activity-based overhead based on a year's history, and project conventional allocation for the balance of the overhead pool.

HOW TO RECONCILE ACCOUNTING RULES WITH NEW-AGE ACCOUNTING

Until the advent of inexpensive computers, keeping the books was a real chore and keeping two sets of books was unthinkable. However, the attraction of Activity Based Costing systems has changed our thinking.

The most important conflict between external accounting rules and internal needs, has to do with how you treat manufacturing overhead. The external rule is that all of the manufacturing overhead of each period must be fully absorbed as an expense into cost of goods sold. A "period" in this case could be a month, a quarter, or a year. Be sure to recognize that this rule applies in the aggregate. There is no legal imperative to apply costs correctly to each product sold, only that all overhead be booked against cost of goods sold.

Because of the problems associated with overhead allocation, some companies are electing to apply no overhead at all to their product costs. Others selectively apply those overheads that are clearly related to the product involved, and allow the rest to go unspread. In this environment you won't absorb all the period's overhead, which does not support external requirements.

Now that it is easy to do, a number of companies have standard costs that are not fully absorbed for inside use, while applying all remaining overhead directly to the period's cost of goods sold for outside reporting. The difference between the two is ignored. Inside the company you use the unabsorbed version for your own benefit. The outside reports, with full absorption in cost of goods sold, don't get much circulation inside the company, and play no part in decision making.

The ABC approach often does not apply all overhead, and may not be usable for external reporting purposes without a second level of traditional allocation to absorb the remainder.

5

RULES TO ENSURE A SUCCESSFUL MRP-BASED SYSTEM

In order for a formal, MRP II-based system to work properly, with or without JIT enhancements, there are a small number of basic elements that you need to keep in excellent order if your system is going to work at all well. In this chapter, we will cover these seven basic rules:

1. Stop abusing your master production schedule.

2. Make your item numbers work.

3. Have a universal item master file.

4. Make one bill of material support everybody.

5. Get control of your design—engineering change control.

6. Designate your factory work centers.

7. Make it the same way every time—good process and routings.

STOP ABUSING YOUR MASTER PRODUCTION SCHEDULE

How to create and use your master production schedule is covered in other places in this book. But one of the basics is to respect its integrity. In consulting engagements, classrooms and lecture presentations, we find over and over that managers are abusing the master schedule.

Abusing the master schedule is the largest single management fault in achieving true excellence in using formal manufacturing systems. Abuse takes two forms.

The first, and most common abuse, is management's bias toward mandating changes to the master schedule inside of lead time. The computer then processes these schedules, using the standard MRP backscheduling rules. This creates schedules that show order start dates past due, and even order due dates already past due.

The result of this abuse is that the schedules are unrealistic, and can't be achieved. This, in turn, destroys the credibility of the computer-generated schedules in the eyes of the planners, vendors, and shop supervisors. Since the schedules are considered rubbish, a separate schedule is develop informally between the parties, and you are back to the expedite mode.

Companies who abuse their master schedules doom themselves to a computer-assisted launch and expedite system. In this environment, the MRP system helps the planners launch purchase and manufacturing orders, and then expediting takes over with the classic shortage lists, supervisors' morning meetings, hot lists, and endless overlapping and conflicting expediting.

The second abuse is overloading the front end of the master schedule. In this situation a manager mandates that more work be put into the master schedule in the early weeks than capacity can produce. Purchased materials arrive within lead time, but the factory simply doesn't have enough capacity to perform to schedule. The consequences of overloading the master schedule are the same as changes within lead time, namely that the schedules become disgraced and useless, and expediting reappears as the substitute method to schedule what truly will be manufactured.

The abusers often are the bosses of the master scheduler. In this setting, schedulers can exhibit only a certain amount of resistance before placing their jobs in jeopardy. In chronic cases, the master scheduler gives up, puts the numbers in as dictated, and lets the computer pump out piles of useless schedules. The users, purchasing and manufacturing, do whatever they can to keep the factory running, and the bosses become frustrated and angry that their orders are not carried out. I am reminded of the motto I have often seen in the planning department, "Sure I can expedite this job today, but does it go ahead of the job you told me to expedite yesterday?" I once worked as a planner in a small manufacturing company where the customers would routinely call the general manager when I couldn't give them an early enough ship date. He would then tell me I had to promise the desired date, or he would get someone on my job who would. I did. As a result we were behind schedule on 60 percent of our jobs, and our vendor rating among our customers was extremely poor.

Management must respect the integrity of the Master Schedule's time fences for each product family, as explained earlier in this book.

HOW TO MAKE YOUR ITEM NUMBERS WORK

A good, clean part-numbering system is an essential ingredient for any properly functioning formal manufacturing system. This requirement is so basic, in fact, that its existence is often taken for granted. People don't pay much attention to part numbering until some outside event brings attention to it. The implementation of a formal manufacturing system is one of those outside events. The development of a new product line could be another cause. Or, merging two plants or two product lines usually demands a reevaluation of the part-numbering schemes involved.

For purposes of this discussion, the term part and item are synonymous, although item is slightly more correct. Also, a part or item refers to any or all of the following:

- Commodity
- Piece part
- Intermediate
- Fabrication
- Sub-assembly
- Assembly

- End item

- Service part

- Owner's guide

- Assembly instructions

- Warranty card

You have to give a number to everything that is to be controlled through your formal system. This includes anything that will be part of the end item.

The subject of a new part-numbering system is always an emotional one. This is true for three principal reasons The first is that people intuitively believe that the part number is the vehicle for providing some sort of discernable information about the part being numbered. This is the significant-nonsignificant argument. Many resist a new partnumbering system out of fear that the differentiation they now expect will be lost. I will cover this topic more extensively below.

The second reason for emotional resistance to a new part numbering system has to do with a perception that conversion will be disturbing to the organization and expensive. This concern, although a legitimate one, tends to be exaggerated. I have seen this one exaggerated to comic proportions. I will cover various conversion strategies below. So, to minimize the emotional reaction, keep the conversion strategy clearly separated from the discussion of the design of the system, during the development and implementation phases.

The third reason for emotional resistance is the classic resistance to change that we see in social organizations of all kinds. Fear of the unknown and fear of a sudden, overwhelming workload contribute to this resistance.

Here are some ideas for a practical approach to a part-numbering system. These ideas assume that a formal manufacturing system is in place or planned, or lacking that, at least that a computerized item master data base is available for use. These ideas are divided into two groups, design features and conversion strategies.

Design Features of a Part Numbering System

A part-numbering system has many desirable features, which add to the quality of the eventual system. Each feature can be evaluated and selected on its own merits. However, discarding any feature will represent a corresponding degradation in the quality of the eventual system.

A system should be as follows:

1. Discrete

2. Complete

3. Universal

4. Clerically Efficient and Accurate

5. Assigned Serially or Randomly

6. Check-Digited

7. Able to Support Tabulated Drawings

8. Durable

9. Administratively Efficient

Feature 1. Discrete

Being discrete means that you give each different part a different number. Most people agree with this in principle. But this rule is violated in practice to a surprising extent, even in high-technology companies. One manufacturer gave spools of lead wire of each gauge the same number, regardless of color coding. Another stored inspected and uninspected printed circuit boards in the stockroom under the same number. Raw and machined castings occasionally can be found in the stock room under the same number. In such an environment, any computerized system will ignore the real differences, process these ambiguities incorrectly, and yield wrong results. These wrong results will in turn cause stock outs and manufacturing errors. The question is only how often these errors occur and how severe they are.

The converse of the discreteness rule also holds. If two items are the same, you must give them the same number. Same in this case refers to the classic form, fit, and function rule. A good test is interchangeability. If one version of an item is interchangeable in all uses, it must have the same part number. If not, a different part number is required. When one part has two numbers, you stock two components instead of one. Lot sizing rules applied separately means more aggregate inventory, and a stock out of one usually cannot be remedied by the other's stock on hand.

Some companies try to avoid the discipline of assigning a new number when the form, fit, and function rule is violated by tying the revision letter to the root part number. Records are kept accordingly, and the different revisions are segregated in inventory. This is a very bad procedure, because every engineering change results in a new part number, and creates a plethora of part numbers. This is the very opposite of standardization, and destroys all recognition of interchangeability. This kind of system violates the discreteness and converse rules above, both at the same time! Every company with this ill-devised procedure asks its inventory control and stockroom personnel to somehow cope and muddle through with an ancillary manual system. You should never tolerate such a muddle-manual system even within a rudimentary formal manufacturing system environment.

Feature 2. Complete

Every item used in production must be given a part number. If it is part of the product, it needs a number. Some companies, indulging in false economies, try to skimp on this rule by ignoring fasteners, packaging, and commodity items such as bar stock and sheet metal. Pallets, banding material, labels, and so forth often are omitted. Unless there is a compelling reason, all items should be included.

Omitting components can easily lead to manufacturing errors. A former client labeled steel rods, bars, and strips only by their dimensions. They recognized their folly after making a large quantity of lawnmower blades out of mild steel, assembling them into end items, and delivering them to retailers. This mistake cost them a product recall!

Some companies attempt to use a vendor's catalog number, the Federal Stock Number, or some other outsider's designation. This leaves you at the mercy of an outside organization who will change specs without regard for your uses. Also, you don't want to be chained to one vendor or change part number just because purchasing switched to a new vendor.

In a formal manufacturing system, if you can't ship without it, it belongs on the system. All parts, no matter how inexpensive or trivial, must be managed somehow. Ignoring them on the main system makes reordering, scheduling, receiving, stocking, issuing, accounting, and payments more difficult, not easier.

You really shouldn't use a powerful, computerized system to manage most of our parts, and have a second, informal, catch-as-catch-can system for the rest. A-B-C concepts do not apply here. Moreover, when the manufacturing system is integrated with the costing system, ignoring trivial and ancillary components will also result in standard and actual cost calculations that are inaccurate because they are too low.

Feature 3. Universal

Your part-numbering system should apply to everything, production items and nonproduction items alike, both present and future. Packaging material, labels, cartons, banding, screws and washers, glue, and so on should all be numbered.

Your procedures even should anticipate use by nonproduction departments. Administrative features and management controls required for MRO (maintenance, repair, and operating) items, for example, are just as demanding as for production items. Many MRO storerooms are disorganized and lack a stock locator. And MRO items often are expensive. Reorder point and safety stock inventory management methods often apply to MRO items. Many commercial MRP II software products have provisions for reorder points and safety stocks for independent-demand items. To make use of the power of these modern systems, MRO items must be numbered.

Even the office supplies function can profit from stock status, stock locator, reorder point, safety stock, issue history, and demand forecasting tools.

Feature 4. Clerically Efficient and Accurate

Part numbers are written or keyed frequently, especially in broad, formal systems. These systems are noted for their extreme accuracy requirements. Part numbers should be easy to read, write, and key, and they should encourage accuracy. Therefore, part numbers should be short, all numeric, one length, and have no punctuation.

- The number should be as short as possible. Short numbers are obviously easier to work with than long ones. Studies have shown that errors occur disproportionately after five digits, and skyrocket beyond seven digits. An odd number of digits seems to yield slightly higher accuracy. You don't need many digits to accommodate a population of items. The telephone company can accommodate a large metropolitan area, with homes and businesses, with just seven digits.

The following shows the maximum populations for three typical lengths:

	Potential Population	
Length of Part Number	*Without Check Digit*	*With Check Digit*
5-digit	99,999	9,999
6-digit	999,999	99,999
7-digit	9,999,999	999,999

● The number should be all numeric. The visual ambiguity of O (oh), Z, I, and l (el), with 0 (zero), 2, 1, and 1, respectively, invites error. Aural ambiguity, though less obvious, is still serious: C with 3; D, B, P, and T with each other; and O (oh) with 0 (zero) are but a few. This problem is still worse when you work with people who don't speak the same language as you do. Moreover, computer languages and software easily and effectively can exclude nonnumeric characters from a numeric field, while in a alphanumeric field anything goes. An all-numeric configuration screens out all these errors. Bar coding using an all-numeric code is much easier to use and more accurate, especially where you need a small bar code label.

● All numbers should be the same length. This eliminates the left-versus-right justification problem. Any number with an extra digit or one missing is obvious to everybody. And in a computerized setting, a simple edit routine will prevent length errors entirely.

● Numbers should have no punctuation. Dashes, slashes, and spaces should be avoided unless you must use more than seven digits. If needed, a simple dash is the best choice and always should be in the same position in the number, just like your telephone number. But punctuation is slow to key and error prone. For example, the computer identifies each of the following numbers as different, while a clerk might not.

123456-789

1234567-89

123456/789

123456 789

123456789

Worst of all would be an alpha-numeric system that allows various lengths, accepts punctuation symbols, and permits them at various places in the numbers.

Feature 5. Assigned Serially

The simplest, most effective way to assign new numbers is serially. It is a trivial clerical job to keep a list of unissued numbers, crossing off each number as it is assigned sequentially. This function is usually performed by an engineering clerk. Some computerized item master systems will even assign the next number automatically when adding a new item to the file. Almost all computerized systems will prevent you from adding a number already on the file.

If logistics require that several offices assign part numbers, then designate one to be the lead office. This office then gives out numbers to the others in small blocks, perhaps a month's worth at a time, thereby preventing others from trying to recognize the design source by reading the part number.

Assigning serially makes maximum use of the numbers available, allowing you adopt the shortest possible number for your population of items. Shortness is an advantage.

Assigning serially also prevents any attempt to attribute significance to the number. This is desirable, since significant numbering never works. Significant numbers are usually long, and often contain nonnumeric characters and punctuation, violating many of the design criteria recommended here. And, even long after the significances have lost their meaning, you are still stuck with its more complicated administration and propensity for error.

Within a system, a data field can have only one use. If you ask one field to perform two services, their needs will gradually diverge, and become mutually exclusive. At this point, one use will be degraded or abandoned. The item number's prime duty is to discretely identify the part. If you ask the number also to tell you something else, you violate this rule. Just remember: one field, one duty; one duty, one field.

Legitimate needs for differentiation, the usual cause of attempts for a significant item number, are correctly dealt with elsewhere in the system, usually on the item master. Drawing size, buyer code, planner code, make-or-buy code, commodity class, design source, for example, are easily accommodated with separate fields on the item master. Where-used relationships, of course, are captured in the bill of material. Similarly, all legitimate needs for differentiation can be accommodated individually, and probably already are, if you are using commercial software.

Resist all attempts to put significance into your part number—it never works.

Feature 6. Check Digited

Input mistakes on the item number are a large source of error in operating computerized systems. Many of these mistakes actually cause two errors: the wrong record is updated, and the right one is not. Using a check digit eliminates virtually all transcription errors. A check digit is computed with a fairly simple mathematical formula and is usually incorporated into the number in the low order (right-hand) position.

There are several ways to compute check digits, but one of the more common ones is called Modulo-11 with arithmetic weighting. Here is how this method works:

Base Number:	8	9	3	9	1	4
Weighting:		7	6	5	4	3	2
Weight:		56	54	15	36	3	8

Total of all the weights: 56 + 54 + 15 + 36 + 3 + 8 = 172.

Divide by 11: 172/11 = 15 with 7 remainder.

Subtract the remainder from 11: 11 − 7 = 4.

Your check digit is 4, which you add to the end, making 8939144 your protected number.

Throw out any number with a check digit of 10.

To check your number, repeat the process, giving the low order position a weight of 1.

When you divide by 11, if the answer has no remainder, the number is correct:

In our example:

```
Base Number:  8  9  3  9  1  4  4
Weighting:       7  6  5  4  3  2  1
Weight:         56 54 15 36  3  8  4
Total:         176
```

Divide by 11: 176/11 = 16 with no remainder, proving that the number is correct.

Using a good check digiting system will eliminate almost all keying errors. The most common errors are adding a digit, leaving one out, entering one or more wrong digits, and making simple and complex transpositions. About the only clerical error that will not be apprehended is where a clerk, keying from a list, keys in an adjacent but legitimate number.

On request, I will send you a program for an IBM or compatible personal computer. This menu-driven program will print a list of protected numbers, as many as you want, with two to nine digits. User instructions are on the disk. Send $2 for postage and handling to:

> John N. Petroff, CFPIM
> Principal
> Raeker, Petroff & Associates
> 5017 Kingsdale Drive
> Minneapolis, Minnesota 55437

Using a check digit in your part number is easier than it looks. If you are doing a crash program conversion (see below), the computer can be programmed to sequentially assign check digited numbers.

Then get a computer run of check digited numbers, sequenced to start beyond the computer-assigned ones. All new numbers going on the part master are taken from this list. This will result in an item master file populated exclusively with correctly check-digited numbers.

When day-to-day operating data are being entered for processing, almost all computerized systems will check to see if the part number coming in is contained in the master. When an erroneous number is keyed, it will be rejected by the conventional "item number not found" editing. This means that the check digit doesn't even have to be calculated at input time, and no new computer programming needs to be added to your system to check incoming items.

Feature 7. Able to Support Tabulated Drawings

A tabulated drawing is one that contains many similar parts. Resistors and sheet metal screws are two typical examples. Color differences is another. Tabulation saves a lot of drafting time and also supports standardization.

There are two ways to manage tabulation. The first is to reserve a generous block of contiguous numbers. For example, if you have 200 resistors, block out 400 numbers. When assigning numbers within the tabulated drawing's block, start with the first number and proceed sequentially, for each new inclusion. Avoid trying to use dimensions or values in the part number, which would violate the "assigned serially" requirement. If you run out of numbers, just take out another block.

Figure 5.1 shows a simple tabulated drawing where the drawing number is the same as the part number.

The second technique is to use a separate drawing and drawing number to contain the various items. Individual entries on the tabulation receive the next part number from the administrative clerk in engineering.

Figure 5.2 shows the same example, but with the drawing number independent of the part numbers. The individual part numbers have been assigned by the engineering administrator in the same way as any other item.

Both techniques work, but the first avoids having a drawing number different from the item number. Both techniques support standardization.

Feature 8. Durable

Changing to a new part-numbering system in a manufacturing company is very onerous. Therefore, when you develop a new numbering system be sure that it will be flexible enough to accommodate growth, product line changes, acquisitions, new software, and changing computer hardware. Moreover, the system should measure up to this task for decades.

Adopting the features shown here, and especially by avoiding significance on the part number is the way to avoid obsolescence. A helpful, common device is to make the part number field in your computer system one or two digits larger than your planned number. This means that the users can start out with a fairly short number, and expand by an order of magnitude or even two if and when the need arises. Computerized input edits can exclude incoming data based on the shorter version. Files

Figure 5.1   Tabulated Drawing
Where the Drawing Number is the Same as the
Part Number

Standard Sheet Metal Screws
Short Length: > 1/4" - 1/2"

Part Number	Diameter	Length	Head	Point	Finish		
8939144	#6	3/8	P	G	C		
8939152	#7	5/16	P	S	C		
8939179	#6	3/8	L	B	P		
8939187	#2	1/4	O	G	C		
8938195	#4	5/16	R	T	C		
8939209	#4	3/8	R	R	P		
8939217	#6	1/2	A	S	B		
8939225	#6	1/2	L	B	Z		

HEADS

P = Pan
R = Round
F = Flat
O = Oval
S = Fillister
A = Allen
L = Phillips

POINTS

G = Gimlet
B = Blunt
S = Self Tapping

FINISHES

P = Plain
C = Cadmium
B = Black
Z = Zinc Dichromate

Standard
Sheet Metal Screws
Short
> 1/4" - 1/2"

Part No.	8939140 thru 8940140

Figure 5.2 Tabulated Drawing
Where the Drawing Number is Independent of the
Part Number

Standard Sheet Metal Screws
Short Length: > 1/4" - 1/2"

Part Number	Diameter	Length	Head	Point	Finish		
1245988	#6	3/8	P	G	C		
1246011	#7	5/16	P	S	C		
1459589	#6	3/8	L	B	P		
1459619	#2	1/4	O	G	C		
1576682	#4	5/16	R	T	C		
1576712	#4	3/8	R	R	P		
1676377	#6	1/2	A	S	B		
2351803	#6	1/2	L	B	Z		

HEADS

P =Pan
R =Round
F =Flat
O =Oval
S =Fillister
A =Allen
L =Phillips

POINTS

G =Gimlet
B =Blunt
S =Self
    Tapping

FINISHES

P =Plain
C =Cadmium
B =Black
Z =Zinc
  Dichromate

**Standard
Sheet Metal Screws
Short
> 1/4" - 1/2"**

Dwg. No.	1246003

and programming logic will start out with the ability to cope with the longer version and won't have to be changed later if a longer number becomes necessary. Computer system developers have been doing this since the beginning.

Feature 9. Administratively Efficient

Almost all computerized systems will guarantee efficient administration of part numbers. The part master's edits prevent using a number twice, and lists sorted and selected on any master file fields are made easily available. Report writer software now is widely installed and make these extractions quick and easy. If a bill-of-material processor is available, it will supply comprehensive product structure and where used lists. Clerical effort is needed only to assign new numbers and in file maintenance.

Three Conversion Strategies to Help You Change Your System

Converting from your old system to your new one is not an easy task. Many emotional problems occur in the discussion of conversion. However, the difficulty of conversion can be and often is grossly exaggerated. With computer assistance widely available, a good, clean, and accurate conversion can be accomplished at a reasonable cost and effort.

There are three main conversion strategies:

1. Crash Program

2. Gradual Phase-In

3. Attrition

Strategy 1: Crash Program

With this conversion approach, you convert current part numbers to your new scheme in one concerted effort. This requires careful planning and preparation.

First, you need a list of active parts. This can exclude service parts not used in active production. Or, as an alternative, the population to be converted can be limited to those required in newer products, on the theory that older products will be retired shortly anyway. Certainly parts neither needed in current products nor for service will be excluded from the conversion. In situations where bills of material and parts information of various kinds are required to be held for historical purposes only, excluding obsolete items will reduce the conversion effort by a large fraction.

If you have significance imbedded in your current part number, each need for differentiation must be evaluated to see if those represented are still needed. Often, you are bringing in new software which will have an enhanced part master file. Because of this, needs for differentiation can be accommodated in your new system, making the part master as useful as possible.

Next, the Data Processing Department writes three programs. One program will assign a new number to each current part on the file and start a new part master for each. It records the old number in a reference field. It also completes as many fields on the new record as possible, either directly or inferentially by using the computer's speedy ability to perform extensive logic. The big problem here is that the new part master probably will ask for more data than the old one has available. In some cases, you will need to "de-combine" one old field into two or more new ones. Sometimes this can be done programmatically with logic, but other times you will have to complete these fields manually. There will also be several new fields, not represented on your old file at all. Part of this computerized conversion process should be a tailored list showing part numbers with blank fields showing up after conversion. The conversion team then assigns each field to one of your functional departments for manual completion.

Although creating these new fields represents a cost, they should not be assessed to the cost of converting to your new part numbering system. Rather, this represents an enhancement to your current condition.

The second program produces two cross-reference lists, one new-to-old, the other old-to-new. These two cross reference lists are made available to all who need them, either on paper or on a terminal.

The third program, or family of programs, takes current files, notably bills of material and routings, and changes all old numbers to their new numbers, and puts the old number in a reference area. The new bills and routings are put into production, and the old ones saved for reference. Using both old and new versions is not possible beyond a very short interim period because you just can't maintain parallel files successfully, particularly ones of this size and complexity. Besides, new numbers come into the system every day, and never would be back-converted into old numbers for inclusion in the old files.

Engineering documents can be changed all at once or gradually with a crash program, as the numbers are called up for other purposes. Current CAD systems probably can make the change easily and automatically.

If you have any amount of service parts business, you will have to take extra steps. The service parts function is severely affected by a crash conversion to the extent that they use parts in current production. Service manuals often have part numbers shown on them. One way to accommodate the change to the new numbering system is to change all of the existing manuals. But this can be quite expensive. Another is to make cross-reference lists available on computer terminals, or the computer could automatically flag out old numbers and show the new one, whenever an old number is keyed in. However, because of the nature of the service function, these cross reference lists will need to be permanent.

A crash program would be appealing in a situation where your product line is stable over the years, with few new products coming in or old products phasing out.

Strategy 2: Gradual Phase-In

With this method, you give a new style number to every new part as it is added to the system. The old parts are changed to the new system gradually as they are revised through your engineering change control process. When a part is being changed to its next higher revision, give it a new part number. Then, after two to four years, you could consider a crash program to clean out the few remaining old style numbers. Some companies have found that 60 percent of their parts undergo an engineering change within two years. This means that given a phase-in rate of 60 percent every two years, you would be left with only 16 percent of the original population of numbers remaining with old numbers after four years.

You must take care to maintain a good cross-reference old-to-new and new-to-old capability. Also, the service parts function is affected in the same way as with a crash program, as mentioned above.

Gradual phase-in is useful for companies that have a somewhat stable product line, but with quite a few engineering changes. This is because the engineering change process is the driving element to changing to new numbers.

Strategy 3: Attrition

With this approach, you assign new style numbers only to new parts, and the old ones are allowed to remain in the system until they disappear through obsolescence. No cross reference is needed, and the service parts function is not severely affected. After two to four years, a crash program can be used to convert any old numbers still in use. This is an especially appealing strategy in a company having a rapidly-changing design, where end items and individual parts have a short life span. There are quite a few companies with end items that have a life cycle of two years or less. This means that almost all old numbers will disappear after just a couple of years.

Recapping Your Numbering System

External influences, such as implementing a computerized formal manufacturing system or an acquisition, often require conversion to a new part-numbering system. A practical part-numbering system can have several features. It can be:

- Discrete, complete, and universal
- Five to seven digits
- Administratively efficient and durable
- Check digited
- Serially assigned
- Insignificant

There are three main conversion strategies:

- Crash Program
- Gradual Phase-In
- Attrition

You should choose the method that will give you the fastest conversion that makes economic sense. You want to minimize the elapsed time to a full conversion and to minimize the expense and dislocations of the conversion.

HOW TO GET THE MOST FROM YOUR ITEM MASTER FILE

In every computerized MRP II-based system, the item master file is a central requirement. You define every item that you want to include in the system. To get control of the item master file and make it work for you, you need two things:

1. Good administration

2. The right fields

How to Achieve Good Administration

Your software provides for add, change, and delete capability, for each field on each record. With modern software and computer hardware, this facility is usually on-line and real time. Most commercial systems take a menu approach to maintaining item master records and are reasonably user-friendly.

Security is another administrative consideration for the item master file. You probably have computer terminals widely available. Your computer system should allow almost every user with a password to view data already on the file. It is widely held that company data is a resource, and allowing broad ability for look-ups is one way to exploit these data. However, only a limited few of your employees should be allowed to add or change records. Most computer environments allow for this degree of security on the basis of user identification codes. Most systems allow this security on a screen-by-screen basis. A better feature, found in some products, allows security by field within screen. This would allow you to restrict update authority based on each field in each screen.

You must assign maintenance authority for each field. In an MRP II-based system your item master record contains many fields, up to 75 or more in some of the mature systems. Each field must be "owned" by one and only one specific department or group. The departments usually involved are:

- Product Engineering

- Manufacturing Engineering

- Manufacturing Operations

- Production and Inventory Control

- Purchasing

- Accounting

- Quality Control

After analyzing the contents of your item master record and demands placed on the data it contains, one of these departments is given add and update responsibility. Within each department there should be at least three persons who know how to maintain their fields. One person is primarily responsible and does most of the input. A second person is needed for backup for vacations, and the like. The third person, perhaps a supervisor, is emergency backup.

Each responsible department should be served by special reports developed by the data processing group to analyze the data they are responsible for, especially blanks or entries that are out of line, based on internal computer editing logic.

You should also designate those few fields that are absolutely mandatory by your systems to function. These would be flags that control logic, as well as those with definite values. An example of a flag would be lot sizing rule. An example of a definite value would be the inventory carrying cost. The other fields usually are display fields, that are more or less handy to various users, but control no logic.

For your mandatory fields you should have strict procedures for their maintenance. Also you should develop an auditing program to routinely test the completeness and accuracy of the mandatory fields. Each field should have its own rules and procedures. Some of the needed auditing should be done by a department different from the one with primary responsibility.

How to Select the Right Fields

If you are using commercial software, your item master record comes to you with definite fields. Most allow you to add extra ones at the end to support any special needs you may have.

When considering the item master record, especially in an MRP II-based system, you have to understand the distinction between the item master and the bill of material (also known as the product structure). For example, where a component is used is a bill of material topic, as is quantity. Storage location and unit of measure are two examples of item master topics. There is much more data associated with an item on the item master than exists on its bill of material.

The following is a "laundry list" of item master fields, commonly found in commercial as well as in home-written software. Some of these fields are mandatory to an MRP II system, others are convenience fields for display. Still others are optional, depending on the features of the software you are using. For example, if you only have one buyer, you could get by with leaving the buyer code field blank on the item master. However, if you have several buyers, you will want each to get their own reports, so populating the buyer code field becomes mandatory.

I will try to designate the following fields as to always mandatory, feature mandatory, or display.

Field 1. Item number

Item number is the key field of the item master record. This is the field that makes each record unique. Every system must have a valid item master record in order to do any processing on that item. This field usually allows around 15 characters, maximum, depending on the software you are using. This is an always-mandatory field.

Field 2. Description

This is a language field, and usually holds the same description used on the engineering drawings. This field is usually around 30 characters long, but some software products allow two or more lines. Although ubiquitous, this field is really not mandatory to the logic of your system. It is a true display field, although your procedures could make it mandatory.

Field 3. Stocking Unit of Measure

This is the unit of measure used inside the company, and is the one used in the stock room for purposes of receiving and issuing. Some software products verify unit of measure at input time. It is fairly easy for one person to be thinking in terms of pounds, and another of feet, for example. The item master record houses the one, official unit of measure to be used throughout the entire system, with the possible exception of purchasing. This is an always mandatory field.

Field 4. Purchasing Unit of Measure

Purchasing uses a unit of measure different from the stocking one when dealing with vendors. If so, you need a special field for it. Advanced software applications will have a separate table containing all the acceptable units of measure, plus conversion factors that allow the computer to convert from purchasing unit of measure to stocking unit of measure and back. This is a feature-mandatory field.

Field 5. Make or Buy Code

This field is used to govern processing and report writing. Regarding processing, the system handles items destined to be purchased somewhat differently from those that will be manufactured. Also, at report writing time, the computer will prepare different reports for purchased and manufactured items.

You may have a number of items that can be either purchased or manufactured, depending on capacity considerations at order placement time. For these items, the standard technique is to use the favored choice, allowing the item's planner to change the designation while the order is in planned status. Better software products allow this "on the fly" alteration on an order-by-order basis, and will act accordingly at the next processing run. This is a mandatory field.

Field 6. Item Life Cycle

Items cycle in and out of your manufacturing scene, and must be administered in different ways at different points in their life cycles. The typical stages in an item's life cycle are:

- Prereleased. This designates an item that is currently under development in engineering. Usually this means that engineering change control procedures do not apply, and serves as a flag to everyone coming in contact with this item. For example, a prereleased item appearing on a requisition in purchasing or manufacturing, would signal a lot size of one and only temporary tooling. Quality control usually is reluctant to allow a prereleased item to be specified into the product line.

- Released. Most of your items will be in released status. Released items are in the mainstream. They are on bills of material, in inventory being purchased, manufactured, and sold to customers, and come under the rules of your engineering change control procedure.

- Service Only. Many companies are obligated to supply service parts for their products long after they are out of current production. Service parts can be either purchased or manufactured, and often will be in inventory. Service items must therefore stay on the system, but are administered differently as to inventory levels, lot sizing, and costing. You may or may not want to allow service items to be structured into new designs.

- Obsolete. These are items that are not called out on any currently-active bills of material, and should be cleaned out. You certainly will not want to purchase or manufacture any more of them, and may want to degrade their value on your general ledger to reflect their true market value. Obsolete items should be investigated periodically and scrapped out as soon as possible.

This is a feature-mandatory field.

Field 7. Design Authority

When you manufacture an item according to your customer's designs and specifications, you don't have the authority to change the design on your own initiative. This situation is common in military contracting. Some companies have several design offices in the plant. Still others get their designs from a central design office, separated organizationally from the plant. In these cases it is important to have an ability to designate the design source for each item. A feature-rich software system could even invoke different logic when processing engineering changes, governed by your design authority code.

This could be a feature-mandatory field, but usually would be a display field.

Field 8. Drawing Number

Companies usually try to have their drawing number be the same as the item number shown. However, other companies having complex products or who use tabulated drawings extensively get forced into having drawing numbers different from the items drawn. If you have this situation, then you will want to use this field. If your drawing numbers are the same as your part numbers, you can ignore this field. This is a display field.

Field 9. Drawing Size

Having the drawing size on a lookup screen helps the design office, and eliminates the usual recipe-card box. This is a display field.

Field 10. Classification Code

This is the field to use if you want to be able to group similar items on reports for analysis and administration. One common use is to use a series of codes that designate the physical characteristics of each item. This is especially useful for standardization, and will help your engineers use existing parts as much as possible in new designs.

Another use for this information is in establishing group technology work cells in the factory, which is a popular Just-in-Time technique. When used this way, items can be grouped to help you plan a flow line type of factory layout.

The classification code also helps purchasing group items for purposes of vendor prospecting and blanket ordering. This is especially important when you contract to buy capacity with short-term releasing, another JIT idea. This is a display field.

Field 11. Planner Code

Purchased items usually are assigned to an inventory planner, and manufacturing items to a production planner. This is done on an item-by-item basis, and you should be able to change this as the work load shifts, planners come and go, and their skill levels increase. These codes are used by the software to route both on-line and paper reports and messages to the designated planner. This is a feature-mandatory field.

Field 12. Buyer Code

Traditional business organization has the inventory planner send a requisition to the buyer. When you have more than one buyer, the system needs this code to route your on-line and paper reports and messages to the designated buyer. A JIT idea is to have one person act as both inventory planner and buyer. In this case, the planner code and the buyer code would be the same. This is a feature-mandatory field.

Field 13. Inventory Cost

This is the cost that you will use for valuing on-hand inventory on your general ledger for financial reporting. This cost traditionally includes fully-absorbed overhead allocation. Using this field allows you to use the same inventory records in all systems, and eliminates the old problem of having general accounting keep a separate set of records of inventory ins and outs. Since MRP II systems must have inventory record accuracy of at least

95 percent, its stock status records, multiplied by this cost, gives a very accurate result. This also eliminates completely the old reconciliation that was required by keeping two sets of records.

If you do not have a separate cost for standard cost rollups this cost will be used for this purpose as well. This is a feature-mandatory field.

Field 14. Cost Rollup Cost

If you have a conflict between full-absorption, activity based, or rate-based overhead allocation, you may be forced to use a separate cost just for standard cost rollups. If so, this field is used for this special cost. However, if you leave this field blank, your standard costing system should default to the inventory cost. This is a feature-mandatory field.

Field 15. Inventory Group

You can use this field if you want periodic reports on inventories grouped into categories. Some typical categories are commodities, components, sub-assemblies, make to stock finished goods, make to order finished goods, and so on. This is a display field.

Field 16. Inventory Account Number

This field allows you to attribute each item to its desired inventory account, according to your current chart of accounts. Having this field available allows flexibility when the chart of accounts undergoes revision. This is a feature-mandatory field.

Field 17. Issue Control

This field is used to designate the items that will be under automatic issue. Automatic issue, also called backflushing, occurs as manufacturing is completed. When you report a completed quantity out of manufacturing, the system explodes its bill of material and relieves items marked for automatic issue in their respective quantities.

Originally intended for use on small items with trivial cost, this technique has become a favorite JIT technique, and works well with frequent vendor deliveries directly to your production areas.

Items not automatically issued must be manually issued from the stock room to support each manufacturing order. This booking usually occurs as the order is started. This is a feature-mandatory field.

Field 18. Cycle Count Interval

Cycle counting is an essential MRP II ingredient. This field allows you to designate the number of working days between cycle counts. Many companies use an ABC approach to this time interval, with A-items being cycled often, B-items less often, and C-items once or twice a year. This field is feature-mandatory.

Field 19. ABC Classification

Although the advent of MRP II systems has drastically reduced the places where ABC ideas apply, this field is somewhat useful, notably for governing cycle counting frequency.

Some software products use this field in processing logic, making this field either feature-mandatory or display.

Field 20. Use-up Flag

This field designates items that you have decided to use up and not order or manufacture again. Using this designation should be part of your engineering change control system. Your planners should get an error message if a use-up item ever appears on a requisition. This field is feature-mandatory.

Field 21. Lot-Size Rule

Every item on your system must be given a lot-size rule. The various rules are explained elsewhere in this book. If left blank, most systems will default to the lot-for-lot rule. This is a mandatory field.

Field 22. Fixed Lot-Size

You use this field if you choose a lot-size rule of fixed. This is a feature-specific field.

Field 23. Minimum Order Quantity

This quantity is used to modify some of the lot-size rules. This quantity is expressed either in units or days, and prevents you from ordering too-small quantities or from ordering too often. This is a feature-mandatory field.

Field 24. Maximum Order Quantity

This quantity is used to modify some of the lot-size rules. This quantity is expressed either in units or days, and prevents you from ordering too-large quantities, or from ordering a coverage that extends too far into the future. This is a feature-mandatory field.

Field 25. Quantity Multiple

This field solves the "55-gallon drum" problem, and causes your requisitions to be recommended in these multiples. This applies to manufactured as well as to purchased items, wherever there is a specific container, vat, tank, reactor, and so on, involved. This field is feature-mandatory.

Field 26. Inventory Carrying Cost

Expressed as a percentage per year, this field is used in some of the more exotic lot sizing formulas. This is a feature-specific field.

Field 27. Setup Cost

This is the setup cost for a manufactured item, or the ordering cost of a purchased item. This is the cost per order, not per unit. This information is used by some of the more exotic lot sizing formulas. This field is feature-specific.

Field 28. Average Order Quantity

This field is used to spread the setup cost per order over the typical order quantity, and is needed only if setup cost is also needed. This is a feature-specific field.

Field 29. Reorder Point

Many independent-demand items can be managed with reorder points. Occasionally you may find a dependent-demand item, that does not fit the MRP II mold, that is better managed with an reorder point. This is a feature-mandatory field.

Field 30. Safety Stock

This is a companion to reorder point. Although it is possible to have safety stock associated with a dependent-demand item being managed through MRP II, this application is very dubious, except in most unusual circumstances. This is a feature-mandatory field.

Field 31. Shrinkage Percent

In some industries there is shrinkage during the manufacturing process. One typical example is a mixing vat, where some product sticks to the walls. In other cases, the need for shrinkage is just poor process or quality control. Using this field has the effect of inflating the size of the manufacturing order. Shrinkage can also be used to inflate purchase requisitions to cover for inspection fall-out at receiving. These are clearly contrary to JIT principles, but may be unavoidable, especially in the short run. You may or may not want to include shrinkage in your standard cost rollups. This is a feature-mandatory field.

Field 32. Move Time

This is the aggregate time needed to move a manufacturing lot from work center to work center, used by MRP II in scheduling. Some software products will populate this field automatically from the routing file. This field is feature-mandatory.

Field 33. Setup Time

This is the aggregate amount of time across all operations needed for setup to manufacture a lot, used by MRP II in scheduling. Some software products will populate this field automatically from the routing file. This field is feature-mandatory.

Field 34. Run Time

This is the aggregate amount of time needed to process one unit in the factory. Some software products will populate this field automatically from the routing file. This field is feature-mandatory.

Field 35. Pick Time

This is the amount of time allocated to pick the components needed to start a lot. This usually is to support a manufacturing order, but some companies also want to supply components to a vendor to support a purchase order. This field is feature-mandatory.

Field 36. Manufacturing Planner Time

This is the amount of time allotted the manufacturing planner to review a recommended manufacturing order before approving or changing it. This is a feature-mandatory field.

Field 37. Inventory Planner Time

This is the amount of time allotted the inventory planner to review a recommended purchase requisition before approving or changing it. This is a feature-mandatory field.

Field 38. Buyer Time

This is the amount of time allotted the buyer to react to an approved requisition. Sometimes this includes selecting a vendor or soliciting quotes. This includes the time needed to prepare a purchase order. JIT philosophy eliminates this function in favor of a permanent vendor relationship, coupled with direct releases to the vendor by the inventory planner. This is a feature-mandatory field.

Field 39. Vendor Leadtime

This is the vendor's quoted leadtime, used in scheduling. The JIT concept of frequent, small deliveries tends to eliminate this as a scheduling factor. This is a feature-mandatory field.

Field 40. Receiving Time

This is the allotted time to process an incoming vendor delivery, and is used in scheduling. The JIT concept of delivery directly to the production line eliminates this factor. This field is feature-mandatory.

Field 41. Inspection Time

This is the amount of time allocated for inspection, either of a vendor delivery, or of a completed manufacturing order. This is used for scheduling. JIT principles call for zero defects and the elimination of this factor. This is a feature-mandatory field.

Special Fields

You can include any number of special fields that you may need to adjust to the individual needs of your company and its plants. You should also have a few extra fields for future needs, so you can avoid re-programming.

Your item master is one of your more powerful tools in tailoring your MRP/JIT system for your company and plants. Don't be intimidated by its size, because each field you choose to use supports a valuable feature. This is especially true for the feature-mandatory fields.

HOW TO MAKE ONE BILL OF MATERIAL SUPPORT EVERYBODY

In the past, bills of material were found on the assembly drawing in the engineering department. Or, perhaps somewhere in manufacturing or accounting, someone had them captured on ledger or Kardex™ cards. Often the details were nowhere to be found except in the heads of the shop supervisors where the items were manufactured. In many companies, this was a never-ending chore.

When computers began to take over the management of bill of material data, and especially since the advent of MRP, bills have become more complete and more accurate. We have moved to a single, universal bill, discontinuing the duplicates and their reconciling. Now you can look at bills not just as a repository of data, but as a powerful tool in helping manufacturing achieve world class, competitive stature.

How to Make One Bill Fit All Uses

One early rule promulgated by MRP is that you can only tolerate one bill of material for the company. This means that all functions in your company that use bill of material data must be served by one central database. The widespread use of modern database management software has made this rule entirely feasible.

Now you will usually find the bill of material in a manufacturing company being administered in the design engineering office, while it contains fields and details to support many, diverse needs.

Once you have the bill of material database built, there are a number of extractions available. Many of these bill of material derivatives available on a computer terminal, on paper or both. Here are seven of the more common bill of material displays.

Display 1, Single Level Bill

After being given the parent's item number, the computer displays all of the components directly structured to it. This reference screen is useful to a wide variety of functions, especially engineering, materials management, manufacturing, purchasing, and sales. In a real-time environment, engineering changes are instantly implemented, and can be viewed immediately.

Display 2, Indented Bill

The indented bill for an end item is very useful, but is available for any level in the bill. It starts with any parent and shows in a step-wise fashion, each of its components, with their components, all the way to the bottom of the bill. This often goes down five or six levels, and some bills go even further.

However, if you have bills more than six levels deep, there probably is a systematic error being done in engineering. The most common error is changing part number after every operation. You should only change part number at a stocking point. This error is usually the result of a faulty accounting system. If you are in this situation, change the accounting system.

Display 3, Product Lead Time

This report is a special version of the indented bill, showing the usual hierarchical parent-component relationships from top to bottom, plus a Gantt chart showing accumulating lead times through all levels, bottom to top. This report is quite useful to master production schedulers. Since it clearly shows the critical path of lead time accumulation, this report is also useful to support your program of lead time reduction. This report has a reputation of taking a long time to process on the computer, and may be available only on paper, after an overnight, batch process.

Display 4, Single-Level Where-Used

This reference shows the requestor every parent where the designated item is used. Almost impossible to maintain in a manual environment, a computerized bill of material system provides this display almost as a by-product. This display is most valuable during the engineering change process. It tells the viewer, every place the item is used, so the impact of a requested change can be completely investigated.

Display 5, Indented Where-Used

When this report is shown for a bottom level item, its usage is traced upward through succeeding levels of all of its bills of material, all the way to all of the end items where it may be used. This makes it possible to do an exhaustive analysis regarding engineering changes. This report, as well as the single-level where-used are also useful for standardization.

Display 6, Pick List

Your stock rooms need to know precisely how much of each item to issue to each manufacturing order. By accessing both the firmed manufacturing order file and their respective bills of material, the computer prepares an up-to-date pick list, extended for the quantity designated on each manufacturing order. The pick list also respects effectivity dates from your approved engineering change orders.

Automatic-issue items are flagged on the pick list, so the stock picker will ignore them at issue time. Some companies use a slave printer in the stock room to print pick lists, saving internal mail time.

Display 7, Costed Bill

Once the source of much duplication and conflict, the cost accounting department is also served by the central bill of material file. They usually want a costed version, showing cost rollups in a variety of ways. Cost rollups can be real time, but in some environments, this is an overnight batch run.

You can make a wide variety of other reports available by merely writing extraction programs, using the one, central, complete bill of material data base.

How to Manage Deep Bills vs Flat Bills for JIT and GT

In a conventional MRP setting you will find bills of material that are usually several levels deep; up to five or six. The sub-assembly breaks represented by each level, model the layout of the factory. The theory is that each work center or shop works on a never-ending string of batches of items, sending each batch to the store room when done. The items then are safeguarded until issued to a manufacturing order for the next higher assembly, and so on until you complete your finished goods and send them off to your customer or to finished goods inventory locations.

Figure 5.3 shows one of these typical bills, for a flashlight, four levels deep, counting the end item as level zero. Here we see four different sub-assemblies to manufacture the flashlight. Four-, five-, and even six-level bills of material are fairly common in factories laid out in the conventional, functional manner.

Just-in-Time and Group Technology concepts suggest a different approach. In JIT, by eliminating queues in front of work centers, and using very small lot sizes, it is possible to deliver the sub-assemblies to the next work center directly, often by hand, without going first in and out of the stock room. This eliminates the need for intermediate stocking and issuing. In such a situation, the sub-assemblies could be designated as pseudos or phantoms on your bill of material. When this is done, they are manufactured under the manufacturing order for the parent, and the pick lists bypass the pseudos. Or, the bills can be restructured to eliminate the pseudo sub-assemblies altogether. In our flashlight example, if this were done for all sub-assemblies, the bill would be one level deep and show just the 12 purchased items.

Figure 5.3 End Item Bill of Material

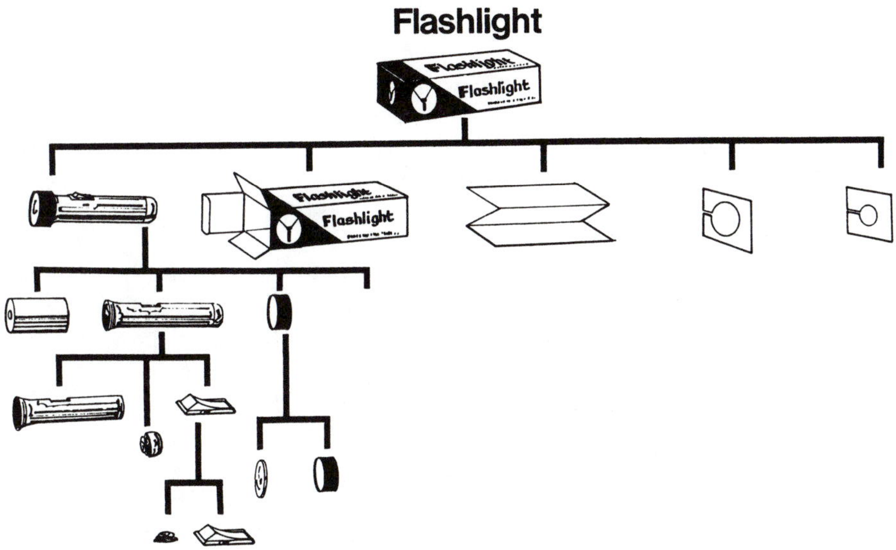

Group technology takes this concept a step further and suggests that the factory be physically rearranged, with the machines lined up according to what is being made. In addition, this puts dissimilar machines together, in a kind of mechanized teamwork layout. This practice also dictates converting your bills from narrow and deep to wide and flat.

How to Control Your Quantities

Differing manufacturing needs often require different treatment of the quantity designation of components. These are the common quantity options:

Option 1. Per Parent

This is by far the most common quantity option for a component. If you want to make one flashlight, you need one switch, and the quantity is designated as one per parent. You also need two batteries per parent.

Your pick list will show each of the components' quantity per parent multiplied by the quantity on the manufacturing order. For cost accounting, the cost contribution is the standard cost of the component, multiplied by the quantity designated per parent.

Option 2. Per Order

Occasionally a component is used just to serve the order. In this case, the quantity is designated as per order. A brush used to apply glue is an example. One brush is used for the order, whether the lot size is 10 or 100. Another use of this option is for setup material. It often happens that some components are spoiled during setup. They would be designated on the bill of material as a quantity per order.

Your pick list shows only the quantity per order, with no recognition of the quantity called for on the manufacturing order.

To serve cost accounting correctly, the standard cost of the per order items are divided by a standard or average order quantity, thus contributing the pro rata cost to the parent.

Option 3. Optional or As Required

Even though it does not square well with MRP, orthodoxy, optional, and as-required components do exist. A realistic bill of material system needs to recognize this fact. In some cases an optional component is seldom used, and this designation is just used to pre-authorize its use if needed. In other situations, the optional item is used regularly, in a predictable number of cases. When this occurs, the percentage of usage should be designated. This then allows MRP to provide for coverage at the stated percentage, and for standard costing to include the pro rata standard cost in the parents' rollups.

Option 4. Reference

Since the bill of material is used widely and frequently, it offers a convenient way to record noncomponents such as specifications, drawings, instruction sheets, reusable tooling, and any other item that can be related to a parent. Reference items are ignored by MRP, usually have no stock status, and are not added to the cost of the parent.

How to Use Planning Bills

The overwhelming number of bills of material are for truly manufacturable items. Figure 5.3 is an example of an end-item bill of material. However, for planning, it is useful to have some special versions, which then allow the user to take advantage of MRP's power with a minimum of inputs. These are the most common planning bills.

Planning Bill 1. Modular Bill of Material

In Figure 5.4, you see a winch family illustrated. If we were to forecast sales and create a master production schedule for all the possible combinations shown, the three drums, six motors, three gear boxes, and three control boxes could be made up into 216 end items.

Some of these 216 combinations will never be sold, others might sell, but in small quantities at unknown intervals. To ask for a sales forecast and to master schedule this array would be a foolish application of MRP orthodoxy.

A far better technique would be to plan the modules one level down from the end item. In this situation you would be working with just 16 items. Then when a customer order arrives, you could assemble a winch in a short time from an inventory of modules. Or better still, you could assemble from modules not yet in inventory, but rather on the master schedule. Selling the master schedule is a good way to cut finished or semi-finished inventory and is possible once master schedule adherence is achieved.

Planning Bill 2. Accessories and Options

Figure 5.5 shows a camera. In this example, every camera takes the same body, but there are three lenses to choose from. The body is entered on the camera's bill at the 100 percent level, while the lenses are specified at the 75 percent, 20 percent, and 5 percent levels. One of these lenses is always required, so the percentages add up to 100 percent. The automatic winder

Figure 5.4 Modular Bill of Material

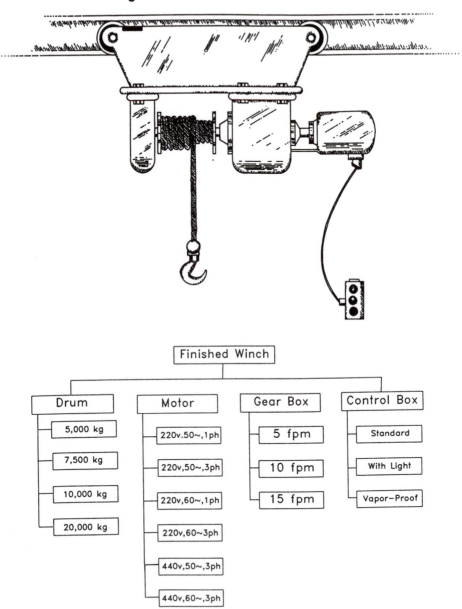

and the flash are options, and experience tells us that they sell at the rate of 10 percent and 90 percent, respectively. This planning technique can even be taken down another level. In our example you see three different flash accessories, each with its own percentage.

Figure 5.5 Accessories and Options Bill of Material

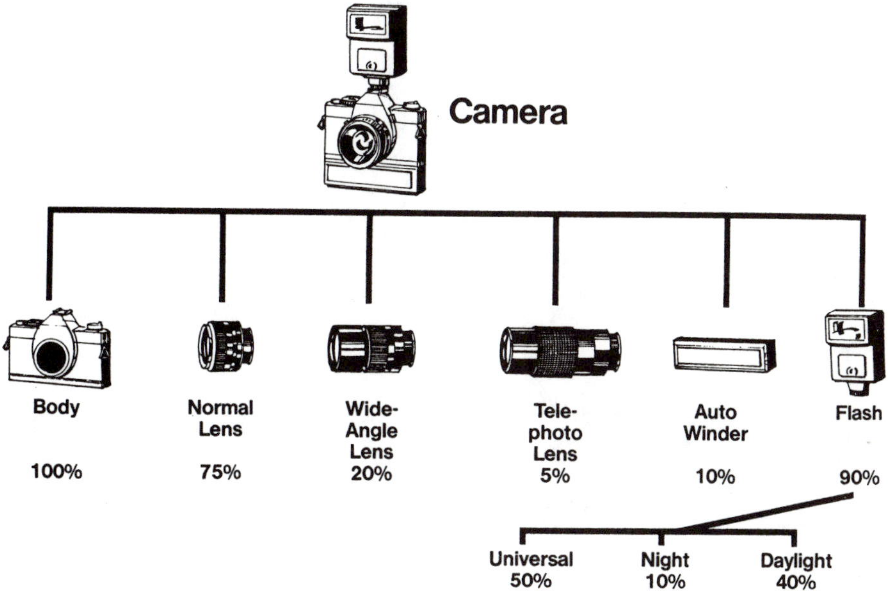

Planning Bill 3. Family Bills

In a like manner you can organize similar end items into family bills for planning purposes. Figure 5.6 shows a family of bicycles, differing in color. Their expected percentage is coded into the family bill, which in turn is master scheduled. MRP now takes over and plans all dependent items, including the actual shippable end items.

How to Use Your Bills for Special Purposes

There are several special categories of items that often are hard to manage using conventional bill of material techniques. But with some enhanced features, these problems can be handled within standard MRP logic. These special uses are:

- By-Products
- Alternate Products
- Liability Items
- Tools
- Starters

Figure 5.6   Family Bill of Material

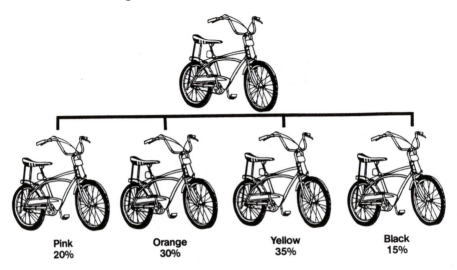

Pink
20%

Orange
30%

Yellow
35%

Black
15%

Use 1. By-Products

Many companies experience by-products. Injection molders have sprues and shorts. Metal working processes often have chips and shavings, sometimes from high-cost stock. Such items can be handled conveniently by including them on the bill of material of the parent, with a separate part number, and with the quantity per parent representing the amount of the by-product. When the by-product can be reused in production, it is called out on the bill of material for the appropriate parents as a normal component. MRP knows open and planned manufacturing orders, and therefore anticipates receipt of by-products. Then MRP plans their consumption just like any other on-order component. In standard costing, the value of the by-product is deducted from the cost of the producing parent. For a consuming parent, a by-product is costed just like any other.

Use 2. Alternate Products

Some manufacturers, notably in electronics, start out manufacturing a parent, only to find at final testing that some in the batch to not conform to the specifications. But the fall-outs do satisfy the specs for one or more other items. These are called alternates, and resemble by products. One difference, however, is that when an alternate is received, the quantity is deducted from the quantity due on the manufacturing order. Using alternates, in effect, creates one manufacturing order which will produce more than one parent.

Alternates are designated on the bill of material for the main parent, and MRP anticipates their receipt into inventory and plans accordingly. The standard cost of the alternates are deducted from the standard cost of the main parent, pro rata.

Use 3. Liability Items

We are in an age of sensitivity to toxic and otherwise undesirable by-products. These are called liability items, because the producer must pay for their disposal. Liability items can be included in the bill of material and act much like a by-product. However, liability items will usually not be used again in manufacturing, at least not without being processed first. The processing or disposal cost of a liability item should be assessed against the parent causing it.

Use 4. Tools

Many manufacturers have multipurpose tooling. When the tool is being used it is not available elsewhere. This often presents a scheduling problem. Tools can be handled by normal MRP logic by coding them twice on the bill of material, once as a normal component, and the second time as a by-product. There must be a time delay designated between these two happenings, representing manufacturing lead time. This is usually done by putting the tool's return on automatic issue, which takes place at the end of the manufacturing cycle. During the time delay, MRP will find the tool unavailable, and act accordingly. Tools, however unlike true by-products have a neutral effect on the standard cost of the parent.

Use 5. Starters

A starter is a component that is identical to its parent, but is required in making the parent. Starters are most common in biological processes. For example, to make yogurt, we need milk and some of yesterday's yogurt to start the process. Structuring a parent as a component of itself is universally prohibited in regular bills of material, so this requires some special logic in your MRP system. The standard cost of the starter is added to the standard cost of its parents just like any other component.

Your bills of material are pervasive and accurate. With imagination and care, they can be called on to serve many of your needs beyond just the traditional MRP explosions.

HOW TO MANAGE YOUR DESIGNS WITH ENGINEERING CHANGE CONTROL

Every manufacturing company experiences engineering changes. It's a fact of manufacturing life. This means that a well-designed business procedure must be put into place to manage them. A good engineering change management procedure can be turned into a competitive tool, because it allows rapid and skillful changes to product design, not only to correct deficiencies, but also to take advantage of new materials and processes, and to seize opportunities in the marketplace. This applies equally strongly to companies who make to order as well as to those who make to stock. A fast, efficient engineering change control procedure is necessary to support both MRP and Just-in-Time practices.

What follows is a general description of a sound Engineering Change Order (ECO) procedure. This procedure assumes the existence of some kind of computerized MRP II-style planning system, or at least some way to precisely manage the synchronization of components structured to parents, recognizing effectivity dates, stock on hand and on order, and lead times. This synchronization is necessary for parent-component relationships regardless of their level in the bill or whether they are purchased or manufactured.

How to Select the Right Control Point

After initial conversion to an MRP-style computerized bill of material processing system, you allow changes and additions only when vouchered by an approved engineering change order. As soon as a design is released for procurement and production, it comes under change control, and is no longer the private property of the designers.

The control point is the insertion of the new data into the computer system. The ECO procedure is focused on updating the computer system, so it can universally and accurately serve all users. Everyone must recognize that the version on the computer file is the only usable one. All other versions are derivative, preparatory, or pirated. The object of an ECO procedure is to manage the preparation of changes, which is the hard part. After approval, updating the computer files is more of a clerical job.

How to Select the Changes that Should Be Controlled

Considering how much data reside in modern MRP systems, it is important that you define exactly what should be subject to the ECO controls imposed. The basic data that always must be controlled are which components are structured into which parents, the quantity of each, and in and out effectivity. You may add company- or industry-specific requirements as needed. Defense contractors and pharmaceutical manufacturers are typical of such companies, and have a long list of requirements.

How to Establish the Right Organization

Since one important design criterion for a good ECO procedure is speed, you need a good organization. I suggest organizing an Engineering Change Control Board with an Engineering Change Coordinator.

The Engineering Change Control Board should have as members decision making representatives from the important functions of the company. This includes:

- Design Engineering
- Manufacturing Engineering
- Production and Inventory Control
- Manufacturing Operations
- Purchasing
- Quality Control
- Sales and Marketing

In some companies, or for unusual circumstances, other functions could be invited to participate. All aspects of the change have to be considered, such as design integrity, marketability, produceability, procurement, scheduling, and costs.

The Board should meet often, and their meetings should be short and decisive. Requested changes already should have been analyzed thoroughly in the various departments. The Board should meet at least weekly. In many companies, especially those with a large volume of ECO's, it meets daily. The Board approach calls for preparatory work to proceed simultaneously in all the departments involved. Then the change is discussed, and the decision made at a Board meeting, preferably the next one. The only other alternative is for the approval cycle to be serial, with the request passing from department to department, from in-basket to in-basket. If you have ever been on the distribution list for a magazine, you know what kind of a delay this process involves. The Board approach is decidedly better.

Defining the Role of the Engineering Change Coordinator

The Engineering Change Coordinator is an administrator and should have the education, aptitude, and leadership ability associated with that kind of activity.

The Coordinator has several functions. First the Coordinator receives raw requests for change, and edits and improves them as needed. In many companies requests come from unusual sources. When they do, they often are not complete or technically accurate.

The Coordinator gives each a control number and distributes copies to the various departments. They, in turn, evaluate each ECO as needed, and prepare for the Board meeting.

The second function of the Coordinator is to facilitate the periodic meetings of the Board. The Coordinator makes sure the arrangements are made and checks to see that the members have done their homework and will be attending or sending a decision-making representative. The Coordinator makes sure that every request is accounted for and processed speedily.

The third function of the Coordinator is to follow up on any unresolved issues from each Board meeting. Perhaps some more information is needed. Or, a supporting decision may be needed from a nonmember. Many details could be left pending after a Board meeting, and the Coordinator takes the initiative to resolve them by the next Board meeting if at all possible.

The fourth function of the Coordinator is to execute the decisions made by the Board regarding processed engineering changes. Some will be accepted, and others will be rejected, and one or the other should be chosen quickly. In all cases the decisions must be communicated promptly and accurately to the functions involved. Since each change is a little different, this promulgation function will need considerable judgement and flexibility on the part of the Coordinator.

After approval, the final function of the Coordinator is to see to it that the computer files are updated immediately and accurately This is the only way approved changes can take effect within the formal system.

How to Request an Engineering Change

Released bills of material for items at all levels, from components to assemblies, to finished products, are used widely. This includes vendors, company personnel, customers, and even regulatory authorities. This means that suggestions for design changes could come from many sources. And considering that we are dealing not just with deficiencies but also with product improvements, the ECO procedure should be receptive to suggestions from all sources.

To facilitate this there should be an established Engineering Change Request Form, easily available to anybody who would like to suggest a change. The form should be as simple as possible, even given the complexity of the task involved.

As a minimum, some fields on your form should be:

- Requestor
- Functional Approval
- Item Number(s)
- Item Description(s)
- Action Requested
- Reason
- Effectivity Requested
- Product Cost Change
- Inventory Obsolescence Cost
- Rework Cost
- Leadtime Impact

There could easily be some additional, company-specific fields that would be included in the request form.

How to Process a Change

The requestor sends the request form to the Coordinator, using the fastest way possible. The Coordinator first assigns a control number and date to the request, and reviews the request for completeness and technical accuracy.

Item Number

Designating the item numbers involved, both parents and components is crucially important. This must be analyzed thoroughly. The Coordinator could easily require assistance from others, notably an engineer. The problem here is to identify the specific parent or parents that will have to be changed to accommodate the request. This is more difficult than it seems because of the need to determine when the parent's item number should be changed versus when its revision level is raised. The phenomenon of upward cascading revisions is the other area where precise technical accuracy is an absolute requirement.

Interchangeability

The interchangeability rule is fairly easy. If the new version is fully interchangeable with the old version, it keeps the same item number, with its revision level advanced by one. If the new version is not fully interchangeable, then the old version is left alone, and the new version is given a whole new item number, with its revision level set at 1. The coordinator makes sure that the revision level is raised, or that a new number will be assigned, as demanded by the circumstance.

Be sure that your procedure follows this rule as corner cutting will lead to problems.

The upward cascading problem can occur if a change at a low level in the bill causes subsequent changes in higher-level parents.

Reason for Change

The Coordinator should categorize the request for later analysis. Some typical categories are:

- Product Improvement
- Customer Request
- New Product Release

- Engineering Standards
- Cost Reduction
- Design Correction
- Field Problems
- Product safety

In your company you will have your own, tailored version.

Effectivity

The coordinator evaluates the requestor's suggested effectivity. Here are the common ones, ranging from mildest to most severe:

- Record Change Only
- Use Up Current Inventory
- Next Order
- In Process
- On Hand
- Product Recall

The effectivity assigned by the coordinator calls for action, and is not just for information. At some severity levels a great deal of effort will be required after approval, while the implementation of the milder ones is usually easy.

Evaluation

The next step in the ECO process is for the coordinator to send a copy of the change request to every Board member and to other departments as needed. Each recipient in turn evaluates the request from the perspective of their department. Implications on product cost, obsolescence, rework cost, lead time, and so on, are considered during this activity. This evaluation must be done promptly, in order to be ready for the next board meeting. The intent should be to have each change request disposed of at the very next board meeting whenever possible.

Disposition

Each change request is considered at the next board meeting, starting with those held over from previous meetings, and continuing through the new ones. The coordinator keeps track of the progress of each request. The Board should strive for speedy consensus which should occur easily in most instances.

Implementation

After the Board has decided to approve or disapprove the request, the coordinator sees to it that the change is implemented correctly and speedily. In case the change has been turned down, the requestor is notified, together with the reasons from the Board.

Approved changes must now be entered into the system, usually a computerized one. The coordinator sees to it that the new data are inserted into the computer system immediately, completely, and accurately. In addition, the coordinator must see to all other details, computerized or not. In the case of some of the more severe effectivities, this could be a big job. The Coordinator invokes whichever company procedures are needed, depending on the details of the change.

JIT Implication

You should notice how JIT principles, particularly the goals of low inventories and fast throughput, drastically reduce some of the undesirable aspects of engineering changes. With low inventories, and fast factory throughput, a changed item will be ready to put into customers' hands quickly, instead of having to wait until present component, work-in-process, and finished goods inventories are worked off. This situation also reduces exposure to obsolescence, as well as the need to rework in-process and on-hand inventory.

HOW TO DEFINE YOUR WORK CENTERS

Defining your work centers is not difficult. The guiding principle is that you must accurately portray your factory within your MRP system. There are two methods.

The first method is the more traditional. If your factory is laid out according to machine similarities, you will use this method. The rule for this method is that each work center contains a machine or group of machines that are so similar in nature, that you could take any job coming into the work center and put it on any machine. I was in one factory where they had

24 automatic screw machines lined up like soldiers and they were all alike. That was one work center.

In another factory, they had three punch presses, small, medium, and large. Those were three work centers. I have seen work centers in many factories designated according to how cost accounting wants to view the scene. If you have this problem, you should use another designation, such as cost center, to group activities and machines to support accounting.

The second method accommodates group technology. Under this rule, a work center is a group of dissimilar machines grouped together especially to produce a family of similar products. Printed circuit lines, and many process-type factories are laid out this way. This definition also takes in your assembly lines.

Many companies have a mixed manufacturing floor, some areas are traditional, others laid out for group technology. Both can coexist in the same MRP system.

HOW TO MAKE IT THE SAME WAY EVERY TIME BY USING PROCESS AND ROUTING

The main purpose of the process and routing effort is to designate all the manufacturing steps for every one of your manufactured items. The details are usually housed in a process and routing file. Each item you manufacture will have entries in the file giving details about each operation needed.

The following are the common data elements you will need for each operation:

- Item Number refers to the item being manufactured. There is usually no provision for designating components. Components are provided by the pick list and are assumed to be accompanying the order as it progresses through the plant.

- Operation Description is a brief description of what to do. Most systems rely on separate drawings, specifications, and instruction documents to give the worker specific details.

- Work Center is the designation of the work center where the work is to be performed.

- Tool Required is used to show if a tool is needed at this point.

- Setup Hours is the number of hours it will take to set up the machine to do this operation. If there is no setup required, this can be a zero, and fractions of hours are allowed. Setup is always for the job, without regard to the quantity being produced.

- Standard Time is expressed in hours or minutes, and fractions are permitted. This is the allowed time to make one piece.

- Usual Lot Size is used for scheduling.

- Labor Grade is used if there is more than one in the work center. Many companies have one labor grade for setups and another for running. For ease of maintenance, the hourly pay rates for each labor grade are on a separate table.

- Operation Yield is used for scheduling, costing, and planning. Some processes, such as in the chemical industry, always have a yield loss.

Some more elaborate systems also allow for alternate routings, operation overlapping and splitting, and outside vendor operations.

The data on the routing file governs how the manufacturing order will progress through your factory, is used for scheduling and loading every work center with planned and released orders, and supplies the labor portion of standard cost calculations.

You need to have all of these seven basics are solidly in place to form a foundation for your MRP-based planning system. Of the ones mentioned, the ones that companies seem to have the most trouble with are Master Schedule integrity, Bill of Material accuracy, and a fast, clean Engineering Change Control Procedure.

6

HOW TO PREPARE
FOR IMPLEMENTATION
OF THE MRP II SYSTEM

Implementing an MRP II-based business system is a difficult
and arduous undertaking. MRP II-based systems affect almost
the entire company, and require substantially different practices,
procedures, and attitudes in many departments. This is often
described in terms of Culture Change. Properly implemented,
such a formal system will be your largest computer-assisted
business system, far larger than any of your traditional systems
such as accounts payable, payroll, general ledger, sales analysis,
and so on. Because of its sheer size plus the required changes
in habits, you must carefully plan and execute your implementation.

In this context, I make a strong distinction between the terms
installation and implementation. Installation refers to getting
the computer code to run on your computer, perhaps including
procuring hardware. Implementation is where you design a whole,
new business system, cutting across most departments, writing
procedures, performing education and training, and getting cut
over. Installation can usually be done in just a few weeks, while
implementation probably will take you from 9 to 18 months,
after you have selected your software.

In this chapter, we will emphasize preparing for implementation, covering the following five points:

171

1. Analyze your business needs.

2. Demonstrate management's dedication.

3. Assemble your project team.

4. Designate a steering committee.

5. Organize for success.

HOW TO ANALYZE YOUR BUSINESS NEEDS

If you are a manufacturer, avoid the "we're different" pitfall. All manufacturing companies have far more similarities than differences. This is what has made MRP II theory and practice possible. This is what has allowed numerous textbooks to be written on the subject. The materials management profession has codified a body of knowledge and certifies practitioners, based on the understanding that any manufacturer, no matter of what size or stripe, will exhibit the universal similarities.

However, since these theories and practices have been around for more than a decade, techniques for tailoring and tuning have been developed to focus the basic concepts for each company, emphasizing some techniques and ignoring others, depending on the individual needs of each company.

The maturing of the commercial software industry is promoting and supporting tailoring with a rich array of features and functions, all operating within the framework of the basic needs for planning, executing, and monitoring, common to all manufacturers.

In order to make best use of your ability to tailor your MRP II-based system, you should analyze just what kind of manufacturer you are. There are several main areas to consider:

- Manufacturing Environment
- Multiplant
- Lot Tracing
- Government Procurement Regulations
- Outlandish Circumstances

Evaluating Manufacturing Environment

Figure 6.1 depicts a three-dimensional manufacturing environment. This illustration asks you to evaluate your company from the market view and from the manufacturing view.

Figure 6.1   Manufacturing Environments

		Process View			
		Single Unit	Batch	High-Volume, Repetitive	Process
Market View	Make-to-Stock	X	X	X	X
	Assemble-to-Order	X	X	X	X
	Make-to-Order	X	X	X	X
	Engineer-to-Order	X	X	X	X

The Marketing View

Taking the marketing view, what kind of company are you? Most companies fall into one or more of the following categories:

- Make to stock
- Assemble to order
- Make to order
- Engineer to order

In a *make to stock* environment, you manufacture end items and put them in finished goods inventory waiting for your customers to order. Consumer products often fall into this category. Most make-to-stock companies promise their customers that they will ship within days or even hours of receipt of their orders. They place a high premium on a very high service level. Forecasting is very important here, and exposure to excessive inventories is a real problem.

In an *assemble to order* environment, you will stock major assemblies which represent building blocks. Your customer places an order by selecting the proper building blocks which you put through final assembly after order receipt. Assemble to order companies often need to route incoming orders through an engineering group to make sure that the order is complete, and that components are compatible. In this environment, you try to hold semi-finished inventory of the components, based on sales forecasts. The same forecasting helps the factory to plan for needed capacities, especially in the final assembly areas. Companies in this environment usually promise quite short lead times, usually days or a week or two.

The *make to order* environment calls for a firm customer order before manufacturing starts. Often the product being sold is according to the customer's specifications and design. Ideally, the manufacturer tries not to keep a supply of raw materials and components because of their uncertain use. Most often, the lead times promised are shorter than your grand total, resulting in the "Lead Time Inversion" common to many manufacturers.

In an *engineer to order* situation, you get a request for a product from your customer, and you design it for them. This environment can take on the characteristics of a project, with the manufacturing section imbedded within it.

The Manufacturing View

Looking at your company from the process or manufacturing view presents different factors:

- Single unit
- Batch
- High volume repetitive
- Process

In *single unit* production, the customer orders one or a very few, and you manufacture just what was ordered. Warships are made one at a time. Machine tools usually are made one at a time. Products in this group tend to be large, complex, and technological.

Batch processing is similar to single units, where the end items are discrete individuals, but usually not so big and complex. They easily could be high-tech however. The size and usage of end items in this category allows for lot sizing to apply. Many components ordered by one manufacturer from another fall into this category. This includes molded rubber and plastic parts, machined and fabricated metal parts, and sub-assemblies. Currently, we are witnessing a lot of emphasis on smaller batches, manufactured more frequently, and delivered quickly to the customer. In these "Just-in-Time" situations, a great deal of emphasis is placed on quality and due date adherence. Daily deliveries is becoming a procurement goal for many companies.

High volume repetitive is characterized by consumer products. Items such as irons or hair dryers are usually put through more or less automated lines in large volumes, with model changes at certain intervals. Fast change-overs and fast throughput are important.

In the *process environment* we usually picture liquids or powders flowing through pipes and valves. Or we can have a few raw materials being dumped into hoppers at the beginning of the cycle. The materials flow from machine to machine automatically. Often, chemical changes occur along the way. Pharmaceutical and personal care products usually are made in a process flow. As well as granola bars and frozen pizzas. One common and important characteristic of a process environment is that production is planned and controlled by rate per shift, not by distinct shop orders. Another important characteristic is that planning and controlling direct labor is minor, compared to the materials and capacities being used.

And finally, in process manufacturing, bills of material (or recipes) have the unfortunate characteristic of being imprecise. The amount of material used can vary by potency, moisture content, interaction with other materials, and even the weather.

When you evaluate your company according to the grid in Figure 6.1, you will be able to circle one or more Xs. Almost every company will circle more than one X. Some companies will circle quite a few of them. This exercise will then point out whether your need a narrow-minded system, or a broad, feature-rich one. This will guide you in developing your business system and in software selection and tailoring.

Establishing Your Multi-Plant Needs

Many corporations have more than one plant. Often, they want consistent business systems across all plants. The multi-plant situation should be evaluated from the aspects, system design, software selection, and implementation.

The implementation issue can be dealt with quickly and easily. The preferred method is to implement one plant at a time, with as much overlapping as possible. Only when there is very high integration between plants, is this typical rule altered.

System design considerations are far more complicated. The most important thing to evaluate is the degree of interdependency among plants. In many companies, each plant manufactures a distinct and different product line. Each plant has within it most of the usual business functions, notably engineering, master scheduling, production and inventory planning, and purchasing. Often, accounting and sales and marketing are at the plant.

A more complex multiplant environment occurs when plants feed one another in addition to having their own outside customers.

Another complicating factor occurs with centralized functions. I have had clients who have central purchasing, where material needs identified at the plant level are communicated to corporate purchasing for fulfillment. To make this environment even more complex, some companies have central purchasing for components and commodities common to several plants, allowing each plant to procure unique items.

Central engineering adds yet more complications, and central sales and marketing are quite common. The most complicated (worst) example I have ever seen, was a company with their factory in Pennsylvania, their marketing organization in Atlanta, and their design engineering function split between Atlanta and the home office in Brussels, Belgium. They had a very difficult time planning because of poor forecasts, and in manufacturing because of the uncertainties of the bill of material.

I have seen many mixtures in operation, and I suggest that you strive to create the simplest, most de-centralized environment possible, even to the extent of some duplication. I believe that support functions should be physically located as close to the manufacturing site as possible.

Establishing a Lot Tracing System

Lot tracing is the ability to trace each lot of incoming materials and components through every stage of production out to the end user.

For example, let's say you are manufacturing automobiles. The brakes fail on one of your cars and somebody is injured. On investigation, you find that a certain metal part in the wheel cylinder failed. Your investigators conclude that the whole manufacturing lot of 500 could be bad. They look up where the other 499 parts are and recall those cars.

Continuing their investigation, they now determine that the bar stock used to make the part was flawed. So now they trace to see where the rest of that lot of bar stock went. Some of it went into other batches of the same brake part, so you put more cars on recall. However, some of those bars were used to make other parts.

The next step in the investigation is to find out all other manufacturing lots that used that bar stock. Now your investigators analyze which of these other parts could possibly fail. Some could, so more cars are recalled.

Throughout this investigation, however, because you had a full lot-tracing system, you were able to isolate to a very small population those cars to be recalled.

Pharmaceutical manufacturers and defense contractors long have had lot tracing requirements. The increasing threat of product liability suits and their huge settlements have made lot tracing an attractive capability for consumer products manufacturers.

Complying with Government Procurement Regulations

Particularly in defense contracting, government procurement regulations impose a broad spectrum of requirements. These requirements have spawned a whole group of professional planners who can plan and manage factory operations with them. A few years ago, the Defense Audit Agency thought they discovered that MRP systems were helping contractors cheat the government, and just about prohibited their use. Soon, however, they came to realize that the MRP systems were only exposing malpractice that were there all along. This was a clear case of blaming the reporter. Then in 1987 the DCAA/DCAS (Defense Contractors Audit Agency/Defense Contractors Administrative Services) decided that MRP was useful after all. They developed 10 key principles that gradually will be required of the planning systems at all defense contractors. These criteria closely follow standard MRP II orthodoxy, and are having the effect of bringing across to the defense procurement arena the good practices that have been developed in the commercial sector.

If you have government business, you must be sure to differentiate which regulations are part of law and quasi-law, and which are merely contractual. The contractual ones can be negotiated. And the government seems to be moving strongly to embrace many of the advanced practices of inventory management and manufacturing planning that are now pretty well-known and practiced in private industry.

Handling Unusual Circumstances

An occasional manufacturer is confronted with one or two unusual circumstances.

I had a client in the spice business. In their raw materials warehouse I ran across a whole bay filled with large gunny sacks. My host explained that they were filled with one of their raw spices. It was an agricultural commodity, harvested once a year, in a politically unstable country. This item only somewhat fit the classic MRP mold, and needed individual attention.

If you have one or two unusual circumstances in your company, be sure to make them recognized. They almost never prevent you from using an MRP II-based system to advantage.

HOW TO DEMONSTRATE MANAGEMENT'S DEDICATION TO MRP

You can contribute to your success by making your dedication to your new system continuous and conspicuous. This isn't difficult, but it is important. You can show your dedication in several ways:

- Support change.
- Exercise leadership.
- Don't cut corners.
- Attend meetings.

Supporting Change

Implementing an MRP II-based system requires quite a few changes in the way you do business, and offers the opportunity and flexibility for making still other changes and improvements. You should adopt the attitude that all current orthodoxies can be challenged. You should imbue this attitude throughout your organization.

In this context I include both changes to current policies, systems, and procedures, as well as to the company's organization chart.

Many things you do now will be done much differently. Other things will be discontinued. Still others will be split up and given to different departments.

Exercising Leadership

Your subordinates look to you for supervision and to set the tone for your department. Everybody has choices to make every day, and by giving direction and setting a good example, people who work for you will "get the message" and govern themselves accordingly.

I held an executive seminar several years ago for an electronics manufacturer. They were just starting their implementation, after having chosen their software product. On the day of the seminar, the president didn't show up. He decided that it was more important to go downtown and meet with some securities analysts. He was wrong. This one action sent a signal to the rest of the company. Everybody perceived the implementation project as a second-class activity and acted accordingly. It took the project manager a full two years to recover from the damage.

Leadership also means promoting the project whenever the opportunity arises, in phone calls, personal discussions, even in conversations with outsiders. I always find that people want to please the boss and are very alert to clues, obvious and subtle, about what the boss wants.

Making Sure Not to Cut Corners

The difference between a sense of urgency and cutting corners is a fine one. During implementation, whenever you are tempted to say "we'll worry about that when the time comes," you may already have crossed the line.

MRP II systems tend to be quite robust, but every time you cut a corner, you will cause the resulting system to be somewhat degraded. And these small degradations stack up, and often result in a system that performs far below its promise. After cut-over, you lose the visibility of the cause and effect relationship of your corner cutting.

Some of the more common areas to watch out for are:

- Sales forecasting and order entry
- Master production scheduling, particularly time fences
- Engineering change control

- Cycle counting
- Time standards
- Material standardization

Attending Meetings

Meetings should be scheduled only when really necessary, and kept as short as possible, usually under an hour. Whoever calls the meeting must have a firm agenda. This makes it feasible to ask for good attendance. In this setting, you should be sure to attend all meetings where you belong. Don't let other distractions make you absent and make sure you send the right message.

HOW TO ASSEMBLE YOUR PROJECT TEAM

The project team is your most important implementation instrument. The goal is to have the team made up of solid, experienced people from most of the functional areas of the company, including:

- Manufacturing Operations
- Production and Inventory Control
- Master Scheduling
- Purchasing
- Design Engineering
- Manufacturing Engineering
- Quality
- Marketing and Sales
- Sales Forecasting
- Cost Accounting
- General Accounting
- Service Parts
- Information Services

The object is to assemble a group of experienced and knowledgeable people from every corner of the company. Their mission is to craft a new business system. The object is not to protect the status quo of the home department. The project manager should be a user. Project managers often come from the Production or Inventory Control Department. Manufacturing Engineering is another good source. I have seen work center supervisors selected. Avoid choosing the second-ranking systems analyst from the Information Services Department. You want to avoid the perception that this is a just a computer project.

HOW TO SELECT A STEERING COMMITTEE

You also need a Steering Committee. This group is made up of the top manager of the business unit, and all of his/her immediate subordinates. In a small company this could be the president and the vice-presidents. In a large company this could be a manufacturing executive and the associated directors. Whatever their titles, the Steering Committee should be made up of the executives who supervise all of the functional areas of the company, generally the same areas shown above for the project team.

Regarding both the Project Team and the Steering Committee, you may find that some of the functions that need to be represented do not report to the top manager at the site. Marketing and engineering often fall into this category, being organizationally tied elsewhere in the company. This factor just adds an additional barrier that needs to be broken. If you expect a high-quality, speedy implementation and subsequent success, you must get the right people involved. This may be untidy organizationally, but is no excuse for allowing functional gaps to exist during this crucial developmental period.

If you are involved in a multiplant implementation, you also should have a Steering Committee at the Corporate level. In this situation, you are sure to have corporate-wide policies and strategies to develop.

The Steering Committee has three main duties:

- It establishes company objectives.

- It sets priorities.

- It provides resources.

Establishing Company Objectives

You must establish the company's objectives in order to clearly and sharply guide the day-by-day activities of the many people, at many levels, involved in the implementation.

Setting Priorities

Almost all employees, especially white-collar ones, have discretionary time during each working day. After their obligatory work is done, they have more or less discretion regarding where to focus their energies. It is up to the Steering Committee to provide the administrative framework to guide everyone's discretion.

Each member of the Steering Committee contributes to promulgating the company's true priorities back at the home department. They manage and guide, assign work and make decisions regarding the implementation project, to keep their subordinates focused on the correct priorities.

I know of a company that hampered its implementation project by not being able to control its priorities. Near the end of one of the early phases, they changed managers in the engineering department. He decided the main priority of his department was to design a new computer monitor. In keeping with this he told everyone in his department to stop supporting the MRP II implementation. As a result, the bills of material started to go bad. They managed to keep the system going by having inventory control provide the computer inputs. This was not really adequate, and in effect took control of the design of the product away from design engineering. They could fume and fuss, but what was in the computerized bill of material was what got built, right or wrong, up to date or not!

Providing Resources

Every company has mutually exclusive contentions for resources. If you have creative, professional people working for you, they always have more ideas to advocate than the company has the ability to implement. The Steering Committee is the body to make sure that the implementation project is provided sufficient resources.

You can view the question of resources as twofold. The first concerns resources needed during project implementation. As mentioned above, the project team takes good people away from their usual jobs, some full time. The part-timers, however often are greatly overburdened. This is especially the case in smaller companies, which chronically have too few people to go around anyhow. The Steering Committee must be realistic in recognizing this rather large increase in the work load, even though it is not permanent. I often recommend to my clients that they go outside and hire temporary, perhaps part-time assistance. Local vocational schools, colleges and universities offer good potential, as do recent retirees. However accommodated, you must provide enough people.

Other resources include equipment such as computer terminals and work stations, and often computer software. These nonpersonnel expenditures usually are fairly minor when compared with the total project, even if you have to buy a new computer.

Then, anticipating the operational phase, the Steering Committee must make whatever arrangements are required for ongoing management of the new system. This will certainly include the correct staffing levels in many departments. Don't succumb to the temptation to cut staff during an austerity drive. I have heard of companies in this situation who lay off such as master schedulers or time study engineers. The result is not immediate nor dramatic. What this kind of false economy causes, however, is a wide, gradual degradation in performance, which could eventually cause the system's failure.

The Steering Committee has a number of other tasks, also important. These tasks include:

- Organizing the Project Team

- Approving Goals and Objectives
  - Project Goals
  - Company Goals

- Approving the Project Plan

- Approving the Education Plan

- Providing a Budget

- Implementing Organization Changes

- Implementing the New Business System

- Demonstrating Support Throughout

- Providing for Continuous Progress

HOW TO ORGANIZE FOR SUCCESS

There are many books on this subject alone. But for our context, there are some organizational and responsibility issues that need to be accommodated. These issues are:

- Develop a good functional organization
- Position the Master Scheduler correctly
- Solve the planner-buyer dilemma

Developing a Good Functional Organization

Group functions in a way that encourages excellence and optimization and minimize conflicts of interest.

For example, I have one client with several medium-sized factories. They happen to be located in geographically the same way that sales territories are drawn. They have each factory report to the regional sales manager. This doesn't work very well because the factory always takes a back seat to the current whim of the sales force. As a result, their factory schedules are chaos, and they are perpetually in a high-intensity expedite state. They should have all the factory managers report to a central manufacturing executive.

Another client broke their export department down into two, just because they had a personnel problem with the manager. This precipitated many problems, and the situation wasn't corrected until that person retired.

How to Position the Master Scheduler Correctly

The master production scheduling function provides the driving input into the operation of a formal manufacturing system. Its importance dictates that this cannot be part of the inventory planning department in the bowels of the basement. The manager of this function should be organizationally and professionally a peer of the data processing manager, the materials manager, quality control manager, and so on.

This is the only way to provide the stature and power to develop and maintain a master schedule with integrity. The master scheduler must be able to say no and make it stick.

Within the organization, the master scheduler is best reporting to the top manufacturing executive as the materials manager, or to the System Proprietor. It never works to have this function reporting to someone in marketing or to information services.

Solving the Planner-Buyer Dilemma

It began with the advent of Material Requirements Planning (MRP I), which automatically develops sound plans for purchasing. MRP plans all purchase orders, time slots them as to due and start date, and computes lot sizes, all at computer speed. This is making the inventory planner obsolete, and eliminates the need for having inventory planning and purchasing as two separate groups. Many companies have merged the inventory planners into the purchasing department to take charge of scheduling shipments from vendors. Others have purchasing concentrate on prospecting, contracts, blanket orders, and general vendor relations, and make the inventory control department responsible for scheduling releases directly with the vendor. The second technique is especially attractive for companies who are moving to single-sourcing.

Every company that plans to have a good MRP system running should get rid of this traditional duplication and overlap.

7

HOW TO EXECUTE A SOUND IMPLEMENTATION OF THE MRP II SYSTEM

"If you can't plan it, you can't do it."

One of the main jobs of the implementation project team is to develop a time-phased implementation plan. Consultants and some software vendors, having helped many clients plan an implementation, have slowly developed a fairly standard approach.

HOW TO MAKE AND USE A TIME-PHASED IMPLEMENTATION PLAN

Every implementation plan starts first by designating major phases. Figure 7.1 shows a typical breakdown into five phases:

- Project Definition
- Implementation Preparation
- Development and Confirmation
- Cutover
- New System Operation

Figure 7.1   Implementation Fast Track to Success

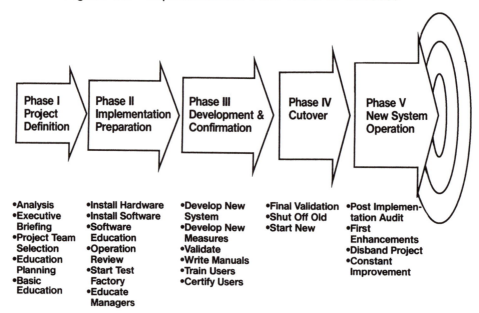

Phase I Project Definition	Phase II Implementation Preparation	Phase III Development & Confirmation	Phase IV Cutover	Phase V New System Operation
•Analysis •Executive Briefing •Project Team Selection •Education Planning •Basic Education	•Install Hardware •Install Software •Software Education •Operation Review •Start Test Factory •Educate Managers	•Develop New System •Develop New Measures •Validate •Write Manuals •Train Users •Certify Users	•Final Validation •Shut Off Old •Start New	•Post Implementation Audit •First Enhancements •Disband Project •Constant Improvement

How to Define Your Project

During the Project Definition Phase, your skeleton project team will perform some basic tasks which could include software selection, a general analysis of your business needs, and begin some basic education. They also finish selecting the rest of the project team and start the Steering Committee. They will also complete the development of the other phases, particularly their due dates.

How to Get Ready for Implementation

During this phase everyone will begin to see some movement. You will install your new software, and whatever extra computer hardware is required. Soon after they are running in the computer room, the project team takes over a special version of the software and begin a Test Factory. The Test Factory is used at first to give the project team members an opportunity to get their hands on the system. At this time your software vendor may provide some technical training on the how to use the software. Soon the project begins to review your current operation to gain a structured idea of how your company now works.

Education continues during this phase, as it will throughout. In this phase they put on education programs for supervisors and managers, not just to inform them, but also to get from them their ideas for inclusion in the new system. This is one of the many ways the project team reduces the inevitable resistance to change. People who contribute to developing the new system naturally take a proprietary interest in it when the time comes to make it work.

How to Develop Your New System

This phase is the most arduous and time-consuming. Your project team will develop your new business system during this phase and this takes time and energy. This is the phase where the project team is working at its highest tempo, with the most participants, direct and indirect. As part of the new system, your project team will also develop new performance measures, supplanting many of the traditional ones you probably inherited from the past. We will cover this theme later in this chapter.

As the project unfolds, and your new system develops, the project team will develop your new business system in all of its details. This will include specifying which pieces of your present system are useable and will be retained, and which pieces are not useable and will be jettisoned. The most important part is to develop the new policies and procedures you will need to complete the definition of your total system.

When the policies and procedures are established and approved by the Steering Committee, the project team also gets the user manuals written, tested and distributed. User manuals tell each person with update authority how to get their piece of the job done. Matthies has written the best book on the subject of manual writing, *The New Playscript Procedure.*[1] Following this procedure makes the job much easier and lends good consistency throughout.

Since your system must be a dynamic one, these policies, procedures, and their supporting manuals must be maintained to reflect the current situation. With the widespread availability of computerized word processing and desktop publishing, this has become a much more manageable job than before.

Validation is an extremely important last step in this phase.

---

[1] Leslie H. Matthies, *The New Playscript Procedure* (Stamford, CT: Office Publications, Inc., © 1977.

How to Validate (Confirm) Your New System

Considering the importance of your new system, and how profoundly it will affect almost every department, you just cannot take any risks that the system won't work as advertised.

Validation falls into these categories:

- Computer System Validation

- Business System Validation

- Data Validation

Computer System Validation

Computer system validation has become much easier with the widespread use of commercial software. You shouldn't have to check for bugs in the programs. What remains is to make sure that the programs work correctly on your computer in your computer room. There are many steps involved.

The first step is to test the various modules. All but the most modest software products come in modules, and they need to be tested to see that they work.

The second step is to test the whole system. You must make sure that the various modules work together. An MRP-based system has lots of data, and it is important so see that the modules pass data back and forth correctly.

Next you will need to test your conversion programs. In this day and age, many companies converting to an MRP-based system already have some computerized data. After cleaning up, they often are converted from the old format to the new, often with home-written code.

Data security must also be assured. This means frequent backups, off site storage, and a whole wealth of procedures. I almost always find that the data processing operations professionals know how to manage data security, and do so without any outside coaching. More important is to make sure that departmental files on personal computers are taken. I rarely find adequate measures here. If you have any important data on these machines, I strongly suggest that you confer with your EDP department and take their advice on data security.

Business System Validation

Here is a checklist for business system validation. Most of these are self-explanatory, but I will elaborate on some:

- Did you get the new organization chart approved?

- Were the policies approved?

- Are procedures written and understood?

- Are audit trails and controls in place?

- Are backups provided?

- Was the test computer system tested for failure?

- Was the business system tested for failure?

Regarding testing the computer system for failure, your project team should develop a comprehensive plan and schedule to test each important field in the system for failure. To do this, they systematically input every conceivable version of bad data: alphabetical characters in numeric fields, very long strings, very short strings, interspersing punctuation, and any other form of "garbage" they can think of. Then, in an equally systematic way, they check to see if the computer programs handle this garbage as intended, sometimes with rejections, sometimes with error messages, and sometimes even with acceptance.

Now your project team must test your business system for failure. They should create a broad range of data inputs that are knowingly erroneous, but that will pass the computer system's input edits. These errors then will flow through to reports for users. Now the project team takes these error-laden reports to the people who will eventually be responsible. The targeted people are then asked to respond correctly, without coaching. If they are able to demonstrate that they able to handle these problems without undue difficulty, the business system passes. If not, there is more work to do, either in training or in fine tuning the system. Moreover, there may be some errors that are created with this testing procedure that have not clearly been assigned to anyone specific. This also requires correction.

Data Validation

You must validate your data before cutting over. You have two types of data, masterfile data and operating data.

Among the masterfiles you have are the Item Masterfile, Bill of Material, and Routing. Your particular software may have some additional ones. How to develop these files is found in Chapter 5.

Your Information Services Department will do its best to write conversion programs to take your present data and transform it into the new format required by any new software you have acquired. In conjunction with this, you should validate the accuracy and completeness of your data as it will appear in the new format.

In order to keep the conversion work load manageable, first you should identify those fields on the new masterfile that are important to your application. For example, if you have only one planner in your inventory control department, you needn't worry about the planner code on the item master. However, if you have several planners then you must put this field on your list of important ones.

Once you have identified the fields your new system needs to operate properly, you should check to see that the entries in each are correct and that these important fields are fully populated. Blanks are not satisfactory. If you are using good software, blank fields will be filled with a default. But that is just to keep your computer programs from failing during processing (usually at 2:00 a.m.). Checking all important masterfile fields for accuracy and completeness is a big job. Your project team probably will distribute this job among several people to get the job done.

The conversion problem is aggravated by the fact that your new software almost certainly will have important fields that your current system lacks. Moreover, you likely will find that one field in your current system will need to be split into two or more fields in your new one. This kind of disaggregation sometimes can be done with logic in your conversion program, sometimes partially so, and sometimes not at all. This means that you could have a number of important fields in your new system that will have to be populated by direct, individual entry.

Your project team also will need to validate the accuracy of your operating data before conversion. The most notable of these is stock status. It is widely recognized that your stock status records must be at least 95 percent accurate for your system to run properly. This means that you shouldn't cut over before you have achieved this level of accuracy. Cycle counting is the conventional way to assure stock status accuracy. Chapter 8 has an extensive section how to develop and use cycle counting.

Other important operating data include open purchase orders, open manufacturing orders (work-in-process), and pending engineering changes. Your software probably will have some additional operating data files that will need validation. Like stock status, these files also must be very accurate at cutover in order for your system to give reliable results.

How to Get Cut Over

Only after the project team has done everything they can think of to make the prospective new business system malfunction can they proceed to the last steps in cutting over. In this setting, cutting over has two important aspects: shut off the old and turn on the new—after adequate validation.

There are a number of strategies available for cutting over. Here are seven of the most important:

- Cold Turkey
- Parallel
- Phased
- Migration
- Test Pilot
- Simulation
- Shake-Down Cruise

1. The Cold Turkey Cutover

In a cold-turkey cutover, you shut off the old and turn on the new without adequate validation. You sometimes see this take place because some executive somewhere has edicted it, no matter what.

I once had a call from the project manager for a client's implementation project. He was distressed because he had been ordered to convert to the new system over the coming weekend. He knew they weren't ready, but was not able to prevail on the boss. After he explained his reasons, I readily agreed that the company would suffer a painful failure of the new system if they cut over that soon.

I managed to find one of our vice presidents who knew the executive at the client site, and he called to warn him about the dangers. The project manager, meantime got an executive from the computer vendor to call too.

Between the two of them, they convinced the client's executive to back off, thus averting what could have been a disaster. That was a cold turkey situation.

In another situation, I was project manager of the implementation. We were going from one computer to a bigger one, and were implementing altogether new software. The data processing manager announced at a project team meeting that in six weeks the old computer would run out of disk space, and we wouldn't be able to process any new purchase orders.

That gave us a deadline that we couldn't meet, but we converted cold turkey anyhow. Luckily, we had done most of our work fairly well up to that point, and we didn't have a catastrophe. We got by with lots of problems and reactive corrections.

2. The Parallel Cutover

In a parallel cutover you run both your old system and your new one, and reconcile the differences. This is a popular cutover strategy among managers and executives who are not involved.

When cutting over to an MRP II-based system, parallel cutover is impossible. The reason for this is that the two systems are always so dissimilar, that it is not possible to reconcile them. The old system could be monthly-oriented, where the new one probably has daily time increments. The new system will have an entirely different bill of material, item master, routings, and several other basic files. Moreover, the new system always has many more features and tools than the old one. And trying to supply inputs to both systems would overwhelm the staff, without even trying to reconcile them.

Even if you could reconcile the old system to the new one, the only conclusion would be that the new system is a lot better than the old one.

The parallel cutover is not recommended.

3. The Phased Cutover

Phased is a very good cutover method if it is available to you. The most likely situation is where you are converting from a mainly manual to a modern, MRPII-based system. In this environment, there are no computerized bills of material, nor an item master. Routings may be lacking or on bits of paper filed in various places. Recipe card and Kardex™ files are used.

In this environment, the new system is used to aid in developing the files needed for the new system. For example, if you have no good computerized bill of material, then your engineers can use the new bill processor to help them get their bills in order. When they are done, they find that they are cut over to the new bill processor. At the same time, the project team is organizing the other files similarly, and the new system gradually takes over. In a phased cutover, there is very little attempt to maintain the old files and interfacing to related systems proceeds along the manual lines already in existence.

No company can use the phased cutover strategy exclusively, but many can use this technique for part of it. It is a very safe and painless strategy, when possible.

4. The Migration Cutover

Migration sometimes can be used in a setting where there already is computer assistance to some extent. Using the bill of material analogy, the users would transfer their old bill to the new format, and complete the transfer by cleaning up bad data, adding missing data, and supplying new data to new fields. After the initial transfer, the old system is discontinued. This migration continues for the several sub-systems, until the whole cutover is complete.

The main disadvantage in this strategy is that during the interim period, the new portions being invoked must somehow be interfaced to the old ones not yet converted. This means that a fair number of computer programs must be written and tested, but which will be used only for a short period of time.

This is often not cost-effective, but when it is the migration strategy is also reasonably painless and safe.

5. The Test Pilot Cutover

In a test pilot cutover you actually start using your new system for an isolated part of the first factory. This technique works best if you have a small department or work center that is fairly independent of the others, and where the components used here are not in much demand in other zones of the factory. This situation is not very common, but if you have a good candidate, you start using the new system in just the pilot department. This limits your startup problems, and gives you a good chance to bring any latent problems into view.

You shouldn't run the test pilot for more than a few weeks because the overlap with the rest of the factory, even if small, is too difficult to work around for a long term.

6. The Simulation Cutover

Your conference room pilot can now be used to do a simulation. For this, you will load complete files—notably bills of material and stock status—for one or two end items, and run the system as if you had cut over. Then you take the results and see if any latent flaws now appear.

A simulation can be repeated as often as needed, and can be expanded to cover a representative collection of end items.

7. The Shake Down Cruise Cutover

A shake down cruise is much like a simulation, except it encompasses the whole business unit. A shake down cruise is executed as if it were a real cutover, except that the old system is not turned off. The results of the shake down cruise are carefully examined to see if any flaws appear. Because this technique requires that all of the files be converted, usually over a weekend, it is onerous to repeat it over and over.

Notice that there is no effort to reconcile the results of the shake down cruise with your current system, which would be a parallel. As discussed earlier, a parallel run is futile.

When a shake down cruise looks right, you can call it the cutover, and shut off the old system. This makes the shake down cruise very risk-free, but costly in the computer room, because they have to go through the whole conversion process more than once.

HOW TO START OPERATING YOUR NEW SYSTEM

Now that you are cut over to your new business system, it is time to use it and make it pay off. It is an upper management function to see to it that the new system is used and respected, and that the old systems and habits be rigorously eliminated. Be sure to guard against backsliding into your old bad habits.

There are six last steps to complete your conversion:

- Make sure the cut over is complete
- Provide first enhancements
- Do a Post-Implementation Audit
- Provide for steady-state functions
- Designate a system proprietor

How to Make Sure the Cutover Is Complete

Here is a list of questions to consider to make sure the cutover is complete.

- Are your data flowing correctly? You have two classes of data—masterfile data and operational. Both have to be flowing smoothly into place as a daily routine.

- Are you all cut over; have the old systems been discontinued? Shutting off the old computer systems is fairly easy, but the old informal techniques and procedures are not.

- Have the shop supervisors stopped holding morning meetings?

- Do the production planners work against their computerized schedules and dispatch lists; no more hot lists?

- Is purchasing working against system-generated quantities and due dates, not from shortage reports?

- Is the receiving dock running incoming shipments quickly into inspection or stock with no pileup and expediting?

- Is your new system really being used?

- Are you respecting your Master Schedule?

- If an emergency order comes in from a favored customer, do you accommodate it on the Master Schedule by delaying an equivalent order or do you just pile in the hot ones and hope that you can somehow muddle through?

- Are your planners and buyers using the action and exception reports to manage their responsibilities?

- Do your shop supervisors choose the next job from the dispatch list, not by cherry-picking the queue?

- Is someone checking the Master Schedule for capacity constraints?

- Are your manuals up to date? The object of having a manual is to be able to have the trained substitute person perform adequately when the primary person is absent, by referring to the manual. You can't allow your manuals to become out-of-date.

- Have you corrected any initial problems that may have escaped the validation process?

After a week or two, someone from the project should audit to see that errors that the system has identified are being handled properly. Sometimes the quantity of error messages is monumental just after cutover, and often is the main cause for not cutting over after a simulation. But cutover is not complete until the users can manage their errors.

The last step in conversion is to see that your system is on cruise control. This means that the system is pretty much running itself, with practically no care and attention from the project team or project manager. Now you can consider your cutover to be complete.

Providing First Enhancements

During your implementation, many good ideas were developed that couldn't be taken care of. You weren't able to stop and start over every time somebody had a good idea. Your project team kept a file of these good ideas, and now is the time to evaluate them. Chances are that the great bulk of them have been taken care of by regular features of your new system, and no longer seem needed. But a few will still be appealing, and they should be evaluated and implemented if appropriate.

You should be very cautious and wary of any desire to change the code in any of your commercial software products. This plain vanilla rule is very beneficial. If you start fooling around with the commercial code, you sink into a never-ending quagmire of changes and de-bugging. You also invalidate any warranty your vendor attaches to their code. And worst of all, you would tend not to take new releases from the vendor, wanting to avoid re-applying all your unauthorized changes.

Extra programs, notably reports, are acceptable as long as they don't violate the basic logic of your system. Don't let yourself slide back to your bad old systems with a report writer attached to your new data.

Doing a Post-Implementation Audit

Your project manager or outside consultant should now make a comprehensive tour through the using departments, to see that the system is working according to plan. Do the department supervisors have any questions, problems, or additional training needs?

Providing for Steady-State Functions

Once cut over, your formal manufacturing system probably is the biggest one in your company and the biggest on your computer. It pervades the whole company more or less intensely. Your company would have a difficult time surviving without it.

Your new system has eight functions that must be performed regularly.

- The first is to have a routine production plan, with its derived resource requirements plan. This is needed to keep your capacities in balance.

- The second regular function that must be made into a regular routine is Master Production Scheduling, with its derived rough-cut capacity plan. This subject is covered in Chapter 3.

- The third steady-state function that must be routine is to monitor data accuracy. Cycle counting stock locations is typical. But all other sources of error should be monitored with a view toward eliminating the causes. Consider the following:

    - Are counts at the receiving dock inaccurate?
    - Are production counts on the floor giving trouble?
    - Do supervisors log completions against the wrong shop order?
    - Do engineers make errors on the bills?
    - Is the stock room issuing wrong parts?

Errors of this kind don't usually destroy a system, but each one is a degradation. Eliminating the causes of errors will help you with your trek toward world-class excellence.

- The fourth regular function is to monitor interfaces between systems. Accounts payable, distribution, traffic, payroll, sales forecasting, are just a few tributary systems that must support, and be supported by your new manufacturing planning and control system.

- The fifth important permanent function is to constantly evaluate how your business system is performing. This routine will help you determine what and when improvements and enhancements are needed.

Manufacturing, especially world-scope manufacturing, is a

dynamic, fast-paced, and very complex environment. Your business system should be able to be changed to support new needs. And it must be able to do this fast, helping you take advantage of new opportunities. Don't ever tolerate turning down a good idea because your system won't allow it!

To keep your business system up to date, you also must keep improving your software and hardware. Commercial software vendors are steadily improving their products and offering new releases. If you are using commercial MRP-based software, you will want to keep your version up to date, even if you can get along without an occasional release. Such releases are usually cumulative, and you will eventually need to implement them all anyhow. Hardware improvements are steadily available, and you should stay up to date with them as well.

Your software vendors often have user groups that meet regularly. You should designate a user to be a member, who should attend meetings regularly. This is an ideal place to network, and is where the vendor gets most of the ideas for enhancements.

• Sixth, you must maintain your manuals up to date. This includes policy manuals that will keep everyone steering themselves in the right direction. This also includes operator manuals to make sure that everyone uses the system consistently, and can support job rotation and personnel backups to take care of vacations, promotions, resignations, and expansion.

• The seventh steady-state function is to provide continuing education and training. The state of the art in manufacturing planning and control systems is moving swiftly, and your company is constantly changing. People come and go and it is necessary to maintain a permanent program in order for your personnel to train for new jobs and get better at the ones they have. You also should encourage participation in professional societies, especially those dedicated to education and professionalism. You should encourage professional certification. Some companies make certification a requirement for certain jobs. In the area of formal manufacturing systems, the most active professional society is the American Production and Inventory Control Society, headquartered in Falls Church, VA. They actively promote professionalism, education, and an extensive certification program. They have a dense network of local chapters, even in smaller towns.

• And eighth, someone must keep your formal manufacturing system coordinated with other technologies such as CAD, CAD and CIM.

How to Designate a System Proprietor

When you consider all that needs to be done to maintain and improve your new formal manufacturing system, it becomes apparent that you need some permanent organizational arrangement to get this important job done. There are two main ways.

One way is to make a new box on the organization chart, of managerial rank, reporting to the most neutral vice president you have, or to the CEO. With a small staff this person then takes charge of the system, and sees to it that it performs. The project manager is the obvious candidate.

The other way is to slim down the implementation project team, and make them a standing committee, headed by the project manager. They meet at regular intervals and are empowered to take action to maintain the system as needed. Now you are fully cut over and can disband the project team.

HOW TO SELECT SOFTWARE THAT SUITS YOUR SYSTEM

We are in the age of commercial software. For all of the common functions of the business, accounts payable, accounts receivable, general ledger, payroll, sales forecasting, and MRP II, there is plenty of good software available in the marketplace.

Abundance of software depends to a large extent on the popularity of the mainframe you want to use. But newer operating systems, database managers, and fourth generation languages are making software more portable.

Remember, you are not different. There is a manufacturing equation. The American Production and Inventory Control Society has done an outstanding job of codifying the basic principles of MRP II/JIT. Software vendors have developed their systems to suit these principles.

To illustrate the point that there is a manufacturing equation, I had a client who makes warships. One ship every two years was fast. At the same time, I had a client making small electro-mechanical parts. They could put 500,000 in one dishpan, and could make that many in an hour. They both were using the same software product.

Every company is a little different, but the basics remain. Software vendors all have built tailorability into their products to achieve wide market potential.

There was a time when MRP II software required a large mainframe or at least what used to be called a minicomputer. But in recent years, systems have emerged that run on desktop computers, especially with networking. There is a commercial software product suitable for you. Don't try to write your own code.

There is conflicting opinion regarding tailoring. My bias is to avoid altering vendor code at all costs. If you want to do something differently, ask why. Don't fall into the trap of writing new code around your current bad habits. After you are firmly implemented, and using your system in the plain vanilla mode, you could consider stand-alone enhancements.

ELEVEN STEPS TO SELECTING GOOD SOFTWARE

You must have a modern data base management software product in operation to support any of the modern MRP II software products. Some work only with one database manager, others work with several. This could be a selection criterion.

Here is an eleven-step software selection process:

- Get good leadership

- Designate a selection team

- Review the basics

- Develop your selection criteria

- Find all the vendors

- Develop a short list

- Validate the vendors

- Have presentations

- Validate the software

- Summarize results and decide

- Get full management agreement

1. Get Good Leadership

You must select someone to be the manager of the selection

effort. This must be someone from the user community, not from data processing. This person often continues as implementation project manager. In addition, you should find a competent consultant to help bring stability and outside knowledge and wisdom. If possible, your selection manager should be APICS certified. But your outside consultant must be certified, preferably at the Fellow level (CFPIM). Your outside consultant should be fully knowledgeable on commercial software and have already done several MRP II-based implementations. If you use a large consulting or accounting firm, be sure that the individual consultant to be assigned is a CFPIM, and you only need one.

2. Designate a Selection Team

Your selection team should be user-oriented. You should have a few seasoned veterans from the most important departments. These include at least:

- Manufacturing Operations
- Materials Management
- Finance
- Engineering
- Marketing
- Information Services

The selection team will develop a realistic set of requirements to support the company after it is fully converted to an MRP II-based system. This is very different from developing a list of requirements to wrap new code around current bad habits.

The selection team will follow through with the selection process ending with a firm recommendation of a specific product or products for management approval.

3. Review the Basics

The members of the selection team must know the basic theories and practices of a computerized MRP II-based system. They must learn how these practices will apply in your company. They must also come to understand where substantial changes will be coming. They also must learn the terminology involved in order to be able to communicate precisely among themselves, with consultants, vendors, and other outside resources including books and trade magazines.

4. Develop Your Selection Criteria

To begin, the team must interview one or two knowledgeable people from each functional area, to get their needs and desires. After this is done, the selection team will collate and analyze them. Some desires are out of keeping with modern systems and must be discarded.

Of the keepers, some are required, others optional, and others cosmetic. The selection team must be very careful to keep the required "knock out" requirements to a minimum.

Outside consultants often have several lists from other clients that can be used as a guide.

5. Find All the Vendors

If you already are committed to a specific mainframe, and/or data base manager, your local salespersons can give you a list. Depending on the combination of computer/data base, this list could be long or short. Also, there are reference publications available. Your information services team member probably as access to these publications.

6. Develop a Short List

Many of the possible commercial software products will obviously not be applicable. One product I know of is designed entirely for process manufacturers, and doesn't work in a job shop. Others may be designed exclusively for military applications and the like. The selection team should quickly be able to prune the list down to less than six prospects.

7. Validate the Vendors

This is very important. Your upcoming MRP II-based system will be too important to take risks with. Here are some points to consider:

● Customer base. The more customers the vendor has the better. Beware of a vendor with just a handful.

● User organization. The better vendors have a organization of users. Some of them have annual national conventions, even augmented by regional sessions and special interest groups. The better user organizations are independent of the vendor. Current users are a very good source of reference and free help during and after implementation.

• Customer service. Find out if the vendor has a hot line, when it is attended, and how effective and knowledgeable they are. An answering machine is not enough.

• Stability. Has the vendor been around a while? Has the vendor survived a recession or two? Find out if the vendor is in good financial condition. One detail to look for is whether the vendor charges current development costs to current expenses, or if they are capitalized. There is dispute in the accounting profession as to which is preferred, but expensing developments certainly is the more conservative.

• Personnel. A commercial software vendor has no assets of consequence except for its personnel. You can check on how many are deployed on the software product you are interested in. You can check on how many of them have professional certification, and how many are active in their professional societies. How many of them teach at local vocational schools, colleges and universities?

• Enhancement. It is very important that the vendor is steadily enhancing the product you are interested in. They should have a history of coming out with new releases at least once a year, and some of them should have been major ones.

Also find out if the enhancements have been incremental to the current product. Some vendors frequently abandon their products at maturity, and bring out a whole new substitute. This is not so bad if you get the new version for free or at a drastically reduced cost. This is not acceptable if you are forced to rebuy your software every few years. I suggest that your upgrade privileges be made part of your eventual contract, and be phrased very much in your favor.

• Local presence. Your success will depend to some extent on the service you get from the vendor's people you will be working with, and their personalities and professional characteristics.

8. Have Demonstrations

Some vendors will ask you to come to their offices for demonstrations. This is marginal, because you can count on them to manage the demonstration to their advantage. A better way is to arrange for a demonstration at the site of a current user. Sometimes the vendor can put some of your data on their demonstration system, for you to try out via remote job entry (RJE) from your office. The term "user friendly" is often used in demonstrations, and is an important idea. During demonstrating, have your own items, bills of material, and volumes in mind. What may look easy for one short item number, becomes onerous if you are confronted have long item numbers and a high volume of transactions per day. Watch out for individual transactions that require you to jump to several screens, especially for high-volume transactions.

9. Validate the Software

Be sure you are considering real software, not vaporware. Vaporware is promised software that is not commercially available. Vaporware also refers to features. Don't believe any statements about modules or features that are scheduled for release next quarter because next quarter may never come.

Only consider software, modules, and features that currently are being used successfully by at least five other companies for important features. For features that are not crucial, you could consider vaporware, particularly if the vendor has a solid history of steady enhancement.

Get a list of other users and call them or visit them. Be sure to differentiate between software working on the computer vs taking good advantage of its tools. You could find companies where the software works just fine, but the company has failed to take advantage of it. Your interest at this point is if the software works.

Another aspect of the validation is bugs. Try to find out from current users if the code is relatively bug free. Beware of buggy software.

Documentation also is very important. Documentation runs from splendid to poor. You should be biased toward well-documented products.

Ask about support services. The better vendors offer consulting support during and after implementation. Some offer training programs in their own classrooms and/or at yours. Since training is a key ingredient to success, this is an important criterion. Good vendors also have a hot line for solving problems.

10. Summarize Results and Decide

The traditional, simplistic approach is to give each criterion a weight, and to score each vendor on how well they meet each criterion. Then simple arithmetic makes your decision. This method is just a crutch to avoid judgment. Doing the arithmetic is useful, but when you get down to three or four candidates, human judgment should take over. The selection team should discuss and argue about the pros and cons. The outside consultant will give broader perspective. After applying judgment from the whole team, they make their choice for presentation to upper management.

11. Get Full Management Agreement

The selection team now makes a presentation to management and reviews the selection process with them. They suggest the one product they have decided on, not a range of three. This is a ratification, not a last step in selection.

It is of utmost importance that all the executives agree, enthusiastically if possible. You cannot tolerate dissention. Some executives may start out with low enthusiasm. But after the decision has been made, it is mandatory that they all support the new strategy. This support must carry forward through implementation.

HOW TO PLAN YOUR EDUCATION AND TRAINING

Before you can cut over to your new system, you must have educated and trained at least 40 percent of the company. And to be truly effective, you will need to cover 80 percent. To manage this you should appoint an education coordinator separate from your project manager. This person could be in your training department, or a person with good administrative and presentation skills. The coordinator's main job is to administer the education plan, but could also do some of the training.

A Seven-Step Program for Effective Training

You can accomplish this ambitious task with a seven-step program:

- Identify your trainees into groups
- Designate the correct level for each group

- Analyze the needs of each group
- Select and develop the right tools
- Schedule and present
- Evaluate
- Repeat

1. Identify Your Trainees into Groups

Your first step is to identify the cadre of users who will lead in the implementation and use of your new system. This group should aggregate to 40 percent of the company. The next step is to put these key users into groups according to how they will be using the new system, and as to how much knowledge and experience they have already.

2. Designate the Correct Level for Each Group

Each group should have similar needs, and this step analyzes how much detail and how broadly they need to be educated and trained.

3. Analyze the Needs of Each Group

Determine the general level of skill and knowledge this group has, and compare this to what they will need to know in the new environment. The difference gives you the needs of the group.

4. Select and Develop the Right Tools

There are two aspects to this topic, namely delivery modes and sources.

You will be able to choose from several delivery modes. The most conventional one is to use a stand-up instructor. This is the public school model. The instructor can lecture, use discussion, exercises, and a variety of visual aids. A stand-up instructor can be from the outside, or one of your own staff. The more the students participate, the more effective is this mode.

Video is a deluxe visual aid. Don't fall into the trap of plug and play. To use video-assisted training, you must have a classroom setting, with an instructor. There must be a generous amount of classroom discussion, quizzes, case studies, and exercises to make this mode work. The rule is one-third video, two-thirds classroom participation.

Computer-assisted education, and especially training is becoming more commonplace. In this mode, one or two students use a computer to step them forward through the material, with a knowledgeable instructor available for consultation. The better versions of this will re-route the student for remedial work if he/she answers a question wrong.

Some vendors are now combining video and computers. In this mode, the student views some video, then turns to the computer for some exercises.

Laser-disc technology is gradually blending video and desktop computer technology together. In the next few years, some vendors will be appearing with cost-effective offerings.

There are a number of sources for MRP II-oriented education and training. Your software vendor may offer some training. Some offer a generous selection.

Schools, colleges, and universities have begun to offer general MRP II/JIT education courses. Vocational and community colleges have had more extensive offerings than the traditional four-year universities.

The American Management Association, independent consultants, and a number of other organizations offer a continuing stream of MRP II education. The cost per student-day can be a discouragement for these sources.

The American Production and Inventory Control Society (APICS) is an excellent source. They offer books, videos, pamphlets, monthly and quarterly periodicals, and a generous mix of conferences and seminars. At least one of your employees should be a member, who would then get all their circulars. For more information contact APICS, 500 West Annendale Road, Falls Church, VA 22046-4274, 703-237-8344.

Your hardware vendor may be able to offer some training, but that will necessarily be oriented toward the computer, and be applicable mainly to the information services group.

The backbone of your education and particularly training will be done by your own employees or a local consultant/educator. In-house training on your system will be required. Since your system will be tailored, no general, canned material will be available for specific training.

5. Schedule and Present

The education coordinator now develops a grid showing your groups of users, and your presentation schedule.

The coordinator arranges for instructors, materials, space, and refreshments. The coordinator makes sure everyone is properly invited, and that participants' supervisors are fully aware of the schedules. The coordinator also is on the scene at the beginning of sessions to make sure that everything goes smoothly. And at the end of every series, the coordinator prepares certificates for the instructor to sign and hand out to all who successfully complete each program. These certificates are welcomed and you will see them pinned up on walls all over.

6. Evaluate

It is difficult to evaluate the quality of your education. The real measure is how well the participants now can do their work. Tests of knowledge and proficiency in the classroom are a substitute for this.

You should also have an evaluation form for the participants to register their comments at the end of every program. Figure 7.2 is an example. Using such a form helps you make the programs better each time.

7. Repeat

Education and training never stop. You have promotions, resignations, transfers, and expansion. People need additional education and training. This seven-point program keeps repeating.

Figure 7.2 Program Evaluation Form

Program Evaluation Form

Program Name _____ Date _____

1. Which topics were most   _____

   most valuable to you?   _____

2. Which topics (if any)   _____

   do you feel should've   _____

   been emphasized more?   _____

3. Facilites	Excellent	Good	Poor	Comments
A. Manuals	☐	☐	☐	_____
B. Visual Aids	☐	☐	☐	_____
C. Exercises	☐	☐	☐	_____
D. Meeting Room	☐	☐	☐	_____
E. On-Site Administration	☐	☐	☐	_____
F. Meals	☐	☐	☐	_____

4. Please circle your overall evaluation of this program   Excellent   Good   Fair   Poor

5. Please circle your overal evaluation of the instrutor

   A. First Instructor (name) _____   Excellent   Good   Fair   Poor

   B. Second Instructor (name) _____   Excellent   Good   Fair   Poor

6. Suggestions for improvement: _____

   _____

7. Additional comments: _____

   _____

8. Your name (optional): _____

8

HOW TO MANAGE WITH YOUR MASTER SCHEDULE

The master production schedule is the keystone of successful MRP and JIT. Without a good, workable master production schedule, all of the other necessary inputs to your MRP system, such as accurate records of inventory and order balances, and accurate bills of materials, cannot guarantee the effective operation of MRP. A bad master plan will not become better merely by being run through an expensive computer program. And, in the world of JIT (where the master schedule results in a uniform plant load) the need for a good master schedule is of even greater importance.

Hundreds of MRP installations have failed partially, if not totally, in that the hoped for benefits of reduced inventories and better control are never realized. While many things may contribute to these expensive nonsuccesses, in nearly every instance the major contributor to failure is a poor master production schedule.

The master production schedule is the final step in planning production operations. It takes the production plan for meeting the production goals which support the overall business plan and specifies the *exact* buildable products, their variety, quantity, and time schedule for their production. The operations plan embodied in the master schedule becomes the driver for those simple but incredibly detailed calculations called material requirements planning.

The fact is, the master production schedule is the key element in turning aggregate plans into action. There are no alternative ways of planning production operations which will support the scheduling, and the execution, of the myriad detailed elements of production with MRP, or for JIT. The master production schedule has been called the control knob or the window on manufacturing which gives management the reliable control over production activities, assuring that they are accomplishing those things which meet the strategic business goals such as flexibility, customer service, and productivity. Regularly reviewed by top management, the master schedule recognizes realistic constraints; and the resulting approved tradeoffs of production, marketing, and financial goals permits the entire organization to work together as a team.

In this chapter we discuss the details of how to do the master scheduling job, how to effectively design and use the master schedule to build teamwork for smoothly taking production needs and turn them into detailed plans which will work on the production floor. We will cover the following:

- The three goals of effective master scheduling.

- How to relate the master schedule to the production plan.

- How to choose the items to be master scheduled.

- The logic of master schedule calculations, and how it can be adapted to various kinds of production.

- How to easily do the crucial job of rough cut capacity planning.

- How to plan the level of flexibility, or to control the amount of change that can be accommodated.

- The unique job of the master scheduler, and what kind of person should do this job.

- How to measure the performance of your master scheduling system; how to tell if it is working.

THREE GOALS OF MASTER SCHEDULING

To make sense of the whole idea of master scheduling it is necessary to understand clearly what it is trying to do. Its basic purposes give meaning to its importance. There are three goals:

1. To make a schedule of production that is achievable within the constraints of existing materials and capacity.

2. To manage customer demand, both new orders and requested or required changes, in compliance with this achievable schedule.

3. To communicate this plan to the planning and production workforce through MRP, continually responding to real world problems as we go.

Making a Realistic Achievable Production Schedule

The first of these goals emphasizes the fact that an impossible plan will not be accomplished. No matter how much you wish you could do, no matter how diligently you throw yourself into the work, no matter how hard you drive the work force, there are realistic limits to your efforts. To plan work that is in excess of our labor or machine capacities, or that depends upon materials that are not available, is to fool ourselves, for the plan will fall apart. Therefore, an effective master scheduling system must help you know what your work load really is, so you may plan additional capacity as necessary, or reduce and rearrange production schedules until you have an achievable plan. Load and capacity, just like supply and demand, must be in balance. A simple example illustrates this:

Suppose you have a production schedule that requires approximately 1,500 hours of machine shop labor in the next month. Further, you know that your normal full-load capacity, limited by people or machines, is only 1,200 hours. It is easy to see that unless something is done, about 300 hours will not get done and will be carried over to the next period. The question is: *which* 300 hours? Master scheduling and MRP cannot tell you. The jobs left behind will be selected by persons or events outside of your knowledge or control: perhaps by the nonavailability of a tool, a shortage of a material, the choice of a foreman or a key operator, or simply, the job gets lost. In summary, it is entirely possible that the specific items not finished would be one for each final assembly you want to ship! By overloading, your shop, you did not lose control of just 300 hours, we lost control of the whole 1,500 hours. Only furious expediting to cover known kit or line shortages, telling the production floor *which* 1,200 of the 1,500 hours scheduled we really do want them to work on, will get you through the month's shipping quota.

By this example, you can see the importance of having a reasonably accurate picture of the volume of work we are planning if we want the detailed steps of production to proceed according to the planned and synchronized schedule we get from MRP. This picture does not have to be accurate to three decimal places—just close. That is why you call the capacity planning connected to the master schedule Rough-Cut capacity planning. It is one of the central problems addressed by master scheduling.

Alternatively, it often becomes known that certain materials will not be available. Maybe the vendor cannot meet the desired schedule, or the parts are defective, needing to be reworked or scrapped. New designs may prove to be too difficult, or unreliable. While action will be taken to correct these problems and try to catch up, confusion and waste can follow if the overall schedule is not changed to reflect the new reality, leaving many other parts to arrive and be ready at a time when they cannot yet be used. The master schedule, driving MRP, can cause a rearrangement of item priorities, so that all the items carry due dates which reflect the realities of the current conditions. A master schedule which represents the best current plan will result in MRP schedules which are credible, believed, and adhered to by the entire production team.

Managing Customer Demand in Complying with an Achievable Schedule

The second goal refers to the need to manage just how we will plan for and react to customer demands. It may be true that customers want everything! But you know your business, you know what you are set up to do, what you can afford. You have your mission and goals for customer service. This is part of your business strategy. And keeping in mind the first issue discussed earlier, what can you do to meet the wishes of your customers? The master schedule is the place where we explicitly and visibly state our plan to cover customer demands. New orders or major reschedules must be reviewed by the master scheduler for materials availability.

The master schedule is not a barricade thrown up around production operations for their protection or convenience. It is the best method for working as a team with marketing to give a reliable level of service. It reflects the best judgment of the entire company on how best to meet its own goal for responding to customers.

Communicating the Master Production Schedule Through MRP

The third goal considers the master production schedule as a tool to communicate, through the calculations of MRP, the detailed and synchronized schedule of each step of the production process. MRP is a priority planning tool. It gives you the relative priority (the due date) of every needed item, make or buy. And better yet, because it plans, and then re-plans, it keeps those priorities current—current to management's most recent commitment as planned in the up-to-date master production schedule. Master scheduling is continuous in its capacity planning, in its response to customer demand, and in its effect on production schedules as it drives MRP.

Using the Computer for Master Scheduling

Are computers necessary for master scheduling? These issues *can* be met with manually prepared master schedules, many firms do. But larger firms, those with more complex production processes, or those with volatile demands, will need to make use of a computer, either an offline micro, or as a module of a larger MRP set of software, to keep track of everything and help with the routine calculations.

But beware, the computer cannot do master scheduling. The master schedule involves judgments about tradeoffs well beyond its ability. The master scheduler, working with management on a regular basis, will incorporate their thinking into the schedule. Then the computer can "run through the numbers" and summarize the plan for further review, calculate the critical load areas for capacity review, and then, upon command, start driving MRP in its re-planning run.

HOW TO USE AGGREGATE PLANNING IN DEVELOPING THE PRODUCTION PLAN

In a formal business system, the master production schedule follows after the production plan. (See Figure 8.1, page 219). The production plan is usually a long range plan, commonly covering a year or more (the length of time is really dictated by the amount of time it takes to respond to major changes in quantity with new plant or machine capacities). The production plan is derived from the company's business plan, its strategic plan for meeting the company objectives. The business plan of course reflects top management's mission and goals as a company, taking into account current and new products, forecasts of sales and market share growth, capital funds availability, and profit potential.

The hierarchy of planning then devolves into the sub-plans which support this business plan. Finance and marketing will make their plans, while production management prepares its plan, the production plan, which outlines the product quantities and scheduled times appropriate to meeting the product sales quantities planned in the business plan, and makes allowance for any desired changes in overall levels of inventory to meet goals for customer service and financial investment. It may also reflect necessary balancing of product schedules to optimize the use of critical resources. It usually attempts to level the rates of production, continuing to build through slow periods so that accumulated inventory will be available to handle peak demands thereby avoiding expensive changes in productive capacity.

There are some companies, even large ones, that have a limited product line, and for them the production plan and master schedule may be one in the same. But more commonly, production management prepares a production plan composed of families, or aggregates, of products. Product family groupings are often used for reasons of convenience. The production plan covers considerable periods of time, so larger blocks of time such as months or quarters are used. Many different scenarios may be constructed through iteration and adjustment, until the rates of production over the planning horizon are deemed to be satisfactory. The use of larger blocks of time and aggregate product groupings simplifies the work, reducing the tedium of calculation, while permitting management to see the whole picture.

For instance, a manufacturer of wheeled sporting goods might group together all bicycles, all scooters, all skates, and skateboards, or perhaps all 3-speed bicycles, 10-speed bicycles, mountain bikes, and all ice skates, roller skates, and so on. The groupings would be unique to any particular firm, because of their unique combination of product offerings and their own methods and processes for producing them. (It is important when creating the groups that each item in the group is reasonably covered by an average item price, cost, and makes a similar

Figure 8.1 The Formal Business System

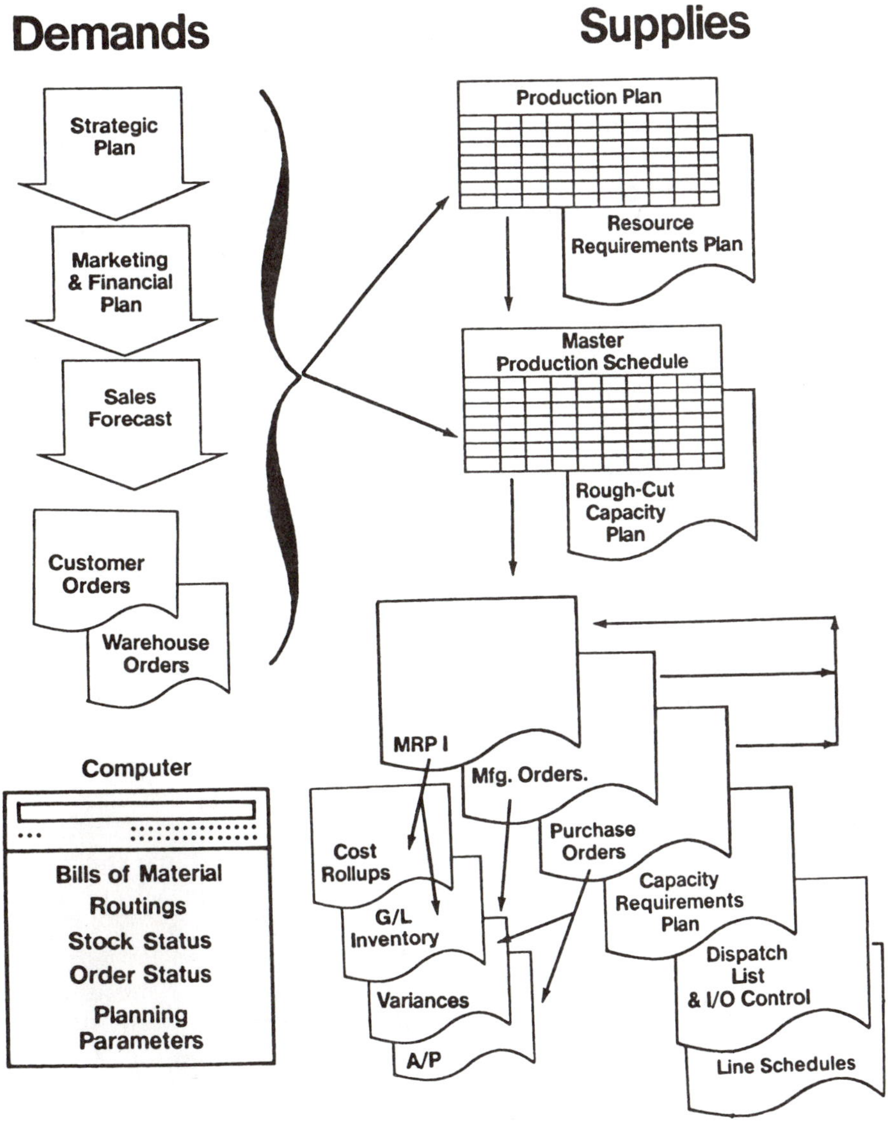

Demands

Supplies

Strategic Plan

Marketing & Financial Plan

Sales Forecast

Customer Orders

Warehouse Orders

Production Plan

Resource Requirements Plan

Master Production Schedule

Rough-Cut Capacity Plan

MRP I

Mfg. Orders.

Purchase Orders

Capacity Requirements Plan

Cost Rollups

G/L Inventory

Dispatch List & I/O Control

Variances

Line Schedules

A/P

Computer

Bills of Material
Routings
Stock Status
Order Status
Planning Parameters

demand on manufacturing capacity.) Then, using an average, or composite price, cost, and manufacturing capacity requirement for the typical item in the group, summaries of the various developing plans are prepared to verify that the plan produces what the business wants. Thus the total costs, total revenue, and total capacity requirements for each period across the planning horizon can be assessed for acceptability to the company goals for sales level, profit, productivity, and capacity capability.

Making Manufacturing Capacity Checks

Of special interest is the area of manufacturing capacity. The total demands on manufacturing capacity must not exceed the provided capacity or the plan will not be achieved. The flowchart in Figure 8.1 shows that a capacity check is made of the production plan, and again, for the master production schedule. The capacity check for production planning is referred to as Resource Requirements Planning, and that for the master schedule is called Rough-Cut Capacity Planning. A spreadsheet program such as Lotus 1-2-3,™ can be used to display the plan and calculate the revenue, cost or load summaries using a technique called Load Profiling, which will be explained later.

What is important is that these capacity checks be made and questions of inadequate capacity be resolved before proceeding to further define the plan in the master schedule, or in MRP. If sufficient capacity is not available, the plan will not work, it won't be credible, and many problems will ensue. Each level in the hierarchy of planning must be achievable, and deficiencies in planning will not overcome by extensive massaging of the details.

To simplify the process it is not necessary that every part of our capacity be examined. There are many areas of production that are not tightly constrained, where capacity is quite flexible. These areas might be service areas such as painting, or plating, or deburring, or any such supporting function where the capability of machinery is not 100 percent utilized or where labor levels can be easily adjusted. But every firm has work centers that are not flexible, limited by the number of capable workers, the output rate of a machine or process, or even in the amount of space available. These "bottlenecks" should be identified for they are then the constraints on our plan of production. Critical resources must be recognized by management, and their capacity either not exceeded, or realistic plans made to increase their capacity or flexibility.

We may discover that unexpected functions can be a capacity bottleneck. For example, quality final test labs (for high technology products), or the customer engineering group (in a design and build to order company) can be overloaded and therefore unable to meet their part of the schedule. Again, the availability of certain raw materials may be a constraint, or the load of work we give a vendor may overload his facility, preventing timely delivery. All of these can be planned for in the load profile.

Resource capacity planning and rough-cut capacity planning are not meant to be finely accurate. They do not use exact labor standards, nor do they allow for some of the work which is in progress, assuming that period to period approximately the same amount of work is already done. They are more like a quick sketch, a forecast, which can chart the effect of our plan over the planning horizon. Wanting and wishing is not enough. Performing these capacity checks is essential to making achievable plans.

PREPARING THE MASTER PRODUCTION SCHEDULE BY DISAGGREGATING THE PRODUCTION PLAN

The production plan, having been approved as meeting the firm's business and production goals, and having been tested as fitting the resources and capacities available, serves to guide the master scheduler in preparing the more detailed master production schedule.

The master schedule is a disaggregation of the family or product groups of the production plan into the exact product quantities and production schedule dates that will drive the MRP calculations. (See Figure 8.2.) There are several reasons for this:

- While product groups are convenient for production (aggregate) planning, in the factory the average item is not buildable. The exact definition of the finished good is required. We cannot build a just a "bicycle" but must know: is it to be a man's or woman's frame, 3-speed or 10-speed, and specify wheel size, handlebar type, and color, and so on?

- In MRP the computer works with specific bills of materials which specify the components required for each unique item. The master schedule must be stated in terms of identification numbers for the desired bills of materials to drive MRP.

- Finally, the master schedule must respond to the most current demands of customers, either as forecasted, or as orders already on the books, or both. The master schedule is management's definitive plan for operations and should take into account the need to give reliable customer service. Managing demand is a key issue for master scheduling.

Figure 8.2 illustrates several other points worth noting. First, the master schedules for each of the family of items, while derived from the master scheduler's review of current demands and current available inventories, should reasonably equal the total for the group as planned in the production plan if the hierarchy of planning starting with the business plan is to be carried through to the production floor (via MRP).

Figure 8.2 Disaggregating the Production Plan

Production Plan

Product	Planning Horizon									
	Firm					Tentative				
	Jan	Feb	Mar	Apr	May	Jun	Jul	Aug	Sep	Oct
A	50				50	60		50		50
B		100			80					

Master Production Schedule

Item	Week 1	Week 2	Week 3	Week 4
B-1	10		10	
B-2		30		
B-3				30

Next is the matter of the *planning horizon*. As you have seen, the horizon for production planning should be as long as the expected period of time it would take to react to major changes in production levels. The horizon for the master schedule may be as long as that for the production plan, but is not required to be so. What is important is that the horizon be somewhat beyond the cumulative lead time for the products we are scheduling.

It is necessary to know just how long it normally takes to procure your raw materials and components, fabricate parts, prepare sub-assemblies, and produce final assemblies. If you do not schedule far enough into the future the lowest levels of your bills of materials will not get priority due dates which allow for proper or dependable lead times. Lead times are very difficult to pin down, especially when there are many levels of construction to the product. Lead times need to be controlled, and padding them with extra "safety" time is counterproductive, because it unnecessarily lengthens the planning horizon, hurts your ability to flexibly meet customer needs, and causes greater reliance on less dependable long-term forecasts. Fortunately, good master scheduling, by making a plan which fits within the available capacity, prevents overloading critical work centers and therefore makes in-plant production lead times more reliable.

Last, notice the "fence" shown on the production plan in Figure 8.2. The purpose of a fence is to control the amount of change that, as a matter of policy, you will allow to your plan. Management can define one or more fences, inside of which differing degrees of schedule change are permitted. Fences are discussed in more detail later. For now, it is important to realize that too much change, too close in to current production operations, will impair the efficiency of production, even to the degree of being impossible to accept. Certainly, you must be careful of accepting changes inside of the cumulative lead time for your production process. The master scheduler must verify that sufficient materials and adequate capacity exist before making changes inside this fence. Fences are an explicit statement of company policy about how you will respond to customer demands and requests for changes in schedule. They will be unique to a firm's production process and strategy for serving customers. And they serve to take some nervousness out of the schedules, making production operations more efficient in execution and more reliable in delivery to the customer.

HOW TO DETERMINE WHAT CAN OR SHOULD BE MASTER SCHEDULED

Because there are a great variety of ways of planning production for your product line it is not always obvious what items should be included in the master production schedule. The most obvious idea would be to schedule the items you sell. But many manufacturing environments can be more efficiently scheduled by basing the master schedule on major sub-assemblies, product families, or at some other level than the complete as-sold item. In some instances, the actual work of master scheduling can be reduced and accuracy and convenience increased by choosing something other than the as-sold finished good.

Whatever is master scheduled must relate to two things: satisfying the customer orders, and the need to plan capacity. Serving the customer, that is, managing demand, will dictate the core of the master schedule. Often, there are other significant demands that consume materials and capacity. It is equally important that all demands on manufacturing resources must somehow be included in your planning. This may broaden the list. The following list will help identify the necessary items.

- Customer orders, or forecasts for orders

- Spare parts and accessories

- Repair parts for service or refurbishing

- Distribution center replenishments

- Interplant transfers

- Significant amounts of rework

Failing to plan for any of these which consume significant amounts of materials or capacity can lead to nasty surprises and result in unplanned overloads which damage the credibility of the master schedule. In many high-technology industries, the need for spares and repair parts will take precedence over regular production, in order that existing installations or equipment can be kept functioning. Good customer service here is crucial. Further, these may constitute a large part of gross revenue and an even larger part of profit. In high-volume distribution operations the key to good service is carefully planned replenishment of distribution center stocks.

If any of these are significant to your operation, either for providing a high level of customer service, or for planning adequate capacity for reliable scheduling, they must be forecasted and managed with the master production schedule.

IDENTIFYING TYPES OF MPS ITEMS

When considering just which items should be master scheduled it may seem that the finished goods items would be the ideal ones to work with. But in reality there are a great variety of ways of planning for production in different companies. Sometimes it may be better to build your master schedule around items that are not at the top of the product structure. You can get better control, gain administrative simplicity, increase MRP effectiveness, and make capacity planning easier if you examine your product line and product structure (bills of materials) and perhaps schedule at some level other than the finished item. This section discusses the possibilities of master scheduling sub-assemblies, semi-finished items, kits of parts, even fabricated or purchased items, as well as the normal as-sold items. They may be mixed, with any of them used with any of the others in preparing the master schedule.

How to Schedule Product Items

We will start with the most straightforward approach to selecting MPS items: using items that are exactly the finished product sold to the customer. Whether you build the item to order, or sell it from shelf stock inventory, the product is completely defined by its Bill of Materials. The master production schedule is then also the final assembly schedule for the plant. MRP is driven by the master schedule, using the planned quantities and due dates to plan component and sub-assembly priorities.

This is the most direct and easiest to understand approach. The master schedule for as-sold items is capacity planned using load profiles for each item (load profiles are described in detail below). A simple spreadsheet program listing the item identities in the first column, with the other columns devoted to the quantities for each planning period, can be flexibly updated to reflect new forecasts or orders and schedule changes as requested, or as required by production realities.

A word about the amount or size of the master schedule. Effective scheduling almost dictates that one person be in charge of arranging the schedule. Coordinating the numerous trade-offs in quantity and time period which will be required to achieve a balanced plan which serves management's needs for service and productive efficiency falls on the shoulders of the master scheduler.

How many items can a master scheduler handle? Of course the answer varies with the business environment, but it probably lies in the range of 100–150. The complexity of the product (the number of components and levels of assembly), the reliability of the forecasts, the volatility of changes in customer order backlog, and the level of flexibility demanded by management, all contribute to the burden of schedule management. Extraordinarily large master schedules are difficult to cope with, and schedules that change frequently are a challenge to the mental powers of oversight by the master scheduler. Very large master schedules may be handled better using some of the techniques discussed below.

Scheduling Product Families

We have discussed the use of product groupings commonly used for ease in production planning. If your product line consists of a large number of products, and each product is offered in many variations of the base model, then it may be possible to master schedule just the base products, letting the master schedule software take care of detailing the schedules for the numerous variations offered for sale.

An example of this might be a company that sells window coverings such as venetian blinds, roller shades, shutters, and the like. Each of the basic products is offered in a wide variety of colors, widths, lengths, or other features. But the manufacturing of each variation is similar or identical on the production floor.

In such a company it makes sense to plan carefully the volume of each base type of product, and use a planning bill of materials to define the variations which will be stocked. Figure 8.3 shows an example of a planning bill for a boy's dirt bicycle. The bicycles are identical except for color. The planning bill of materials does not represent a buildable product, but a concept of the base product. In this bill the quantity per assembly is the percentage of the total group forecasted to have that feature. The individual item percentages will of course total to 100 percent.

Master scheduling for product families is a two-level process. The master scheduler plans a quantity for the basic product based on forecasts. This is the quantity used for capacity planning, and represents what management wants to build in each period. The master schedule software then "explodes" the planned quantity of the base item into the individual buildable items which now become the master production schedule to drive MRP.

This technique, useful for these special situations, is not very common. These software programs are more complex and therefore not all master scheduling programs will include the features necessary to perform this kind of planning.

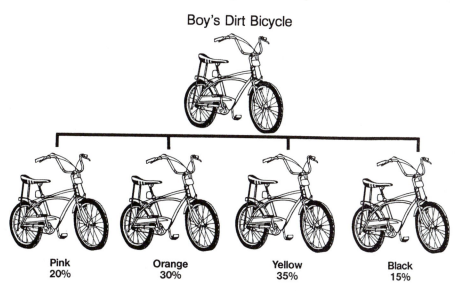

Figure 8.3 Planning Bill
Boy's Dirt Bicycle

Boy's Dirt Bicycle

Pink
20%

Orange
30%

Yellow
35%

Black
15%

Forecasts for groups of items are usually more accurate than the individual forecast for each item. This gives an advantage to this kind of planning, since the basic schedules will be better and the capacity planning more reliable. But don't forget that the percentages used in the planning bill are forecasts themselves. Therefore, companies must develop procedures for monitoring actual sales and updating the planning bill percentages. While these percentages may change, and schedules for actual production be changed, the overall product group plan for capacity and material does not need to change.

Establishing Final Assembly Schedules Using Major Sub-assemblies

Much more common is master scheduling using various sub-assemblies or modules that will be used to assemble a customer order (using a Final Assembly Schedule). An example of this might be a computer system consisting of a central processing unit offered with customer choices of types and quantities of memory, various modems, keyboards, monitors, printers, and so on. The as-sold product can therefore be flexibly sold by building quantities of the major modules, and then quickly assembling them when the customer order is received. This is referred to as a "configure to order" situation.

For example, in Figure 8.4 you see a hypothetical 35mm camera. This camera can be purchased in many variations, including choice of lens, film advance, and type of flash. The customer selects the components desired and the final unit can be assembled on the spot. A similar circumstance would be the selection of components of a home entertainment high fidelity system.

Figure 8.4 Accessories and Options Bill for a Camera

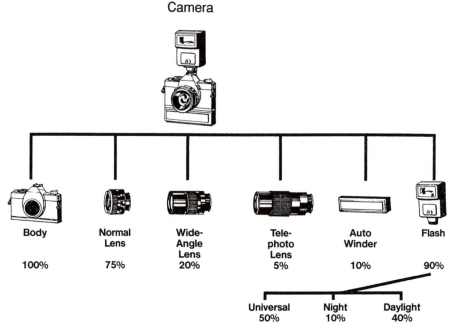

Camera

Body — 100%
Normal Lens — 75%
Wide-Angle Lens — 20%
Tele-photo Lens — 5%
Auto Winder — 10%
Flash — 90%

Universal 50%
Night 10%
Daylight 40%

There may be an uncountable number of variations of the final product, but planning and production is clearly simplified by master scheduling at a lower level. Rather than a very large number of top level bills of materials for all the possible permutations, a much smaller number of bills for the major modules is maintained. These buildable and stockable modules then become the forecasted and master scheduled items. Using this technique results in large gains in sales flexibility, in being able to exactly meet customer specifications. Also, forecasting, master scheduling, and configuration management through engineering change control become much simplified. Using this technique results in the fewest number of bills of materials, and the smallest number of items which will be forecasted and subsequently master scheduled.

The ability to forecast, plan, and schedule in this manner depends on the way the product is designed and sold. If the original design for the product contains this type of configuration, so much the better. But if variations of the basic product are becoming so numerous as to cause problems it may necessary but worthwhile to examine the product structuring and redesign existing structures to use interchangeable modules. This is never easy to do, but it can lead to tremendous savings and greatly increased control of planning and customer service.

Essential to this process is a customer order entry system that captures the exact customer specifications. The line items of the customer order represent, in effect, the bill of material for the final assembly, and the forecasting system bases its forecast on the line item sales. The customer order is then scheduled for the (usually short-term) assembly in the Final Assembly Schedule (FAS), and the line items become the pick list for releasing the required modules from stock. In essence, this technique permits a high level of customer-unique service, while master scheduling and production operations are based on a build-to-stock basis to satisfy forecasts for the modules. It accomplishes a de-coupling of final demand from the production process, permitting efficiency in final product assembly and in component or module production.

An important part of the order entry process is the checking of each incoming order to verify that all the desired components are available in stock. This should be done before a firm delivery commitment is made to the customer. In many situations this can be routinely done by the order entry clerks, using the regular master schedule reports (described later) showing stock on hand and especially, the available-to-promise.

In some instances the master scheduler should review the new order before committing to a delivery date. Perhaps, only nonroutine problems will be referred to the scheduler for problem solving and planning for items that are not available in a timely manner. It is clear that an order included in the Final Assembly

Schedule that does not conform to the master schedule availabilities will create problems in production and furious expediting within regular production operations.

Scheduling by Using Kits of Parts

Sometimes an optional module or feature is not buildable or stockable as an assembled item. In this case a kit-of-parts technique can be used to master schedule the necessary set of parts. For example, a final product such as a forklift truck may be alternatively configured to use gasoline, propane, or diesel fuels. Each of these requires a different set of parts in the engine, fuel, and exhaust systems. Each combination of these parts is not a buildable assembly in itself. However, the full sets of these parts need to be master scheduled so that their demands on capacity can be allowed for, and their availability guaranteed by proper forecasting and production.

This situation can be managed by creating bills of materials for the necessary combination of parts in each kit, and deleting them from the regular engine, fuel and exhaust system bills of materials. This kits are then forecasted and master scheduled for production to stock. In final assembly the proper kit is withdrawn to complete the required customer configuration.

Scheduling Service Items

Service Items and repair parts may sometimes be inconsequential and easy to obtain. But if their ready availability is a matter of concern, if they require long lead times to fabricate or procure, and if they represent more than a token demand on manufacturing capacity, they must also be master scheduled.

Sub-assemblies or parts at lower levels of assembly that are required for after-market support are therefore proper items for master scheduling. Thereby, their need will be forecasted, production planned, and capacity to produce them made available, so that shop priorities can be scheduled and remain valid, and customer service goals can be met. The tools available in master scheduling make this easy to do.

Scheduling Semifinished Items

In some industries a large variety of final products are produced from a limited number of materials, or through a standardized process requiring a fixed number of steps. These process type industries approach master scheduling through the important common ingredients rather than the intense variety of finished products possible.

An example of this might be the paper box manufacturer who can provide an infinite variety of box sizes (or for other industries, the flavors, colors, or sizes, etc.), all of which are made from sheets or rolls of corrugated board made from relatively few raw paper materials. What is important here is that there is a common element for materials and capacity planning that can be most easily used for master scheduling.

Master scheduling is based on the semi-finished product (in this case, the corrugated board). The square feet of board to be consumed by production schedules is the common measure of load against machine or process capacity, and defines the quantity of raw materials needed.

This kind of master scheduling is quite special and unique to each firm, closely designed for the product and process of manufacture in use. By focusing on the raw materials or on the semi-finished products within the process and translating sales demands and final production schedules into quantities of the common material or process used, the job of master scheduling is simplified while still meeting its goals of meeting customer demands, providing productive capacity, and planning for materials required.

Scheduling Fabricated and Purchased Items

It is sometimes desirable to include certain component items in the master production schedule in order to give them extraordinary visibility in the planning process. Such items as gold for contact plating, or tool diamonds, or any item that has very long or unreliable lead times, or which is sole-sourced, may be included in the master schedule. Doing this assures constant review by management and the master scheduler to avoid problems of cost and availability, while maintaining minimum inventory.

HOW THE MASTER PLANNING ENVIRONMENT AFFECTS THE MASTER SCHEDULE

Before looking into the calculations involved in planning each master schedule item, we must look at the general kind of planning basis used by the firm. The manufacturing environment, such as make-to-stock or make-to-order, not only affects which items we master schedule, but also affects, to a degree, the specific kind of procedure to be used. The basic form of logic is adjusted to account for the differences in planning basis.

Describing the Make-to-Stock Environment

The make-to-stock environment plans production to replenish stock. Sales are shipped from finished goods ready in the warehouse, and production planning is based solely on forecasts of item sales in a volume or at a rate that will replace those sold and result in an inventory balance that covers expected forecast errors (safety stock) and meets management's financial goals for investment in inventory and customer service.

The master scheduler's efforts are aimed at reviewing the master schedule reports that display the current forecasts, the balance on hand, and actual and planned production. The report's basic information is called the Projected Available Balance for each period in the future, and the master scheduler reviews each item to verify that production covers the forecast needs (a positive balance) or, if not, what production orders need to be planned, released, or rescheduled in order to remove any negative balances. Conversely, reductions in the forecast will cause orders to be scheduled out or canceled. The corrected schedule then may be given to the Material Requirements Planning module for explosion and update of component priorities.

Because the forecast is the basis for planning, the master scheduler must be the most careful watcher of the forecasts, continually watching for sales changes which could affect the forecast, and regularly consult with marketing to review the forecasts. The scheduler will set safety stock levels to cover expected forecast error, levels which are also in line with management's goals for inventory investment and customer service.

Complications can arise if shipments are normally made from stock but customer orders are booked and held for future shipment. When this happens the master schedule will show how much of the forecast has been consumed by these backlog orders, and how much of future production is available to promise in future periods.

Distribution requirements to warehouses or dealers also add to the complexity. Ideally, the rate of sales from distribution points directly to customers has been included in the forecast level. The master scheduler will then monitor warehouse replenishments to fairly distribute production.

Describing the Make-to-Order Environment

In the make-to-order environment the planning is based not on a forecast but on the backlog of booked orders. The master scheduler schedules the orders based on the customer requested due date, in full cognizance of the realistic lead time to produce the product.

There is a broad range of possibilities in this make-to-order world. At one extreme of the spectrum, the product is totally customer specified, engineered for production, and then scheduled. In this case there will be no item forecast beyond that forecast implicit in the fact that the firm is open and ready for business. Master scheduling in this case is really project or program management. The difficulty will vary depending on how much of previous designs and products can be used in capacity and materials planning. In the aerospace or defense industries, for instance, new or add-on contracts for items previously designed and built can easily be incorporated in the master scheduling because the bills of materials, as well as process and routing data are available for capacity planning. But if the design is new the master scheduler must seek out available historical data on similar or common sub-assemblies previously built. For an entirely new design, only estimates (often found in the bid and quote process) are available to help with loading and capacity planning. Finally, the scheduler will cope with changes in design, changes in schedule, and conflicts with other programs and projects.

At the other end of the make-to-order spectrum the items sold are of proprietary design. They may even be catalogued. Bills of materials, as well as process routings, are available to help guide the master scheduling process. In this environment a rather regular list of items is produced, but not until a customer order is received. There may even be a forecast, used to plan capacity over a long horizon, but a real production order is not released until a customer order justifies it.

There is considerable variability in the degree that raw materials, components, and sub-assemblies are stocked, depending on management's policy for inventory investment and customer response time. Because forecasting is difficult, critical-path lead times, as tempered by current material availabilities, are important. The master scheduler will carefully review incoming orders and check lead times, material availability, and manufacturing capacity before giving a delivery promise. This requires not only a deep understanding of product and process, but close coordination with marketing to prevent overloading and nonperformance to schedule.

Often management will want to improve response times by authorizing the procurement of materials, or the manufacture of sub-assemblies with long lead times. Here the master scheduler will likely want to master schedule sub-assemblies on a more nearly forecasted basis. But keeping track of the status of these orders and their availability for use on future orders, as well as responding to management's changing policies in this area, will add much complexity to the master scheduler's job.

Using Combination Environments

In order to gain greater flexibility and responsiveness management will want to combine elements of the two previous environments. Make-to-stock companies often wish to increase their market by offering a greater variety of products, and do it without great increases in finished goods inventories. Therefore, for part or all of their product line they will move towards using a configure-to-order or assemble-to-order approach (with modular bills of materials, discussed previously). Master scheduling is more complex here, especially if the firm continues to schedule its as-sold product at the same time it is scheduling the lower level sub-assembly modules. At a minimum they will need to re-identify the modules, giving them their own bill of materials so that dependent demand for modules arising from the as-sold finished item will not be confused with the forecasted demand for the configuration modules.

Conversely, make-to-order companies may want to reduce their order response lead times (to meet competitive pressures), or decrease certain manufacturing costs by running larger lots of production. They can do this by forecasting and authorizing the production of stockable sub-assemblies. Customer orders can then be more quickly assembled from the available stock. The master scheduler must suggest the most advantageous items to treat this way, trading off lead time for inventory costs, and work to be certain that the modules so built are consumed in a timely way.

Either of these approaches can bring benefits, but only if they are carried through well. If not carefully merged, the use of two planning bases can lead to wasteful confusion. In any case, the introduction of a master production scheduling system may trigger a worthwhile analysis to streamline operations by restructuring bills of materials and starting new forecasts.

Describing Repetitive Manufacturing and Just-in-Time

Repetitive manufacturing, or assembly line production, is a special case of make-to-stock, quite often with a limited variety of products. In JIT, the assembly line is supported by other producing functions controlled with visual signals such as Kanban. But in either form these organizations require good master scheduling. The master scheduled items are the products that consume the capacity of the repetitive operation. And in JIT the master schedule represents the Uniform Plant Load which is critical to smooth product mixing and level loading of work throughout the plant.

This capacity may be defined by the rate or cycle time of the assembly line itself, or by gating operations which may have machine capacity limits. It generally is difficult to alter capacity in these environments for they are inefficient when operated at significantly higher or lower volumes. For instance, overstaffing or understaffing assembly lines upsets line balance, increases delays, and leads to increased unit cost.

In this environment the master scheduler must have a thorough understanding of the capacity constraints, so as to balance production to satisfy current customer demands, and to fully utilize capacities. Capacity planning, customer demand management, and master scheduling are clearly linked together in the repetitive environment.

HOW TO APPLY THE LOGIC OF MASTER PRODUCTION SCHEDULING

The master production schedule reports prepared by computer systems are based on a simple set of calculations that are in many ways similar to the mechanics of MRP planning. Much of the terminology used is similar. And the fundamental logic the computer uses is identical: for each master schedule item the quantity of supply must equal or cover the quantity of demand.

In another important way computer master scheduling is also just like the computer planning of MRP—it is a mechanical process of calculating, blind to many of the realities present within the production system. The computer will scrupulously review the data for each item and then plan or suggest production orders that will ensure coverage of the demands. Like the sorcerer's apprentice it rolls on without knowing whether the data is accurate (for demands and/or supplies), whether the materials or capacity are available to work the plan, and whether the more or less fixed rules for planning really represent the current management policies for flexibility, customer service, production efficiency, and inventory investment.

The computer calculates with unswerving accuracy, but the value of the results depends on the quality of the input. The goals of master scheduling, to meet customer demands, to uncouple production for productive smoothness and efficiency, require that there be tradeoffs in schedules to balance the goals of service with the available resources. These policy decisions must be made by management, by reviewing the master schedule prepared by the master scheduler, making necessary changes in the inputs, and reiterating the master schedule until it becomes a workable and achievable plan. Only when this management responsibility is complete should the master schedule be used to drive the detail planning of MRP.

Required Inputs for Calculating the Master Schedule

The data used by the computer to calculate the master schedule for each item falls into three main areas:

1. Current Status of each master schedule item:
   - Inventory balances of the items selected for master scheduling
   - Quantities of these items now released in production
   - Any inventory in transit from other locations or vendors
   - All existing demands for these items:
     - forecasts of sales
     - existing backlogs of sold but not shipped orders
     - any distribution replenishment orders
     - forecast and orders for spares and repairs items
     - any demands for interplant transfers

It is helpful if detailed information about these demands, such as order numbers, scheduled due dates, and so on, is easily available to the master scheduler. When reviewing the schedule and solving problems the master scheduler needs to have full knowledge of the details about who and what will be affected by changes and replans.

2. Current or existing plans:

   ■ Planned production orders over the planning horizon—the existing master schedule

   ■ Forecasts over the horizon—either directly for each item, or exploded from family groups using the planning bills of materials

3. Planning rules, and information to guide computer processing, either global (for all items) or for each master schedule item:

   ■ Lead time for assembly of the item

   ■ Lot sizing rules to be used

   ■ Time fences and how they will be applied

   ■ The cumulative or critical path lead time

   ■ Load profile data for each item for capacity planning

This last category contains much of the data that defines the management policies, the boundaries set to control the degree of responsiveness and therefore the customer service within the system. The load profile data is used subsequently to the master schedule process in testing the loads planned against the resources and capacity available.

Using the Planning Worksheet to Calculate the Schedule

In order to explain the method of calculation we will make use of a planning worksheet (Figure 8.5), carrying through several examples which will illustrate the process. This worksheet is meant to be characteristic of any master schedule report, containing information which is typically found on actual system outputs, although it has an arbitrarily short planning horizon of only eight periods. It will serve as a framework for stepping through the basic arithmetic as well as several variations which are used to tailor a system to a specific manufacturing environment.

First, a few words of definition and description will be helpful before proceeding to use the form. The form is used for an individual master schedule item so the part number of the finished good (or the master scheduled subassembly if modular planning is used) will identify the worksheet at the top.

Figure 8.5 Planning Worksheet

Part _____
Lead Time _____
Lot Size Rule _____

	Period							
	1	2	3	4	5	6	7	8
Forecast								
Backlog								
Gross Requirement								
Master Production Schedule (MPS)								
Projected Available (PAB)								
Net Requirement								
Planned Order Receipts								
Scheduled Receipts								
To MRP								
Available to Promise (ATP)								

The lead time comes next. This is the normal lead time to assemble the item, not its cumulative lead time, which may be used to offset the starting date for a planned order. The lead time is important to the master scheduler in deciding what changes in schedule date might be possible or can be accommodated. While not shown in this example, the cumulative lead time is often displayed also, giving the reviewer a feel for the potential problems of taking new orders or increasing quantities of old orders inside of this critical path.

The lot size rule will be used by the computer to calculate the size of a planned order which the system is suggesting in order to cover the demands. Simple rules are all that are required for master scheduling, especially because orders will be carefully reviewed by the scheduler. Possible rules commonly used are:

- Fixed Lot Size—a regular size of production run set by the master scheduler, or by production management, as being reasonable is most cases. This quantity can be changed when the order is firmed by the planner if necessary to cope with some problem such as limited material or capacity.

- Period Order Quantity—the size of the order is set by considering the demands over a fixed or defined future period of time, the order being sufficient to cover all demands in this period. This is a useful rule as it does not overplan production through periods of low demand, but also responds to increasing demands.

- Lot-for-Lot—sometimes called discrete planning, this rule plans production lots exactly equal to period demands. It is useful for make-to-order situations where additional production beyond the customer order quantity is not wanted. However, it is a poor rule in other situations such as make-to-stock because it changes with every change in demand, causing the production lot size to change, which, in turn, will require MRP to re-explode the changed order through all levels. This creates undue "nervousness" in an MRP system.

The remaining titles or headings in Figure 8.5 relate to the data used in the calculation, or the results of a step in the process.

- Forecast—this is the period by period forecast for the item, essential in planning the make-to-stock environment. It also may be of value in monitoring received order levels in a make-to-order situation. Here also will be forecasts for spares and repairs items which are master scheduled.

■ Backlog—this is the actual customer order backlog, essential in make-to-order planning, and necessary for showing book-and-hold orders in make- to-stock situations.

■ Gross Requirements—this important line represents the demand which actually will be used in the calculation of needed production. The source of gross requirements changes and may be *either* the forecast, the backlog, or some combination of the two. *It is the definition of this line which is the major tool used by management to tailor the system to its own basis for planning (make-to-stock or make-to-order) and to control how responsive the system will be to customer demands.*

■ Master Production Schedule—this line shows the existing master schedule, the management approved current schedule for production. It is the correctness, or adequacy, of this schedule which is being reviewed now by the master scheduler using the master schedule module of the system. In a sense similar to some MRP systems, the master schedule is a "net change" schedule, always in existence, but subject to incremental corrections as needed to cover new, more current, demands.

■ Projected Available Balance—this line has the same meaning it would in MRP. It is the amount of the item at the *end of the period* after deducting demands (gross requirements) from the prior inventory balance. Some or all of this quantity has been committed and should not be confused with already available to promise (see below).

■ Net Requirements—after the computer has scanned and reviewed the master schedule, it calculates the net requirements (where the Projected Available Balance is negative) which are not covered by the current production schedule. The computer will recommend new, planned order receipts using the applicable lot sizing rule to cover these requirements.

■ Planned Order Receipts—this line shows the planned orders recommended by the computer to the master scheduler for his review and subsequent approval as scheduled receipts.

■ Scheduled Receipts—this line shows production orders which have been written and released with a firm due date.

- To MRP—this line shows the quantities which will be sent to MRP as the master schedule to drive the explosion.

- Available to Promise—this last line is a separate calculation which shows the quantities which are not committed to any sales order and are truly available for sale to incoming orders.

Please note that there are many master scheduling software systems available. Not every one of them will have all these lines in its reports, nor always use exactly the same titles for them. Nevertheless, the logic will be similar, and we may look on this form as a sort of generic pattern for the master schedule calculations we will now examine.

How the Arithmetic of Master Schedule Calculations Affects Planning

The basic logic of master schedule calculations by the computer is to verify that Demands (from forecasts and orders) are fully covered by Supplies (released production orders, and quantities which have been master scheduled). Whenever coverage is incomplete, supplies do not cover all demands, the system will prepare "Planned Orders" sufficient to provide coverage. These planned orders may be viewed as recommendations to the planner to adjust or increase the master schedule to provide the necessary coverage. In this way the master scheduler is notified to fully examine the status of a particular item, verify that the demands are proper, and then prepare a planned response that will meet the need and at the same time carry out the policies of management for production and inventory levels. Usually management will review and approve the corrected master schedule before it becomes the driver of the MRP explosion.

While this is the basic logic of the system, there are several ways in which it is adjusted to allow for the unique planning policy of the individual firm. For instance, firms that make-to-stock for sales from their warehouse will use a different procedure for calculation than will firms that follow a make-to-order planning basis. And of course there are many variations in between these two extremes.

We will go through examples of the master schedule calculation that illustrate how the procedure can be tailored to the company's planning basis.

Using a Make-to-Stock Planning Basis

Figure 8.6 shows a typical review of a master schedule item, Item G, for a company that uses a make-to-stock planning basis. This item has an assembly lead time of three periods and it has been decided that the most common or reasonable lot to schedule for production is 20 units. The system will use this quantity rule whenever it needs to plan a new production lot. The master scheduler may change this recommended quantity when he or she adds it to the master production schedule.

Figure 8.6   Make-to-Stock Plan

Part ___G___
Lead Time _3 Periods_
Lot Size Rule _20 (Ffixed)_

	Period							
	1	2	3	4	5	6	7	8
Forecast	10	10	10	10	10	10	10	10
Backlog	6	5	2		1			
Gross Requirement	10	10	10	10	10	10	10	10
Master Production Schedule (MPS)		20		20		20		
Projected Available 18 (PAB)	8	18	8	18	8	18	8	18
Net Requirements								2
Planned Order Receipts								20
Scheduled Receipts		20						
To MRP				20		20		20*
Available to Promise (ATP)	12	13		19		20		

* Recommendation to Planner

For the make-to-stock company planning is based on a forecast of sales. The forecast is prepared by any one of a number of methods, often by the materials management staff using exponential smoothing of historical data, and may be entered manually or automatically in the master schedule system. It is important that if the forecast is not made by marketing that the marketing people review and approve its reasonableness before master scheduling. In this example the forecast is a level one at 10 units per period. See Appendix V for a full explanation of forecasting techniques.

A safety stock level should always be set to cover the expected random forecast error. In this example the safety stock calculation has been ignored to simplify this demonstration. The master schedule system would handle safety stock the same as it does in MRP.

In the line below the forecast we can see that there are customer orders which have been booked for delivery in periods one, two, three, and five. Since this firm mainly ships from stock we would expect these order quantities to be only a fraction of the total forecast level. Should the backlog exceed the forecast the master scheduler should have marketing review and correct the forecast.

It is the definition of what constitutes the demands on the third line, Gross Requirements, which is unique to the make-to-stock situation. As we see in this example, the demands which must be covered by the master schedule are exactly the same as the forecast. In the make-to-stock planning environment the forecast demands are what must be covered with master scheduled supplies. The order backlog is shown to give confidence in the forecast level.

The system, now having defined the demands to be covered, proceeds to compare the supplies available, the stock on hand (18 in this example) plus the quantities master scheduled, to verify that all demands are covered. The first master schedule quantity for 20 in period 2 is, in fact, a scheduled receipt, meaning that this scheduled lot has already been released as a production order.

Starting with the inventory of 18, the system performs successive calculations, deducting gross requirements, adding the master scheduled production, and for each period calculates the Projected Available Balance (PAB) at the end of that period. The PAB then becomes the starting quantity available at the beginning of the next period's calculation. For the second period the PAB of eight in period one is added to the master schedule production of 20 while the 10 units of gross requirements are deducted to result in an end of period balance available of 18. The third period has no planned production but the PAB is sufficient to cover requirements with a balance of eight projected to be on hand.

This process of calculation continues until, as in period eight, the Projected Available Balance does not cover the demand of 10. The shortage of two is recognized as a Net Requirement for two, which the system must now plan to cover. Using the decision rule assigned to this Item G, it plans an order for 20. The system then assumes that the scheduler will add this to the master schedule, and therefore accepts the 20 units as a supply order, which after covering the net requirement for two, results in a balance of 18 at the end of the period. The system then goes on subtracting demands and planning supplies across the whole planning horizon.

When supplies do not match demands (as in this example in period eight) the system will recommend a new planned order, or perhaps, a reschedule of an existing master schedule, and a message about this exception will be sent (usually in the form of a complete status printout of this item) so that the scheduler can review the record and consider changing the master schedule. In this example the master scheduler could master schedule a new quantity of 20 in period eight, or even, if possible (material and capacity being available) increase the 20 master scheduled in period 6 to 22 which would cover the net requirement of two in period eight. This is a judgment call by the scheduler, but if possible, would result in changing the PAB in period 6 to 20, period 7 to 10, and the PAB in period eight to zero. Of course, if there is a specified safety stock required the schedule in period six would have to be enlarged enough to cover it also so that the safety stock quantity would be projected to be available in period eight. Such a change in the master schedule six periods in the future would result in lower future inventories, and with less disruption of current production schedules than would a reduction of a more current schedule in periods two or four.

The system would also report messages to the scheduler to suggest rescheduling out master schedules that result in excessive inventories, or even to cancel scheduled quantities not needed. It should be clear why the master schedule system must work through the master scheduler, and not be allowed to automatically generate new instructions to MRP. The scheduler must consider a great number of things, such as disruptions to the production floor, the availability of materials and capacity, and the company's policy about customer service levels, before choosing what to schedule in response to the net requirement caused by uncovered demands. To allow computer planned production orders to be automatically carried through MRP to the production of component parts and subassemblies would be quite dangerous.

Some systems have the capability to show what quantities will be sent to MRP from this master schedule. The scheduled receipt of 20 in period two is not going to be sent to MRP because it is a released order which has its components and they no longer need to be planned. The master scheduled quantities in periods four and six must be exploded through MRP to cause planning to provide the components to build Item G when these quantities are released to assembly.

A last comment about the planned order receipt of 20 in period eight. Whether or not this quantity is to be sent automatically to MRP depends on how dependably the system is working. In a mature system, and if the master scheduler is conscientious in reviewing the suggested planned orders and updating the master schedule, it may be possible to allow this automatic transfer of a potential master schedule quantity to drive MRP. The cautious policy would be to insist that only after review and update by the master scheduler would the now master scheduled quantity be exploded through MRP.

The *Available to Promise* (ATP) line is a helpful display for order entry to use in accepting orders and making delivery commitments. It is calculated by all systems in a manner which is different from the Project Available Balance, so as to emphasize the quantities which are truly available for shipment. The ATP is only calculated in the first period, and then only in those periods which have a planned master schedule quantity. The method of calculation is as follows:

- In the first period the ATP is calculated by adding the quantity on hand to any production scheduled in the first period, then subtracting *customer orders* on hand until the next time there is a master schedule quantity. In this example there are 18 units in stock, none are scheduled, and there are 6 units in backlog, resulting in 12 being available to promise.

■ In all subsequent periods where there is a master schedule, the customer order backlog which needs to be shipped before there will be more production will be subtracted from the master schedule quantity. Again, in this example, in period two the master schedule quantity of 20 will have the five units ordered for period two and the two units ordered for period three deducted resulting in a ATP for periods two and three of 13 units. The master schedule quantity of 20 in period four has only one unit committed, so 19 are available to sell. An order entry clerk can easily see that 12 units are ready for instant sale, 13 more are available during periods two and three, and 19 more in periods four and five.

The Available to Promise report in an on-line system is updated continuously as customer orders are booked, so that the current status of availability is always known. If the ATP is not available on-line, then the order entry people must pencil in orders accepted on the report so they do not over commit shipments. The next printed report will bring the report up to date. Requiring customer order entry to refer to the Available to Promise report before committing to any order is a way to give better, more reliable, customer service.

Using a Make-to-Order Planning Basis

At the other end of the spectrum of planning bases is the firm which makes to order, that is, it produces final product only after a firm order is received. In extreme examples of this kind of planning, nothing is purchased or fabricated until a order is in hand. Then material is ordered, parts fabricated, subassemblies built, and finally the complete unit is built and shipped. In most cases the final product is special or unique to the specific order, with similarity but little commonality to other products shipped. Often the cumulative lead time to produce is quite long. Forecasting is difficult because specific items can vary greatly. Yet some forecast of sales must have been done in order that the firm could even be in existence, with its manufacturing capacity and human resources in place, ready to accept any order.

Sometimes companies in this extreme environment feel that they cannot really use master scheduling effectively. Certainly, coping with many, and varying, demands is not their greatest problem. Yet they have as much concern for capacity planning and scheduling reliable deliveries competitively as any other firm. Even here some kind of master scheduling, especially to preview their capacity needs, is useful.

More commonly, many firms that make to order deliver a fairly standard product, perhaps even from a catalog, but do not wish to commit to building the product before an order is received. In many cases these firms will stock certain raw materials and long lead time component parts in order to have them on hand, thereby shortening the lead time from order receipt to delivery, making them more competitive. And in this environment a forecast of hoped-for sales, maybe only by product family or type, is regularly made to aid in planning materials purchases and preparing proper capacity for the expected volume.

Figure 8.7 represents this kind of make-to-order master scheduling. Item H has a forecast which is useful for some planning purposes, but which is not to be used to commit orders to production in advance of customer orders. This kind of master scheduling is used any time that management does not wish in invest in inventory of sub-assemblies or final assemblies, yet wishes to effectively schedule production lots across the planning horizon. In this example the master schedule results in planning for reasonably regular sales with a minimum of finished goods inventory.

In this example of make-to-order scheduling, the Gross Requirements are identical to the backlog of orders, the forecast is not involved. In the first period the Master Scheduled quantity is 20, evidently planned some time ago, which is now a Scheduled Receipt, that is, a released order in production. This 20, added to the four on hand in inventory, results in a Projected Available Balance of 16, which just covers the backlog in periods two and three.

In period four the Gross Requirement of nine has caused an order for 20, based on the fixed lot size rule for 20. This, and the similar order planned for period six, were planned in a prior review period. The Master Scheduler could easily have reduced the suggested order to 17, leaving a balance of zero in period five. But perhaps because 20 is a preferred lot size to run through production and assembly, he/she did not lower the quantity, and the management review of the master schedule has not overridden this decision, resulting in a small inventory of finished goods. Note that these two planned orders are being carried through to MRP in order to cause the required parts and sub-assemblies to be planned.

Figure 8.7 Make-to-Order Plan

Part ___H___
Lead Time _3 Periods_
Lot Size Rule _20 (fixed)_

	Period							
	1	2	3	4	5	6	7	8
Forecast	10	10	10	10	10	10	10	10
Backlog	8	6	10	9	8	12	7	13
Gross Requirement	8	6	10	9	8	12	7	13
Master Production Schedule (MPS)	20			20		20		
Projected Available (PAB) 4	16	10	0	11	3	11	4	11
Net Requirement								9
Planned Order Receipts								20
Scheduled Receipts	20							
To MRP				20		20		20*
Available to Promise (ATP)				3		1		7

* Recommendation to Planner

The ending Projected Available Balance of four, being applied to the Gross Requirement of 13, results in a Net Requirement of nine in period eight. Responding, the computer has suggested another planned order of 20. At this point the system sends a message, usually with a printout of this status, so that the Master Scheduler can decide what should be the planned quantity. The Master Scheduler is familiar with the management policies for this Item H, and would be aware of future orders which would be covered by another order for 20. For instance, he can see that because the Projected Available Balance is not growing, the level of production is consistent with the level of demand. Further, the orders are approximately equaling the forecast. Therefore, in this example, an order for 20 in the eighth period will be added to the Master Schedule.

In order to complete its processing, the computer system will assume that the order for 20 will be entered. Therefore, it calculates that after satisfying the Net Requirement for nine, there will be a Projected Available Balance of 11. Again, whether or not this order is automatically carried through to MRP is a choice to be made based on confidence in how the system is working. The cautious position would be to require the Master Scheduler to actually enter the planned order into the Master Schedule, to be approved by management review before MRP explosion causes production to start.

On the Available to Promise line the entire lot of 20 in period one is committed to orders in periods one, two, and three. The lot of 20 scheduled for period four has orders for nine and eight against it, leaving three available for new and urgent orders which might be received during the next five periods. Also there is one piece of the next lot of 20 not yet sold, while only 13 of the last, newly planned order have been committed with nine available.

In summary, this make-to-order example shows how the schedule calculation uses the sold backlog as the basis for Gross Requirements. Yet the Master Scheduler is able to schedule reasonable and regular production lots which permit production operations to run more smoothly, and provide a very small level of inventory to handle rush orders. Of course, all of this must represent the policy of the management which basically considers itself a make-to-order company.

Using the Greater of Forecast or Orders (Assemble-to-Order) Basis

The two prior examples show the extremes of the planning bases, complete make-to-stock and make-order. In each case we saw how what sources are used to define the Gross Requirements controls the master scheduling of the items. It is usually possible that management could set a specific policy for planning each item where some are on one planning basis and others are planned in the alternate way.

But this is not the limit of the possible ways to define Gross

Requirements. There are many other creative ways to define how we will want to respond to demands, either orders or forecasts. By carefully thinking through what we want to do management can devise other algorithms for calculating Gross Requirements which will accomplish their goals of giving some degree of customer service responsiveness while controlling the timing and quantity of changes fed to the manufacturing operation. Keep in mind that complete, forever accurate, models are not possible. And it is for this reason the master schedule must be created by a competent Master Scheduler and thoroughly reviewed and approved by management.

We will now examine a method which gives a high level of customer service when both forecasts and order backlogs are known. In this example (Figure 8.8) the company regularly books orders for Item J with a four-period delivery lead time, usually to complete a customized assembly from previously assembled major sub-assemblies which have been produced to meet a forecast. Therefore it wants to build final product only to existing orders, not forecast, in the near term, but build to the greater of forecast or known orders in later periods. This gives a higher level of customer service (with resulting slightly higher inventory levels) by planning to cover known orders even if they exceed forecast, while still using the forecast level to drive MRP planning for the future.

In this example a "fence" has been created at the start of the fifth period. Because this company does not expect to receive further new orders during its normal four-week delivery cycle, it has decided that inside this fence it will treat only existing orders as Gross Requirements. In this particular example, existing orders are slightly lower than what was forecasted. Therefore, near term production is geared to this level. Beyond the fence, Gross Requirements will be considered to be the greater of either forecast or orders.

In the first period through the fourth periods the order backlog defines Gross Requirements. The first master scheduled production of 20 is a released order in production and, including the four units in stock, covers demands in periods one and two, with a Projected Available Balance of eight at the end of period two. The next master scheduled production of 20 has also been released which covers periods three and four. These released orders have claimed their component parts from stock and therefore are not carried to MRP for explosion and planning.

Figure 8.8 Assemble-to-Order Plan

Part __J__
Lead Time _4 Periods_
Lot Size Rule _20 (Fixed)_

	Period							
	1	2	3	4	5	6	7	8
Forecast	10	10	10	10	10	10	10	10
Backlog	9	7	11	8	7	14	7	12
Gross Requirement	9	7	11	8	10	14	10	12
Master Production Schedule (MPS)	20		20		20			
Projected Available 4 (PAB)	15	8	17	9	19	5	15	3
Net Requirement							5	
Planned Order Receipts							20	
Scheduled Receipts								
To MRP							20*	
Available to Promise (ATP)	8		1		-1		1	

* Recommendation to Planner

Starting with the fifth period the system will choose either the forecast or booked orders as Gross Requirements, whichever is greater. In periods five and seven the forecast of 10 is considered demand to be covered, while in periods six and eight the larger quantities of the booked orders will be used as demand. There is a master scheduled order already planned for period five, and the system is recommending an addition of an order to the Master Schedule in period seven.

The Master Scheduler can see that the total schedule is slightly over-planned as orders are below forecast in the first four periods (35 orders versus 40 forecast) but that in the next four periods orders equal the forecast, with the possibility of more orders yet to come.

The Available to Promise is interesting. Order entry, working with the Master Scheduler, can see that currently released production orders will leave eight units available for sale (4 on hand plus 20 in production less the nine plus seven *sold* before the next master schedule of 20 equals eight available). Likewise, the next 20 units of production cover the 19 units sold before the next master schedule lot. This next master scheduled lot has been oversold by one unit, which, in this instance, is not a problem. This visibility of commitments makes it easy for Order Entry to respond to new order requests, even if they are asking for less than normal delivery lead time.

Whether or not the suggested master schedule order for 20 in period 7 (and in the future periods extending through the planning horizon) is carried automatically to MRP for explosion and planning of the lower level components, or must be confirmed by the Master Scheduler and management review, is a policy to be determined by the confidence in the system operation. Of course, the order could be automatically carried through, and then cut back by a subsequent review, however, this causes a lot of "busy work" for the MRP computing system.

Summary of Calculating Gross Requirements

These three examples in no way exhaust the possibilities for the kinds of decision rules given to the computer system for planning production. Another common algorithm simply asks that the greater of forecast or sales orders be used as Gross Requirements from the beginning, with no fence. This would tend to cause higher levels of production, but with a higher level of customer service, while essentially planning at the forecast level in the more distant future for which no orders have yet been received.

But they illustrate the idea that the method of calculating Gross Requirements is the way of affecting the suggested master schedule quantities, causing them to reflect the management policy for proper planning basis for each item. The variety of algorithms available varies with the software used. Usually several are offered which cover the range of possibilities. Exact specification to cover a unique company's situation could possibly be programmed. But realistically an approximate algorithm will be sufficient, leaving adjustment in the hands of the Master Scheduler, which ultimately is the only dependable way of handling the infinitely varied real-life situations affecting production planning. Computers don't think and they shouldn't be allowed to automatically run production.

HOW TO USE CUMULATIVE LEAD TIME AND FENCES IN PLANNING

A serious matter in planning your master scheduling system is the effect of lead time on your ability to be responsive to changes in demands. Each firm has its own realistic constraints to the degree with which it can change its course. These constraints need to be understood by all. Then management should recognize that these limits exist and, by policy, effectively require that they be recognized in the planning process.

Lead time is a difficult thing to specify, having great variation, depending on reliability and cooperation of suppliers, levels of raw materials and components regularly stocked, and the production capacity of the manufacturing process. Each of these is unique to a firm, its process, and its marketing policies, and is subject to change over time to meet competitive pressures and financial capabilities.

Disagreements over what are the lead time constraints abound. Manufacturing feels that current capacity does not permit accepting additional work, or knows that sufficient materials cannot be procured by the requested due dates. Marketing, on the other hand, feels that its efforts to increase sales by responding to customer needs should be paramount. And there is no one definitive answer. The problem is: there has to be design tradeoff. If manufacturing is to be productive and efficient it cannot change its plans with every new order. Yet some inefficiency and cost must be accepted or marketing will be strangled in its effort to be competitive. Therefore management is responsible to decide just how this tradeoff is to be made. And the Master Production Schedule is a place where management policy can be effectuated, using the idea of time fences.

Figure 8.9 illustrates the concept of time fences keyed to the components of cumulative lead time. Cumulative lead time can be defined as the total time to manufacture a product through normal processing if no materials or components were yet avail-

able. It is like a "critical path" through the levels of buildup of
a product, adding the lead times for assembly to the longest
fabrication item lead time, and then adding the longest procurement lead time to that. Even if the lead times have not been
excessively loaded up for convenience, this lead time may be
surprisingly long. And if lead times have been "padded" for comfort the cumulative lead time can become ridiculous.

Figure 8.9 Master Production Schedule Time Fences

Horizon →	Planning	Change	Firm	Due Date
	↓	↓	↓	↑

Material Lead Time		Fabrication Lead Time	Assembly Lead Time
Planning Time	Cumulative Lead Time		
Open	Trading Area		Emergency Changes
	Material Availability	Capacity Availability	Only

Manufacturing has an obligation to examine lead times and
assure that they are reasonable, that is, there is a good likelihood
that each component, fabrication, and assembly can reliably be
produced in the stated time. If there is any doubt about this,
manufacturing can expect continual pressure to perform in less
than the stated lead time (and they will often do so as sufficient
pressure leads to furious expediting). Marketing then has an
obligation to honor the realistic lead time, incorporating it into
is sales efforts.

Commonly, marketing cannot be effective if full lead time is
required. Only in strict make-or-order situations is full lead time
common. But what generally happens is that management allows
some level of investment in inventory, such as long lead time
components, or perhaps fabricated parts and sub-assemblies,
above the levels strictly required for scheduled final production.
This reduces or removes these elements of an over-long lead
time. For instance, a long lead gray iron casting would be overstocked so that it would not be an insurmountable limit on a
new sale or an increase in an existing order. Or further, a part

could be partially fabricated in large quantities, as when a machined casting is held awaiting one of several alternative finishes. The Master Scheduler working with all the materials planners would identify these possibilities for shortening the cumulative lead time, and get management approval for stocking in excess of exact need. This planning to reduce overall lead time is a key function of the Master Scheduler, contributing to the competitive capability of the firm's marketing.

A "Firm" lead time fence could be defined by management at the assembly lead time (see Figure 8.9), setting a policy that no changes, or emergency ones only, would be accepted once assembly has started—the schedule is frozen. It is easy to see why this kind of policy has to be made by management or serious infighting will start.

Other fences could be defined at the time fabrication starts, or when materials must be ordered. A "Change" lead time fence could restrict schedule or quantity changes to a certain amount, say 10 percent, assuming that inside this fence capacity is available to produce the new or changed order. Marketing might be allowed to "trade" one order for another during this time frame, based on capacity availability. Then a planning fence could define the period when new orders or changes in quantities are covered by materials inventories, or, again, marketing could substitute one order for another. Further out into the future, the schedule is open for orders or changes in larger amounts.

By defining these fences, for each item in the master schedule or as a blanket general policy, management greatly eases the master scheduling process. How many fences to create, and where they take effect, are not easy decisions to make. But by firmly honoring the fact that there are limits to the changeability of production, the teamwork which arises from good planning and the efficiency gained from smooth production will pay off in less conflict and more reliable customer service.

HOW TO USE ROUGH-CUT CAPACITY PLANNING WITH LOAD PROFILES

To be effective a master schedule has to be a reasonable and achievable plan. An overloaded master schedule, for which sufficient and timely capacity does not exist, *can* be exploded through MRP, and too often is! The result is a large volume of detailed shop and purchase orders carrying due dates which are not credible to the production and purchasing departments, causing confusion and leading to missed customer schedules, energetic expediting, and poor morale. The plans don't work.

Before exploding the schedule a Rough Cut test of capacity availability must be made. This capacity test is called Rough Cut Capacity Planning because it is just that. Three decimal place accuracy is not required. What is demanded is only that we be sure that for certain, critical, work centers sufficient capacity is roughly available to work the plan.

The tool for doing this is the Load Profile. Basically, for each item in the Master Schedule we define what demands (load) a unit of the item places on any work center which has limited, or perhaps, inflexible capacity. As we will see in the following example, there are other volume or capacity numbers that are also useful to management.

Figure 8.10 shows the data base of load information about a master scheduled item. In this example it is a kitchen blender. We have decided that there are three critical resource areas for our manufacturing: Final Assembly, Subassembly, and the Machine Shop. We are also interested in the volume of the copper wire, a commodity we use in large volume, and the dollar volume of our costs of manufacture as well as the approximate revenue our production will generate.

Figure 8.10 Detail of Unit Load Requirements

	Critical Resource Units to be Loaded					
Blender	Assembly Labor (Hours)	Subassy. Labor (Hours)	Machine Shop Labor (Hours)	Copper Wire (Pounds)	Cost of Goods ($)	Revenue ($)
Final Assy	.10				11.25	15.80
Motor Assy		.20	.40	.81		
Switch		.15				
Base Assy		.10	.20			
Total	.10	.45	.60	.81	11.25	15.80

We examine each part of the product, calculating the standard hours of labor required to fabricate and build each element as well as the assembly time consumed. These standards may be built up from the engineered labor standards for each part, or, if these are not available, from historical records of manufacture, or even from estimates. If history or estimates are used the numbers can be refined by calculating the total loads for the last several months' master schedules and comparing these to the actual labor hours used in these prior periods and then re-estimating so that the load figures are more realistic. The cost of goods comes from the costing system, and the revenue from an average selling price of the item.

A unit load profile such as this is prepared for each item in our master schedule. In Figure 8.11 we have summarized the total unit load required to produce each of our products: the blender, the food processor, and the hand mixer. Having prepared our database we are ready to assess the capacity requirements of our Master Production Schedule.

Figure 8.11 Unit Load Profiles

Resources	Capacity Requirements per Unit		
	Blender	Food Processor	Hand Mixer
Final Assembly (Hours)	.10	.15	.15
Subassembly (Hours)	.45	.40	.30
Machine Shop (Hours)	.60	.50	.65
Copper Wire (Pounds)	.61	.68	.51
Cost of Goods ($)	11.25	18.00	13.00
Revenue ($)	15.80	26.50	17.50

Having prepared our trial master schedule, we multiply the quantities of each product in each period by the critical resource load values in our data base. These extended values are then summarized into the Rough Cut Capacity Load report as shown in Figure 8.12. The 500 blenders, 300 food processors, and 1,000 hand mixers will require 245 hours of assembly time, 645 hours in the subassembly department, and 1,100 hours of shop time during the first period, and so on across the planning horizon.

The master scheduler then compares the results with the planned capacity for each area to verify the plan is workable.

Of interest is the amount of fluctuation in the loads. Does the 20-hour variation from 228 hours of assembly required in period three to 248 hours in period five represent a problem? Can period five be covered with a little overtime? Or should a small part of the fifth period's schedule be pulled forward to periods two and three to level the load? And if this is done, will materials be available in time to do this? If part of the schedule is pushed out to period six, will we have sufficient production to cover the sales orders for period five? These are the questions which the Master Scheduler will research and answer.

Figure 8.12   Rough-Cut Capacity Load Report

Master Production Schedule						
	Units by Time Period					
	1	2	3	4	5	6
Blenders	500	600	550	400	600	550
Food Processors	300	250	300	325	300	250
Hand Mixers	1000	900	850	1025	950	900
Rough-Cut Capacity Load						
Resource	Total Load Requirements by Period					
Final Assembly (Hours)	245	233	228	243	248	228
Subassembly (Hours)	645	640	623	618	675	618
Machine Shop (Hours)	1100	1070	1033	1070	1128	1040
Copper Wire (Pounds)	1019	995	974	988	1055	965
Cost of Goods Sold ($)	24,025	22,950	22,638	23,675	24,500	22,388
Revenue ($)	33,350	31,855	51,515	32,870	34,055	31,065

Knowing the rate of use of the copper wire over the planning horizon gives purchasing the information to negotiate better long term delivery and pricing. And the cost of goods figures are useful for calculating working capital needs, while the revenue can be compared to the business plan and production plan to verify that the current master schedule is in synch with these plans, carrying out the wishes of management in meeting the objectives of the company.

This example is quite simple, to show the flow of the work. For small master schedules it would be possible to prepare a spreadsheet program on a personal computer which would easily carry out this procedure. For larger master schedules, the greater power of master scheduling software is required.

This process is called Rough Cut because we are dealing with larger blocks of time (such as weekly periods), and no allowances are being made for those parts already in stock or somewhere in process and which have already consumed their required capacity. There is an assumption that the amount of already completed work will be offset at the end of the horizon by having some other, similar work done for future production.

Modern master scheduling software permits offsetting the elements of a load profile to reflect the fact that fabrication precedes subassembly which precedes final assembly, and so on, thereby putting the load more closely to the period when it will actually occur. This is important if you experience large shifts in product demands over the planning horizon.

Rough Cut Capacity Planning is a powerful tool in helping the Master Scheduler see that the master schedule is truly achievable. The capacity requirements must be within the bounds of the realistic, demonstrated capacities of the factory. The effort of doing it is amply rewarded by the better planning which results.

DEFINING THE ROLE OF THE MASTER SCHEDULER[1]

We have covered the mechanics of master production scheduling. What remains is to discuss how we bring it to life. And the essential ingredient has to be the master scheduler herself or himself. The master schedule is the final operations planning tool, all that follows is mere execution. A manager, or managerial-thinking person, must be in charge of this planning. The

---

[1]This discussion is derived from the paper, "Master Schedulers Are Made—Not Born" by Richard Kust, given at the 1984 International Conference of the American Production and Inventory Control Society, published as Readings in Management and Personal Development, pp. 200–204.

failure to understand the duties of the job, and the requirements, the skills and the background of this top operations planner, leads to a poor definition of the job, its position in the organization, and subsequently to poor selection of the person who should be responsible for making it work.

What should we look for in a master scheduler? What personal qualities are needed? The master scheduler should be a professional, a business manager, a manager perhaps of things more than people, but nevertheless a manager. The master scheduler makes plans, leads in their execution, and monitors results—certainly the basic essence of what we call management. This will become clear as we look at the multi faceted role which the master scheduler plays in effective operations planning. The master scheduler has a measure of authority—even power—that comes from possessing information.

Effective master scheduling occurs at the focal point of the information flows of several major systems (see Figure 8.13). It is the position which connects these systems, by creating a path whereby information is allowed to flow between the major functional areas. The information flows through the master scheduler. Without the master schedule function the flow and interchange of information between these groups is impeded, much as if there were static and electrical resistance in a circuit. And this leads to the common failings of poor team play which characterize badly run manufacturing organizations.

The master scheduler is the receiver of all this information, absorbing it and redirecting it. And using the tools we have described before, the scheduler makes the "game plan" which balances and coordinates these diverse components of the total business, carrying through the management policy.

Seen in this light the role of the master scheduler becomes more clear. The master production schedule does not spring fully grown in the mind of the master scheduler, but results from the skillful use of judgement in using this information flow. Therefore the master scheduler will possess the abilities to deal with this volume of information, and especially, to deal with the people who both create it and use it. Whatever be his or her place in the organization chart, the master scheduler must be a generalist, understanding of the workings of the entire organization.

How the Master Scheduler Interfaces with Major Systems

We can have a better appreciation for the role of the master scheduler by examining how the master scheduler interfaces with these major systems. The basic problem is the fact that the ordinary goals of each functional area, marketing, manufacturing, finance, etc., are often in conflict. Marketing has a deeply felt need to provide good customer service. The obvious way to accomplish this is with sufficient levels of finished goods in inventory, plus considerable flexibility in scheduling. But the higher inventory levels often upset the plans of finance, whose own goal is to minimize investment and obtain a greater rate of return on the capital employed.

Figure 8.13 The Focal Point of the Master Scheduler

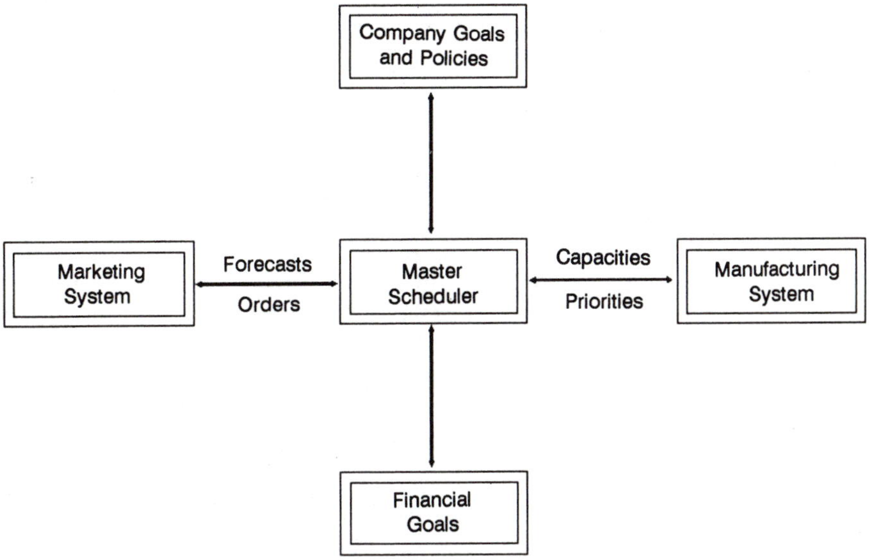

And, while flexibility in responding to customer demands is also a worthwhile goal, it runs counter to the goals of manufacturing. Manufacturing usually pursues a goal of reducing unit production costs to the lowest possible level, thereby contributing to profitability. Ordinarily this is pursued by using larger and faster machinery, and planning longer, and steady, production runs to overcome the costs of set up. Of course, this results in larger inventories, both of components and work-in-process, as well as finished goods.

Again, conflicts are apparent, and the longer production runs tie up more of the capital finance is trying to conserve. Further, they make it more difficult to respond to changes desired by marketing. Flexibility in manufacturing has its costs, and must be carefully planned for in the design of the product, the choice of the production process, and on the methods for scheduling and controlling work. There are limits to the amount of change a production system can accept, as we saw in our discussion of fences. Large lot sizes, very efficient from manufacturing's point of view, are a major restriction on changing schedules. In Just-in-Time systems where lot sizes are minimized, thereby reducing work-in-process inventories, shortening throughput time and increasing flexibility for minor changes, the overall production volume must be held steady. Production always wants stable schedules.

What is required is a design tradeoff. The normal goals of each of the major areas cannot all be maximized. If the business is to work as a team each area must modify its goals for the benefit of the whole. Just as the highly specialized players on a football team blend their efforts to carry out the game plan, working to the specific plays called, the successful company must have its game plan (business plan and production plan), and communicate it in detail to the team members for execution through master scheduling and MRP.

The key to making this tradeoff work is the master scheduler. As the focal point for information from the major functional areas the master scheduler is able to make the game plan for production operations which balances the goals of each area, carrying out management's policies, while keeping everyone informed of what they must do to accomplish the plan. This is the ultimate purpose of master scheduling: to permit the entire organization to work as a team. The master scheduler's role is one of continuous liaison with the entire organization, communicating the plan, striving for balance.

Let's look at a few examples of the kinds of interfacing the master scheduler does. This will help define what kind of person the master scheduler should be.

Interfacing with Marketing

Forecasts, by their nature, are usually wrong at any point in time, and we plan safety stocks to handle upside errors in demands. The master scheduler must be a continuous monitor of forecasts, alert to the possibilities that demands are coming in consistently over or under the forecast. If the master schedule is unequal to the level of customer orders, the master scheduler must initiate review of the forecast, and to re-plan production schedules to cover customer needs. The master scheduler must have a clear understanding of the forecast techniques used, and be able to communicate with marketing about their correction. Of course, manufacturing must be consulted about the effect of increased, or reduced, schedules.

Another major interface with marketing is the job of giving promise dates for delivery of customer orders. The available to promise quantities are shown on the master schedule report. But the problem occurs when quantities are insufficient to cover all orders. While examining every possibility for meeting customer demands, working with planning, purchasing, and manufacturing, the master scheduler must recognize the realities of production and be able to say no—cannot do. Marketing must then give their final priorities for shipping final product, and respect the master schedule by not insisting on the impossible. Only by having credibility with marketing can this problem be handled effectively.

When distribution is a large part of the firm's business, the additional challenges to meet demands from multiple stocking locations adds to the problem. The master scheduler will need to interface with marketing as to how to allocate product to the best locations to maximize good, but not perfect, customer service.

Interfacing with Engineering

The master scheduler interfaces with engineering in those businesses which modify or engineer their product to customer specifications. The capacity of engineering to produce the new bills of materials, drawings, and procedures, is key to the proper scheduling of smooth production. This interface may start with the pre-release of certain long-lead items, but has to continue until all engineering information is ready in a timely manner.

Interfacing with Accounting and Finance

A regular interface with accounting is caused by the policies for granting credit approval before shipment. Policies are demanded here: shall we schedule production of invoiceable items only? How much time is to be allowed for moving an order from credit hold back onto the schedule? And what is the effect of the addition or removal of large orders on materials availability or manufacturing capacity? What alternate orders can be shifted to accommodate the inclusion of newly released orders, or the removal of work load from the production floor.

Another major interface with accounting and finance is the impact of inventory caused by any plan to level production through periods of slow demand. Leveling production greatly benefits manufacturing. The master scheduler is in the position of having the forecasts and the production schedules. He or she can make the plans but finance has to approve the level of funds to cover the buildup. The concurrence of the whole business team should be obtained for such a plan.

Interfacing with Manufacturing

Of course, manufacturing must agree to build the master schedule, and the issues are ones of materials availability and proper capacity. If the hierarchy of planning has been followed the overall capacity will have been balanced to the production plan through Resource Requirements Planning. What remains is to verify that the master schedule conforms to the production plan, exactly. Rough-cut Capacity Planning applied to the master schedule verifies that critical resources will be available when needed. The master scheduler, working with manufacturing management, must design and oversee the use of the load profiles used in this process. Whether prepared from process engineering standards, or knowledgeable estimates of key managers, the credibility of the capacity planning, and of the master scheduler, is necessary to making effective schedules.

Another involvement of the master scheduler in manufacturing is the preparation of the Final Assembly Schedule. In those firms where master scheduling is done at the modular, or sub-assembly level, this can be difficult. It is important that the Final Assembly Schedule be prepared with the master schedule in view. The master scheduler will prepare the schedule from the sales orders scheduled after examining carefully the availability of the component modules and necessary critical final assembly capacities, such as the final quality testing of the product. Final assembly must be scheduled with work that is producible. Therefore, the master scheduler must prepare the Final Assembly Schedule as well as the master schedule.

Interfacing with Production Planning and Inventory Control

Although scheduling is done from the top down, production proceeds from the bottom up. As production proceeds from the lowest level fabrication to higher assembly, things can go wrong. The intricate network of supporting schedules of the dependent demands can be upset by any single item failing to be done on time. The planners and schedulers will be monitoring performance and will become aware of deficiencies—late deliveries, rework, scrap, or loss of production capacity. They will bring these to the attention of the master scheduler. He must verify they have been thorough in their attempts to regain missed schedules by compressing lead times, using alternate materials or processes, until the scope of the problem is clear. In some cases, the master schedule is impacted, and it must be changed, with alternate work scheduled to replace the lost production.

If production planning and master scheduling has been well carried out there are usually sufficient capacity and material to make the solution manageable. But if lead time fences have been generally ignored, or capacity plans not made and adhered to, the problems will be many and insurmountable.

If the master schedule must be changed, the master must interface with marketing and manufacturing to communicate the scope of the problem. Marketing will interface with the customer and manufacturing will respond to the new priorities communicated through MRP. The master scheduler must have the strength and skill to make the master schedule work.

Defining the Skills and Background of the Master Scheduler

The following is a review of the most important qualities to be desired in a master scheduler. Everyone cannot possess a full measure of every skill desired. And the need for each skill varies greatly with the business and planning environment. But these descriptions will help in identifying the potential for success of the person who would be a master scheduler.

Intelligence

This difficult to define quality underlies all the rest. Master scheduling is a thinking process, a problem solving and decision-making process, requiring above average intelligence. It is not simply a technique which once learned can just be repeated over and over again by filling in the blanks of some form. The breadth and volume of information processed in the mind of the master scheduler requires good learning and thinking ability. To gather the facts, and "reading between the lines" when there is not time to gather every relevant piece of information, and then to process this information with the knowledge of company goals and policies provided as direction by the top management of a company, requires considerable analytical skill. The ability to look forward and foresee the effect of any particular decision is crucial.

The master scheduler is an everyday problem solver. The various members of the team look to scheduler for quick decisions. The problems are large, or trivial, but the decisions must be consistent to the company's objectives. Quick wittedness is an asset. Sometimes the problem is a major change in marketing policy, or the introduction of a new product line, or a corrective action to the inevitable errors in a forecast. Perhaps the problem is a loss of needed components through scrap or delay, or the sudden loss of capacity in a critical work center. The master scheduler will assess the extent of the problem, and lead in finding a reasonable, workable, solution.

Deeper analytical skills will used in improving forecasting methods, or planning how to respond to the irregular flow of customer orders. Product families must be arranged for production planning which may be different from the groupings used by marketing in their planning. The master scheduler will realign the items into aggregates which make similar demands on manufacturing capacity. For instance, cold pills and aspirin in their many packaging forms may be two product lines for marketing, but whether they are offered as tablets or liquids makes a great deal of difference to capacity planning. The master scheduler has to understand both the marketing aspects and the manufacturing processes before good judgement can be applied.

Education

It is helpful if the master scheduler is educated in several areas. Knowledge of accounting principles will help in understanding the flow of cost information, as well as the calculation of manufacturing profitability. A knowledge of marketing is important to understand the goals and pressures for customer service and distribution. This general business knowledge prepares the scheduler to understand the goals of top management which will guide daily decision making.

In the area of manufacturing the master scheduler must have solid education in how MRP works and the function of the master schedule in the hierarchy of operations planning. The production plan, the master schedule, MRP, and their concomitant capacity planning procedures must be thoroughly understood.

The master scheduler's education should include the knowledge of the need for, and proper level of, safety stocks, and where they should be placed. The master scheduler, as top planner, will lead others in the use of all the techniques for inventory control for independent demand. He or she will understand how to use bills of materials effectively for planning purposes. The master scheduler will assess cumulative lead times, and how to plan for long lead items so that there can a greater level of flexibility in operations schedules. In summary, the education of the master scheduler in manufacturing systems will be extensive.

Knowledge

Beyond understanding of manufacturing systems, the master scheduler must have intimate knowledge of the systems and processes of his or her own company. The planning basis must be understood, whether make-to-stock, make-to-order, assemble-to-order, or any mixture of these.

Most important is the master scheduler's thorough knowledge of the company's products, their bill of material structure, and all the steps in the process of manufacture. Whether it is marketing requesting an order in less than normal lead time, or a planner fighting a problem of a delayed component, knowing what makes up the full chain of events in the creation of a product is an absolute prerequisite to applying judgment to finding a useful solution. The range of possibilities for recovery of missed schedule, or the degree of flexibility towards handling a new and important order, can only be known to the master scheduler who really understands the production capabilities. It is not possible for an outsider to step in and make credible decisions in the master schedule.

Experience

The knowledge described above usually means that the master scheduler has spent several years in planning or manufacturing in a company. The principles learned in formal study of business systems, and relevant training in MRP, master scheduling, and Just-in-Time, will be honed into usable sharpness by experience in applying them. Considerable experience in material planning and scheduling, purchasing, shop floor control, and order processing is the norm. It is helpful if these experiences have been in the company for which he is to master schedule. Extensive experience in state-of-the-art electronics assembly is not of much value in a high volume metal fabrication shop. And the pressure for quick decisions places a premium on experience in using the information available in a modern, computer-based MRP system.

The amount of experience required is extremely variable, having a lot to do with the quality of the experience and the intelligence and resourcefulness of the master scheduler in learning from this experience.

Communication Skills

The position of the master scheduler at the interface of the major functional parts of the business, balancing their conflicting goals, requires a best possible skills in communication. This includes listening as well as speaking and writing. Acting as a mediator, looking for a balanced solution, requires a high degree of persuasiveness. He or she must have marketing understand the reason and benefit of honoring time fences. At the same time, manufacturing must understand the occasional need to respond to a crisis in order to meet legitimate urgencies. These are not easy points to get across, especially if the atmosphere has been combative.

With good communication skills the master scheduler can credibly present solutions based on broad understanding, user inputs, and judgment. Experience, and good past performance contribute a great deal to the scheduler's communications. In interfacing with management the master scheduler will meet with managers who have good communication skills, and they expect effective communication in others.

Pressures

If the master schedule is working well, and the firm is generally successful, pressure on the master scheduler will not be too great. But if the company is moving out of a prior mode of poor planning, continual firefighting, and combative attitudes, trying to build a healthy master schedule is a difficult job. There are much too many problems to solve, all at once, and not by removing symptoms, but rooting out the causes.

The master scheduler, working in the real world of dollars and cents, must bear up under pressure. The bright side of this is that success in master scheduling brings a degree of relief. He or she must successfully avoid "overloading" the front end of the master schedule with backlog. He or she must be able to tell the truth to marketing and customers about the reality of delivery (no significant negative available-to-promise!). An if the master scheduler can achieve a measure of stability to the schedules which permits planners to really schedule work through MRP, the gains in productivity will serve to reduce the pressures under which the master scheduler and everyone else in manufacturing must work.

CONCLUSION

Master scheduling has great power to affect the levels of inventory, the quality of customer service, and ultimately, the competitive productivity which assures business success.

The computer techniques for managing the data of order backlogs, forecasts, and the production orders which will cover them are readily available. But the computer cannot think, at least not well enough to manage the course of a business.

- To make the system work, everyone must understand the power the constraints residing in the master schedule.

- Marketing management, manufacturing management, and top management must understand what is required to get the benefits of master scheduling; they must fully support the company-wide goals and objectives.

- Master scheduling is a process, led by the master scheduler; it is not a technique to be automatically applied.

- Master scheduling is the major process for communicating about problems and their solutions, so that the whole team, from management to the machine operator is working together on the right things.

- The master scheduler is leader, interfacing with marketing management, manufacturing management, finance, engineering, and top management.

- The master scheduler brings the major players together and insists that they agree on the plan of action.

- Master scheduling helps a business avoid wallowing along in the "order launch and expedite" mode, struggling to get full sets of parts to make shipments, yet living with bloated inventories.

- Continual "end-of-the-month cramps" destroys productivity, customer service, and the morale of everybody in manufacturing.

■ Whether operating in MRP or Just-in-Time, all the parts and systems have to work; the master production schedule is the required technique to have them work together.

9

MANAGING YOUR INVENTORY INVESTMENT

Inventories, at all levels, are a very large item on your balance sheet. For some companies inventory is the largest single item, while frequently it is the second largest. Helping you minimize your inventory levels is one of the major reasons for having an MRP II-JIT system. But beside the financial aspect, there are other dramatic advantages to managing your inventories skillfully.

HOW ZERO INVENTORY IMPROVES PERFORMANCE

Intuition often suggests that large inventories are necessary to achieve efficiency and customer service. To the contrary, starting in the 1970s and beyond, it has become clear that bloated inventory usually goes with poor efficiency, constant stock outs, and customer service in the 60 percent range. The reason is that the old, ineffective techniques cause us to be overstocked on items we don't need and out of stock on the items we do need. With MRP II and especially as enhanced with JIT ideas, we now know that inventory just masks problems. And by removing inventory you can actually improve performance.

How Zero Inventory Increases Your Inventory Turns

Companies that have not implemented a dynamic inventory reduction program often have inventory turns in the 2.0–2.5 range. Other companies that have embraced JIT philosophies, including zero inventories, seldom do poorer that six turns, and often get into the double digits. You should realize that every time you double your turns, you cut inventory in half.

How Zero Inventory Helps You Bring New Products and Enhancements to Market Faster

Time compression is becoming a competitive tool, on a par with total quality. Very low inventories help you to bring new products and enhancements to the market faster. If you have large purchased, work in process, semi-finished, and finished goods inventory on hand, you have to wait a long time for this pipeline to clear itself of the old things before a new product will come off the production line ready for your customers. The alternative to waiting is to accept having an excess and obsolete inventory write-down.

Another zero inventory principle that helps get innovations to the market faster, is to develop close relations with your suppliers, who themselves have achieved shorter leadtimes. This will help you get your new purchased items quickly. When you need a new part or a change to an existing one, you supplier can act in days instead of weeks or months.

If your manufacturing cycle is just a day or two, and your suppliers are responsive, you should be able to have an enhanced product ready to ship in a week.

If your carry finished goods, you will want to sell off current stock. Good forecasting and Distribution Requirements Planning should allow you to keep a bare minimum of finished goods. This will shorten the delay time for this pipeline to clear.

How Zero Inventory Sharply Lowers Your Excess and Obsolete

If you haven't bought it yet, you can't get stuck with it as obsolete. Engineering changes are a fact of manufacturing life, and coordinating a use-up situation with many parts involved will almost always leave you with leftovers. Whereas, if you are running very low on inventories, the coordination is much easier, and you reduce your exposure to large pools of excesses after effectivity date.

How Zero Inventory Reduces Clutter and Confusion

I once visited a potential client, a small manufacturer. They believed that because they were small, they were forced to buy lot sizes that lasted them months. At the time of my visit, the stock room was jam packed, to the point that it was difficult to get around. Worse yet, in the factory, inventory was stored under workbenches and above workbenches in makeshift shelves and racks. They weren't able to put these lots near where they were to be used, and they had no effective stock locator system. Fortunately, they were small enough so one or two expediters could usually find what they needed.

Once in a while you will see several semi-trailers parked near a receiving dock. Whenever I see this, I imagine the company renting the trailers as temporary storage for their bloated inventories.

How Zero Inventory Reduces Administration

This advantage is not widely recognized. If you can get close to zero inventories, especially if you store items on the floor next to their first point of use, you can close some stockrooms. This reduces your administrative storeroom staff, plus many of your material handlers.

If you install receiving docks strategically around the plant, you can have the supplier's truck driver deliver the goods to the line, and curtail your traditional receiving docks.

In this environment, you will have substantially fewer computer terminals, and perhaps even simpler computer systems.

Cycle counting and inventory reconciliations are drastically reduced or eliminated, and you take at least one day out of lead time.

HOW TO MINIMIZE PURCHASED, WORK IN PROCESS, SEMI-FINISHED, AND FINISHED GOODS INVENTORY

In this context we are dealing with the physical presence of inventory, as opposed to the bookkeeping definition. If you expense an item as it is received, it goes off the books. But the items are physically present and represent value, even if your accounting books don't show it.

How to Minimize Purchased Inventory

The best way to minimize purchased inventory is to develop blanket, long term orders, and release incrementally, based on your MRP II-generated schedules. The goal is to have daily deliveries. You earn the privilege of having daily deliveries from selected suppliers, by developing close relations with them, and by having stable schedules, particularly in the short term.

Daily releases by Electronic Data Interchange (EDI) is becoming more widely used, and will be the norm in a few years. This speeds the process still more.

If daily deliveries are not possible, you should choose the smallest economically-feasible lot size. In your MRP II-based system, you may have several lot sizing formulas available to you. If you have a choice of rules, try to apply the one that recognizes MRP II's future requirements, and plans purchase increments that will leave no remainders. This will protect you from remainders of lot sizes, which is particularly important if you have intermittent production and/or seasonality.

How to Minimize Work in Process Inventory

The four main factors of work in process are move, queue, setup, and run. Most discussion of these factors concentrates on lead time reduction and schedule improvement. Often escaping notice is that every throughput time reduction gives you an equivalent inventory reduction. Each factor can be a source for reduction.

Move time is related to how your factory is laid out. Conventional, job shop style factories usually have long and complex move patterns, governed by the routes for the items you produce.

Group technology flow production, in addition to many other merits, eliminates many moves.

Relocating stock rooms closer to the point of use also will reduce move time, and JIT philosophies suggest that you can stock your inventory at the point of use, which eliminates many moves.

Queue time is the largest of these four factors. Queue is work, already started into work in process, standing idle at the entrance to a work center, waiting to be worked on. In a conventional job shop layout, queue time often is 80 to 90 percent of total work in process time. Queues have been instituted over the years to mask problems. Some of the common problems we hear about are quality defects from previous work centers or suppliers, unreliable schedules, parts shortages, unplanned machine down time, and waiting for common setups.

You can remove considerable inventory by analyzing the reasons that cause queues and gradually eliminate them. When the causes are removed, the corresponding queues can be reduced.

You can analyze how much queue is actually needed at a work center by a simple technique: For a work center, select a representative time span, one month for example. Next measure the queue each day. At the end of the month, subtract the lowest queue from the highest one. That is how much queue is really needed at that work center during the month. Figure 9.1 illustrates an example:

Figure 9.1 Daily Queues in Hours

20	25	15	10
15	20	25	30
25	20	10	10
15	20	10	25
30	35	30	30
15			

The highest reading is 35, the lowest is 10. The difference is 25, which is the correct queue for this work center.

Remember, however, that this queue size is valid only until you make your next improvement.

There is a worker motivation and training aspect to queue reduction. Historically, shrinking queues have been a sign to workers of an impending layoff. As a result, when queues go down workers slow down. This means that to have effective queue reduction, you must get the workers on your side, by promising no layoffs as a result of this project.

How to Minimize Semi-Finished Inventory

Semi-finished inventory are items you have manufactured to the piece-part or sub-assembly stage; not yet at a finished goods level. Semi-finished inventory is governed directly by the levels in your bills of material.

The first way to reduce this class of inventory is to simplify your bills of material. Under MRP II control, every bill of material level is a stocking level, represented by an item number. MRP II will plan shop orders for these items. At the completion of the shop order, the item goes into stock so MRP II can issue it later to the next higher assembly. Therefore, every time you can take a level out of your bill of material, you eliminate that item from stock. Bills with few levels are called shallow, and those with many are called deep. Shallow bills, 2 or 3 levels deep, is a powerful JIT technique.

If your bills have more then five or six levels, you probably have an error in your bill structuring procedures. If you routinely have more than six levels, you probably are making a level break after each operation, usually as a result of a cost accounting requirement. This is wrong, and should be corrected.

Another way to reduce semi-finished goods inventory is to reduce lot sizes. We cover lot sizes later in this chapter. The best lot size is one lot per day, also called lot-for-lot. With this rule, you use up tomorrow what you make today, and semi-finished goods inventory falls to zero for items managed by this lot sizing rule. For items that don't yet qualify for Lot for Lot, daily production, choose a rule based on MRP II's planned requirements; one that does not leave remainders.

Scrap, rejects, material in review, and other categories of non-usable inventory frequently are carried on the books as good inventory and should be disposed of promptly.

How to Reduce Finished Goods Inventory

These comments apply only if you are a make to stock company.

The best way to reduce finished goods inventory is to ship off the line, directly to the customer, without ever stopping to be stored. You can do this if you can simplify your bills of material, and shorten your manufacturing throughput time sufficiently.

Even if you can't reduce your throughput time enough to match your advertised lead times, the faster your factory, the less finished goods you need. If you can replenish your stocks in a week instead of a month, your inventory falls from an average of ½ month to ½ week. Moreover, the resulting shorter forecasting horizon automatically makes the forecast more accurate.

Smaller lot sizes also contribute to less finished goods inventory. For example if you reduce your lot size on an item from 1,200 to 500, your average inventory for this item falls from 600 to 250.

Using modular bills, as described in Chapter 3, also can eliminate large quantities of finished goods. Using modular bills, you build sub-assemblies to the level just below final assemblies and store them ready for final assembly. When a customer order arrives, the appropriate modules are drawn from stock, assembled, and shipped, often the same day or the next day. This technique represents an ideal application for a kanban (pull) system. The large inventory saving comes because there are far fewer modules than there are end item possibilities,

HOW TO CRAFT THE RIGHT LOCATION CONTROL TECHNIQUES

Location control is a method for governing how and where you store your inventories. There are four main location categories. The first three deal with closed stockrooms. They are Random, Fixed, and Controlled. The fourth location control method is open floor stock. In all cases a computerized inventory record keeping system is needed.

Using Random Location Control

Random location control is the loosest of the three stockroom techniques. With this control level, the material handler stores the incoming material any place where space is available. The data entry clerk records the location address and the quantity into the inventory records. Bar code reading laser guns and radio frequency (RF) transmitters are starting to be used directly by material handlers to record transactions as they occur. This eliminates the separate clerical keying step, and speeds the process by several hours. If you have a lot tracing system in force, the lot number also gets entered.

Under random control, the location could be anywhere, and the computer does not check to see if the location is an authorized one. You could designate the employee parking lot.

Random is the easiest to use, and could be useful for some of your inventory. Its advantage is that this control level allows you to make the most intensive use of your spaces, because anything can be stored anywhere. The disadvantage, is that a material handler can invent a location designation, which could make it hard to find for retrieval.

Using Fixed Location Control

Fixed is at the other end of the spectrum. With this control level, the material handler must put the incoming inventory in a location that has already been specifically designated for that item in the computer system. An item is allowed to have multiple fixed locations.

When a transaction is entered into the system, it checks to see that the incoming location is authorized for that item. Otherwise an error message is sent, and a correction is needed.

Fixed is very useful or even an absolute requirement for some items. Inventory that must be kept frozen, for example, must be put in a freezer. Some companies have controlled substances or precious metals that must be kept in a safe. Toxic and flammable inventory must be kept in special spaces. Although the most stringent, fixed location control is very important for many companies.

I had a client who makes biological cultures, mainly for the pharmaceutical industry. They have a number of products that must to be kept at 0°F. For this they have several large walk-in freezers. In addition, they have a few items that require a storage ambient of –70°F. The accommodate this by having a special, –70°F freezer located inside one of their 0°F walk-in freezers.

This is the best example of the need for fixed location control I have yet seen.

Using Controlled Location Control

Controlled is a compromise between random and fixed. Under this designation, inventory can be put away in any location that has previously been identified as an authorized stocking location. This prevents the material handler from unnecessarily creating new locations, or from using space not intended for inventory.

Using Open Floor Stock Location Control

Open floor stock is gaining in popularity. This control technique has the inventory stored next to the using work center instead of the traditional enclosed stockroom. The workers help themselves as needed according to the day's production schedules. In this environment, a standard item, used in many places, could be stored in many places. Although open floor stock and automatic issuing are often paired, this is not a requirement. You can have open floor stock tied to manual issue. Supporting manual issue from floor stock, however, takes a good bit of discipline and training.

Open floor stock with automatic issue is a favorite JIT practice. Once confined to low-cost items, automatic issue now is being used more widely for items of substantial value.

HOW TO ACHIEVE 95 PERCENT INVENTORY ACCURACY WITH CYCLE COUNTING

One of the few unforgiving requirements of MRP II has to do with inventory accuracy. The rule is that to work effectively, MRP II needs 95 percent stock status accuracy. And you must keep this level constant during the year.

The 95 percent level is harder to achieve than you might at first believe. If an item should have 100 in stock, and you count 95, you do not have 95 percent accuracy. That item has zero accuracy. The rule is that you have 95 percent accuracy when you count 100 different items, and find 95 of them absolutely accurate, within the tolerance you have for your counting scales.

Cycle counting is the practice of counting a few items every day. Your program must be organized such that everything is counted at least once a year, with some items counted oftener.

A correct cycle counting program consists of two parts, error correction, and cause elimination.

The first step is to conduct a daily or weekly cycle count of selected items. After each count is taken, you compare it to the book record on the computer and make corrections as needed.

The second step, error elimination, is the more important of the two. This requires that you put the cycle counting errors into categories for analysis. Where are the errors coming from? Why are they being made? Then you pick the worst causes, and take action to eliminate them. You may have a procedural problem. You may have a training problem. You may need better equipment. This is a constant improvement technique.

How to Select What to Count

Your computerized system should have features that automatically create a cycle counting list each day or week, based on the selection rules you designate. Since you probably have multiple stocking locations, you need a cycle counting list organized by location, and counts are reconciled location by location.

The favorite selection rule is to use an ABC analysis. Appendix IV shows how to do an ABC analysis. The ABC principle suggests that you count more important, expensive or fast-moving items, more often than cheap, or low-volume ones. Most cycle counting programs have A-items counted fairly often, even monthly. B-items are usually counted two to four times a year, and C-items once or twice. If you have a modern MRP II system, it probably has the ability to automatically print daily cycle count lists, according to the rules you have designated.

There are several other techniques that you can use to augment the basic ABC interval described above.

When inventory in a location falls to zero, that is a good time to count, since it is very easy to do so. The counting clerk just needs to confirm that the location is empty.

Another good flag for a cycle count is negative stock status. Since it is impossible to really have a negative quantity, this is an error condition, deserving a cycle count.

Some companies do a cycle count on items scheduled to be received the next day. The idea here, is that the quantities are at their lowest at this time and easier to count. This also has the effect of counting more frequently those items that have the most activity. This technique, however, is not very useful for those items having very frequent deliveries.

I had one client who cycle counted every thing that had a transaction the day before. The theory was that if an item had no transaction, the balance couldn't have gone wrong. They had very low traffic, which made this a very useful method for them.

Another good way to dramatically reduce the effort needed for cycle counting, and keep accuracy high, is not to break bulk in the stockroom. You can ask your vendors to ship items to you in a package you can issue directly to the line. If a carton has, say, 1000 screws in it, you can put it into storage as 1000 and issue it as 1000, without opening the package. One carton in, one carton out. This makes it very easy to maintain high accuracy.

I had a client who did this in his automatic storage and retrieval stockroom. One carton in, one carton out. As a result, he routinely had 100 percent record accuracy, year after year. At first the auditors wouldn't believe it, and had to send in a couple of Vice Presidents from their Chicago office before they would believe that the locals (in Iowa) had really found 100 percent accuracy.

The control group is a very good technique to help you quickly identify major sources of error. Under this method, you select a small group of items, each of which has frequent transactions, and represents a good cross section of all of your inventory categories. Then you cycle count these items every day, and keep careful records on the errors that have occurred. This will allow you to discover systematic errors quickly so they can be eradicated. When you run out of errors, you can select a new control group. This technique is best applied in a new implementation. It also is useful in an old system that is not working well, and needs rejuvenation.

All of these techniques enhance the basic ABC approach, and can be applied on an item by item or category by category basis.

Using Motivational Techniques to Enhance Record Accuracy

As a motivational technique, some stockroom supervisors assign zones to each stockroom person, who takes personal responsibility for that zone, including stock status accuracy. This has achieved excellent results.

Another excellent motivational tool is to keep a large graph in the stockroom showing the accuracy level of each day's cycle count. Selected supervisors, managers, and executives also should receive this information.

Cycle counting to support an MRP II-based system is incompatible with the old, year-end physical. The year-end physical requires a crash program to count everything usually over a weekend. This involves closing up the stock rooms, drafting low-level office workers, and working all weekend. Then the accountants take over and try to reconcile everything.

Over the years there have been several papers presented at professional society conventions stating the classic year-end physical results in an inventory accuracy of about 85 percent, and it takes them three months to repair the damage. The reason for this poor showing is because of the characteristics of the personnel involved. Most of them are not familiar with the inventory, and don't know what they are doing. Besides, the warehouse is dirty and cold (or hot), and they would rather be somewhere else. Training and pep talks help some, but the problem remains. Your MRP II-based system can ill-afford this sharp degradation in one of its most important data bases.

As a substitute for the year-end crash program, the auditors should spot check your records and procedures, and confirm that you really have 95 percent accuracy. This certainly justifies eliminating the year-end physical.

HOW TO SET GOALS, MEASURE INVENTORY TURNS, AND ATTACK EXCESS AND OBSOLETE INVENTORY

Many say you get what you measure. It is fairly easy to develop quantifiable inventory goals.

Using Dollar Amounts for Inventory Goals

The financial tradition focuses on dollars. You can develop an inventory plan, based on your MRP II-generated schedules, in terms of dollars. You can monitor your progress on a monthly basis.

Your MRP II system analyzes many factors, one of which is a planned on-hand balance for all items under its control. Since these items have a standard cost, it is easy to calculate a planned inventory balance, in dollars, by month. You can even have this subdivided by whatever categories you find useful. Since dollars is the common denominator in business, this method does communicate well. However, since it is monthly, it could be too tardy to help correct problems.

Another important thing to recognize about inventory goals, is that in an MRP II-based system you do not control inventory directly. In order for your MRP II system to function, you must honor its planned orders. Inventory happens because of rules you set, such as lead times, lot sizes, queue sizes, scrap allowances, and safety stocks. This means that if inventory is too high, you must look to the rules you have given MRP II, and improve them. You cannot act directly against the inventory.

Another weakness in aggregates is that you can't very well compare your company's performance to other companies inside or outside your industry, based on these aggregate dollars.

How to Measure Inventory Turns

Inventory turns is a measure that is independent of volume,

and can be made to be sensitive to seasonality and cycles. Manufacturers of discrete items such as cars, toasters, and electric motors have a much lower turn ratio than do processors, such as oil refining, chemicals, beverages, and so on, where material spends just a few minutes being processed from raw to finished state. This measurement is more useful when applied to the manufacturing of discrete items.

The easy way to measure inventory turns is to take your yearly financial statement and compare total inventory from the balance sheet to the cost of goods sold (CGS) from the profit and loss (P&L) statement. Divide inventory into CGS to get turns. This technique allows you to check your performance against your competitors, other companies, or the economy as a whole.

Yearly, published financial statements often contain quite a few adjustments, some of which could affect the turns calculation. Moreover, this is necessarily only an annual measurement. You should measure turns every month, and the data are available from your accounting records. First you total the monthly cost of goods sold for the last 12 months. Next you calculate average inventory for the same 12 months. Divide the average monthly inventory into your 12-month CGS, to get your turns.

Some companies take the inventory turns measure to a more detailed level. Some calculate inventory turns by product line, others by categories such as purchased, semi-finished, work in process, and finished goods.

The United States is frequently compared to Japan with this measurement. Figures vary widely, and there may be some selective reporting, especially from Japan, where we hear about a few spectacular successes. My own observation is that U.S. discrete manufacturers average about three turns, but with a wide variation from less than one to double digits. The statistics we see about Japan usually refer to the best, end-item manufacturers, such as autos, consumer electronics, and heavy industrial equipment. We do not see much about how well the lower tiers of the supply network are doing; those who supply components to the big companies. There is some evidence that they do not do nearly as well as the big companies,

However, just about everyone agrees that Japanese manufacturers in the aggregate, do better than their U.S. counterparts.

How to Attack Excess and Obsolete

Engineering changes and large inventories are the two biggest causes for excess and obsolete inventory.

Every company has engineering changes. Many of them represent genuine product improvements. However, many represent error correction. The U.S. has the reputation of cutting corners during the design phase of a new product, and then correcting flaws as they are identified by our customers. Correcting these flaws often requires a crash-program, that is expensive and usually leaves orphaned inventory behind.

For this and many other good reasons, you should insist that the design and development of a new product be complete and thorough. Products should be rigorously tested under your control, not that of your customers. In this way you will have many of your engineering changes during the design cycle, where the impact on inventory is slight.

Your engineering change control procedure should have a provision for determining how much inventory will be obsoleted by the change. This becomes one of the factors to consider when deciding on an effectivity date. Large inventory, which your inventory turns help you measure, is another prime cause of excess and obsolete. Obsolete is defined as those components in inventory that your MRP II system has no use for in the next 12 months. Excess inventory is that which MRP II will not consume in the next n months. You set your own time horizon for the n factor. If you implement the JIT ideas of small lot sizes with frequent deliveries, small queues in the factory, short lead times, and no safety stock, your exposure to excess and obsolete will diminish sharply.

HOW TO CHOOSE AND USE LOT SIZING RULES

Lot sizing rules all attempt to optimize setup cost with carrying cost. The larger your lot size is the lower your setup cost per piece, but your carrying cost goes up. If you lower your lot size too much, you pay too much per piece for the setup.

In all of these discussions, for a purchased item, the cost of placing an order is used in place of the setup cost.

Traditional lot sizing approaches have attempted to minimize setup and carrying cost. Some operate on past history, assuming that last year is an acceptable predictor of next year. More modern lot sizing techniques take into account future, specific, periodic demand, which you get from your MRP II system. We have seen a number of formulas evolve, especially out of college campuses and from mathematically-trained practitioners.

Since JIT principles have gained in popularity, particularly the idea of zero inventory and small lot sizes, our emphasis has shifted from fancy formulas to setup reduction. We no longer take the factors such as setup cost as an immutable given. Rather we now know that setup can be reduced, often sharply.

However, until we can reach zero setup on everything, we still need to choose lot size rules carefully. Your modern MRP II-based system probably offers several of the common lot sizing rules.

Appendix II shows detailed calculations on each of the following rules.

Using the Fixed Order Quantity Rule

This is also known as the "nice round lot" rule. Usually these quantities are set by guess and whim. In Purchasing, they want to get the lowest unit cost, so they select a large quantity in order to get a price break. Similarly, shop supervisors and inventory analysts often prefer large lot sizes. They believe that large lots reduce setups, and give better coverage of future needs. Experience shows, however, that the fixed order quantity method usually results in a lot size five to ten times larger than one calculated by formula.

The Fixed Order Quantity rule usually will leave a remainder at the end, which means if this item is ever phased out, or if it is seasonal, these residual amounts stay in inventory. This is not a very good lot sizing method.

Using the Economic Order Quantity (EOQ) Rule

This is the well-known square root formula that attempts to calculate a balance between carrying cost and setup cost. Balance is achieved when the setup cost per unit is the same as the carrying cost per unit. This formula uses annual usage, setup cost, and unit cost to arrive at a recommended lot size. You can use annual usage from the past, or future usage from you MRP II system. Using future, planned orders is much better, because this takes into account phase ins and phase outs.

This formula has one serious flaw. It assumes straight line usage. Some finished products or service parts might show straight line usage during the month and during the year. But in an MRP II setting, component usage is rarely constant. When you start a shop order, you want all the components at the beginning of the run, and may not need any more for several days or weeks. This is called "lumpy" demand. The larger your lot sizes and the deeper your bills, the lumpier the demand gets. There is an irony here, in that this formula, which assumes straight line usage, defeats itself by creating lumpy demand when it is applied.

The main advantage of the EOQ formula is that it is well-known, and the first one laypersons think of when lot sizing is mentioned.

Also this formula usually will leave a remainder at the end, to carry forward in inventory until the next demand triggers a new order.

Although of limited use compared to the other formulas available to you, EOQ is useful for items having independent demand, such as service parts, and to validate other methods.

Using the Period Order Quantity Rule

To get around the lumpy demand problem EOQ has, you can use period order quantity. This is a simple extension of the EOQ idea. It is easy to understand and to use. This rule adjusts the lot size to cover a fixed period. To arrive at a period order quantity, take the EOQ and divide it into the annual usage. This will tell you how many times a year to order. Divide that number into 50, or 250, to get the time interval between orders in weeks or days, which is the period to be covered (the lot size).

For example, if an item's EOQ is 250 pieces and its annual usage 1,600, you should order it 6.4 times a year. Divided into 250 working days in a year, gives us 38.5 days. In this case the period between orders will be about 38 days. Precision is not necessary.

Used with an MRP II system, when a net requirement occurs, Period Order Quantity has the system look forward 38 days, and recommends an order sufficient to cover total requirements to that point.

Even if a time period has no demand, it counts as a period. This means that Period Order Quantity will leave no remainders at the end to carry over to the next order.

The period of coverage sometimes is set by edict or whim. The shop supervisor may not want to run certain items more often than every six days, for example.

Period Order Quantity is preferable to EOQ and Fixed Quantity, because it recognizes lumpiness.

Using the Lot for Lot Rule

Lot for lot is the favorite JIT lot sizing rule. This rule suggests a lot size to cover each planning period.

If your MRP II system is a newer one with daily planning increments, using Lot for Lot will give you daily quantities for purchasing and for manufacturing. Daily quantities is the cornerstone of the zero inventory idea.

You have to earn the privilege of using Lot for Lot sizing by bringing setup time to near zero. When you can justify this rule, your MRP II system should be updated to use it, and your stockroom inventory will fall to zero on those items you have so designated.

There are no mathematics involved outside of standard MRP II logic, and Lot for Lot is very easy to understand. This rule also tends to smooth out lumpiness.

You should have a heavy preference for Lot for Lot sizing, whenever you can justify it.

Using the Least Total Cost Rule

Like EOQ, least total cost balances carrying cost per unit and setup cost per unit. The best lot size is the one where those two costs are equal. This formula looks at MRP II's future requirements and calculates a setup cost and carrying cost for just the first week. Then it reiterates the process using a lot size enough to cover the first two weeks. It repeats the process, adding a week each time, until the carrying cost and the setup cost per unit are the same. The recommended lot size will be the total requirement to that point.

Because Least Total Cost looks at future requirements, it takes lumpiness into account, and leaves no remainders at the end of the lot.

Using the Part Period Balancing Rule

This method is almost the same as Least Total Cost. It starts with an inventory carrying cost for one part for one period. Then it analyzes the carrying cost associated with a lot size of one period, two periods, three periods, etc. It constantly asks, how many parts will be carried for how many periods. It has found the lot size when the total part-period cost is closest to the setup cost.

Using the Least Unit Cost Rule

This method is similar to Least Total Cost, except it takes an extra step and calculates a unit cost, based on setup and carrying cost per unit for the succeeding lot size steps. This also is a reiterative process. It suggests the lot size that gives the lowest unit cost (setup + carrying cost + lot size).

This method usually gives the same result as Least Total Cost.

Describing Other Rules

There are a number of other lot sizing rules that are substantially more complicated than the above. They mainly are used for teaching, and have very limited practical use. The most famous one in this category is the Wagner-Whitin formula.

Using Lot Size Modifiers

Depending on the lot sizing rule you select, you may want to employ a modifier selectively. The first modifier is a maximum, expressed in quantity or in days. This simply means that no matter what the lot size calculation shows, you don't want to order or make more than the maximum.

The second modifier is minimum, expressed in quantity or days. You use this to set a floor under the lot size.

The third modifier is a multiple. This solves the 55-gallon drum problem. If your lot size calculation shows you should order 10 gallons, you will order 55 anyhow. If the calculation asks for a lot size of 60 gallons, you will order 110 gallons. A multiple also is needed if you have vessels in your production process. Usually the vessel must be filled for the process to work correctly, regardless of what the lot size rule suggests.

There is not much difference among the mathematically sophisticated formulas. This means you should choose the simplest formula that will work for you. To some extent this is software dependent, because your MRP II system might not feature all of these formulas.

You should try to move to zero setups so you can use the lot-for-lot rule. Otherwise select a rule that people can easily understand, and leaves no remainders. Period Order Quantity could be a good contender.

10

HOW TO INCORPORATE GROUP TECHNOLOGY AND STANDARDIZATION

At one time, Group Technology and MRP were considered incompatible. But Since MRP I evolved into MRP II, and especially with the increasing popularity of Just-in-Time and Zero Inventory ideas, Group Technology is becoming recognized as a complementary and supporting technique. Group Technology has a number of pseudonyms, including cellular production, continuous flow production, and flow shop.

There is some confusion on definition of Group Technology. The American Production and Inventory Control Society defines Group Technology as, "An engineering and manufacturing philosophy which identifies the 'sameness' of parts, equipment or processes. It provides for rapid retrieval of existing designs and anticipates a cellular type production equipment layout."[1] Hyde says "Group Technology is a technique for manufacturing small to medium lot-size batches of parts of similar process, of somewhat dissimilar materials, geometry and size, which

---

[1]*Dictionary*, Fifth Edition; American Production and Inventory Control Society; Falls Church, VA; 1984, p. 13.

are produced in a committed small cell of machines which have been grouped together physically, specifically tooled, and scheduled as a unit."[2] I like Hyde's definition better, mainly because it recognizes that Group Technology is being used so this definition will be used in this book.

The opposite of Group Technology is the traditional job shop factory layout, where machines are grouped by similarity of machine.

Figure 10.1 depicts how shop orders travel through a factory with a conventional layout. Here we see that the factory is arranged with machinery and equipment grouped according to similarity without regard for the sequence and flow of work through the facility. Notice that even in this simple example, the pathways are very complicated, and the total travel distances great.

Figure 10.2 shows a similar factory laid out according to Group Technology. Here we see the factory laid out according to several common work sequences that accommodate the families of products being produced. In this example we see that the product lines fall into four main groups, with the machines laid out in sequence without regard for the type of machine involved.

HOW GROUP TECHNOLOGY WORK CENTERS OUTPERFORM THE TRADITIONAL JOB-SHOP LAYOUT

There are many advantages that come with Group Technology. They are as follows:

- Queue time is reduced.

- Factory leadtime is reduced.

- Work-in-process is reduced.

- Lot sizes are reduced.

- Just-in-Time performance is enhanced.

- Quality is enhanced.

- The impact of engineering change orders is reduced.

---

[2]William F. Hyde. *Improving Productivity by Classification, Coding, and Data Base Standardization* New York: Marcel Dekker, Inc., p. 152.

Figure 10.1 Conventional Job-Shop Layout

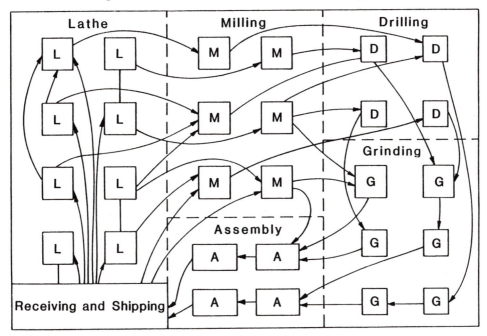

Figure 10.2 Group Technology Layout

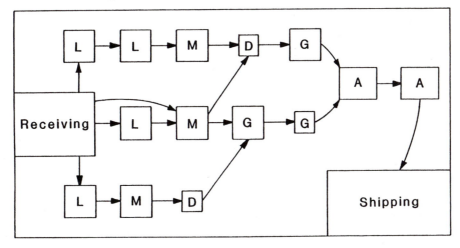

- Manufacturing costs are lowered.
- Standardization is fostered.

Reducing Queue Time

One of the principles of Group Technology is that once a shop order is started in a work center, it flows from operation to operation, from machine to machine, directly with no waiting in a queue. Taking one of the lines from Figure 10.2, we see that a shop order is processed on five machines, but experiences a queue only once, at the beginning of the manufacturing cycle. This reduces the queue by four-fifths, or 80 percent.

Reducing Factory Leadtime

In factories with the conventional, job-shop layout, queue time is usually 90 percent of factory leadtime, and processing time 10 percent. In our example we eliminate four of the five queues, thereby reducing leadtimes by 80 percent of 90 percent, or 72 percent.

Reducing Work-in-Process

Since shop orders in a queue are part of work-in-process, any reduction in queue will result in an equivalent reduction in WIP. The cost of carrying inventory is high. Although there is no consensus as to inventory carrying cost, many practitioners use 36 percent a year, or 3 percent a month. Even a modest-sized manufacturing company can have $1,000,000 of work-in-process inventory. Taking this hypothetical company, and our same Group Technology example, reducing queue by four fifths also will reduce WIP by 72 percent, or $720,000. Using the 36 percent annual carrying cost, this gives a yearly saving of $259,200. Notice that this is a contribution to profits before taxes, the popular bottom line, and recurs every year. This is in addition to the permanent reduction in inventory investment, a balance sheet item.

Reducing Lot Sizes

Because of the partial dedication of machines and equipment in a Group Technology layout, major setups disappear, and only minor setups remain. This should result in a corresponding reduction of lot sizes. In an early implementation, one French company grouped two lathes, one vertical drill, and one milling machine into a Group Technology cell. They found setup time dropped 85 percent.[3] One of the supporting techniques leading

---

[3]Ibid., p. 155.

to zero inventories is the reduction of setup time in order to achieve lot-for-lot lot sizing.

Enhancing Just-in-Time Performance

Shortening factory leadtime by 72 percent will certainly lead to much better performance in finishing manufacturing schedules on time. Shorter leadtimes mean that orders will be started much later than before, drastically increasing the likelihood that the entire pick list will be on hand at release time for the next order or for final assembly. Also, shorter manufacturing time reduces exposure to scheduling and production anomalies.

Enhancing Quality

In a job shop, a manufacturing quality problem often is first discovered when a lot of parts is issued to a subsequent work center for further processing. In this case, the entire lot is rejected. Then the bad parts are sorted out for rework or scrap before normal processing can resume once again.

In a Group Technology setting, the same flaw would be discovered a few seconds after it was made, because each workpiece is passed along singly. In this environment, the process is stopped until the problem is corrected, and only a few parts are spoiled.

Reducing the Impact of Engineering Change Orders

A few companies have a stable product line and few ECOs. They are in the minority, however. Most companies have a significant traffic in them, and many companies are plagued by them. Effectivity severity of ECOs range from next order, to in-process, to in stock, to product recall. There is very strong incentive not to recall products in process or in the field for rework. By starting shop orders much later, many ECOs already will have been accommodated before manufacturing starts.

Lowering Manufacturing Costs

The Machinability Data Center found references claiming a 40 percent reduction in manufacturing cost per piece.[4] The re-

---

[4] Machinability Data Center, a Department of Defense Information Analysis Center; Group Technology, an Overview and Bibliography, (Cincinnati, Ohio, MDC 76–601, c/o Metcut Research Associates, Inc.) p. 18.

duction occurred mainly in operating cost. They also found evidence of a 47 percent reduction in manufacturing operating costs, Group Technology over conventional layout.[5] These studies are not recent, but nevertheless demonstrate that significant cost savings, beyond WIP inventory reduction, come with Group Technology.

Fostering Standardization

The analysis techniques developed to implement and sustain Group Technology automatically lead design engineers to current components, and encourage common usage and similar designs.

HOW TO ANALYZE THE DISADVANTAGES OF GROUP TECHNOLOGY

Almost every new technique exhibits some disadvantages, Group Technology included. The main ones are:

- Extensive analysis is required.

- Factory rearrangement is required.

- Supervisors need retraining.

- The system is inflexible.

Requiring Extensive Analysis

In order to convert to a Group Technology factory layout, you must analyze your existing items. They must be grouped according to similarity of production steps. Since this has never been a strong requirement in traditional manufacturing, analytical tools usually are not in place. This means that some type of analysis provision must be developed and put into place, even before analysis can begin. This usually requires the addition of some kind of classification code to a new field in the item master. For companies with thousands of manufactured items, this could be a formidable job.

Another approach could be through your process and routing system, if that is suitable. This approach requires computer programs to analyze the similarities, and develop groupings.

---

[5]Ibid., p. 19.

Requiring Factory Rearrangement

Carried to its logical conclusion, conversion to Group Technology requires that the whole factory be uprooted and rearranged. This takes time and money. Most companies move gradually, establishing a few Group Technology work centers at a time. Some factories never complete the process, because they want to keep some job-shop capability for those items that don't fit into any family.

Retraining Supervisors

Under a conventional layout, a work center supervisor usually has only one type of machine or equipment to supervise. In a Group Technology environment, the supervisor will have to know how to supervise operators working on a wide variety of equipment.

Recognize Inflexibility

When set, a Group Technology cell has a degree of specialization that may inhibit or make more costly the introduction of new products, especially to the extent that they are dissimilar to current ones.

HOW TO ANALYZE YOUR MANUFACTURED ITEMS USING THE CLASSIFICATION CODING METHOD

Bearing in mind the basic needs of Group Technology and standardization for classification codes, the following requirements emerge for a good classification coding system:

- It must be universal.

- It uses physical characteristics.

- It is discrete.

- It is computable.

- It has a separate field on the item master.

Cataloging the Universe

Your classification coding system should be able to catalog the universe. Change is a fact of life, and a number of writers and lecturers point out that the pace of change is accelerating. This means that a classification coding system must be able to expand to encompass unexpected, new demands. This includes developing drastically different product designs, buying product lines from other companies, and buying other companies.

Using Physical Characteristics

Your code must classify each item according to its physical characteristics which are permanent over time, regardless of application. Classification can not be according to how used or where used. For example, *standoff* is a description of use and is no good for analysis. Nor is bolt, bracket, hold down clamp, washer, or doorbell wire. A standoff is really a piece part, made of steel, threaded at both ends, approximately two inches long, and one-fourth inch in diameter.

Developing a Discrete System

Your system must bring similar items together, and exclude interlopers. Mooveover, it is very useful that your system allow selection and listing at cascading levels of detail, from fairly general at one end of the spectrum to quite specific at the other. In addition it is necessary that each item have only one code.

Using the Computer

In this day and age, you can assume that a computer is available for use. This is especially true of companies using MRP II software, which universally have an item master file already available. Your classification system should be crafted so storing, sorting, selecting, and listing information is easy and on demand. Listing should be on a terminal's screen if possible, and in every case available in printed form.

Establishing a Separate Field on the Item Master

Many companies make the mistake of trying to imbed some sort of classification into either the part number or the description. Neither can or ever works. It is necessary to have a separate field on the item master (or elsewhere) to house the classification code. (For a full description of a good item numbering system, see Chapter 5).

The above requirements describe an ambitious classification system, one that would be very difficult to develop by a company with its own resources. It would be a major development project. Luckily there are a number of serviceable commercial products on the market that can spare you from reinventing that wheel.

These systems are analogous to commercial computer systems, that most companies use whenever possible.

An Example of a Classification System

For this example I will draw most heavily from the Brisch-Birn system, which is one of the several products available in the United States and abroad.

Figure 10.3 shows how the manufacturing universe can be divided into a hierarchy, and is the first step in allowing the computer to retrieve data from the general to the specific. The world of production is divided into the categories of "by, from, into, by means of, and with the help of."

Taking one of production's general classes, 1000, Primary Materials, Figure 10.4 shows them broken down into the next level of detail, Nonmetallic and Metallic, which are subdivided into nine classes, 1100 through 1900. Not shown are the further subdivisions which would go two more levels deep.

Figure 10.5 shows Commodities, class 2000, broken down into its nine divisions, 2100-2900, And Figure 10.6 shows the same for class 3000, Piece Parts. There is a similar breakdown for each of the other members of the manufacturing universe.

To illustrate how a common piece part would be classified, we can refer to Figure 10.7, which shows a typical machined component. It has a 3½" diameter, and is 5¾" long. Figure 10.8 shows how you step through a hierarchy of detail. First you see that our component is round with multiple diameters. Within that group you further refine your definition by designating that the part has a straight centerline and blind holes. Within that class you quickly determine that its maximum diameter is at one end, and between three and four inches.

This example illustrates that it is easy to give a component its correct code. Although easy for one component, converting an existing population of thousands of components is a major undertaking, that must be cost-justified against the huge advantage of Group Technology and standardization.

An Example of Cost Justification

To illustrate cost justification, in 1979, one medium-sized company discovered that they could save $1,500 each time they avoided making a new design, and $1,400 when they could modify an existing one. In one year they made 150 searches, 50 of which resulted in design avoidance. Their measurable cost

Figure 10.3 The Manufacturing Universe

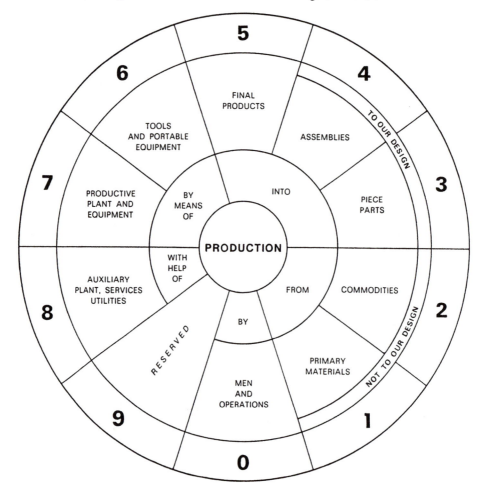

savings were augmented by noticeable improvements in other areas such as procurement, tooling, and general manufacturing flexibility.

Notice that the hierarchical approach would allow you to do different analyses based on the scheme. For example, you could ask the computer to give you a list of all straight, round parts, with multiple diameters. They would all have the code $341nn$ and $342nn$. All you do is look at the index of codes to develop your selection arguments. Then you enter these parameters into your computerized lookup system for an instantaneous display of all items that match.

Figure 10.4 Primary Metals

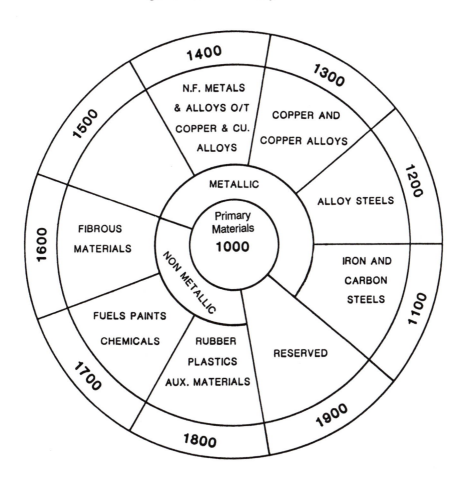

Figure 10.5   Commodities

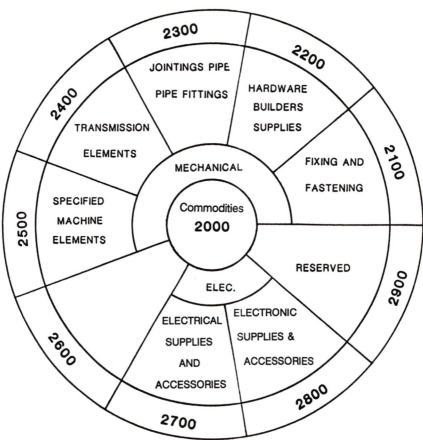

Figure 10.6 Piece Parts

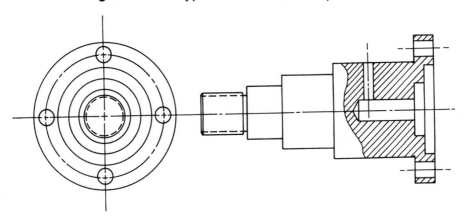

3200

3100

3300

3900

SINGLE
O/D

IRREGULAR

RESERVED

ROUND

Piece
Parts

3400

MULTI
O/D

REGULAR

3000

SPECIFIED

3800

O/T
ROUND

FLAT

BENT

3500

3700

3600

Figure 10.7 Typical Machined Component

Figure 10.8 Classifying a Typical Machined Component

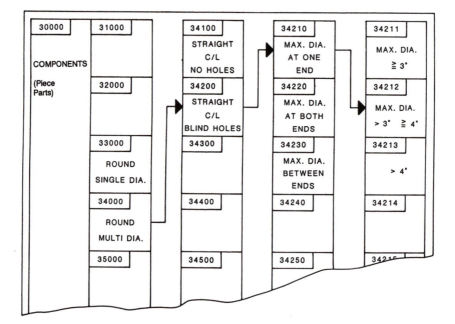

There are several commercial products available. Figures 10.9 through 10.13 show how some of these products would code a flat washer.

HOW TO INCLUDE STANDARDIZATION IN YOUR SYSTEM

Standardization can be an engineering specialty on its own, but simply put it, means don't reinvent the wheel.

A standardized approach to component design proceeds in the following sequence:

1. Use an existing component as is.

2. Slightly modify an existing component. If the modified version is interchangeable all around, keep the same item number and raise its revision level. If the modified version is not interchangeable, keep the old component with its same item number, and give the new component a new item number. In this latter case, it probably would have the same classification code.

Figure 10.9 Brisch-Birn System Example

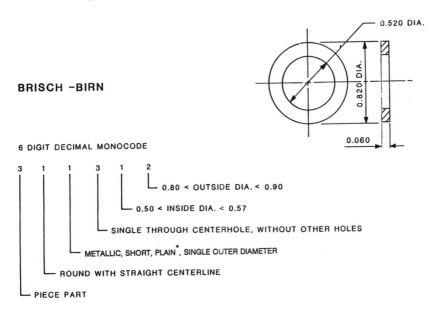

BRISCH –BIRN

0.520 DIA.

0.820 DIA.

0.060

6 DIGIT DECIMAL MONOCODE

3 1 1 3 1 2

└ 0.80 < OUTSIDE DIA. < 0.90

└ 0.50 < INSIDE DIA. < 0.57

└ SINGLE THROUGH CENTERHOLE, WITHOUT OTHER HOLES

└ METALLIC, SHORT, PLAIN*, SINGLE OUTER DIAMETER

└ ROUND WITH STRAIGHT CENTERLINE

└ PIECE PART

*NO THREADS, SPLITS, KEYWAYS, FLATS, GROOVES, SLOTS, KNURLS,
OR SWAGED OR ANGULAR ENDS

3. Take design tips from existing designs. The resulting new component often will have the same classification code as the sample.

4. When all else fails, design a new component from scratch.

The advantages of standardization are very attractive and include such things as:

■ Lower design cost.

■ Faster design process.

■ Less inventory: fewer stock locations, less inventory investment.

■ Planning efficiency: fewer items, fewer stockouts.

■ Easier administration with customer designs, government contracts, and regulatory authorities.

Figure 10.10 CODE System Example

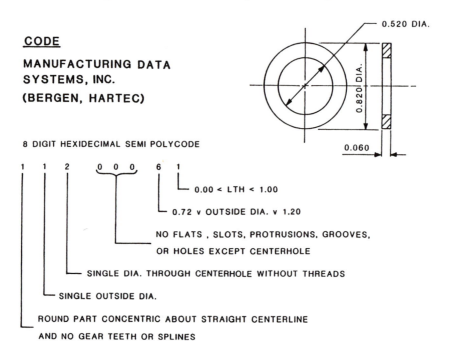

- Fewer tools, better tools
- Group Technology and more standardization of machines and equipment.

Design costs are lower because new designs are avoided. Starting a new part costs anywhere from hundreds to thousands of dollars each. Using an existing part avoids this cost altogether. Using a revised version of an existing one sharply reduces the design cost.

Standardization results in many fewer components used in manufacturing, thereby avoiding inventory on each. With higher usage of fewer components, inventory usage becomes more stable and manageable, leading to lower investment. Higher volume also leads to lower unit cost.

With fewer items to manufacture or purchase, planning is less cumbersome, and usage less lumpy. This results in fewer stockouts, and in a Just-in-Time environment, makes daily increments the more viable.

Figure 10.11 MICLASS System Example

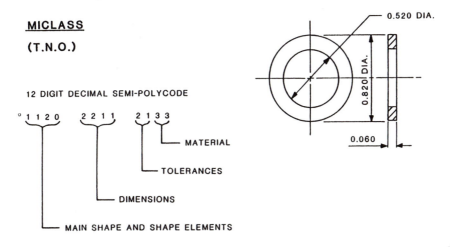

MICLASS

(T.N.O.)

12 DIGIT DECIMAL SEMI-POLYCODE

° 1 1 2 0   2 2 1 1   2 1 3 3

— MATERIAL

— TOLERANCES

— DIMENSIONS

— MAIN SHAPE AND SHAPE ELEMENTS

ROUND PART WITH SINGLE OUTSIDE AND DIAMETERS
WITHOUT FACES, THREADS, SLOTS, GROOVES, SPLINES,
OR ADDITIONAL HOLES. THE OUTSIDE DIAMETER AND
LENGTH ARE WITHIN CERTAIN SIZE RANGES.

Figure 10.12 TEKLA System Example

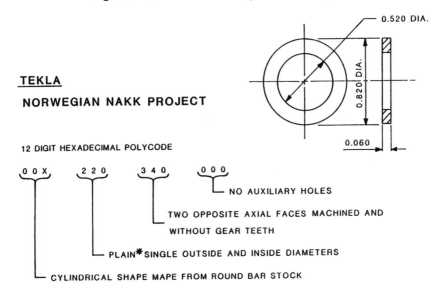

TEKLA

NORWEGIAN NAKK PROJECT

12 DIGIT HEXADECIMAL POLYCODE

0 0 X   2 2 0   3 4 0   0 0 0

— NO AUXILIARY HOLES

TWO OPPOSITE AXIAL FACES MACHINED AND
WITHOUT GEAR TEETH

— PLAIN✷SINGLE OUTSIDE AND INSIDE DIAMETERS

— CYLINDRICAL SHAPE MAPE FROM ROUND BAR STOCK

✷NO THREADS, GROOVES, OR SLOTS

Figure 10.13 Opitz System Example

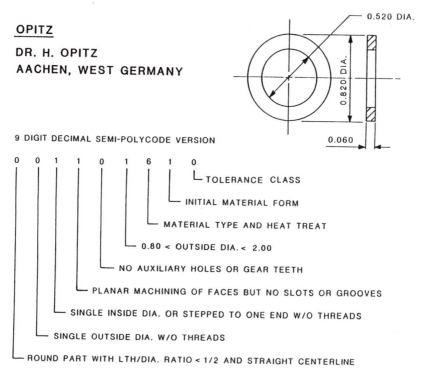

OPITZ

DR. H. OPITZ

AACHEN, WEST GERMANY

9 DIGIT DECIMAL SEMI-POLYCODE VERSION

```
0   0   1   1   0   1   6   1   0
                        └─ TOLERANCE CLASS
                    └─ INITIAL MATERIAL FORM
                └─ MATERIAL TYPE AND HEAT TREAT
            └─ 0.80 < OUTSIDE DIA. < 2.00
        └─ NO AUXILIARY HOLES OR GEAR TEETH
    └─ PLANAR MACHINING OF FACES BUT NO SLOTS OR GROOVES
  └─ SINGLE INSIDE DIA. OR STEPPED TO ONE END W/O THREADS
└─ SINGLE OUTSIDE DIA. W/O THREADS
└─ ROUND PART WITH LTH/DIA. RATIO < 1/2 AND STRAIGHT CENTERLINE
```

In a government procurement environment, it often is very difficult to get permission to use a new component. Getting for approval for one already being used is far easier.

Standardization has an impact on tool design. Higher volume of fewer variations means that better tools are affordable. This also supports the Just-in-Time principle of fast changeover. Equipment and machine purchase is affected similarly. Standardization and Group Technology taken together create many new selection and design considerations with respect to both tooling and equipment.

In a plant where classification coding is already in place, the designer first examines all existing similar parts, using the hierarchical retrieval tool. In some cases there will be a component that will suit the application with no alteration. In other cases, an alteration can be made to suit the new application without spoiling the interchangeability in existing applications. This represents a clear saving of a new design.

In other cases the designer can take an existing part, modify it to suit, and give it a new number because it is not interchangeable. This results in a new part, but design time and effort are minimal.

HOW TO ACCOMMODATE FEATURES AND OPTIONS WITHIN GROUP TECHNOLOGY

To be able to handle features and options in the easiest way, you must design the product influenced by three criteria. These criteria are:

- Modularity

- Ease of manufacture

- Incorporating options as late as possible in the manufacturing cycle

Developing Modular Approach

Modularity is the building block approach. Figure 10.14 shows a camera with accessories and options. Each is a module, which is manufactured independently of each other, and assembled together after the customer order is received. In this case, every camera takes the body and one of the three lenses. These are the options. Some customers take the automatic winder or the flash unit. These are accessories.

In a Group Technology situation, each of these modules could be built in their own cell.

Establishing Ease of Manufacture

Notice that the flash has three different versions—universal, night, and daylight. The principle of ease of manufacture would require that they all are similar enough that they can be manufactured in the same Group Technology cell, and that the differentiation be designed to be as simple as possible, preferably just by installing the appropriate flash tube.

Incorporating Options as Late as Possible in the Manufacturing Cycle

This principle asks that products be designed such that the available options be incorporated as late in the manufacturing cycle as possible. For example, if you are making computer video terminals, contrive to have the components that are voltage-specific go on last. This means that commonness of production persists until the very last moment, when the differentiating components are applied. In a Group Technology setting, the different components could be applied at the end of the line, or unfinished items could be sent to different work centers for finishing.

Figure 10.14 Accessories and Options

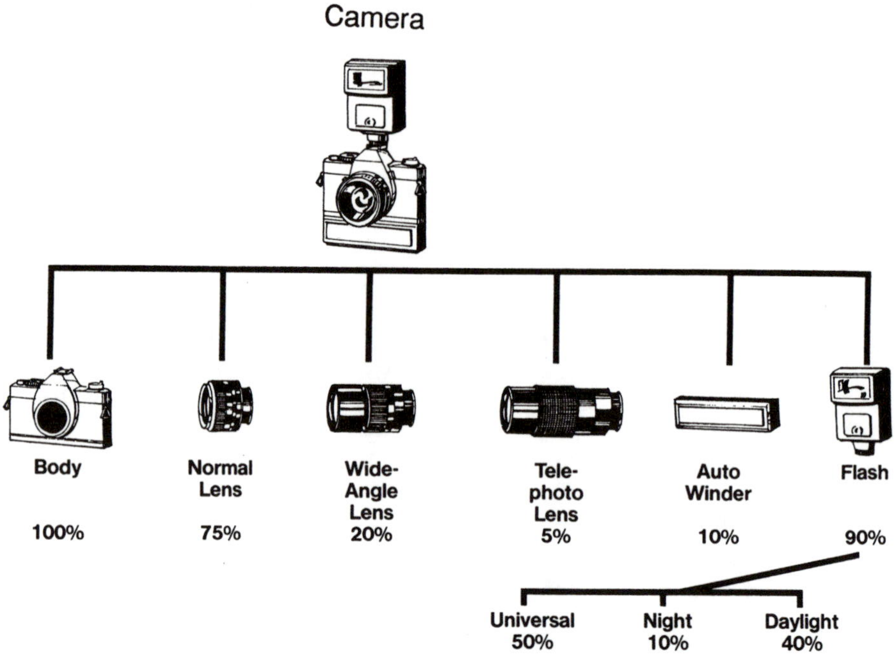

Camera

Body	Normal Lens	Wide-Angle Lens	Tele-photo Lens	Auto Winder	Flash
100%	75%	20%	5%	10%	90%

Universal	Night	Daylight
50%	10%	40%

HOW TO INTEGRATE GROUP TECHNOLOGY WITH MRP/JIT

Regarding Just-in-Time, Group Technology is a backbone concept. It is the MRP II aspect that has caused some confusion.

There is no fundamental incompatibility between MRP II and Group Technology. When implementing Group Technology, however, there are four adjustments to MRP files that must be made; no logic changes. These four areas are:

- Bills of Material
- Item Master Records
- Work Center Master Records
- Routings

Adjusting Bills of Material

Group Technology often eliminates stocking levels, also known as subassembly breaks. This means that the bill of material for every item to be manufactured in the new environment must be corrected to eliminate the levels that no longer are to be stocked. Remember, the bill of material must match production. If this makes other departments uncomfortable, their systems are faulty and must be updated.

Adjusting Item Master Records

There will be a number of item numbers that will no longer be used, because sub-assembly breaks will be eliminated. Perhaps these should be flagged for purging.

Recognizing that Group Technology is a very different way to manufacture, the lot sizes of all items going through these work centers must be adjusted appropriately.

Adjusting Work Center Master Records

Since a Group Technology layout is altogether different from its predecessor job shop, you will have to redefine and renumber your work centers. The new characteristics of each Group Technology cell must be entered into their respective work center master record.

Adjusting Routings

All routings must be updated to recognize the Group Technology cells as being one work center each. The route details how manufacturing proceeds through each cell.

Finally, the Group Technology cell must be supervised properly. Group Technology work cells are designed so that once started, each workpiece proceeds directly through all of the machines to the end. This is in sharp contrast to the job shop tradition of finishing the whole batch at the first step before moving on to the second one. Supervisors must be trained to practice this important principle.

HOW TO ELIMINATE THE FIXATION ON DIRECT LABOR

Since the dawn of the Industrial Revolution, manufacturers have been progressively successful at reducing the direct labor content of finished goods. Today, most companies have less than 20 percent direct labor in Cost of Goods Sold. Many companies have less than 10 percent, and a few have less than 5 percent. Group Technology helps continue this trend.

Many Group Technology cells have workers tending several machines. There are a few Group Technology cells that have no direct labor in them whatever, relying instead on transfer devices and robots to move the work pieces through.

Another thing to recognize immediately, is that in a Group Technology cell, one of the machines is the slowest one. This machine will set the pace of the entire cell, and all other machines will perforce be operating at less than maximum.

You should develop new performance measurements for Group Technology cells, based on quality, schedule adherence, and no downtime; less on labor or machine utilization or efficiency.

HOW TO LINK GROUP TECHNOLOGY INTO COST ACCOUNTING

Traditional cost accounting absorbs indirect expenses as a percentage of direct labor. Since Group Technology cells often have expensive machines contributing to overhead, and little direct labor, items benefitting from these cells tend to be under-costed, while hand-assembly operations with little equipment bear the brunt of being over-costed. This results in erroneous standard costs which can and do lead decision makers astray.

In order to know how profitable Group Technology practices are for your company, you will have to develop a more accurate method of allocating overhead. Some emerging techniques are Activity-Based Costing and Rate-Based Costing. In a Group Technology setting, machine hours could be used to apportion the depreciation portion of overhead to items processed there. This would more accurately assess the right cost to items benefiting from the machines in the Group Technology cell.

CONCLUSION

Group Technology and job shop layout are the two ways you can lay out your factory.

- The more traditional job shop is functionally organized:

  - Work centers are established with one or a group of similar machines, with no regard for the items being manufactured.
  - There is a routing for every manufactured item to guide each lot through the various work centers as needed.
  - Each lot of items is completed in each work center before being passed on to the next.

- Group Technology takes the opposite approach:

  - The factory is laid out specially to accommodate the families of items being manufactured.
  - The cells have dissimilar machines grouped according to the manufacturing steps for the family of items belonging to the cell.
  - In a Group Technology cell, each workpiece is passed on to the next work station individually, not waiting for the whole lot.

- Group Technology offers many benefits:

  - Queue time is sharply reduced.
  - Throughout time is reduced.
  - The reduced setup allows for smaller lots.
  - Quality is enhanced, because a flaw, discovered in a downstream operation, causes an immediate correction, before the entire lot is spoiled.

- There are some disadvantages to Group Technology:

  - Detailed analysis is required in preparation of a major rearrangement of the factory.
  - Supervisors, who have been accustomed to one type of machine, now must be trained to watch over dissimilar ones.

- – It is more difficult to retool for new models, especially if they will be manufactured differently.

- A correct classification coding system helps support both Group Technology and standardization:

  - – The code belongs on a separate field on the item master, and there are several good commercial systems available.

- Group Technology is the backbone of the Just-in-Time concept; MRP II-based systems can be updated to support it.

  - – All you need to do is update your bills of material, item masters, work center masters, and routings. You don't need any logic changes.

- Group Technology tends to have a minimum of direct labor; you should try to eliminate the mechanism of spreading overhead as a percentage of direct labor.

- You should develop new performance measures to suit and encourage the new environment.

11

HOW TO APPLY
JUST-IN-TIME (JIT) IDEAS

The Just-in-Time Bandwagon is rolling full tilt. When this "roll" got started in the early to mid 1980s, many observers and practitioners asserted that JIT and MRP were incompatible; mutually exclusive. Sober reflection and study has revealed that most Just-in-Time ideas apply to the execution phase, while MRP II shines as a planning tool. Moreover, it turns out that JIT ideas do not represent a closed-loop system, as MRP II does, but rather a long list of good ideas; ideas for achieving manufacturing excellence. MRP and JIT for the most part support and compliment each other.

I have concluded, therefore, that the main appeal of JIT is that it is a clarion call to excellence. MRP II for the most part is very forgiving. It will allow you to continue having long lead times, large lot sizes, bloated inventories, functional factory layout with spaghetti bowl routing, inspection at every turn, scrap, shrinkage, and quality measured in defects per hundred. JIT focuses our attention on performing manufacturing functions not by perpetuating current bad practices, but rather on doing all functions well. Moreover, JIT admonishes all of us to keep doing better, no matter how much we may have achieved already. JIT also emphasizes the importance of steady, incremental improvements, rather than on block busters.

JIT ideas apply to many of your company's functions. It goes well beyond the factory, into such functions as:

■ Material Control

■ Production Control

■ Engineering

Implementing JIT also will demand some changes to your current environment:

■ Traditional Administrative Rules

■ Traditional Management Attitudes

Even JIT fanatics admit that there are some problems and limitations with the concepts; these are covered later in this chapter.

HOW TO APPLY JIT TO MATERIAL CONTROL

In applying JIT to material control, you should do the following:

■ Establish small lot sizes.

■ Achieve zero defects.

■ Eliminate receiving inspection.

■ Get frequent deliveries from suppliers.

■ Have material delivered directly to the line.

Establish Small Lot Sizes

The urgency of small lot sizes applies both to purchased and manufactured items. You should have small lot sizes on cheap items as well as expensive ones; on simple piece parts as well as on complicated assemblies; on small items as well as on big ones.

There are two main ways to set lot sizes—guesswork and by formula. Many companies use the guesswork approach. You can always spot them by simply asking how lot sizes are determined. I often get "I don't know", or "that's the size I inherited from my predecessor." I am also suspicious of nice multiples of hundreds or thousands. These techniques result in what is often called the "nice, round lot." Before JIT helped us focus on inventory excesses, this was considered to be an ok technique. But the current emphasis on zero inventories and high inventory turns, has made the intuitive, wet finger in the air, approach to lot sizing totally unacceptable. I frequently find that these lot sizes are five to ten times too high, compared to the lot size indicated by a suitable formula.

The other main way to arrive at a lot size is by formula. The main ones are detailed in Appendix II. There are several factors used in these formulas, such as usage pattern, inventory carrying cost assessment, setup cost for manufactured items, and the cost of placing a purchase order for purchased items.

Analyzing the usage pattern traditionally took the form of looking backwards to historical usage, and projecting this forward for the coming year. This method is barely useful, because it is totally unable to accommodate year-to-year increases or decreases. Worse yet, it is blind to design changes. Items being discontinued often appear in inventory anyhow, and go directly into obsolete inventory. With MRP-based systems, future usage is known based on dynamic bills of material and the Master Production Schedule. This known, future usage pattern for each item, is used by many of the better lot sizing formulas, and result in much more precise lot sizing, and dramatically lower inventory by using the smallest possible lot size and by eliminating lot size remainders and obsolete inventory.

Calculating Inventory Carrying Cost

Inventory carrying cost assessment is difficult to specify accurately. From professionals, I hear figures from 24 percent a year to 100 percent. From rookies and laypersons, I often hear much smaller numbers. Notice that the higher the carrying cost, the lower the lot size. This means that if you impute a too-small inventory carrying cost, you buy bigger lot sizes than you should I have even run into an occasional accountant who thinks that carrying cost should be 1/2% over prime. Inventory is expensive to own. Factors such as shelf life, reinspection, rework, damage, scrappage, storage cost, material handling, insurance, pilferage, obsolescence, and the opportunity cost of the cash tied up, are a few costs that contribute to inventory carrying cost. You probably would be wasting your time to try to do a scholarly job of defining this cost, because there are many places for judgment and conjecture. This makes for endless disagreement. Better to pick a number, making sure it is not too low. If your product line is mature and stable, perhaps 36 percent would do. If your product line is high-tech, or otherwise volatile, you should use a higher number.

Setup Cost

Setup cost is a big factor in lot sizing. Before JIT, we took whatever setup time the manufacturing engineers gave us, dollarized the time, and applied it to our formula. Closer observation shows that many planned setup times were just guesses with fudge factors built in. In many other cases, the engineer just put a stop watch on a current sloppy, thoughtless procedure, and passed it forward. JIT has directed us to reduce setup times. As this is successful, lot sizes must be reduced, and the better formulas will do this automatically. We cover setup time reduction later in this chapter, in the production control section.

The setup cost factor for a purchased part is represented by the cost of writing a purchase order. You can arrive at this figure by taking the annual cost of the purchasing department and dividing it by the number of purchase orders written in a typical year. Your cost accounting or Industrial engineering department can help figure a correct amount or eliminate purchase orders. One applicable JIT concept here is to have but one supplier for each item, and to have a blanket agreement with each. In this environment, you can quit sending purchase orders altogether, substituting releases by phone calls, or by sharing your MRP schedules with the supplier. Using Electronic Data Interchange is rapidly taking over here. Soon most companies will not be mailing out very many purchase orders, especially for production items.

To summarize, then, small lot sizes are very desirable. You earn a small lot size by reducing setup costs, recognizing the true cost of carrying inventory, and by streamlining the purchasing cycle.

Achieve Zero Defects

The idea of an acceptable quality (or un-quality) level has largely disappeared. Zero defects is rapidly becoming a commercial imperative.

The advent of World War II caused a preoccupation with volume production, with quality, as well as other considerations, taking a back seat. Under this environment, we witnessed the quest for large runs, with the worker preoccupied with volume. Then, after the batch was completed, the inspection department, using statistical sampling methods, decided if the batch exhibited the minimum quality level in terms of defects per hundred. What did we do if the batch failed? Sort. We sorted out the bad ones and sent them back for rework if possible, otherwise sent them to the dumpster. The inspection department was responsible for quality, manufacturing was responsible for bulk. In this environment, the focus was inspecting to see of the batch was ok. If not, we sorted out the bad ones. In this way, we inspected quality into the product.

The new wave, and the much better one is to control the manufacturing process so well that we avoid making bad parts. Inspecting individual parts is done not to accept the batch, but rather to make sure that the manufacturing process stays within tolerance. The new wave is to make sure that we make no bad parts.

One key ingredient is to make sure the machinery and equipment can hold tolerances. Another key ingredient is to make the worker responsible for quality production. Quality control provides the tools and training. The workers monitor production. And most important, the worker is empowered and expected to make adjustments or call for help as quality begins to wander and to shut down the equipment of bad parts are imminent or are being detected. Many traditional supervisors and managers have a difficult time accepting this requirement, but it is still a requirement. The worker must be trained to shut down in anticipation of bad production.

Current practice calls for statistical process control techniques to be used to equip the worker with the knowledge and information to make these judgements. More advanced practices include having equipment so good, that the traditional "x-bar, r" charts of statistical process control can be dispensed with. We now have available self-checking devices built in to machines and processes that are able to diagnose and apprehend impending un-quality and spontaneously shut down.

These modern techniques are widely, commercially available; and cost effective. There no longer is much excuse for manufacturing un-quality, and true zero defect production is a practical reality in most environments.

Finally, flawless quality has become so widely available and used, that it is now being made into a minimum threshold for continued viability in the marketplace. Zero defects is no longer a competitive tool, but rather a minimum requirement for staying in business.

Eliminate Receiving Inspection

We now can expect our suppliers to be able to deliver flawless quality, and to have internal procedures to assure this. As a result, after negotiation and demonstrating their capability, vendors gradually should be tagged as not needing receiving inspection. From the suppliers earning this rank, their deliveries go directly to stores, or better yet directly to the production line. JIT thought calls receiving inspection a waste and should be vigorously eliminated by developing quality suppliers. There are many companies today who have a strategy of gradually eliminating suppliers who do not qualify for no inspection status. This is a manifestation of the zero defect imperative.

Get Frequent Deliveries from Suppliers

You should note that the JIT lot size of choice is "lot-for-lot." Regarding suppliers, this means a lot size of one planning period. Most modern MRP II-based systems have daily planning periods, often called *buckets*. If you have a daily-bucketed system, you can switch on daily supplier deliveries by setting the corresponding flag on the item master record for that part to lot-for-lot. If daily deliveries don't make sense, then choose a lot size rule that will result in a delivery in multiple days. But make them as frequent as conditions allow.

Regarding planning periods, commercial software publishers probably will begin to allow planning by shift or even hour. When this happens, the lot-for-lot rule will result in deliveries by the shift or even hour.

For example, in Japan, the Busan company supplies seats to one of the Nissan factories. As the car body enters the painting station at Nissan, a signal is sent to Busan, who assembles the corresponding seats. They load them into a truck in the correct sequence and drive the 20+ kilometers to the assembly line, where they unload them directly on the assembly line in the correct sequence, just in time for assembly into the car. This kind of close coupling of supplier to customer will find more and more applicability.

Distance between supplier and customer, container sizes, transportation costs, and a number of other considerations should be taken into account, but you should have a heavy bias to eliminating excuses and striving for more frequency, with daily increments being the goal for today.

Have Material Delivered Directly to the Line

As you achieve no receiving inspection and frequent delivery from a decreasing number of suppliers, the traditional dock to stock to tracking system loses its merit. For these selected suppliers, you should deliver directly to a designated drop zone at the entrance to the work center needing the item. Multiple usage merely would call for multiple drop zones.

Factories embracing this practice have installed receiving docks around the perimeter of the factory. The supplier's truck driver pulls to the right door, and moves the material directly to the proper drop zone. This is detailed in the driver's delivery ticket. The driver then logs the delivery in to the customer's MRP system, which satisfies the planned receipt. And in some of these plants, the supplier is paid on this basis, automatically, with no invoice. The supplier has previously earned the trust of the customer with respect to counts and quality.

This system and subsequent derivatives are currently in occasional use, and the use is growing apace.

HOW TO APPLY JIT IN PRODUCTION CONTROL

The following ten ways should be used in applying JIT to production control:

- Demand short lead times.

- Use zero queues to get a close-coupled factory.

- Use single-cycle setups.

- Achieve zero defects by implementing statistical process control.

- Implement planned maintenance.

- Use standard operations.

- Use computer-aided process planning.

- Balance final assembly scheduling.

- Use a mixed model final assembly.

- Use the push system, the pull system, or both.

Demanding Short Leadtimes

Time compression is the new watchword for the 1990s, and shortened leadtimes in the factory are leading the way for the whole company. To shorten leadtimes, you should be constantly on the lookout for delays in the factory as well as in the office. Many companies now can do a final assembly and ship the product in a couple of days.

I have a client who makes fine, high precision metal components for the computer industry. A few years ago it took them 12 days to manufacture an end item from the time the work order hit the factory floor to its appearance on the shipping dock. Now they do the same thing in eight hours. And quality has improved because their product happens to be susceptible to contamination.

When the factory can now measure factory throughput time in hours instead of weeks, it is grotesquely out of proportion for order entry to take four days, credit check an additional three, configuration engineering four more, and scheduling two additional days!

You should continue to goad the factory to shorter throughput times, but now is the time to start dramatic improvements, or eliminations, in the back room.

Using Zero Queues to Get a Close-Coupled Factory

Especially in a functionally organized, traditional factory, queue time represents around 90 percent of factory through put time.

You can check out this percentage by doing a quick statistical analysis of some representative closed shop orders. Pick a good sample of closed orders across peaks and valleys, across products, and across work centers. Note their clock on and clock off times into and out of the factory. Look at the shop calendar for those dates and jot down the number of elapsed factory hours. Then look at the route sheet and note the number of standard direct and indirect labor hours authorized for the order. Add up the two figures for your samples, and divide total available hours into total standard hours, and the result will be your queue ratio. In a functionally organized factory this will usually be around 90 percent. In a process flow factory, queue time is usually not as severe.

As your MRP II-based system takes hold, and your plans become good and reliable, you should start a formal, vigorous program to reduce queues. Here's how to start. Select a few target work centers to start with. Measure the queue in front of each once or twice a day for a month or two. Subtract the lowest queue during the period from the highest one. The difference is the correct queue for that work center. That is the queue time to use on your work center master file.

The next step is to have your workers and supervisors analyze what factors are at work that require that residual queue, and take steps to eliminate them. Quality, upstream schedule adherence, material handling time, common setups, and whim are some of the main reasons. They should be analyzed and eliminated, which will allow further queue reductions.

A strong word of caution: In the classic factory, dwindling queues are viewed as a harbinger of a coming layoff, and workers slow down. You must tie a queue reduction program with an education program to prevent this common syndrome.

Using Single-Cycle Setups

We have stopped accepting long setups as an immutable given. Long setups are evil and must be eliminated. There are many solid techniques for making drastic setup time reductions, and often they can be implemented with no capital expense.

The first step is to invoke an ongoing, vigorous program for setup reduction. The most successful ones are centered around workers and supervisors. Manufacturing engineering plays a support role, and has no veto power. The whole atmosphere must be to say yes, not "no, it wasn't invented in engineering." In the last decade many companies have had conspicuous success with setup reduction by using worker-directed and worker-empowered teams.

There are several good techniques that can be used. The first technique is to videotape the setup. Then using the people closest to the scene, critique the setup. It is amazing how many good ideas come from such a simple approach.

First of all, all the hand tools and other equipment should already be at the workplace, so the worker doesn't have to run all over the factory just to get ready to start the setup

Internal vs. external setup is another technique. All possible setup operations possible should be done to the tool while the previous operation is running. Sharpening, adjusting, and aligning a few other activities that should be done externally.

The incoming tool should be at the work site. If the tool needs to be heated, this should be done beforehand if possible.

A fellow consultant had a client where dies needed to be warmed, which took almost an hour after being mounted in the press. On his first walk around the plant he noticed a large oven standing idle, and was told it no longer was used. He suggested that all the dies that needed to be warm, be stored in the oven. In the aggregate this has taken a huge bite out of setup time. It also made scheduling very flexible, since any die can be called for at any time with no warm-up penalty.

Another technique is to arrange the machine so the current tool can be rolled out the back as the new one is being rolled in from the front. I have seen photographs of large presses served by roller conveyor belts. On these belts are lined up the next dies, in the proper order. Another set of rollers take the old die out the back.

Having dies all the same height reduces shimming after it is in place. This allows the use of locator pins to precisely position the tool in place, where quick clamping devices are used instead of hex bolts.

Chapter 10 covers Group Technology. One very important benefit of this factory arrangement is that is nearly eliminates major setup. Since a Group Technology work cell is dedicated to a similar family of items, you will have only minor setup for succeeding orders.

Achieving Zero Defects by Implementing Statistical Process Control

Many experts now say that flawless quality has ceased being a competitive advantage, but rather it has become a minimum requirement. Many companies have achieved zero defects, and many others are working to achieve it. Customers are demanding flawless quality as part of their JIT efforts, and have proclaimed a strategy of not buying from suppliers who cannot demonstrate their ability to achieve zero defects.

You achieve zero defects not by better inspection, or by admonishing your workers. You achieve zero defects by process control. This requires that you provide machines and processes that do not turn out bad product. Then you provide tools, organization, procedures, and training to assure that your workers either call for help or shut the process down when un-quality is about to occur. The worker is responsible for quality and is empowered to stop production rather than make a bad part.

This puts a heavy responsibility on management to make sure that your production machinery, equipment, and tooling can maintain tolerances and routinely turn out good parts. This also requires a change in management style; one that empowers workers to participate in managing the company.

In this environment, the quality control department changes from being an enforcer to being a facilitator. They take the lead in implementing statistical process control, in extensive educating and training, and in continuing improvement.

Implementing Statistical Process Control

● Step one is to analyze your current processes. This is a statistical analysis to determine if your current machinery, processes, and tools are able to hold to your tolerances.

● Step two is to correct those processes that are deficient. Alternatively, you can investigate the tolerances to see if they are realistic.

We had a client who was having a hard time holding tolerance on a certain product. Finally someone asked the customer why the tolerance was so tight. Their answer was that it wasn't their idea, and they always wondered why the engineers had made them so tight. It turns out that the engineer who had designed the item just picked a tolerance that looked about right at the time. When they loosened up the tolerance, the problem disappeared, even though the production environment remained as before.

● Step three is to prepare control charts for the items that will be processed. There are two different kinds of data, measurable and countable. Measurable data works with items that can be evaluated with fractional numbers. Weight, length, speed, time, temperature, viscosity, and volume are some examples. The other kind of data are countable, where whole numbers are involved. Eight out of round, four short pins, five torn bags, five paint chips, and go-no go gauges are in this group. The statistical approach to each is somewhat different, although equally valid.

Control charts are set up statistically to show the operator when production is tending to an out of control condition, or has already crossed the line. The operator monitors output periodically, plots the new numbers on the control charts, and takes action if production is going out of control.

- Step four is to train workers, supervisors, and everybody also who will be directly or indirectly involved, in the new ideals and techniques. This requires education on the whys, and training on the hows. Part of this education process is to instill a new supervisory style, empowering the worker to take unilateral action either to get help, or to actually shut down production.

As an example, we will use a measurable item. Figure 11.1 shows a fabricated stud, with an outside diameter of 1.600 ± .0005". In order to prove that our machine can hold our tolerance, we measure 100 studs at random over a representative time span. Figure 11.2 shows our frequency distribution.

Figure 11.1 Fabricated Stud

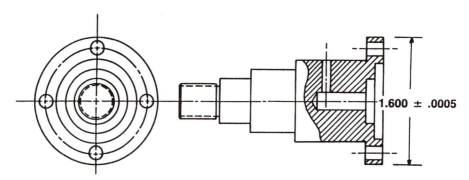

On it we have tallied our findings and determined that our average measurement is 1.6.

Next we prepare a histogram showing our measurements, shown in Figure 11.3. This displays the well-known statistical phenomenon of central tendency.

By applying the common standard deviation formula (not shown in our example), we can add the stud's standard deviations to the histogram. This is shown in Figure 11.4. Notice that three standard deviations, which account for 99.7 percent of our output, still fall within tolerance. From this histogram we can decide that the machine making this stud can hold the ± .0005" tolerance.

Figure 11.2　Stud Frequency Distribution

Measurements	Tally	Freq.	M * F
1.5993	///	3	4.7982
1.5995	Ж ////	9	14,3955
1.5997	ЖГ ЖГ ЖГ ЖГ ///	23	36.7954
1.5999	ЖГ ЖГ ЖГ ЖГ ЖГ ЖГ ЖГ /	36	57,6000
1.6001	ЖГ ЖГ ЖГ //	17	27.2034
1.6003	ЖГ ЖГ	10	16.0030
1.6005	//	2	3.2012
		100	159.9967

$$\overline{x} = 1.6$$

Figure 11.3　Stud Histogram

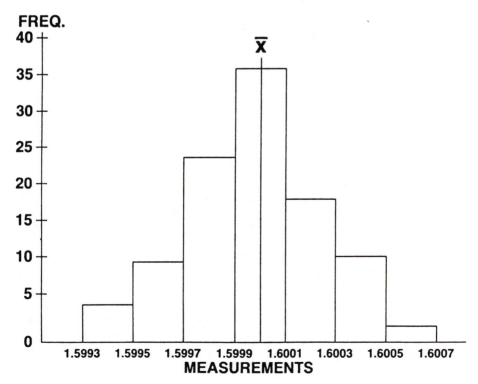

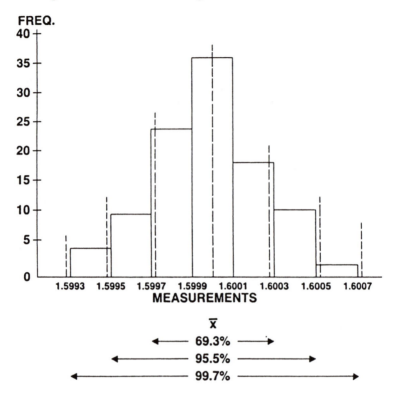

Figure 11.4 Stud Histogram with Standard Deviations

Now we can develop our control charts. We start by measuring 16 samples of seven parts each, shown in Figure 11.5. We note the average of the seven measurements in the x-bar column, and the range of the measures in the r column. When we are all done, we average the two columns and find that our x-double-bar (average) is 1.6000, and our r-bar (average) is .0008.

Our next step in developing a control chart is to calculate upper and lower control limits for x-bar and an upper control limit for r, shown in Figure 11.6.

We don't calculate a lower control limit for r, because a zero variation within one of our samples is acceptable. The factors A_2 and D_4 are selected from a guide book, and in this case represent approximately three standard deviations. Completing our calculations we arrive at an upper control limit of 1.6004 and a lower control limit of 1.5996, both within our basic ± .0005 tolerance. Also our upper control limit for the variation we will allow within a sample is .00162".

Figure 11.5 Stud Sample Measurements

SAMPLE NO.	1	2	3	4	5	6	7	$\bar{x}$	r
1	1.6003	1.5999	1.5993	1.5999	1.6001	1.5997		1.5998	.0005
2	1.6001	1.5997	1.5999	1.5997	1.5999	1.5981		1.6003	.0010
3	1.5995	1.5999	1.6005	1.5997	1.5993	1.5'		1.5999	.0008
4	1.6003	1.5997	1.5995	1.6001	1.5997			1.5997	.0006
5	1.5997	1.5997	1.6003	1.5999	1.6			1.5998	.0012
6	1.5997	1.6001	1.5999	1.5995				1.6003	.0011
7	1.5999	1.5999	1.5997	1.6003				1.6202	.0003
8	1.5997	1.5999	1.5999	1.600				1.6000	.0005
9	1.5999	1.5999	1.5997	1.5				1.5997	.0010
10	1.6003	1.5997	1.6005					1.5998	.0009
11	1.5995	1.6001	1.5					1.5999	.0002
12	1.6001	1.5999						1.6001	.0011
13	1.5999	1.59						1.6002	.0008
14	1.59							1.6002	.0007
15	1.6							1.5999	.0005
16	1.5							1.6001	.0009
								$\bar{\bar{x}} =$ 1.6000	$\bar{r} =$ .0008

Figure 11.6 Computing Control Limits

$$UCL = \bar{\bar{x}} + (A_2 * \bar{r})$$
$$= 1.6000 + (.483 * .0008)$$
$$= 1.6000 + .0004$$
$$= 1.6004$$

$$LCL = \bar{\bar{x}} - (A_2 * \bar{r})$$
$$= 1.600 - (.483 * .0008)$$
$$= 1.5996$$

$$UCL = D_4 * \bar{r}$$
$$= 2.004 * .0008$$
$$= .0016032$$

In Figure 11.7 we have drawn our control charts including the 16 samples that supported them.

Now we are ready to use the new control technique. From time to time, the operator takes a sample of seven, averages the measurements, and plots the average and range of each sample on the control chart. The operator already has been trained to watch for five conditions. They are the following:

- Shift

- Trend

- Periodicity

- Hugging

- Beyond Limit

Figure 11.7 Stud Control Chart

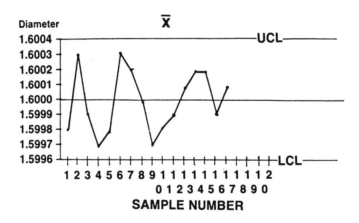

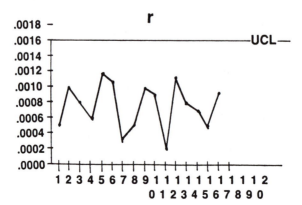

We already have empowered the worker to take action when things are getting out of control, and the first four conditions call for the operator to call for help, while still allowing production to continue. The last one, beyond limit, indicates that bad parts are being produced, and the operation is shut down immediately, and then help is called for.

● Figure 11.8 shows a shift. A shift has occurred when seven consecutive measurements fall on one side of the average. In our case we see that the r (range) measurements from samples 14 through 20 all fall above the average, r-bar. The operator signals for help.

Figure 11.8 Shift

Sample Weights —
Line 12, Lot 2367

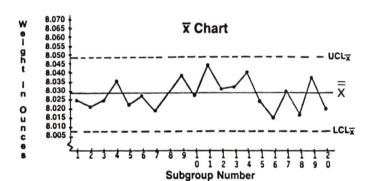

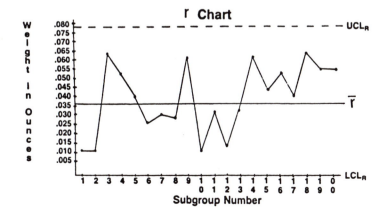

● Figure 11.9 shows a trend. Similar to a shift, a trend is underway when seven consecutive measurements are in the same direction. In our example, the range measurements 14 through 20 all are going down. The operator signals for help.

Figure 11.9   Trend

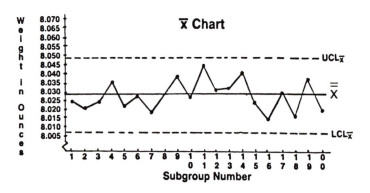

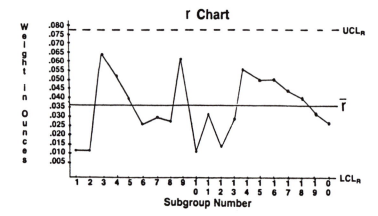

● Periodicity, shown in Figure 11.10, shows a regular wave pattern. This usually means that two things are being blended together, and result in an invalid control chart. This requires the operator to call for help, or for additional training.

Figure 11.10 Periodicity

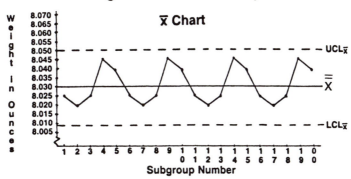

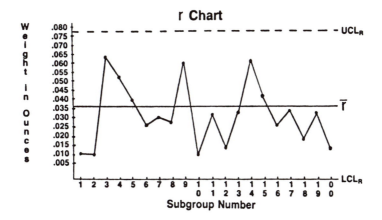

● Hugging, although not an indication of un-quality, does show an invalid control chart. As shown in Figure 11.11, the x-bar measurements all fall very close to the average; hugging it. This probably means that the process has been improved, and the control chart has not been updated to match.

● Any time a point beyond a control limit occurs, as we see in Figure 11.12, bad parts are being produced and the operator shuts down and calls for help.

Developing and using control charts for countable data are very similar, and equally valid.

Figure 11.11   Hugging

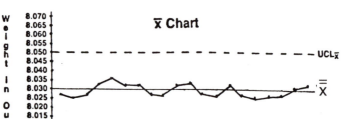

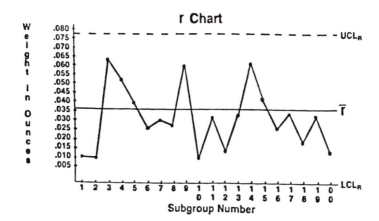

Implementing Planned Maintenance

Run it until it breaks is no longer a viable strategy if it ever was. But as we really get serious about zero inventories, small lot sizes, and schedule performance in the high nineties simply will not work if your machines are breaking down randomly.

Planned maintenance in a JIT setting requires that the operators consider that they own the machines, not the maintenance department or some amorphous they. In JIT factories, the workers do the daily, easy maintenance. This includes simple adjustments, oiling, checking fluid levels, and keeping the equipment clean. The worker also sweeps and cleans the immediate area. When this is adopted, the worker can notice when things are going wrong. Are there any leaks? Are there any vibrations? Are there any funny noises? When the operator takes ownership

Figure 11.12 Point Beyond a Control Limit

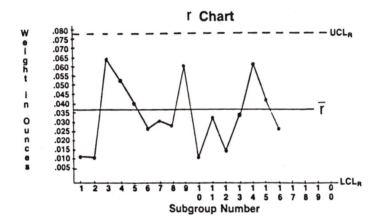

of the equipment, you find a dramatic improvement in machine performance.

The second level of maintenance is usually done by the maintenance department on a fixed schedule. This level occurs on an off shift if available, otherwise takes the machine out of service for a short while. In second level, maintenance adjustments are made and simple repairs and replacements made.

The third level is major maintenance, often teardown, inspection, and rebuilding. Third level maintenance usually can't be finished on an off shift, takes the equipment out of service for one or more days, and is scheduled accordingly.

Preventive maintenance works well with your zero defects program, because most of the signals recommended occur before the machine has to be shut down.

Steady, preventive maintenance also assures you that the factory routinely and permanently is in condition to manufacture perfect quality.

Using Standard Operations

Standard operations grow naturally out of Group Technology work cells. In these work centers, all items manufactured there are very similar, and could possibly use the same routed operations. JIT environments seldom have piecework payment methods, so highly precise time standards are not necessary. Standard, close approximations are good enough for scheduling and monitoring progress.

If your computer systems permit, these standard operations can merely be entered once in your files and then invoked when needed, thereby reducing considerably the work load of the Industrial Engineering Department, and perhaps even the Cost Accounting Department.

JIT strongly emphasizes flexibility, and using standard operations adds to flexibility.

Using Computer-Aided Process Planning

Modern technology already has put Computer Aided Design (CAD), Computer Aided Manufacturing (CAM), Numerical Control (NC) of machines, and MRP II based systems in common use. Unfortunately, there is little interfacing between these systems. Any cooperation among them usually is done through the brute-force method of reentering data from one system to the next.

We are beginning to see some integration of these technologies, and in the 1990s we will see more. The coming scenario will have the design team create the design using CAD. The data from this system will be down loaded to the MRP system's item master file and bills of material. At the same time the NC machines will have their programs created, and standard operations will be flagged. Then when the MRP system calls for a shop order, a bar coded signal will start the manufacturing process, where parts will be picked or automatically deducted from inventory, and NC controlled machines will be started up. Small lot sizes will come out the end of the manufacturing cycle in minutes instead of weeks.

Balancing Final Assembly Scheduling

One good way to reduce lead time is to stock sub-assemblies and do final assembly only after the customer's order is received. This requires two schedules, one resulting in the sub assemblies being on hand, usually represented by the Master Production Schedule. The Assembly Schedule is a second schedule with many of the same characteristics as the MPS. It consumes material and capacity.

In a JIT setting, where short lead time is emphasized, using the Final Assembly Approach is allowing many companies to ship the same or next day. This also has the effect of reducing inventories drastically, when compared with holding finished goods.

As is the case with Group Technology work cells, the final assembly line or lines need to be balanced in order not to create idle time, especially for workers. Good forecasting and good industrial engineering help keep this problem under control.

Using a Mixed Model Final Assembly

This powerful JIT idea is to make something of everything every day and to make them one at a time in rotation. In this way, you can ship them out in the sequence they are manufactured. Where possible, this gives you a very good level of customer service, with little if any finished goods.

Figure 11.13 shows a mixed model schedule for a television line. They make three models, a 14-inch, a 17-inch, and a 17-inch with a built-in video-cassette recorder/player.

Figure 11.13 Mixed Model Final Assembly Schedule

Model	Per Month	Per Week	Per Day	Per Hour
14"	500	125	25	4.2
17"	400	100	20	3.3
17"/VCR	300	75	15	2.5
Total	1200	300	60	10.0

Model mix in in 5,4,3 proportion
Mixed Sequence:
14", 17", 14", 17", 14", 17", 17"/VCR, 14", 17", 17"/VCR, 14", 17"/VCR

The principle here is to manufacture in the same tempo that the customers are buying your TV sets. The tempo should be as shown per day per hour. In this way you will avoid finished goods inventory, because you will ship each day's mix. You can easily make corrections for variations in daily mix, either the same day or the next one.

Using the Push System, the Pull System, or Both

The pull system has the advantage of eliminating the conventional work orders and shop order packets. Pull's principle is to send a signal to the upstream, supplying work center, when a subsequent, downstream department needs more.

Kanban is the classic form of pull. Kanban means card in Japanese. Kanban asks that a signal (card) be sent back to the supplying department when a replenishment is needed. The kanban authorizes the supplying department to make another batch, presumably a small one, and send it forward. A signal is not confined to a card. It often is an empty tote pan. I have heard of signals as varied as colored golf balls to electronic signals.

You can pull from a vendor just as well as from a prior work center.

Pull systems work best in focused factories or in straight-line flow production settings. It is less workable in the traditional, functionally-organized job shop, with it spider-web routings. This is where MRP II, which has great planning and scheduling power work best.

In many factories, especially where Group Technology flow production and job-shop layouts both exist, both pull (kanban), and push (MRP II) can be used, side by side. In these environments, some alteration needs to be done to standard MRP II, to shut off its shop floor control features for the pull work centers. This should not be difficult, and you should not hesitate to have a mixed factory.

HOW TO APPLY JIT TO ENGINEERING

Many of the advantages of JIT ideas start in Engineering, emphasizing once more that JIT, and manufacturing in general, are company-wide concerns, not just manufacturing ones.

Designing for Manufacturing/Concurrent Design

Until JIT principles put the spotlight on this activity, many design engineering departments did their work in relative isolation from the rest of production; somewhat of an ivory tower condition. In this environment, the engineers designed end items with no special regard for how they would be produced in the factory nor how the components would be procured. Many was the design that couldn't easily and profitably be manufactured in the existing facility. Nor were some components readily and economically available in commercial quantities.

I have seen companies that take the engineering drawings and specifications and redo them elsewhere. Usually manufacturing engineering, production control, and purchasing sit down and re-do engineering's work, putting the sub-assemblies in the right places, and designating commercial equivalents to exotic components.

When I run into such a situation, I always ask the executives who has control over the designs? Certainly not design engineering.

With the current emphasis on world-class performance and JIT, this situation is swiftly disappearing. The substitute is to invoke a design team made up of engineers, but also including knowledgeable people from manufacturing operations, sales and marketing, manufacturing and industrial engineering, production and inventory control, and purchasing. The objective is to deliver a design that will result in a product your customers want to buy at your profit margin, can be manufactured in your factory at the necessary cost, and for which components can be bought economically in commercial quantities. Also the design should be so ripe, that few engineering changes will be necessary to correct bugs.

Concurrent engineering also has the very good advantage of cutting design time sharply. In the auto industry, this technique is reducing the time to design a new car from five years to two. In less complex products, concurrent design can get a new product in the hands of your customers in weeks instead of months or years.

How to Do It Right the First Time and Allow the Time to Do So

I have often seen slapdash designs sent over to manufacturing because design engineering simply has not been allowed enough time to do the job right. I have never talked to an engineer who wanted to do shoddy work, but I have known many who were forced into it by unrealistic due dates. On investigation, I usually find that the planned total design lead time was adequate, but upstream functions ate up too much time and engineering was forced to make up some of the slack.

It is a duty of upper management to see to it that the project to design a new product is well planned and monitored. Every function must be allotted enough time and resources to do the job right, and then kept on schedule.

Figure 11.14 shows a graph of when engineering changes occur during the life of an end item in the typical Japanese company. Notice that the bulk of engineering changes come during the design and pre-production cycle, before the product is shipped to their customers. Contrarily, as shown in Figure 11.15, U.S.-designed products have a large bulge of engineering changes just after the product starts to be used, and follows its life cycle. This means that customers using U.S.-designed products are finding problems, whereas the Japanese manufacturers find most of their flaws before introduction. This is one big cause of the bad reputation U.S. manufacturing is suffering under today.

Figure 11.14 Ratio of Engineering Changes to Units Produced - Japan

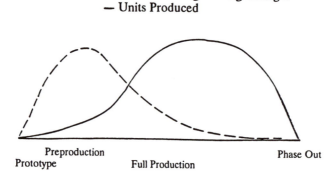

--- Number of Engineering Changes
— Units Produced

Preproduction
Prototype
Full Production
Phase Out

This reputation will persist long after the problem is eliminated, as has already happened in many U.S. companies.

The legendary penchant of American managers to be preoccupied with the short term is manifested here, much to the
disadvantage of manufacturing in the U.S.

Figure 11.15   Ratio of Engineering Changes to Units Produced -
U.S.A.

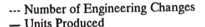

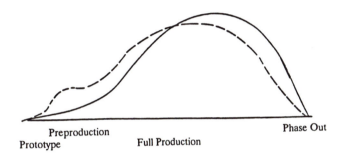

Preproduction Prototype Full Production Phase Out

Using Plant Layout and Group Technology

Chapter 10 is devoted to this subject, but it remains an
engineering function. Factories laid out functionally are basically
less efficiently than those laid out according to process. You
usually find long travel time, large batch sizes, large queues,
poor quality, inaccurate schedules, missed customer due dates,
and excessive inventory in these facilities. Whenever possible,
organizing your factories according to how you manufacture your
families of products is a far superior approach. Although usually
associated with high-volumes and narrow product lines, the
Group Technology flow line approach can be applied more extensively than many realize at first.

The new emphasis on time compression as well as those of
JIT should give all of us a bias toward continuous, flow production.

How to Develop and Use Good Time Standards

When the implementation of your JIT ideas begin to take
hold, your inventories will drop, your queues will evaporate, and

your schedules will be good. Good scheduling requires that loads and capacities be well balanced. This means that there will not be a generous buffer of work in front of each work center just in case. In a JIT environment, the next job will arrive just as it should be started. This means that if a worker finishes up a job faster than expected, the next job likely will not be there waiting. Workers being very clever about these things, will slow down just enough so the next job will be there waiting.

In a closely coupled factory with skimpy queues, time standards become much more important than before, both to help calculate load and to provide setup and run times for scheduling.

The problem of developing usable time standards for machine-paced activities is not very difficult. Any competent industrial engineer can figure out the cycle pace of a machine or process quickly and accurately.

The difficulty in arriving at time standards occurs with labor-paced activities. There are several ways to develop labor-paced time standards:

- Ask the Supervisor

- Historical Average

- Just Like a Similar Product

- Stop Watch

- Predetermined

If you ask the supervisor or a production worker how much time to allow for an operation, their natural tendency is to make it generous. It is to their advantage, particularly if they are accustomed to being evaluated based on these standards.

Historical averages use the time taken for the same or similar item over time, and average them. Supervisors and operators always try to hide indirect activities in run times, and historical data is always inflated.

Companies who make a new time standard out of a similar, existing one, usually allow a little extra time to each one.

I once worked for a company whose product line was updated on a yearly basis. The new items were very much like the old ones, so Industrial Engineering took last year's standard and allowed a little extra time. I discovered that they had been repeating this practice for more than 20 years, adding allowance on top of allowance each year. Their time standards were so grotesquely incorrect, that they were entirely useless.

The stop watch approach to setting standards at least tries to be professional and precise. One trouble with this approach is that at the end of the process the engineer must make a subjective judgement as to the performance of the operator being timed. Is this operator working at 100 percent, or at 80 percent, or at 125 percent? It is well-known that most machine operators can put on a show for an engineer and make themselves look like they are really whizzing along, when in reality they are going slower than they usually do. The result is that stopwatch standards are chronically loose.

Predetermined time standards are available for all manufacturing activities. Started in the 1940s, these standards have been built up, refined and validated over and over. At the present time there is a good time standard for every movement your body can make, at the same time taking into account the difficulty of the activity. For instance, it is a lot easier to pick up a hex bolt than a flat washer from a flat surface.

The modern versions of these predetermined standards are computerized to point where all the engineer needs to do is identify the movements and key in their code identifiers. The computer takes over and prints out a good routing and accompanying time standards. And to make the job still faster and easier, the most common combinations of activities have been grouped into macro elements.

The challenge in using predetermined time standards is in training the engineer to be able to observe and record *all* activities. Otherwise the result will be a standard that is too tight.

There are many versions and suppliers of these systems. The most well-known is a technique called MTM (Methods Time Measurement) and its macro versions. This is public domain data and is managed and promulgated by the MTM Association for Standards and Research.[1]

Predetermined time standards can have a bias toward being too tight, if the practitioner misses an activity. All the other methods mentioned above have a strong tendency to being too loose; 40 to 60 percent loose, actually.

---

[1]MTM Association for Standards and Research; 16–01 Broadway; Fair Lawn, NJ 07410.

In a close-coupled, JIT factory, running lean on inventory, you will be forced to live down to your time standards if they are too loose. And compounding the evil is that it will look to your system as 100 percent performance. Beware!

THREE CHANGES YOU NEED TO MAKE IN YOUR TRADITIONAL ADMINISTRATIVE RULES

JIT principles by nature deny business as usual. There are three important administrative procedures that need to be changed in moving to JIT, some of them quite contentious and radical.

How to Make Your Suppliers Family, not Adversaries

Ever since business schools were invented, it has be *de rigeur* for purchasing to have three current competitive bids for each non-trivial item used in manufacturing. Suppliers were treated as if they were crooks trying to short you on counts and slip you shoddy goods at inflated prices. As a result you were expected to play off one supplier against another and beat them down as much as possible on price. Then to make sure they don't slip anything by, you sent them elaborate specifications and set up an equally elaborate receiving inspection department to police adherence.

JIT calls for just the opposite. Suppliers are to be treated as the outside factory. You should strive to have just one supplier for each item. And their shipments are not inspected either for quantity or quality. Their items can go directly to the line.

This kind of relationship must be developed and earned mutually with a formal systematic program. Communication is broadened. Anybody can talk to anybody; the buyer loses this monopoly. Engineers help engineers, and quality departments work together. You develop a long-term commitment to keep buying from that supplier as long as performance holds or gets better. Cost decreases are shared.

Suppliers in this status are called Class 1. Suppliers who are actively working with you to achieve Class 1 status are Class 2 suppliers. Class 3 suppliers are not making any effort to work with you on this process. There are many companies, including some very large ones, who have a corporate strategy to have no Class 3 suppliers within just a few years.

The obvious lesson here is that routinely being a Class 1 supplier will soon be a condition of survival. In the mean time being Class 1 with one customer will help you sell your products to other JIT oriented customers.

How to Make Your Workers Family, Not Adversaries

Since the 1930s with increased militant unionism, there has developed a strong adversarial relationship between management and labor. It is now very clear to both parties that this is not possible anymore considering the demands of being world-class. JIT principles also cry out for worker empowerment. Factory workers are supplying the bulk of the ideas for setup reductions. Worker empowerment is a necessity for process-based flawless quality.

We no longer can afford to ask our workers to check their brains at the time clock and act like robots once they start work. Moreover, increased automation and use of computers to control our factory operations demand that workers think for themselves.

Some companies are developing self-directed work groups. This is a work group with no supervisor. As a group they make the decisions normally associated with a work center supervisor, including training, counseling, hiring, and even firing. Companies who do a good job of implementation are achieving excellent results in terms of costs, quality, and quantity; besides the obvious morale factor. Some companies even have stopped calling themselves employees. They now are associates (or something similar).

Such an environment requires substantially less supervision, and most of the bureaucracy associated with dispute resolution can be disbanded.

These and other overhead activities are properly called waste in JIT lore.

In the 1980s we have seen a dramatic turn-around in the traditional militant attitude of many if not most unions, and the managements of most companies. We now realize that a partnership is one way to keep jobs and even whole industries from being exported.

How to Establish a Focused Factory

A focused factory is a manufacturing facility, purposely kept small. It focuses on one product, product line, or a group of similar ones. The key is that there is similarity. The focused factory can be thought of as a logical extension of the Group Technology process flow techniques of factory layout.

The focused factory is usually has under 1,000 employees, and often fewer than 500.

Until recently, orthodox thinking concentrated on economies of scale. It was widely thought that the bigger the factory and its machinery, the lower the cost of the product. This also included emphasis on vertical integration.

In an era of standard products, with stable designs, and a high labor content, this may have been true. However, in the last decade we have evolved to a point where direct labor is usually less than 20 percent of cost of good sold, and occasionally less than 5 percent. In addition, we now have a large proliferation of varieties within a product or product line. This applies to consumer products as well as to industrial ones.

When you are forced to run a wide variety of versions, features, and options through a large and vertically-integrated facility a number of disadvantages happen.

Larger machines usually take longer to set up. This means we either spend more money on setups, or resort to large lot sizes. Many manufacturing managers are accustomed to turning a blind eye to inventory carrying cost, and create some large inventory pools. At 36 percent a year carrying cost, this is an expensive way to buy your way out of high setup costs.

The complexities of such facilities are very hard to plan for, even with elaborate MRP II systems.

Large factories have large administrative functions. These functions grow disproportionately as variety increases. Sales, Order Processing, Purchasing, Production Planning and Control, Engineering, Quality Control and Accounting are classic functions that have to be able to cope with the complexity of a wide product line. It seems also that administrative functions increase faster than output, as factories get bigger.

The focused factory avoids some of these problems. The first one has to do with vertical integration. The focused factory emphasizes assembly and shallow bills of material. Such a facility will have a larger purchased component in their end items than the vertically-integrated one. This fits very well with the concepts of single-source, cooperative vendors.

Implementation of the focused factory idea can vary greatly. Taken to its logical extreme, a focused factory would have its own engineering, sales, accounting, purchasing, and field service functions, beyond just manufacturing. Some corporations have product lines that allow this, others not. Usually, how many activities to focus is a matter of judgement.

One client decided to focus their factories, but to keep purchasing centralized for common parts and commodities. This meant that each factory has its own purchasing department for its own parts, but had to requisition central purchasing for the items they have assigned to them. This resulted in fairly smooth purchasing through the local function, but some real difficulties with the central office. There was a necessary delay in getting the requisitions to them. Other channels of communication such as status requests, engineering changes, expedite messages, and quality problems got slow and difficult.

I believe that if you move toward the focused factory approach, you should include all possible functions, even when some efficiency is lost. This loss probably will be more than made up by better communication and shorter manufacturing and administrative times. Besides, you can still get many of the benefits of large-scale purchases by organizing a corporate blanket, with individual factories releasing their own requirements as needed.

The big advantage of the focused factory is that everybody and everything is focused on a narrow range of products and get very good at producing them.

HOW MANAGEMENT NEEDS TO CHANGE TO IMPLEMENT JIT

The need for top management participation and support applies broadly. It is obvious to all of us who have spent any time in the corporate world that people do what pleases the boss. If management is conspicuously dedicated to implementing and enhancing JIT principles, it will affect the daily activities of everyone in the company. However, if you display an attitude that it is somebody else's bailiwick, then everybody will be waiting for that mythical somebody else to get JIT ideas installed.

Educating and Training Managers and Executives

Just because you are a vice president does not make you perfect. I am continually surprised at the resistance of middle and upper management to admit that there are things they don't know. Yet, for JIT ideas to give you their promises, you have to know how to use them. Local consultants, colleges and universities, seminar promoters, and professional societies all offer quality seminars and lectures on JIT, many oriented toward managers. In addition, there are a number of good books on the subject.

Setting Quality as a Priority

The day of the acceptable quality level, measured as a percentage of good parts is now over. Your customers will soon reject you as a supplier if you deliver that degree of un-quality. The new imperative is for zero defects. Instead of defects per hundred, we now are expected to measure our performance in terms of defects per million parts.

Statistical Process Control is the answer, as expressed earlier in this chapter. Still, insistence on quality at this level is a managerial responsibility.

A natural extension of this new fixation on quality has extended to all areas of the company. We now realize that every employee has a customer, from the telephone operator to the receptionist. To have a quality-oriented company, you must instill a perfectionist drive in everyone.

In the 1990s, quality in all activities is certain to become the new norm.

Allowing for Idle Workers and Idle Machines with JIT

In the traditional factory, supervisors are rated on how well they keep their direct laborers busy. This is more the case in functional, labor-paced factories than in process industries, or factories that have adopted Group Technology process flows.

JIT principles however rate too soon as almost as bad as too late. This means that if a work center has completed its schedule of work for the day, they stop production. It is no longer acceptable to start on tomorrow's work, just to keep the workers occupied.

As with many JIT ideals, you earn this condition with good schedules and good adherence to them. You earn this with flawless quality from vendors and upstream work centers.

But the traditional utilization reports that managements have used since the dawn of the industrial revolution must be discontinued to make everything truly just in time. Otherwise supervisors and workers will keep producing inventory you don't need now, and may even never need.

Just-in-Time principles also quarrel with the accountants' desire to keep all machines running all the time. In a JIT factory, you purposely build in a little extra capacity to allow you to recover from daily upsets that otherwise would prevent schedule adherence. JIT factories regularly schedule their work centers at less than capacity. The rule is if you are not done, keep producing beyond normal quitting time, and if you get done somewhat early, stop.

These two principles do not mean that your workers will be sitting on their hands at the end of the day. There are many desirable indirect activities to be performed, such as housekeeping, training, setup reduction, and small group improvement meetings.

These time spans can also be used for cross training. Or, a cross-trained worker can quickly jump over to another work center to help out if they are running late.

Making Your Workers Versatile

The JIT ideal is for any worker to be able to do any job in the factory. This calls for cross-training. You can't just leave cross-training to chance. To achieve widespread cross training requires a formal, structured program, administered by the Human Resources Department. Some companies raise workers to a higher labor grade as they become cross trained.

It is easier to achieve universal cross-training in a focused factory than in a large complex one. But the principle applies, varying only to the possible extent of cross-training.

In the last few years, the idea of cross training is being applied to managers and administrators, especially in areas where specific technical training is not required.

Part of the versatile worker idea also is that the worker owns the machine and area immediately surrounding it. JIT ideals call for the worker to take charge of housekeeping in the immediate area.

Beyond just keeping the machinery clean, versatile workers also do first line maintenance, as mentioned earlier in this chapter.

Traditionally, in unionized factories, this amount of versatility has been prohibited. But in the last few years, unions have become much more understanding about the need to adopt efficient JIT practices as a matter of survival. Contractual restrictions to versatility are disappearing fast.

Adopting JIT Performance Measures

The specific performance measures are covered in Chapter 12. But this is a Management-level JIT topic. You need to address three important management issues regarding performance measurements in a JIT setting.

The first issue concerns current, orthodox measurements. Every company has performance measurements. Many emanate from the accounting department, others are performance measures imbedded in your salary administration systems. Manufacturing operations and industrial engineering frequently measure various performances. In order to implement good, comprehensive JIT-oriented performance measures, you must develop a complete list of all measures and where they come from.

Step two is to evaluate all of these measures. Those that conflict with JIT performance must be eliminated.

Step three is to create as few new measures as needed to keep the company on the JIT track. These measures should be published regularly and actively used to motivate the entire company. These new measures definitely should become part of your compensation program. In this area, the new emphasis is to reward teamwork more and individual performance less, than has been traditionally been the case.

Handling Inventory and Safety Stock with JIT

Inventory and Safety Stock are Naughty. This attitude is a radical JIT departure from traditional thinking. The zero inventory ideal of JIT is not frivolous. Almost all inventory covers up problems, errors, and sub-optimal performance. It is a managerial responsibility to continually monitor inventory and analyze why it occurs. You will find a large list of excuses, some more realistic than others. The managerial imperative is to analyze the causes of inventory and safety stock levels, and to systematically take steps to eliminate their causes. Some common reasons are that safety stock buffers against schedule and quality problems from suppliers and previous work centers. Functionally arranged factories usually have generous inventory queues in front of each work center to buffer against machine breakdowns, schedule problems, tooling problems, to name just a few. Large lot sizes always leave residual inventory.

Whenever and wherever you observe inventory, you are observing a degradation from perfection.

Accounting also has a flaw in their current conventions. Accounting theory calls inventory an asset. This is not true. Inventory is an expense waiting to happen, and should be labeled as such. If your plans are sound, eventually you will use your inventories to manufacture products and sell them to your customers. When this occurs, inventory becomes cost of goods sold, an expense. But you are not always so lucky. If your inventory becomes obsolete or becomes unusable, you sell it for scrap, which certainly is an expense.

We are all taught to consider assets as desirable, and calling inventory an asset obscures the fact that it is truly undesirable.

HOW TO USE TIME COMPRESSION, THE NEW COMPETITIVE TOOL

In manufacturing, we have made great strides in reducing lead times, using JIT ideas. One of the big gains is in laying out the factory according to production flows instead of by function. We covered this in Chapter 10. Many companies have reduced their manufacturing throughput time to hours or days instead of weeks or months. In such environments, you can no longer tolerate taking several days to process and schedule an incoming customer order, several more days to make a shop packet ready for the factory, another day or two to get the end items packed and shipped, and finally days or weeks in transit.

Because this is an emerging technique, we can't be sure where it will lead, but our experience in the factory can show us the way. To achieve a time-compressed factory you will go through three phases.

Analyzing and Streamlining Your Present Operations

The first phase in compressing your administrative activities is to analyze your current operations. Industrial engineers all have studied work flow charting, with the classic symbols; an "O" for operation, a box for inspection, an arrow for a movement a "D" for delay and a triangle for storage. Figure 11.16 has a simple example of a typical process analysis chart.

Figure 11.16   Flow Progress Chart

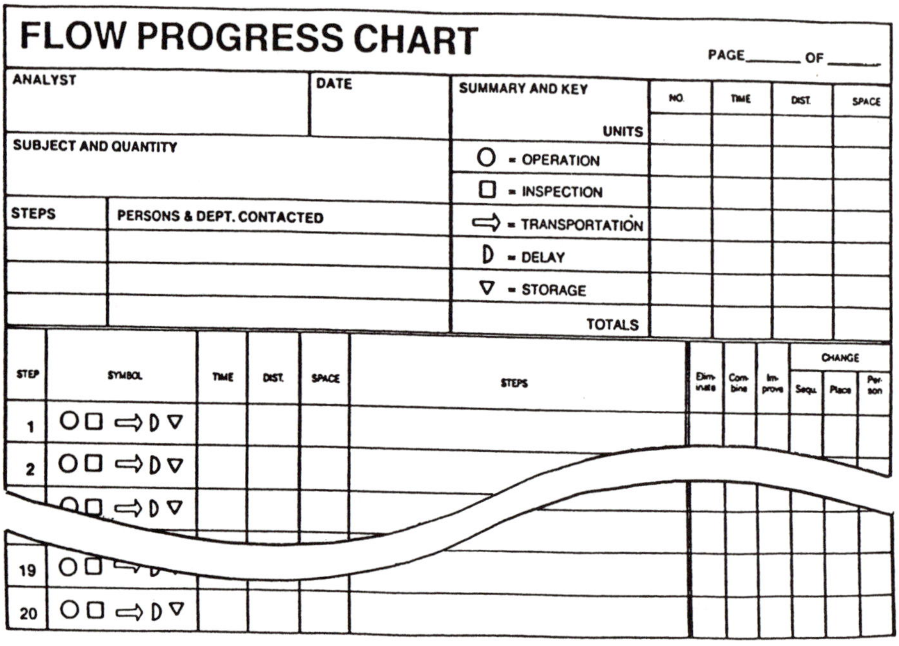

FLOW PROGRESS CHART

PAGE_____ OF _____

ANALYST		DATE		SUMMARY AND KEY		NO.	TIME	DIST.	SPACE
				UNITS					
SUBJECT AND QUANTITY				O = OPERATION					
				☐ = INSPECTION					
STEPS	PERSONS & DEPT. CONTACTED			⇨ = TRANSPORTATION					
				D = DELAY					
				▽ = STORAGE					
				TOTALS					

STEP	SYMBOL	TIME	DIST.	SPACE	STEPS	Elim-inate	Com-bine	Im-prove	Sequ.	Place	Per-son
									CHANGE		
1	O ☐ ⇨ D ▽										
2	O ☐ ⇨ D ▽										
	O ☐ ⇨ D ▽										
19	O ☐ ⇨ D ▽										
20	O ☐ ⇨ D ▽										

Although this analysis tool has been around for decades, it almost always is used to analyze factory operations. But now with the need for time compression upon us, we can call on this tried and true technique to help us improve.

Choose a small, but frequent activity, such as approving an invoice for payment, and analyze it. Any competent industrial engineer can do this. The new aspect of the analysis, however, is to be highly sensitive to activities that do not need to be done. You should justify every operation and every inspection. Certainly moves and delays are conspicuous candidates for improvement.

You can fairly quickly streamline your present operations by doing this IE analysis of your main activities.

Establishing Tiger Teams

Once you have identified your main work flows, you can set up some Tiger Teams. A Tiger Team is made up of knowledgeable people, one from each main department involved. The Engineering Change Control Board, which many companies use, is a model.

The Tiger Team meets periodically, daily or more often. Picture the customer order processing Tiger Team. They could meed two to four times a day, depending on how often it is efficient to pick up the mail. The Tiger Team sits down at a conference table and processes all the orders through all of the steps on your streamlined flowchart. The Tiger Team is empowered to make decisions, binding on the home departments of the members as well on the whole company. In the example of customer order processing, the task is done in minutes, and the next activity can begin immediately. This eliminates transportation and many delays. And because the participants are all together and confer with one another, the quality of their work is better than before.

How to Reorganize the Company

This will be the contentious phase, because it will require a drastic change to your conventional organization chart. Currently you are organized functionally, the way old-fashioned factories are. You have an accounting department that takes care of accounting for all products. You have functional departments for sales and marketing, design engineering, personnel, data processing, purchasing, production control, inventory control, industrial and manufacturing engineering, and manufacturing operations. This could be called vertical organization.

The time compressed company will have a horizontal organization based on Business Teams. We will take our lesson from the group technology process flow organization in the factory. Under the GT model, we line up dissimilar machines together to produce a family of very similar items. Building on this, and your experience with Tiger Teams, you will develop Business Teams focused on a narrow scope. This focus could be by customer group, product lines, or even geography. Most likely it will be by product group.

Ideally, each Business Team will have its own sales and marketing, accounting, design engineering, production and inventory control, and the all the rest. The Business Team also will control the Group Technology work cells. In this environment, the traditional organization chart just about disappears. The only remaining tasks for the skeleton that will be left will be to do the few things that apply to the company as a whole. You will need an accounting group make outside reports as required by law. Engineering may need company wide standards, although that could also be done by a committee. Some personnel and finance issues are inherently company wide, and will continue.

Carrying this logic forward and backward, the Business Teams would form "partnerships" with suppliers and customers, and time-compress the entire supply chain.

Retailing is leading the way in supply chain time compression. *APICS—The Performance Advantage*, in its December 1991 issue, has a story about a KG Men's Store who sends a summary of their day's sales of Levi's, back to them by Electronic Data Interchange (EDI). Levi's manufacturing system automatically schedules replenishment, then signals Milliken, their denim factory, by EDI, who automatically replenish Levi's. Then Milliken, in turn, flashes the news to DuPont, whose system takes action to replenish the yarn.

This is the wave of the future, and could easily become the United States' answer to the interlocking Japanese supply chain companies called *keiretsu*.

EXAMINING THE DISADVANTAGES OF JIT

JIT romantics would like us to believe that JIT applies everywhere. While these principles and ideals are very broadly based, they still do have some disadvantages and areas where they don't apply themselves well.

Analyzing Where Pull (Kanban) Doesn't Work Very Well

Kanban, probably the most famous JIT idea, does not fit as well in job shops as in smooth process flow shops. Job shops need complex routings, and usually have a large number if different work orders for quite different parts open all the time. Group Technology flow lines and focused factories, on the other hand, lend themselves well to the kanban idea.

Engineering changes are a little hard to time phase, especially when one change order applies to several parts. Synchronizing a complex change requires personal attention on the floor, because there is no centralized control. Use-up effectivity of several parts at the same time also is hard, and you easily could be left with some obsolete items.

Product phase-in and phase-out can give some of the same synchronization problems as engineering changes do. Again, in a focused or GT environment, this is less of a problem, but still significant.

Low volume and nonrepetitive products lend themselves better to a job shop, and not to kanban. Nonproprietary designs, where you make a product to your customer's specification, often are also not amenable to the smoothness needed by kanban.

Government work, especially defense work, are governed by procurement regulations and contract stipulations which can easily prevent you from using kanban, and other JIT ideas. For example, many military contracts require material to be procured separately for each contract, and stored in segregated areas.

Off-shore procurement usually requires large lot sizes. Ocean transportation usually has poorer schedule reliability than trucks and trains. Import customs is also legendary around the world for delay and no scheduling. I have had more than one client who allows as much time for customs clearance as for ocean transit time, and their throughput times are widely variable. This makes using kanban and a number of JIT ideas hard to use.

How to Integrate JIT with MRP II

There are a number of classic MRP II functions that need to be changed after JIT, especially a pull-oriented one, is implemented.

Capacity planning at the Production Plan, Master Production Scheduling, and Shop Floor levels, currently focus on providing resources according to discrete time periods. Under JIT the focus changes to assuring capacity to achieve and maintain the correct rate or tempo of production. Similarly, Master Production Scheduling concentrates on rates.

Material Requirements Planning (MRP I) could possibly change quite drastically. JIT efforts can make bills very shallow. Zero inventories and just in time receipts could eliminate inventory, just as manufacturing shortens up leadtime to a day or so. In such a setting the complex logic of MRP I which back- schedules using lead times, lot sizes, and inventory on hand, could become superfluous. It could be that MRP I will confine itself to a one-pass explosion, in effect just a gross explosion, all time-phased for the same starting date. When your parts come in today and the end item ships tomorrow, you won't need the elaborate planning that MRP I is justly famous for.

Shop floor control currently manages execution with a daily or hourly schedule, shop orders, and a dispatch list. In an advanced JIT environment, this gives way to the pull signals of kanban or its substitutes. This function shrinks considerably

Manufacturing engineering's job will be far easier. They will develop standard routes to govern the limited number of flow lines in the factory, instead of having to maintain a route for every item going through the plant.

The role of quality control changes dramatically. No longer will they inspect quality into batches and measure acceptable quality levels in defects per hundred. Rather they will monitor the manufacturing machinery, equipment, and processes to make sure that no bad quality is being made. Moreover, they become mentors and coaches to the workers, not police.

Cost development will continue much as it now is being done, except that we will see overhead applied by activity instead of direct labor. But the bill of material will still provide the material portion and the standard routing the direct labor portion of your standard cost.

Production cost monitoring, however will be quite different. Currently, we like to monitor actual cost by shop order. In a pull system, there likely will be no shop orders to record costs against. Therefore, cost monitoring will be by the processes that we have developed under Group Technology and Focused Factories.

Production Control, in a JIT environment, will quit tracking work in process, because it moves so fast, and confine itself to planning and monitoring production rates.

On the inventory side, we already see much more automatic issuing, also called backflushing. This is the technique that automatically decrements inventory, according to a bill of material explosion factored for the amount completed. This means that if you make 100 little red wagons, you take 400 wheels out of inventory as production is completed. Backflushing is becoming very popular in non-JIT and nonpull factories, and works very well after proper education and training.

Purchasing in the JIT environment has suppliers become members of the family, as mentioned earlier in this chapter. This means purchasing professionals quit being preoccupied with creating a purchase order for every increment. Rather, they take the lead in negotiating Class 1 status. The purchasing activity becomes much more professional under JIT!

Releasing increments for shipments from the supplier will be by some sort of kanban-style signal. Electronic Data Interchange (EDI) is becoming widely used, and will supplant releases almost universally, even for companies using few other JIT ideals. EDI makes releases paperless, instantaneous, and integrates the customer's and supplier's systems.

12

HOW TO IMPLEMENT
A PROGRAM
FOR CONTINUOUS
IMPROVEMENT

They say that the pace of change is accelerating. The Cold War and the Berlin Wall suddenly evaporated. Economic cycles come and go. Who would have thought a few years ago that we would export our entire consumer electronics industry to the Pacific Rim? How old is the personal computer, and how many basic upgrades has it gone through?

I had a client a few years ago, in the medical apparatus industry. They had an electronics-based product. We all were horrified that the lifespan of their product line was two years. By the time they got a new product into their marketing channels, it already was obsolete. They had to have the next model in the development pipeline, even before the current one was established.

In more recent years, a two-year life span for a technology-oriented product is medium; many products are shorter.

For your company to succeed and remain successful, you must have an environment that asks for constant improvement. If you aren't gaining on your competitors, they are gaining on you.

HOW TO DEVELOP A CHANGE-RECEPTIVE ENVIRONMENT

The Prussian or military command-structure type of environment is naturally hostile to change, especially coming up from lower levels of the organization chart. Especially resulting from the JIT influence, organizational rigidity is softening, and in some companies has become downright soft. J.C. Dithers rightfully belongs in the funny papers.

Take a Long-Term View

American business continues to take a lot of criticism for being transfixed with quarterly reporting to the securities analysts. This might be appropriate in the Treasurer's office, but not in manufacturing. I have had several clients, particularly large ones, where upper managers are looking at this quarter's or this year's results, while middle managers are working on projects and ideas that take more than a year to bring into being, and longer than that for the payback to come in. This is known as Horizon Inversion. The proper perspective is for higher managers to be looking farther out into the future, middle managers less far, while group supervisors and work center leaders look out just a few weeks. In order to make your environment receptive to change, the horizons should be correctly in place.

Establish the Concept of "Plateaus of Excellence"

When a new idea comes along, it is very easy to ask, "Why haven't we been doing this already?" This carries an implied criticism of those in charge. This reaction should be resisted, because it will stifle innovation, and raise the hackles of defensiveness.

A good case in point is the difference between the performance of reorder point/safety stock systems compared to MRP II-based systems. MRP manages inventories much better, and it is easy to poke fun at the excesses, poor schedules, and stock outs endemic to the old techniques. I strongly believe, however, that this is just cheap-shooting. The fact is that between the dawn of the Industrial Revolution, and that of the MRP Crusade, ROP was the only way we had to plan and schedule manufacturing activities. And many companies achieved world-wide prominence running their factories this way. I like to recognize these accomplishments as Plateaus of Excellence, and to give praise to companies and individuals who worked hard to achieve them. We should be made to feel good about how far we have come.

No matter what the situation, or how bad things seem, you can usually identify the current status as a plateau, and now is the time to spring upward to the next one.

In the areas of production planning and control, in the last two decades we have witnessed the plateau of ROP used as a basis to climb to MRP I. That in turn gave way to the MRP II plateau, which now is allowing us to climb to a new plateau with JIT ideas and practices.

What's next? This is difficult to predict, but another plateau will come in sight sooner or later; probably sooner. We should all be on the lookout for whatever that might be, and be ready to go for it when it appears.

Plateaus of excellence apply both to individual departments and people, as well as to the plant and whole company.

The concept of plateaus of excellence builds a picture of a dynamic and exciting company, one that can progress and lead into the future; one that can succeed and thrive.

Decentralize Authority

In my many years of consulting, I have seen centralized and decentralized organizations. My opinion, which is steadily reinforced, is that decentralized works better. Even in the face of assertions of economy of scale and demands for managerial control, when possible, decentralize the planning and execution activities as much as possible.

For example, for many years, companies and their external auditors developed an elaborate authorization procedure for purchase orders. Trivial amounts could be ordered on the strength of the buyer's signature. Large amounts had to be signed for by the head of the department. Larger dollar amounts had to be bucked upstairs to some vice president to be counter-signed. This kind of bureaucracy became ingrained in many decision-making processes.

Then MRP came along. For MRP-controlled items, purchase requisitions come out of the system, derived from the Master Production Schedule. It doesn't matter what the dollar amount is, the requisition has to be honored or the MPS will fail. In this environment the only monitoring that should be done regarding the buyer's commitments is how well he/she is fulfilling the requirements calculated by MRP.

Yet I still see many companies still burdened with the outmoded dollar/escalator approval rules.

Decentralization puts the decision making where the facts are. Employees will almost always make good decisions. I can't remember the last time I met an employee who wasn't strongly committed to the company's welfare. All they need is good tools and information to work with. Contrarily, I often get the feeling, that if you send a decision upstairs, it will be made on the basis of whim, ignorance, politics, or bad habit.

Another part of decentralization is to allow small expenditures, especially for improvements, to be made with no approval.

I heard of one company that used this principle in its setup reduction program. Each reduction team was authorized to spend $250 with no further approval. To stay within this ceiling, they scrounged around for discarded material and fixtures inside the plant, and even went bargain hunting at used equipment stores and junk yards. And this was on their own time!

The potential of unleashing the creative and motivational power of employees can be awesome, and decentralization is part of this process.

Threat

Today, people are worried about losing their jobs. Employees soon learn to shut off ideas and stall improvement projects when recent experience shows that they lead to layoffs. If you are fortunate, and your business is growing, you often can absorb displaced people in other jobs. In a steady or declining environment, this is not so easy. Attrition is the favored solution, if that is feasible.

The Harley-Davidson saga has it that they promised their workers no layoffs as a result of their dramatic JIT implementations. The result was that they did have some idle workers. To absorb them, they began to do job-shop work for other manufacturers, taking advantage of available workers, vacated floor space, and their high plateau of excellent quality.

Keep Your Organization Small and Simple

One way to keep your organization small is to have focused factories. The current thinking is to have plants of around 400 workers. In this environment, it is possible for the managers to know just about everybody by name. It is probable that they will have first-hand knowledge about the details of the plant's operations, especially its problems.

This work group also tends to have fewer layers in the organization chart, with the general manager having one or two intervening layers of management between him/her and the workers.

It often is more effective to have support functions at the plant level as well. This includes design and manufacturing engineering, purchasing, accounting, personnel, and even sales, when the distribution channels permit. Losing economies of scale often is more than made up by losing the diseconomies of bloated central bureaucracies and the extra lead times they impose.

Another emerging concept is using speed as a competitive advantage. In a focused factory, decisions can be made on the spot. This cuts out the time taken in larger organizations for the classic approval cycle. Changes can be made quickly. Customer service improves, as does your competitive posture.

To get small, you don't have to change brick and mortar.

I visited a large factory building, one of many of a huge U.S. manufacturer. The building had been divided into a number of focused factories, under the one roof. To delineate the different entities, they had short railings around their perimeters, and banners hanging from the rafters. Their office workers, including enclosed offices, were located inside the perimeters. They shared a lunchroom and the parking lot, but not much else.

This simple expedient gave them the advantages they were looking for in a focused factory, with almost no capital expenditure.

To stay simple, cut out as much staff as possible. Some writers are even suggesting that graduate business schools be closed, because all they turn out are staff technocrats who confuse the issues at headquarters. That may be too harsh a conclusion, but it is a good idea to eliminate as much staff burden as possible. Central staffs have a built-in tendency to block progress, especially improvements needed in the field. They tend have a strong "not invented here" problem.

Eliminating central staffs blends nicely with the ideas of focused factories and decentralization.

Cautioning Against Taking Success for Granted

Many companies grow from nothing to success and prominence in a short time, on the strength of a technical innovation or a marketing niche. This environment can lead to a degree of self-satisfaction and arrogance that blocks further innovation and progress.

I once worked for the XYZ Corporation that was a pioneer in the word processing marketplace. They got started before there was such a thing as a personal computer, using an IBM Selectric typewriter and some extra electronic devices that recorded keystrokes as they were being typed. Then, on replay, corrections could be made on the fly, and the new version captured on a second tape.

Then they progressed to an all-electronic device with a dedicated computer terminal, floppy diskettes, and a daisy wheel printer.

They designed and built their own computer, wrote their own operating system, and their own word-processing software. For a while they were an industry leader.

Then Apple appeared on the scene, and IBM introduced their first personal computer. Good software appeared quickly. This new combination of a good personal computer and good word processing software sold for a fraction of the cost of XYZ's product.

In spite of ample warning, XYZ took the attitude that they must be doing things right, proved by their success so far. They continued with business as usual.

Their arrogance was soon followed by humiliation. The newcomers took away all of their business. XYZ closed its two factories, and laid off all their manufacturing personnel, and just about everybody else. They are in Chapter 11, as this is being written, with a likelihood that they eventually will be liquidated. This whole scenario occurred within a 15-year period. This failure was due largely to the hypnotic effect of fast, conspicuous success.

Good management dictates that you use your success as a plateau, from which to climb to the next one. The arrogance syndrome is easy to spot. You may hear someone reject a new idea by saying, "We must be doing something right, look at how successful we are." That is the telltale symptom. The better response should be, "Let's take advantage of our success so far, and build more success for tomorrow."

How to Handle Resistance to Change

Resistance to change in a social organization is always present, more or less severely. Lewin[1] and Schein[2] developed a theory

---

[1] Lewin, Kurt. "Group Decision and Social Change," in *Readings in Social Psychology*, Maccoby, Newcomb and Hartley (Editors), Holt, Rinehart and Winston, New York, 1947, pp. 197–211.

[2] Schein, Edgar H. "The Mechanism of Change," in *Interpersonal Dynamics*, Bennis, Shein, Steels and Berlew (Editors), The Dosey Press, Homewood, Il., 1964, pp. 362–378.

for dealing with this real problem. Their approach seems to make sense, and can be used in the context of developing and implementing an MRP/JIT system.

Their approach has three phases:

- Unfreezing

- Movement

- Refreezing

Unfreezing has to do with creating an awareness that change is desirable. Unfreezing can be because competition is taking away business. Or it can be based on the idea that we want to step up to a higher plateau of excellence.

Movement is the development of the new environment or idea. This could be a simple improvement in a department, or a move to a major new system. In an MRP/JIT setting, the movement is the development of the new business system, with all of its new procedures, measures, and results.

Refreezing is the operation of the new system, according to its new procedures and measurements. This is accomplished by education, training, and hands-on use. This is also accomplished by discontinuing the old procedures.

The problem with this approach seems to be another frozen situation, and the whole cycle will be need to be repeated next time.

I have an improvement to suggest, and that is to refreeze in a "slushy" condition. This means as the new systems are developed and implemented, together with their measurements of success, that the developers build in a continuing, routine mechanism to review progress and to make corrections and improvements steadily. My idea is to refreeze a condition that is permanently bent on constant, steady improvements. Maybe this is just a way of saying the unfreeze, movement, refreeze cycle is never-ending.

HOW TO MAKE MRP/JIT PART OF YOUR COMPANY-WIDE MISSION

MRP I and II started the movement toward manufacturing excellence, and JIT has taken the concepts to higher plateaus. To achieve their promise, these ideas should pervade the whole company. You can achieve this by using these techniques.

Define Your Company Vision

It may sound corny to hard-bitten autocratic-style managers, but this works. You should work up a company vision statement. Do you want to be the industry technology leader? Do you want to be the world's lowest cost producer? Do you want the shortest leadtime in the industry? Do you want to be the highest quality house? Employees at all levels should know what the company vision is. This is especially important in an environment that consciously decentralizes decision making.

Establish Your Strategy

We covered the mechanics of Strategic Planning in Chapter 2. We want to emphasize it here in the context of setting the stage for employee involvement, and steady improvement. You want employees to spontaneously make small- and medium-sized improvements on a daily basis. In order to keep the focus of all these people correct, a cogent, and publicized strategy is needed. This strategy should support the company's vision, and be rejuvenated every year.

Reinforce Planning and Scheduling

At the executive level, this homework means realistic forecasting, production planning, and resource planning. It also means insisting on a realistic Master Production Schedule with integrity and respect. These topics are covered in Chapters 2 and 3. It is very important to have these activities correctly in place and functioning. They help set a tone of orderliness and rationality for the whole company; a tone that invites thoughtful, good ideas. The contrast is a company whose strategic plan is only on paper and the master schedule is abused by the executives on a daily and hourly basis. In such a chaotic and irrational environment, good ideas for improvements never get beyond the lunch table in the cafeteria.

How to Use the System at All Levels

The famous Oliver Wight report card requires that all levels of the company use the established system, including top management. MRP-based systems are inherently complete and accurate, and have a fast response time. One consistent system means that improvements can be communicated and implemented quickly and routinely, without a lot of fuss.

Using the system also requires that competing and overlapping systems be discontinued. You can't have morning shop meetings to decide on the day's priorities. You must use the dispatch list. If the dispatch list is not workable, it should be fixed, not worked around.

Using the system also means that all work in the factory be but through the system.

Well, almost all work. I did a short engagement with a company that makes cast iron stoves. In one corner of the factory I saw a sailboat. I asked about it and was informed that it belonged to the owner of the company. It seems that they were going to refinish it during idle hours. I grudgingly admitted that it would be ok to do this off the system.

Promote Teamwork Inside the Company and Competition Outside the Company

Computer-based MRP/JIT systems now give us the ability to have current, accurate, and coordinated plans for the whole company. It is now easy for everyone to know, precisely, what their share of the total task is and their due dates. It becomes feasible to the point of being easy for everyone to govern their actions to optimize company performance. Before the advent of these computer-based systems, the planning process was very cumbersome, slow, and fraught with inaccuracies. In this environment, it was generally held that if each department would optimize itself, the company would automatically be optimized.

Departmental optimization was the best we could hope for in those days, but usually led to sub-optimization of the company. We had heavy emphasis on "controls", usually emanating from the accounting books. This led to the monthly ritual of cooking the input numbers, making lame excuses for variances beyond a certain percentage, and blaming other departments for short-comings. When carried to an extreme this led to constant bickering and finger pointing. Ambitious department managers tried to gather power in what has become known as empire building. In such an environment, much creative time and effort is wasted in competing with the next department, while the competition runs away with the business.

Now that we have the luxury of superior tools for planning and synchronizing the activities of a manufacturing company, we should emphasize teamwork and harmony. We should be encouraged to help one another achieve our goals, and unleash our competitive drive only against our competitors.

Another good concept is to blend the departmental borders. Every department on the organization chart has dealings with several others. The traditional idea of sharp, clean delineation of departmental responsibilities can quickly lead to turf wars. Better to have these borders purposely fuzzy, which will encourage flexibility and cooperation at these interface points.

Get Consensus

Webster[3] tells us that consensus is "an opinion held by all or most; general agreement". This is not necessarily unanimity. In our manufacturing setting, this means that new ideas should be given some incubation time, until they achieve broad acceptance. The more radical, the more "soaking" time is needed.

I had a client recently who appeared at first to be "meeting happy." They had a constant stream of meetings. I gradually noticed that when department managers were present, they would sit at the back and not say much. The participants in the meeting often were hastily recruited because they were directly involved. They often started out naive, but during the discussion the real issues were thoroughly examined. As a result, the conclusion, reached by consensus, was pre-sold, and the resistance to change factor never had a chance. Their decisions usually were good ones. I suppressed my "Dutch Uncle" act, and let them get to a conclusion themselves. Sometimes I had to interject a technical comment, or an outsider's observation, but they gradually zeroed in on a good solution. Somebody kept minutes, and they were promptly published. What looked like time being wasted, was really consensus developing. This company has become their industry leader, in a global market, partly because of this process and its underlying management strategy.

Get Employee Involvement

One good way to get employee involvement is to adopt the "say yes" attitude. When someone has an idea for an improvement, look for ways to say yes to it. Put the burden of proof on those who would turn it down. This is in sharp contrast with

---

[3]*Webster's New World Dictionary,* Third College Edition, (New York: Simon and Schuster, Inc., 1988).

the old orthodoxy of cost-justification, payback in a few months, discounted cash flows, and paralysis by analysis.

Employee involvement is not just for white collars. There have been some remarkable improvements suggested by blue collar workers. This is especially so in the area of setup time reduction. Other consultants and practitioners in the field report that the actual workers make far more suggestions than the manufacturing engineers in devising setup reductions.

HOW TO DEVELOP WORLD-CLASS GOALS

In order to achieve real success in manufacturing, you must measure your progress and performance correctly. Many of the old standbys, often imbedded in accounting systems, do not support your new goals, especially Just-in-Time ones. Actually, many of these traditional goals are counter-productive.

Achieving true excellence in any MRPII-based system, especially JIT-modified ones is a management issue and responsibility. This means that managers and executives must use the system properly and respect it. Above all, the Master Production Schedule must be strong and respected.

Seven Steps to Develop Goals

You can develop excellent world class goals by following these steps:

- Select the right mix.
- Discontinue the wrong goals.
- Make sure the goals are measurable.
- Start now.
- Publish results promptly, and distribute them widely.
- Tie goals to personnel performance.
- Review and adjust annually.

1. Select the Right Mix

To select the right mix, you must first understand your company's business strategies. Only then can you develop a spectrum of goals and performance measures to cover the company completely. You should take care not to overdo goal-setting, nor to concentrate on just a few functions. Since world-class performance is a company-wide activity, all functions should be covered.

2. Discontinue the Wrong Goals

This is the most important step in the preparation of good goals. You must eliminate counter-productive goals, no matter where they come from, no matter why they originally were developed. This easily could require some profound changes in your accounting concepts and systems, as well in your whole salary administration apparatus. Some examples of bad orthodox goals are setup variance and machine utilization. Both influence shop supervisors and planners to take actions contrary to the best interests of the company. Some other bad ones are the classic monthly "dollars out the door" shipping bogey, and labor utilization.

3. Make Sure the Goals are Measurable

In order for a goal to be effective you must be able to measure it objectively, and be able to report on it.

4. Start Now

This applies no matter where you are in your development cycle. Just establishing them and measuring them will cause improvement. The 3M company found direct labor efficiency often went from 40 to 60 percent just because measurements were instituted. If you are at the beginning of an implementation program, starting now creates a baseline from which you demonstrate progress.

5. Publish Results Promptly and Distribute Them Widely

You should publish your results as soon after the event occurs as possible. Gone are the days where we can satisfactorily manage ourselves with last months's information, 15 days late. Instantaneous feedback on computer terminals is one method. Visual boards and lights also are used. Reports that still fit the weekly or monthly cycle can be distributed via the company newspaper, on bulletin boards, in pay envelopes, and so on.

6. Tie Goals to Personnel Performance

Personnel administrators' orthodoxy notwithstanding, you get the performance you pay for. If your shop supervisors get their raises because they consistently have favorable machine usage variances, then forget your Just-in-Time ideas of making only what you need.

I had a student in one of my classes once, a work center supervisor. He confided that if a worker finishes the day's work he starts on the next day's, regardless of the schedule. Worse yet, if there is no work in the queue, he has the worker make scrap, to keep his labor and machine utilization high. His performance and pay raise was rated in part on utilization.

This may be an extreme example, but it does illustrate the problem.

To make your goals and objectives really work as a motivational force, you should make sure that everyone's personal goals, usually incorporated in your salary administration process, are coordinated with them. Counter-productive ones must be discontinued. Everyone should take personal and group goals and targets that fully support your dynamic move toward world class and beyond.

7. Review and Adjust Goals Annually

Your company's environment changes, so your company goals must be dynamic. I suggest that you review and rejuvenate your spectrum of goals each year as part of both your annual budgeting process and your salary administration procedures.

SIX NEW MEASURES YOU CAN START

Following are some suggestions for new measures that support MRP and especially JIT concepts. This is not a comprehensive list, but one to start you thinking. Notice that we usually are not thinking about the absolute numbers, but rather what your trend is month after month. Start measuring now, and insist on steady improvement.

1. Asset Efficiency

● Inventory Turns = Annual cost of goods sold average inventory held during the year.

A variation on this is the month's cost of goods sold, annualized ÷ this month's inventory. This is one of the best measures of all. You can't hide pockets of inventory as if they don't count or don't exist.

I have known several companies who thought they had six

inventory turns. But when applying this formula, they had to admit that they were omitting things as excess and obsolete, service parts, return to vendor, and hold for material review. After recognizing these hidden pockets of inventory, their real turns were about three, which was my guess after touring their factory facilities.

You can elaborate on this measurement, by using it on categories of inventory, such as raw materials, work in process, or finished goods. If you have a variety of product lines in your factory, you might be able to take advantage of measuring inventory turns within each major product line. There even are some industry and national figures available.

The United States is often compared to Japan with this measure, and we come up looking bad. I frequently ask my clients what their inventory turns are, and often get answers in the 2.0 – 3.5 range, rarely higher. In Japan, they say, many companies claim to have double-digit turns.

● Factory Turns = Annual cost of goods sold ÷ total plant and equipment.

Automation is fine, but we should be just as concerned about using our investment in plant and equipment intensively as we are about inventory.

● Asset Turns = Annual cost of goods sold ÷ total assets.

This is a measure of the company's total performance regarding all assets.

2. *Business Planning*

● Marketing Plan = Sales Forecast?

Do our sales forecasts add up to the marketing plan? This is not a hard measure, but forces you to keep these two plans in synchronization with each other.

● Sales Forecast = Production Plan?

This is a capacity issue. The production plan is your top level plan for supplies to match your demands coming in through the sales forecast. Are you planning enough material and capacity to manufacture the sales forecast?

● Production Plan = Master Production Schedule?

The Master production schedule is the driving force for all of your subsequent MRP II plans. In a good MRP II-based system you will be producing what is shown on the MPS. The production plan usually shows families in monthly time slices, while the MPS often is daily or weekly, and usually shows shippable end items. Using these two as a team, you can support product introductions, product eliminations, and seasonality. If can't get the capacity to produce all your orders, these plans are your vehicle for allocation.

- Forecast Accuracy.

Current techniques for measuring forecast accuracy have a decided statistical component. They measure the mean absolute deviation of forecast to actual, and derive a tracking signal from these deviations. When the tracking signal exceeds a certain value, your forecast probably is flawed and needs to be reexamined. George Plossl covers this technique very well in one of his books.[4]

- MPS Index = MPS orders completed today ÷ orders scheduled today.

This measure is one of the most important of all. It is very important to manufacture your master schedule at least every week, preferably every day, at a very high success rate. Only by achieving your master schedule can you qualify for many of the desirable benefits of MRP II/JIT.

3. *Manufacturing Operations*

- Schedule Adherence = Mfg orders completed today ÷ orders due today.

If you are going to adhere to your master schedule, you have to complete your sub-assemblies and piece parts on schedule. This becomes especially critical in a JIT environment with small lots and diminished queues. A JIT factory is a synchronized one, and fulfilling your daily schedules is very important.

- Vendor Performance = PO's received today ÷ PO's due today.

This one should be approached carefully. If you are in an expedite mode, your best vendors are responding to phone calls,

---

[4]George W. Plossl, Production and Inventory Control, Principles and Techniques (Englewood Cliffs, NJ.: Prentice-Hall, Inc.), pp. 107–108, © 1985.

not your schedule. I suggest that you use this measure mainly with your partner-vendors, and then only after you can demonstrate that your schedules to your vendors have integrity and are valid.

- Materials Index = Pick lists scheduled and completely filled today ÷ orders to be started today.

If you can't start your orders with full sets of parts, you probably won't be able to compete them on time. Starting work orders into the factory knowingly short of parts is the main reason why tradition-bound factories, with their monthly shipping bogeys, ship 60 percent of their output at the end of the month. These operations routinely start orders short of components, and expedite the missing ones. Orders stall in the factory for lack of parts, until the last week when the expediting starts to pay off. In a last minute rush, as many orders as can be, are completed and shipped. There was little regard for the promised ship date, only getting dollars out the door. The rule is not to start an order until its pick list can be fulfilled entirely.

- Inventory Accuracy = Cycle counts correct ÷ item #'s counted.

This is one of the essential basics. Your accuracy should be 95 percent or better. One thing to notice here is that you are measuring by item number, not quantity. For example, if your stock record shows that you should have 1,000 of an item on hand and your cycle counter finds 950, this is not 95 percent accuracy. The rule is that if you count 100 items in the stockroom, 95 of them should be absolutely correct ± your counting scale inaccuracy. This is how you eliminate the obsolete year-end-physical.

- Bill of Material Index = (Unplanned material issues + returns) ÷ open orders.

This is not the same as BOM accuracy which. but is somewhat easier to track.

- Bill of Material Accuracy = Single level bills fully accurate ÷ single level bills audited.

To really be sure you have bill of material accuracy, you should initiate a cyclic audit of their accuracy, along the lines for cycle counting inventory. Concentrating on active bills, Engineering should select a few bills to audit each week. This procedure should cover all active bills once a year. There are several ways to conduct an audit. You could try to assemble one unit to see if the factory is adding or deducting anything. You could examine or disassemble one unit. Some companies compare the bill to the assembly drawing. More recently computer-aided-drafting (CAD) systems are providing the source to cross-check bill of material entries.

Fully accurate refers to the components called out and their quantities. In your application, you could also designate other crucial fields to be included. This is another essential index, and the norm is 98 percent accuracy. As in cycle counting, this measure is more stringent than might appear. If you have a single level bill with 100 components, and 98 of them are accurately shown, this is not a 98 percent bill. The rule is that if you audit 100 single level bills, 98 of them must be fully accurate.

- Inventory Plan Index = Planned inventory ÷ actual inventory.

This measures how well you are hitting your inventory targets. But you should recognize that in an MRP II setting, you don't manage inventories directly. Your inventory levels are governed by such things as lead times, lot sizes, queue sizes, safety stocks, and so on. If you aren't satisfied with the size of your inventory, you have to look to see what the causes are and correct them.

4. Customer Service

- Orders or lines shipped today ÷ those promised.

Whether you choose orders or lines depends on your industry and your customers. Orders is the more demanding. You could have a customer who needs the whole order to get started in their own factory. If you are short one or more items, they can't get started anyhow, so they don't want any of it. In this case you should use orders promised. Or, the customer's order could have line items that are not mutually related. Then you could use line items as the basis for your measurement. However you choose, your score on this index should be in the high 90s.

- Orders or lines shipped today ÷ those requested.

You should use this measure if you frequently promise a ship date different from the one your customer requested. You could be hitting your promises quite reliably, but routinely be disappointing customers.

- Aged Backorders.

This is like aged accounts receivable that the accountants have been using for years. A one-day back order is not as bad as a one week one!

5. Personnel Cost Indices

- Parkinson's Index = Net income + number of employees.

This index will show if your bureaucracy is growing faster than your income, as often happens, particularly in mature industries.

- Department Index = Net income + department payroll.

This puts each department in the perspective of the total company. Are some departments growing relatively, while others are shrinking?

- Direct Labor Index = Net income + direct labor payroll.

This measure puts your labor payroll in a company perspective. This is the JIT substitute for the old labor utilization measure.

- Composite Labor Index = Net income + total factory payroll.

Ever since accounting started measuring direct labor performance, factory supervisors have busily been converting direct labor activities into indirect. A dollar spent on indirect labor is just as expensive as one spent on direct labor. This index puts both direct and indirect together under one measurement.

- Composite Labor Cost = Total earned hours + total factory payroll.

This gives you your aggregate labor cost per hour. Earned hours come from the time standards on your routings on the month's manufacturing orders.

6. JIT Performance

- Actual Lead time = Elapsed factory hours + number of orders.

You could do this for the whole factory or for product lines, as a way to get a general measure of your true lead times.

- Average Lot Size = Units produced + number of shop orders.

This measure is especially important if you are on a lot size reduction program. Here again, you could have one measure for each major product line.

- Queue Index = Total queue hours + throughput hours.

Throughput hours is (pick + move + queue + setup) + (standard time routed for the order's operations × standard lot size). Many companies find that queue is 90 percent of throughput time, and represents a prime target for lead time reduction.

- Move Index = Total move hours + throughput hours.

This is not a crucial measurement, and useful only if you have long move times.

- Setup Index = Total setup hours/throughput hours.

This is especially important in a JIT setting, and will help you monitor your setup time reduction program.

HOW TO MAKE THE QUEST FOR IMPROVEMENT PERMANENT

After you are fully implemented and have disbanded the project, you are ready to start making your new system fulfill on its promises.

Establishing the Operations Control Department

One very significant characteristic of an MRP II-based system is that it is the first, and often only, business system that is integrated company-wide. All other computerized systems wrap new code around existing systems. Forecasting, order entry, accounts payable, accounts receivable, sales analysis, and personnel are but a few common ones that come to mind. In every case, they are designed for a specific department, computerizing what they had been doing all along.

MRP II, on the other hand cuts across departmental lines freely, and influences how many departments function. Accounting gets labor and material costs for their cost roll-ups. Purchasing gets good schedules. Sales gets on line, real time order promising; then fulfillment of these promises over 90 percent. Manufacturing gets good material and capacity plans. Engineering gets iron-clad control over the execution of their designs, and the list goes on. And all departments become closely interdependent.

Based on the fact that an integrated MRP II-based system does not naturally belong to any of the functional areas of a company, there appears the problem of who to put in charge of this business system, which is part of the lifeblood of the company. None of the conventional departments qualify, because they all have their own parochial interests ingrained into their activities.

The need to manage this pervasive business system asks for a new box in the organization chart. Perhaps we could call this the Operations Control Department. The head of this department would be a Director, an organizational peer with the Directors of Information Services, Personnel, Materials, and Sales. The Director should be APICS-certified, degreed, and have demonstrated several years of successful experience, including supervisory. Staffing would include the Master Production Scheduler and a clerk or two.

This new department would need to report to an executive, preferably a vice-president; one who can provide a "neutral corner" to operate out of. If you have a Vice-President of Administration, this would be a good choice. Lacking that, the Director of Operations Control should report to the Chief Executive (or Operating) Officer. This new function couldn't be effective reporting to marketing, manufacturing, finance, engineering, or any other operating function, because they do not provide the necessary neutral corner. Nor does the purview of any one of them encompass the whole company.

The operations control department would have a number of operational as well as system management duties.

Providing Steady-State Operation

The operations control department assures that your new system is on cruise control. Part of this is to perform three important periodic activities—production planning, master production scheduling, and capacity management.

Production Planning

In Chapter 3, we described production planning. Essentially, the production plan is a monthly statement of what you will be manufacturing, by family. The production plan also is the basis for resource requirement planning.

The production plan will be prepared in the operations control department, probably by the master scheduler, who also will validate it with resource requirements planning. When done, the Production Plan is submitted to upper management for discussion and approval. This is a monthly activity.

Master Production Scheduling

In Chapter 3, we also described the master schedule. This the most crucial operational input into MRP II, and must be managed with great skill and judgement. Depending on product line, managing the master schedule must be done in close co-ordination with sales order administration. The time slices on the master schedule can be daily or weekly, but no greater.

Capacity Management

In addition to Resource Requirement Planning, the Master Scheduler also makes a Rough Cut Capacity Plan from the Master Production Schedule. Any capacity shortages must be resolved before proceeding further. This process is described in Chapter 3.

Managing the System

The Operation Control Department actively oversees that the system is functioning properly, striving to be better all the time. The three important oversight activities are data integrity, performance audits, and error elimination.

Data Integrity

In Chapter 5, we described the important data files that must be managed correctly. They are:

- Item Master
- Bills of Material
- Engineering Change Control
- Work Center Definition
- Process and Routing

And in Chapter 9 we discussed stock status accuracy and cycle counting.

The Director of Operations Control establishes communication channels to be notified when anything goes wrong. This function also controls the systematic, ongoing reporting of operating performance. The director sees to it that data integrity is maintained and improved.

Performance Audits

Part of the implementation effort was to establish a spectrum of periodic reports to gage how well the system is performing. We covered this in Chapter 1. The Director of Operations manages any of these performance reports that do not naturally flow out of one of the conventional departments.

Error Elimination

We first learned about the power of this idea when the concepts and techniques of cycle counting were developed. Now all of your performance measures should be coupled with steady, systematic performance improvement. This department takes the lead in making sure that these steady improvements continue.

Monitoring and Improving Your Business Systems

Your company is dynamic. You want your business systems to be at least as dynamic as your company. This means that the components of your MRP II-based system must be constantly monitored and improved wherever possible. There are several main areas to be addressed:

- Software Enhancements
- Hardware Improvements
- Yearly Redefinition of Goals
- Education and Training
- Maintaining Documentation
- Relations with Other Business Systems
- Relations with Other Technologies

Software Enhancements

Particularly if you use commercial software, your supplier probably will be offering you enhancements periodically. The Director of Operations Control must examine and evaluate each revision as it is published. It is a very good idea to keep up to date. This will allow you to benefit from improvements, even though seemingly minor. This will also keep you current with the supplier's hot line, publications, documentation, and education programs.

Also, each release usually requires all previous releases to be in place. This means that when a feature comes out that you really want, you should be current.

Hardware Improvements

The computer hardware environment is dynamic to the point of being in turmoil. New things are offered, and existing components are getting better and cheaper by the day. The Operations Control Department keeps up with developments and together with the Information Services Department, judges when it is time to bring in new devices.

Yearly Review of Goals

You should review your performance goals every year. This is best done in anticipation of your yearly financial budgeting cycle. The Operations Control Department takes the lead in reviewing each measurement, adjusting each as needed. This is one of the more important tools to keep the constant improvement momentum going.

Education and Training

Your company is in a competitive environment, and your business systems must be dynamic. You have personnel changes; promotions, hires, and transfers. Evolving systems and different faces demand that education and training continue permanently. Absent a strong training and development group, the Operations Control Department oversees this important function. Even if you do have a strong training and development department, they will need technical and subject matter support. Ongoing education and training is an important, permanent activity of the Operations Control Department.

Maintaining Documentation

Good, written procedures and users' manuals were an important deliverable during implementation. Considering the dynamic nature of the business and computer environments, these documents must be constantly maintained to keep them current.

I had an amusing experience at a consulting company where I once worked. I took over an educational program we were offering from a vice-president. After I had done the program several times, my secretary showed me a page from the travel section of the policy manual. It clearly stated that whoever did this program was authorized to fly first class. Taking advantage of this new-found privilege, I booked myself first class for my next assignment. The travel agency reported this to the controller who called me to ask what was going on. When I read him the procedure he laughed and replied, "Oh, we don't follow that procedure anymore." So much for the whole manual!

Most companies have word processing facilities readily available to make updating and redistribution efficient. I have a client who has put their documentation on a linked network of terminals, making their documentation available on line. The distribution of updates effectively is real time. They have eliminated printed copies except for those not on the net.

Technology has made it easier to keep documentation current, and the operations control department performs this activity.

Relations with Other Business Systems

Most companies use commercial software, which reduces sharply the demands on the information services group. One big effort that remains is the interfacing or integrating of separate commercial systems, even when they come from the same supplier. Your MRP II-based system is very large and central to your company's operation. This requires frequent adjustment to the interfaces between it and other computerized systems. It is very important to keep your systems as dynamic as your business environment.

Relations with Other Technologies

Bar coding is the first of these technologies that comes to mind. I have had several clients who bar code their products for their customers, but don't use them themselves. This is changing fast, and most companies that don't use bar coding now are at least evaluating it.

Another technology that is becoming popular is hand-held terminals. They are useful making inventory and cycle counting transactions.

The Operations Control Department takes the lead in evaluating and implementing new technologies that apply to your MRP II-based business system.

Appendix I

HOW TO CALCULATE REORDER POINTS

Reorder points are used to govern when to reorder certain inventory items. This method is best used on independent demand items, but not on dependent demand ones. Dependent demand items are those structured in your bills of material and managed by MRP II. Dependent demand items are by far the more numerous. There are, however, many items needed in a manufacturing company that are not dependent on bill of material structures. These are called independent demand items.

There are several main groups of independent demand items:

- Finished Goods

- Service Parts

- Machine and Equipment Spare Parts

- Plant Maintenance Parts and Supplies

HOW IT WORKS

The reorder point (ROP) formula is very simple: ROP = demand during lead time + safety stock. When the inventory balance drops to the reorder point, an order is sent for one lot size.

This technique uses several simple factors, namely:

- Average Demand Rate

- Lead Time

- Lot Size

- Safety Stock

The average demand rate is usually set a year at a time from the prior year's experience. This rate is usually expressed in units per day. The lead time is usually taken from the supplier's catalog or from the standard factory lead time.

The lot size is usually established by the square-root EOQ formula, although often it is just fixed by the planner at an arbitrary number. See Appendix II for a more complete explanation of these two lot sizing rules.

Safety stock is needed to cover when actual demand is greater than the average. See Appendix III for more details on how to calculate safety stock.

Figure I.1 shows a graph of stock status for an item being managed by the reorder point technique. In the first cycle, actual demand conforms to the average. When stock status falls to the reorder point, the planner notifies purchasing to place an order for one lot size which is sent to the supplier. At the end of lead time, the order is received and placed into inventory, just as stock status reaches the safety stock level. Then the cycle starts over.

Figure I.1 Reorder Point Cycle

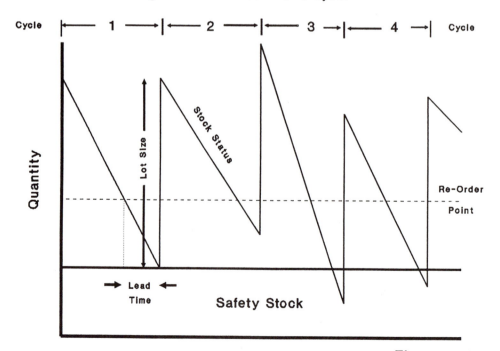

In the second cycle, actual demand is less than average. When stock status reaches the reorder point, the planner notifies the buyer to send another order for one lot size is sent to the supplier. As before, the order is received and placed into inventory. But this time stock status has not reached the safety stock level, because demand was slower than planned.

In the third cycle, actual demand is substantially more than average. At reorder point, another order is sent to the supplier. But in this case some safety stock is consumed before replenishment comes in, because demand is higher than planned. But safety stock was sufficient to prevent a stockout, and the new shipment was received before a stockout occurred.

In the fourth cycle, actual demand was the same as forecast, but the supplier was tardy in making delivery. In this case some safety stock was used to cover this delay.

It should be noted that the reorders occur at irregular intervals, and that the quantity is always the same, until the lot size is updated. Also, because the system has no way to realize that actual demand is running faster or slower than planned, the replenishment order was sent sooner than needed in the second cycle, and later than needed in the third.

The average inventory for this item is ½ lot size + safety stock. The same is true for the aggregate of inventories under reorder point control, which makes budgeting easy.

ASSUMPTIONS AND PROBLEMS

There are several assumptions that underlie this method, which may not always be true. The first assumption is that consumption is a straight line, and in small increments. In fact some items have "lumpy" demand. This is where there are no demands for several days, followed by one large withdrawal, followed by several days more of no activity. If the lumps are sufficiently far apart and severe, it could cause frequent stockouts, and probably will cause excess inventory to be held between lumps.

Some independent demand items have seasonal demand. If seasonality is severe, using this reorder point technique could result in stockouts during the season of high use, and surely will result in excess inventory during the slow months.

The lot size used is assumed to accurately reflect a balance between ordering costs and storage costs. In reality, the lot size is usually set and then neglected for years. This will result in a higher inventory cost than is needed. To keep this system working well, the lot size should be recalculated at least once a year, or when one of the controlling factors changes.

The lead time is assumed to be correct and fixed. Practical experience shows that lead times are flexible and manageable. The planner should strive to use the shortest practical lead time, and to review it annually.

Managing designated lead times, reorder points, and lot sizes for these items is subject to abuse. Planners find they are criticized for running out of stock far more often than they are for having too much inventory. The natural tendency for planners is to give their items higher reorder points, lot sizes, and generous lead times to help avoid the grief of having a stockout.

Regarding finished goods inventory, because of their expense and large numbers, there have become available several good forecasting techniques, and computer software to support them, that are frequently used to manage this category. When a forecasting tool is available, it is a better way to manage finished goods inventory than reorder point.

THE TWO-BIN VARIATION

The example above assumes stock status records that are updated as inventory is received and issued, and than an inventory planner takes actions based on these records. This whole clerical load can be eliminated by using the two-bin method.

The two-bin method takes the quantity equivalent to the reorder point, and places it in a second bin, separate from the main one. Issues are made from the main bin until it is empty. The stock picker then starts to use inventory from the second bin. Inside the bin is a traveling requisition card which is sent to the planner or directly to purchasing for action. The card is returned for reuse.

A refinement of this system is to have the safety stock quantity segregated in a third bin, leaving just the lead time quantity in the second bin. If the second bin gets emptied before the replenishment is received, the stock picker goes to the third bin, which has an expedite card to be sent to purchasing.

The two-bin system is widely used for small parts of trivial value. It works very well for these items with a minimum of administrative expense.

Appendix II

HOW TO CALCULATE AND USE LOT SIZES

Every time a purchase order or a manufacturing order is planned, either by MRP II or manually, a lot size quantity must be chosen. To arrive at a sound quantity requires a balance between two main conflicting costs, namely order cost (either setup cost or purchase order cost, plus related order processing costs) versus inventory carrying cost. The larger the lot size, the smaller the order cost per unit, but the higher the inventory carrying cost. A small lot size will minimize inventory carrying cost per unit, but cost too much per unit in order cost. Over the years a number of lot sizing methods and formulas have been devised. Most of them attempt to optimize the order versus carrying costs.

Manufacturing is a very complex activity, and various categories of inventory can exhibit different characteristics. Some have straight line usage, while others have "lumpy" demand. Some items are expensive per unit, others almost trivial. Some items are used widely in the factory, others very focused.

Some items are in your bills of material, others not. These are but a few factors that can influence the choice of the most appropriate lot size.

Since the JIT movement started, another factor has appeared. JIT ideals call for a strong emphasis on setup reduction in order to earn smaller lot sizes.

Good MRP II-based systems have several lot sizing rules available in them. The planner is responsible to select the right rule for each item, and to change it when circumstances change. The planner must also maintain the specific values used in the calculations, notably standard cost, inventory carrying cost, and order cost.

Many formulas and algorithms have been published, many coming from universities. From these, there have evolved several formulas that have found practical application, some more, others less, in manufacturing planning and control systems.

The most common rules are:

- Fixed Order Quantity

- EOQ (Economic Order Quantity)

- Period Order Quantity

- Lot-for-Lot

- Least Total Cost

- Part-Period Balancing

- Least Unit Cost

- Others

There is also a family of lot size modifiers that can be used to accommodate unusual circumstances.

In the following examples, the periods shown are weekly, even though some systems work with daily time intervals. We use weekly periods to make the examples easier. The logic is the same with either daily or weekly time periods, but daily planning periods are preferable.

FIXED ORDER QUANTITY

Fixed order quantity is probably the oldest of all of them. Also called nice round lot, this rule has no formula or algorithm. The planner or buyer just arbitrarily selects a lot size. Sometimes price breaks play a role, and work center supervisors often voice their opinions. Lot sizes set with this method often are far higher than any of the mathematically based ones would suggest.

Figure II.1 shows an MRP II-style planning report using a fixed order quantity of 100. Whenever a new order is needed, as occurred in periods 1, 3, 4, 5, 8, and 12, the system suggests a quantity of 100.

Notice that in most periods, there is some ending inventory, which carries across to the next requirement. In period eight, for example, the ending inventory of 90, carries across period nine which has no demand to period 10 and beyond, and is not consumed until period 11.

This rule makes no effort to minimize inventory, nor to optimize the ordering cost against inventory carrying cost.

Although no longer very popular, this lot sizing rule may be useful in circumstances where an item has an extremely high order cost, when there is a fixed batch constraint, where tool life must be considered, and sometimes for very low cost items where the inventory carrying cost is minimal. It also is widely used for independent demand items; those not under MRP II control. Independent demand items include:

- Service parts

- Finished goods

- Machine and plant maintenance parts

- Manufactured or purchased parts for destructive testing

Figure II.1 Fixed Order Quantity

Period	1	2	3	4	5	6	7	8	9	10	11	12
Gross Reqmts	40	60	70	80	65	45	35	15	0	30	60	100
Planned Orders	100		100	100	100			100				100
Beginning Inventory	100	60	100	130	150	85	40	105	90	90	60	100
Ending Inventory	60	0	30	50	85	40	5	90	90	60	60	0
Average Inventory	80	30	65	90	118	63	23	98	90	75	30	50

EOQ (ECONOMIC ORDER QUANTITY)

The Economic Order Quantity formula was the first widely-used one for balancing order cost with carrying cost. The formula is:

$$EOQ = \sqrt{\frac{2AS}{ic}}$$

The factors are:

A = Annual usage
S = Order (setup or purchase order) cost
i = Carrying cost rate expressed as a decimal (24% = .24)
C = Unit (standard) cost

This formula can also be expressed an graphic form, which is shown in Figure II.2.

Figure II.2 Economic Order Quantity
(EOQ)

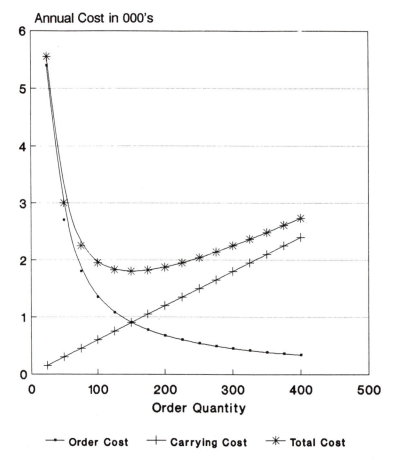

In this graph you can see that the order cost, per unit, decreases as the lot size increases. At the same time, inventory carrying cost increases as the lot size increases. Total cost, the sum of both, is a curve that bottoms out where the order cost line crosses the carrying cost line. Another way to express this is that the lowest total cost occurs when the order cost equals the carrying cost. This is an important consideration, because some of the more sophisticated formulas have this as their goal.

From the point where the two lines cross, you read the lot size on the x-axis and the total cost on the y-axis.

Figure II.3 shows an MRP II-style planning report showing this EOQ formula being used.

In this example, whenever a new order is needed, MRP suggests the EOQ of 150 units. Depending on the features of the software being used, the computer possibly could automatically re-calculate the EOQ during every planning cycle. In other software environments, the EOQ is fixed, and periodically updated manually by the planner after calculating a new EOQ using some off-line method or report. This is the most usual.

In this example, and all the following ones, the factors are:

A = Annual usage = 2400 units
S = Order (setup) cost = \$56.25
i = Inventory carrying cost = .24 per yr. = .02 per mo. = .005 per wk.
C = Unit cost = \$50.00

Carrying cost per period for 1 part = \$50.00 × .005 = \$0.25
Solving the EOQ formula:

$$\sqrt{\frac{2 \times 2400 \times 56.25}{.24 \times 50}} = \sqrt{\frac{270,000}{12}} = \sqrt{22,500} = 150$$

Figure II.3 shows the lot sizes of 150 planned for periods 1, 3, 5, and 11. Notice that zero inventory occurs only once, and that the average inventory in each period often is close to a period's worth. In this example the EOQ formula is planning too much inventory.

This formula has the big advantage that it is well-known. It is the lot size rule that lay persons usually think of first when the topic comes up. It is easy to calculate, and can help validate other, more elaborate methods. Also the EOQ is used by the Period Order Quantity formula.

Another advantage for this formula is that it is useful for independent demand items that are not under MRP II control.

Figure II.3 EOQ (Economic Order Quantity)

Period	1	2	3	4	5	6	7	8	9	10	11	12
Gross Reqmts	40	60	70	80	65	45	35	15	0	30	60	100
Planned Orders	150		150		150						150	
Beginning Inventory	150	110	200	130	200	135	90	55	40	40	160	100
Ending Inventory	110	50	130	50	135	90	55	40	40	10	100	0
Average Inventory	130	80	165	90	168	113	73	48	40	25	130	50

This classic EOQ formula has some serious drawbacks, however. The first is that it does not drive inventories toward zero. In Figure II.3, ending inventory is zero in period 12. The first lot is mainly consumed in periods one and two. There is a remainder of 50 carried over to period 3, but not enough to cover the requirement of 70. Similarly, there is a remainder after each of the subsequent lots, except the last one, which is entirely consumed but just by coincidence.

The second weakness of this formula is that it assumes straight-line usage. In an MRP II-based system, however, many components have the opposite, "lumpy" demand. In Figure II.3, period nine has zero demand, while period 12 has 100. This is a mild example of lumpiness, and more severe situations often occur. Lumpiness is worse with large lot sizes and deep bills of material.

It is interesting to note that using this lot sizing formula in an MRP II setting causes the lumpiness that erodes one of its own assumptions.

PERIOD ORDER QUANTITY

Period order quantity calls for a specific number of periods to be covered whenever MRP II creates a planned order. The key to success here is to determine the economical time span to cover, attempting to balance order cost per piece against carrying cost. This is done by calculating an EOQ according to the previous example. Dividing the EOQ into the annual usage, tells how many times per year to order. Dividing that number into 52 (weeks per year), will give the interval of coverage.

Using the previous example, 2400 ÷ 150 = 16 times a year. 52 ÷ 16 = 3 weeks coverage per order.

Figure II.4 illustrates this lot size in use. The first planned order is needed during the first period. The system looks at the needs for three periods, in this case periods 1, 2, and 3, with quantities of 40, 60, and 70, respectively. This totals to 170, which is the recommended lot size. The next order is needed in period 4, so the requirements for periods four to six are totaled, and 190 becomes the quantity for the second order. The next order is needed in period seven, so seven to nine are totaled. Notice that system does not skip period 9 because it has no requirement.

Figure II.4 Period Order Quantity

Period	1	2	3	4	5	6	7	8	9	10	11	12
Gross Reqmts	40	60	70	80	65	45	35	15	0	30	60	100
Planned Orders	170			190			50			190		
Beginning Inventory	170	130	70	190	110	45	50	15	0	190	160	100
Ending Inventory	130	70	0	110	45	0	15	0	0	160	100	0
Average Inventory	150	100	35	150	78	23	33	8	0	175	130	50

A disadvantage of this formula is that it does not try to balance order cost and carrying cost. Instead, it is derived from the EOQ formula, which is very weak in this regard when applied to dependent demand items.

This formula does recognize lumpiness by looking ahead to actual demands. As a result there are no remainders, and the entire lot is consumed before another is received. In Figure II.4, this occurs in periods three, six, and nine. If this item were to be discontinued, or if were to experience large cyclic variations, there would be no excess or obsolete inventory left over.

Period order quantity is very useful for items with a definite shelf life. It can also be used for trivial items that you don't want to bother with more than twice a year. This is accomplished by setting the period interval to 26 weeks.

LOT FOR LOT

This is the favorite formula for JIT applications. The lot for lot rule plans an order sufficient for one planning period. This rule does not give a lot size of one, as you sometimes hear. This rule occasionally is called *discrete.*

This means that whenever MRP II identifies a requirement, it plans an order to be received in that period and just for that period's quantity.

Lot for lot sizing works well when the order cost approaches zero. However, if order cost is still sizeable, then this rule will result in too much time and expense spent on setups. This is the companion to lot size reduction, one of the JIT ideals now being emphasized. In a JIT implementation, when setup time is reduced, the lot size setup time factor must be updated. When setup finally is minimal, and no longer is an impediment to productivity, the Lot for Lot rule can be switched on.

Figure II.5 shows an MRP II report using this rule. Its application is very simple. For every requirement, there is an order planned for the same quantity.

Figure II.5 Lot for Lot

Period	1	2	3	4	5	6	7	8	9	10	11	12
Gross Reqmts	40	60	70	80	65	45	35	15	0	30	60	100
Planned Orders	40	60	70	80	65	45	35	15	0	30	60	100
Beginning Inventory	40	60	70	80	65	45	35	15	0	30	60	100
Ending Inventory	0	0	0	0	0	0	0	0	0	0	0	0
Average Inventory	20	30	35	40	33	23	18	8	0	15	30	50

The great advantage of this lot sizing rule is that it results in a zero inventory at the end of each planning period, and will give the lowest average inventory compared to the other rules.

This would result in daily lot sizes if you have your MRP II system working with daily time periods.

A minor advantage is that this rule has no complicated mathematics or computer logic associated with its use.

LEAST UNIT COST

The least unit cost lot size rule relies on a reiterative process. It takes the first quantity from MRP II's calculated demand array, tests it as a lot size by and analyzing the resulting unit cost (order cost + carrying cost ÷ lot size). It repeats the process for the first two quantities, then for the first three quantities, until it finds the lowest unit cost. The total demand for those consecutive periods is the recommended lot size. Then it repeats the reiterative process starting with the next series of demands. It repeats the process, order by order, to the end of the MRP II planning horizon.

Figure II.6 shows an MRP II planning report that used this lot sizing rule, and Figure II.7 shows the details of the calculations that yielded the lot sizes.

This formula tries to minimize unit cost. It recognizes lumpiness and leaves no remainders at the end of each lot. In this example, ending inventory fell to zero in periods 3, 5, 8, 9, and 12.

Figure II.6 Least Unit Cost

Period	1	2	3	4	5	6	7	8	9	10	11	12
Gross Reqmts	40	60	70	80	65	45	35	15	0	30	60	100
Planned Orders	170			145		95				190		
Beginning Inventory	170	130	70	145	65	95	50	15	0	190	160	100
Ending Inventory	130	70	0	65	0	50	15	0	0	160	100	0
Average Inventory	150	100	35	105	33	73	33	8	0	175	130	50

Figure II.7 Calculation of Lot Sizes in Figure II.6

Setup cost = $56.25, carrying cost = $0.25/unit/period

Period	Net Reqmnts	Periods in Inv	Trial Lot Size	Carrying Cost This Lot	Cumul. Carrying Cost	Carrying Cost per Unit	Setup Cost per Unit	Total Unit Cost
1	40	.5	40	$ 5.00	$ 5.00	$.13	$1.41	$1.54
2	60	1.5	100	22.50	27.50	.28	.56	.84
**3	70	2.5	170	43.75	71.25	.42	.33	.75
4	80	3.5	250	70.00	141.25	.57	.23	.80
4	80	.5	80	10.00	10.00	.13	.70	.83
**5	65	1.5	145	24.38	34.38	.24	.39	.63
6	45	2.5	190	28.13	62.51	.33	.30	.63
7	35	3.5	225	30.63	93.14	.42	.25	.67
6	45	.5	45	5.63	5.63	.13	1.25	1.38
7	35	1.5	80	13.13	18.75	.23	.70	.93
8	15	2.5	95	9.38	28.13	.30	.59	.89
**9	0	3.5	95	0	28.13	.30	.59	.89
10	30	4.5	125	33.75	61.88	.50	.45	.95
10	30	.5	30	3.75	3.75	.13	1.88	2.01
11	60	1.5	90	22.50	26.25	.29	.63	.94
**12	100	2.5	190	62.50	88.75	.47	.30	.77

** Recommended

LEAST TOTAL COST

The least total cost formula works on the proposition that when the order cost and the accumulated carrying costs are equal, the total cost is minimized. This is similar to the basis for the EOQ formula. See the EOQ formula graph, Figure II.2, for an illustration of this condition.

The least total cost formula is a reiterative process, working on the requirements computed by MRP II. It takes the first requirement as a trial lot size, and calculates its total carrying cost. It compares the carrying cost with the order cost. Then it takes the first two requirements as a lot size and analyzes its total carrying cost, again comparing it to the order cost. Then it takes the first three requirements and repeats the process. It selects as the recommended lot size the one that gives total carrying cost closest to the order cost.

Figure II.8 illustrates an MRP II planning schedule using this rule. Because least total cost recognizes planned orders and their schedules, it will leave no remainders at the end of the lot. There is zero inventory at the end of periods 3, 6, 10, and 12.

Figure II.9 shows the calculations supporting the schedule in Figure II.8. Notice that total carrying cost most closely equals the setup cost of $56.25 in periods 3, 6, 10, and 12.

Figure II.8　Least Total Cost

Period	1	2	3	4	5	6	7	8	9	10	11	12
Gross Reqmts	40	60	70	80	65	45	35	15	0	30	60	100
Planned Orders	170			190			80				160	
Beginning Inventory	170	130	70	190	110	45	80	45	30	30	160	100
Ending Inventory	130	70	0	110	45	0	45	30	30	0	100	0
Average Inventory	150	100	35	150	78	23	63	38	30	15	130	50

THE PART PERIOD BALANCING FORMULA

The part period balancing formula is the same as least total cost. However, it does have an enhancement feature, called look-ahead and look-back. With this feature, after a lot size has been calculated, the system looks ahead to the next demands, and backwards to previous demands, and may re-evaluate the current lot size recommendation. This is useful when an item has very erratic demands, interspersed with low or zero demands. The

Figure II.9 Calculation of Lot Sizes in Figure II.8

Order Cost = 56.25, Carrying Cost = $.25/unit/period

Period	Net Reqmnts	Periods in Inv	Trial Lot Size	Carrying Cost This Lot	Cumul. Carrying Cost
1	40	.5	40	$ 5.00	$ 5.00
2	60	1.5	100	22.50	27.50
**3	70	2.5	170	43.75	71.25
4	80	.5	60	10.00	10.00
5	65	1.5	145	24.30	34.38
**6	45	2.5	190	28.13	62.51
7	35	.5	35	4.38	4.38
8	15	1.5	50	5.62	10.00
9	0	2.5	50	0	10.00
**10	30	3.5	80	26.25	36.25
11	60	4.5	140	67.50	103.75
11	60	.5	60	7.50	7.50
**12	100	1.5	160	37.50	45.00

** Recommended

look-ahead, look-back feature examines to see if a nearby demand will become isolated amid several periods of no demand. If so, the isolated one is incorporated into another iteration of the analysis to decide if it is more economical to include or to exclude this isolated demand in the current lot. This is the only lot sizing formula discussed in this section that analyzes the mutual relationships between two or more adjacent recommended lots. All the others examine the future demands, recommends a lot size and moves on to the next series of demands.

OTHER LOT SIZING FORMULAS

There are a fair number of much more sophisticated lot sizing formulas, usually discussed on university campuses. The most famous of these is the Wagner-Whitin algorithm. It is reputed to do the best job of optimizing order cost and carrying cost. However, it is so complicated and opaque, that it is almost never used routinely in any company. It does, however, provide a valuable way to validate other, more straightforward rules, for teaching, and to stimulate thought and discussion.

There are several others available, and the *Production and Inventory Management Quarterly Journal*, published by the American Production and Inventory Control Society, in Falls Church, VA, publishes a continuing stream of variations on this theme.

LOT SIZE MODIFIERS

For some selected items you may need to use lot size modifiers. The first modifier is for a minimum quantity, either in terms of days or units. Even in an extensive JIT environment, there will continue to be situations where it is not reasonable to order less than a certain minimum.

The second modifier is for a maximum quantity, either days or units. Although the emphasis on smaller lot sizes is eroding this issue, even in a JIT environment, there still may be heavy or bulky items that never should be ordered over a certain quantity.

The third modifier is for multiples. This is to solve the 55-gallon drum situation. No matter what the lot size rule suggests, you must order in increments of 55 gallons. This also often applies to pails, bags, and tankers. Moreover, some manufacturing operations involve vats, vessels, and kettles that must be filled up in order for the process to work correctly. Your MRP II software could feature these modifiers.

HOW TO CHOOSE THE RIGHT FORMULA

In a computerized system, particularly an MRP II-based one, each item on the system must be given a lot size rule by its planner. All commercial software products have several to choose from, but perhaps not all of them. These software products will either force the planner to designate a lot size rule when adding a new item to the file, or will default to one rule, usually Lot for Lot.

Independent demand items only qualify for the Fixed Order Quantity or the EOQ rule, because all the others depend on analyzing future demands from an MRP II schedule. Independent demands are outside of MRP II. Between the two, the EOQ formula is by far the better, because it tries to recognize the balance between order cost and carrying cost. Fixed Order Quantity tends to be set by whim and usually is five to ten times larger than the lot size calculated by the EOQ formula.

For dependent demand items, avoid Fixed Order Quantity and EOQ. Dependent demand items are all of those in your bills of material; those planned by MRP II. This is by far the larger category.

The whims surrounding Fixed Order Quantity have no place in a world-class system, and the EOQ formula, although making an attempt to balance order cost with carrying cost, has no way to adjust for future demands being planned by MRP II. Because it assumes straight line usage, it is powerless to deal with erratic, lumpy demands, and almost always will leave a remainder at the end of a lot.

In an MRP II-based system, Lot for Lot is clearly the best choice, because it schedules one order per planning period. But you must already have significantly reduced order costs to qualify for this rule.

This rule also results in zero inventory at the end of each planning period, which makes it the favorite for JIT applications. If you are on a daily scheduling system, Lot for Lot will schedule daily increments to be consumed that day. This will give you zero stockroom inventory for those items where this rule is applied.

The next best choices are Least Total Cost and Least Unit Cost, which do a good job of balancing order cost with carrying cost, by analyzing the up-coming demands calculated by MRP II. Period Order Quantity does not do this, making it the poorest choice.

Part Period Balancing with the look-forward and look-backward feature should be selected only for items that exhibit erratic demands interspersed with no demands. This will avoid having a lot size just for an isolated quantity. However, because this rule takes somewhat more computer time, it should be selected only when appropriate.

All but Fixed Order Quantity and EOQ will result in zero inventory at the end of each lot, leaving no remainders. This is important to keep inventory investment as low as possible, and to reduce exposure to obsolescence due to product phase-out or engineering changes.

Selecting an appropriate lot sizing rule, occasionally in conjunction with a modifier, will result in almost all orders recommended by MRP II making sense, and will minimize manual intervention from the planner.

BEWARE OF NERVOUSNESS

Except for Fixed Order Quantity, and EOQ, all these lot sizing rules can re-calculate all recommended lot sizes with every MRP II run. Many companies are running MRP II every night, which could lead to slight or even large changes to the recommended orders and their timing every day. This is called nervousness. This problem gets worse deeper into the bills of material, and are especially evident in purchasing, at the end of the chain. If your master production schedule is changed in the near term, you are very likely to have a nervous system.

There are several defenses against nervousness. The first one is to make sure that your master production schedule is professionally-managed and has integrity. Make your lead times as short as possible, establish time fences in your master schedule to match, and make sure that these time fences are respected. If lead times are sufficiently short, an event that would fall into the nervous zone falls outside of that lead time fence and becomes routine.

The second defense is to emphasize shallow bills of material, which reduce the number of planned orders and reduces lead time.

The third defense against nervousness is to have your MRP II process respect firmed orders. In this environment, as soon as the planner accepts the lot size and due date recommendation by firming an order, MRP II should not change either quantity or due date without permission from the planner.

The fourth defense against nervousness is to invoke filters, which some commercial software products provide. These filters introduce extra rules for MRP II to use when recalculating lot sizes and due dates. These filters can govern what changes are tolerable inside of lead time, and also can exclude trivial changes throughout.

Appendix III

HOW TO MANAGE SAFETY STOCKS

Safety stock is a buffer against problems. Recognizing this, safety stock presents fertile territory for the JIT ideal of constant improvement.

Before the advent of MRP II-based systems, the reorder point/safety stock (ROP) method of inventory control was used extensively. MRP II took over managing the components in your bills of material, and eliminated ROP for most items used in manufacturing. These items are usually referred to as dependent demand items. Current thinking says that you should not have safety stock for dependent demand items. Rather, you should concentrate on making your MRP II system work correctly, and avoid covering up inadequate performance with safety stock. If you need safety stock, you should use it sparingly, on an item-by-item basis, either at the end item, master schedule level or at the purchased component level, but not for manufactured piece parts, components, sub-assemblies, and intermediates.

Regarding end items, if your manufacturing throughput time is fast enough to satisfy the customer, even if you do have a manufacturing upset, you may be able to recover by manufacturing another batch rather than relying on safety stock.

Independent demand items, such as service parts, maintenance, and repair parts are appropriate places to use safety stock.

WHY HAVE SAFETY STOCK?

Manufacturing is a very complex activity, and events often to not adhere to the best of plans. Safety stock is added to inventory to protect you from stock outs caused by these imperfections, anomalies, and upsets. The most common sources of such problems are:

- Forecast error

- Vendor off schedule

- Vendor short quantity

- Factory off schedule

- Factory short quantity

- Unplanned machine down

- Quality fallout, especially random

SAFETY STOCK TO COVER FORECAST ERROR

There are some simple statistical tools that can help you calculate quite accurately how much safety stock you need to cover your historical forecast error. These techniques apply only to items that are forecast, or which are under reorder point control. This excludes low-level, purchased items, planned by your MRP II system.

In this context you have two types of forecast. The first is a conventional forecast, which takes past history and attempts to extrapolate from that into the coming future. There are many, good techniques for this which are discussed in Appendix V.

The second type of forecast is the one implicit in the logic of the reorder point technique, discussed in Appendix I. The implied forecast is the rate of consumption used to establish the reorder point. This simple forecast uses historical demand during lead time (+ safety stock). The historical demand is usually expressed in units per week or day.

The statistical method employed to develop a correct safety stock level relies on the well-known idea of standard deviation. If your actual demand varies only slightly from your forecast, you don't need much safety stock to cover. If your actual demand varies greatly around the forecast, you need more safety to cover these aberrations.

Calculating Control Factors

Figure III.1 displays a twelve-week forecast for an item on reorder point, and the weeks' actual sales. Also shown are the individual deviations (errors) of the forecast, and those deviations squared. These factors are needed to calculate the Mean Absolute Deviation (MAD) and the Standard Deviation (σ). These two calculations are shown at the bottom of Figure III.1.

Using MAD and σ

MAD and σ are two similar ways to measure the historical inaccuracy, (deviation, or error) of the forecast Of the two, σ is somewhat more accurate, but MAD is easier to calculate. If the data have a normal distribution, they correlate very closely, and σ usually equals MAD multiplied by 1.25, as is shown at the bottom of Figure III.1.

Calculating the Safety Stock

Calculating safety stock requires a statistical analysis of historical deviation from the forecast. Figure III.1 shows an example of a part being managed by the ROP method. As usual there is a deviation between actual sales and the forecast. In this case the deviations are not very wild, which means that a modest safety stock will buffer us against the deviations we are experiencing.

To calculate the required safety stock first requires a management decision on how high customer service we want to provide. Will we be satisfied with 90 percent coverage of stronger sales demand, or do we want 95 percent? By using either MAD or σ, for this specific item, we can calculate exactly how much safety stock is needed.

Using this example where MAD = 38 units, if you want 90 percent of incoming customer orders covered by inventory, by looking at Figure III.2, you need 1.6 MADs of safety stock. Therefore, safety stock = 1.6 × 38 = 61 units. If your management decides to have 95 percent coverage, Figure III.2 shows that this requires 2.06 MADs; 2.06 × 38 = 78 units of safety stock. 99% coverage will require 2.91 MADs, or 110 units. 99.99 percent coverage would require 5 MADs, or 190 units. In this manner, you can calculate a safety stock to cover any pattern of forecast error, for any independent demand item you choose to maintain inventory for.

Figure III.1 Calculating Control Factors
for an Independent Demand Item

Wk.	Forecast Sales	Actual Sales	Devia-tion	D²*	RSFE**	TS***
1	500	450	-50	2,500	-50	1.3
2	500	400	-100	10,000	-150	3.9
3	500	550	+50	2,500	-100	2.6
4	500	525	+25	625	-75	2.0
5	500	550	+50	2,500	-25	.7
6	500	525	+25	625	0	0
7	500	525	+25	625	+25	.7
8	550	500	-50	2,500	-25	.7
9	600	575	-25	625	-50	1.3
10	600	600	0	0	-50	1.3
11	600	650	+50	2,500	0	0
12	600	600	0	0	0	0
Total	6,450	6,450	450****	25,000		

* D² = Deviation Squared.
** RSFE = Running Sum of the Forecast Error
*** TS = Tracking Signal
**** Ignoring Sign
Mean Absolute Deviation (MAD) = 450 ÷ 12 = 37.5
Standard Deviation (σ):

$$\sigma = \sqrt{\frac{\Sigma D^2}{n}} = \sqrt{\frac{25,000}{12}} = \sqrt{2,083.33} = 45.64$$

MAD x 1.25 ≈ σ; 37.5 x 1.25 = 46.9

Figure III.2 Safety Factors
for Calculating Safety Stock

Service Level	Safety Factor Using MAD	Safety Factor Using σ
50.00	0.00	0.00
75.00	0.84	0.67
80.00	1.05	0.84
84.13	1.25	1.00
85.00	1.30	1.04
89.44	1.56	1.25
90.00	1.60	1.28
93.32	1.88	1.50
94.00	1.95	1.56
94.52	2.00	1.60
95.00	2.06	1.65
96.00	2.19	1.75
97.00	2.35	1.88
97.72	2.50	2.00
98.00	2.56	2.05
98.61	2.75	2.20
99.00	2.91	2.33
99.18	3.00	2.40
99.38	3.13	2.50
99.50	3.20	2.57
99.60	3.31	2.65
99.70	3.44	2.75
99.80	3.60	2.88
99.86	3.75	3.00
99.90	3.85	3.09
99.93	4.00	3.20
99.99	5.00	4.00
100.00	∞	∞

Notice that the increase in safety stock at ever-higher levels of coverage is geometric, not linear. Figure III.3 shows a graph of safety factors vs coverage. As desired service level gets into the high 90s, safety stock needed to cover grows geometrically. At 100 percent coverage, safety stock would need to be infinity.

By applying a reasonable inventory carrying cost, you can easily calculate the cost associated with whatever level of coverage you desire, and management will have facts to work with when deciding on how much coverage to have.

How to Monitor Forecast Validity

In the calculation above, the actual rate of usage was fairly close to its forecast. The safety stock we calculated depends on the continued accuracy of that forecast. However, because circumstances change, the forecasted rate could gradually become inaccurate over time.

The Tracking Signal is the way to monitor the continuing accuracy of the forecast. Figure III.1 shows the Running Sum of the Forecast Error (RSFE) and the Tracking Signal (TS). The RSFE shows the cumulative error between forecast and actual. The Tracking Signal is RSFE ÷ MAD.

Figure III.3 Safety Factor vs. Service Level

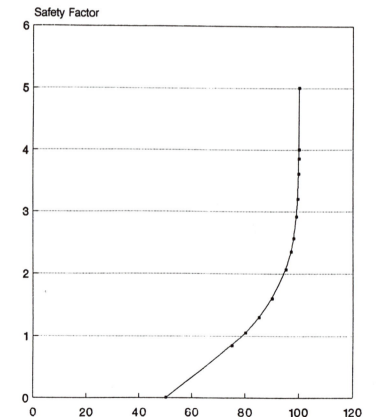

The bigger the TS, the worse the deviation of actual from forecast. The toleration limit for the TS is set between four and eight. A low number is less tolerant and a high one more so. You might choose a low number with an item of high value, one that merits close supervision, and a high TS limit for low value ones. A volatile product that historically exhibits erratic swings could be given a larger TS limit, where a stable product a low one.

When the TS exceeds its assigned tolerance, a planner should be signaled to examine the situation. Usually, the demand pattern of the item has changed, requiring a new forecasted rate of consumption.

In the example of Figure III.1, only one reading comes close to being out of tolerance, that of week two, with its tracking signal of 3.9. All the other weeks' readings show the situation proceeding nicely according to plan.

SAFETY STOCK TO COVER OTHER PROBLEMS

You may need to use safety stock to cover other problems such as poor schedule adherence, unplanned down time, short quantities, and quality fallout.

Determining the Safety Stock Level for Other Problems

Unlike setting safety stock to cover forecast error, there are no Standard Deviations and MADs, nor safety factors to help the planner set safety stock at the proper level to cover these problems. The planner is left to exercise judgement. In such an environment, the tendency is to designate too much safety stock. It is, after all, much more visible and therefore painful to be out of stock on an item than to have too much safety stock on it. As a matter of fact, most companies don't measure planners' performance regarding too much safety stock, while many have elaborate monitoring and measuring techniques regarding stock outs. Especially if tied to your compensation program, this situation can lead to large excess inventory.

Monitoring Correct Individual Safety Stock

If you have your reorder point and safety stock system computerized, there is a way to measure how much safety stock is enough to cover. Take a representative time span, and subtract the high value and low value of safety stock during the period, which will give a more appropriate safety stock. This is illustrated in Figure III.4.

Figure III.4 shows a typical situation. Safety stock is set at 75 and the reorder point is 175 units. Reorder point is usage during leadtime (100) plus safety stock (75). The high safety stock remains at 75 during the 12 week study, and the low was 65. The difference is 10 units, which becomes the new safety stock.

Figure III.5 shows the same example using 10 for safety stock and 110 for the reorder point. Ten seems to be adequate, with period nine being the only one with a low ending inventory.

In the first example, average inventory for the 12 week period (excluding the 175 ending inventory from week 0) was 160, while that of the second example was 85, a 47 percent reduction with no degradation of service level!

Figure III.4   Safety Stock Study Before Adjustment

Lot Size: 150
Lead Time: 2 Weeks
Consumption Rate: 50 per Week
Safety Stock: 75
Re-Order Point (ROP): 175

Week	Sales	Receipt	Ending Inv	ROP ?
0			175	
1	45	150	280	
2	45		235	
3	50		185	
4	45		140	ROP
5	50		90	
6	55	150	185	
7	60		125	ROP
8	60		65	
9	60	150	155	ROP
10	55		100	
11	50	150	200	
12	40		160	ROP
Avg			160	

Highest Safety Stock: 75
Lowest Safety Stock: <u>65</u>
Recommended SS   10

Figure III.5 Safety Stock Study After Adjustment

Lot Size: 150
Lead Time: 2 Weeks
Consumption Rate: 50 per Week
Safety Stock: 10
Re-Order Point (ROP): 110

Week	Sales	Receipt	Ending Inv	ROP ?
0			175	
1	45		130	
2	45		85	ROP
3	50		35	
4	45	150	140	
5	50		90	ROP
6	55		35	
7	60	150	125	
8	60		65	ROP
9	60	150	5	
10	55	150	100	ROP
11	50		50	
12	40	150	160	
Avg			85	

Monitoring Correct Aggregate Safety Stock

Since all safety stock is used to cover a deficiency of some sort, and since inventory is very expensive to own, you should have a permanent procedure to monitor the use of safety stock. This procedure should include investigation into causes and their eradication.

With a computerized system at your disposal, periodically the inventory control department should have a report prepared showing dollar value of safety stock levels assigned to all items. This list should be in descending order by safety stock level. This puts the worst offenders at the top of the list. The planners should choose the top 20 percent for investigation and improvement. Gradually, causes of safety stock will be eliminated, or at least recognized as being intractable.

Appendix IV

HOW TO DO AN ABC ANALYSIS

The idea behind an ABC analysis is to segregate the important few from the trivial many. In a manufacturing company, inventory is often analyzed this way.

WHAT IS AN ABC ANALYSIS?

The ABC concept was developed by Viflredo Pareto (1848–1923), a Swiss economist and sociologist. He noticed that a few very wealthy people controlled a big fraction of the wealth. Thus was born the graduated income tax.

Applied to manufacturing inventory, we always see the pattern shown in Figure IV.1. The top ten percent of your items usually account for 65 percent of the dollars spent on inventory items. The bottom 70 percent only account for 10 percent of your expenditures.

CALCULATING AN ABC ANALYSIS

You can do an ABC analysis fairly easily, especially if you have a computerized inventory system. Simply multiply the annual usage by the standard cost. Then sort the result in descending dollar value. In the listing, show the cumulative dollar value, the percent of items, and percent of the total dollar value for each line item. Figure IV.2 is an example using 1,000 items.

In Figure IV.2 you can see that the top 100 items, 10 percent of the total, account for 64.1 percent of the year's total expenditure. These we designate as A items. The next 20 percent, 250 more items (350 items and 35 percent total), account for 25% more of the dollars, for a total of 90 percent to this point. Finally the bottom ranking 650 items only account for 10 percent of the dollars spent on inventory.

USING AN ABC ANALYSIS

In an MRP II environment, there are only a few reasons to apply the ABC principle, because MRP II's logic eliminates the need to segregate items by importance. MRP II makes it easy to manage all inventory with equal intensity.

Cycle counting interval is the main remaining use for an ABC analysis. Many companies will count their A-items once every month or two, their B-items quarterly, and their C-items once or twice a year.

Lacking a mathematically-based procedure, some companies determine lot sizes based on the ABC ranking of the items. A-items would be purchased weekly, B-items monthly, and C-items six months at a time. This method of determining lot sizes, also is widely used for independent items being managed by the reorder point method.

Some companies put C-items into floor stock, some put C-items on automatic issue, and some do both.

Accounting systems often have designated C-items as expensed items. Under this procedure, C-items are expensed to cost of goods sold in the accounting period they are received in. A and B items only are booked into inventory and incrementally issued. This eliminates the tedious recording of frequent stocking and issuing transactions for C-items, which account for 70 percent of your total population.

Figure IV.1 Typical ABC Distribution Pattern

Class	% of Total Items	% of Total $
A	10	65
B	20	25
C	70	10

Figure IV.2 ABC Analysis

Line No.	Part No.	Unit cost	Annual Usage	Annual Usage Value	Cumulative Usage Value	% Total Value	% Total Items
1	691811	281.22	366	102807.47	102807.47	2.6	0.1
2	996751	943.16	82	77138.68	179946.15	4.6	0.2
3	970555	17.65	4204	74206.21	254152.36	6.4	0.3
4	949693	492.88	144	70923.07	325075.43	8.2	0.4
5	456249	15.98	4242	67777.27	392852.70	9.9	0.5
6	990316	390.39	161	63008.90	455861.59	11.5	0.6
7	812156	39.82	1546	61548.56	517410.16	13.1	0.7
8	255191	42.38	1368	57970.91	575381.07	14.6	0.8
9	693796	150.62	366	55156.90	630537.97	16.0	0.9
10	960086	370.93	145	53649.17	684187.14	17.3	1.0
11	651650	13.84	3711	51381.83	735568.98	18.6	1.1
12	380511	19.90	2542	50592.41	786161.38	19.9	1.2
13	131045	13.53	3428	46373.91	832535.29	21.1	1.3
14	266090	113.84	404	45941.56	878476.85	22.2	1.4
15	457386	105.54	409	43196.94	921673.79	23.3	1.5
16	882142	338.07	121	40954.56	962628.35	24.4	1.6
17	724684	304.26	123	37563.37	1000191.71	25.3	1.7

Figure IV.2, *continued*

.							
.							
.							
97	753695	60.01	152	9139.00	2507947.54	63.5	9.7
98	659196	10.21	885	9040.34	2516987.88	63.7	9.8
99	886724	90.09	99	8950.87	2525938.75	63.9	9.9
100	449063	72.92	122	8871.97	2534810.73	64.1	10.0
101	21654	13.03	678	8831.54	2543642.27	64.4	10.1
102	712892	45.70	193	8828.79	2552471.06	64.6	10.2
103	782041	24.16	365	8819.99	2561291.04	64.8	10.3
.							
.							
.							
298	616340	19.15	119	2275.76	3451435.60	87.3	29.8
299	452661	8.44	269	2268.66	3453704.26	87.4	29.9
300	729316	31.63	72	2264.68	3455968.94	87.4	30.0
301	780371	5.97	377	2253.76	3458222.71	87.5	30.1
302	720635	10.94	203	2218.10	3460440.81	87.6	30.2
303	685729	7.58	292	2216.18	3462657.00	87.6	30.3
.							
.							

Figure IV.2, *continued*

348	986699	9.17	206	1891.08	3554205.76	89.9	34.8
349	285579	32.37	58	1867.96	3556073.73	90.0	34.9
350	724774	43.29	43	1859.25	3557932.97	90.0	35.0
351	295393	26.12	70	1839.56	3559772.53	90.1	35.1
352	615875	14.89	123	1834.61	3561607.15	90.1	35.2
.							
.							
.							
992	92040	0.05	25	1.25	3952050.17	100.0	99.2
993	841350	0.04	27	1.08	3952051.25	100.0	99.3
994	653091	1.20	1	1.20	3952052.44	100.0	99.4
995	563470	3.58	0	0.00	3952052.44	100.0	99.5
996	5630	5.27	0	0.00	3952052.44	100.0	99.6
997	344575	17.30	0	0.00	3952052.44	100.0	99.7
998	153708	0.08	0	0.00	3952052.44	100.0	99.8
999	946731	1.37	0	0.00	3952052.44	100.0	99.9
1000	984059	0.72	0	0.00	3952052.44	100.0	100.0

Appendix V

FORECASTING

Why do you need a forecast? Why not just wait for the orders to arrive and make what the customers order? Or even better, make some of every item listed in the product catalog and have plenty of each on hand! You can't sell from an empty wagon, right? Wrong!

Today's competitive, global markets do not allow for either of these alternatives. Customers are unwilling to wait for what they want so a you must reduce lead times by anticipating customer needs. Yet, you cannot afford the luxury of bulging finished goods warehouses. Most companies simply do not have the cash you would need to carry such an inventory, and inventory carrying costs would eat up your profits.

Moreover, competitive lead time is but one of your issues. Future planning for facilities, for financial budgeting, for product development, and for anticipating change are each good and necessary reasons to develop forecasts.

HOW TO PREPARE A FORECAST

I am approaching this topic under the assumption that you can have computer software available to assist in calculating any forecasts that are developed. To me this is a more than reasonable assumption because a wide selection of software programs are available at what I consider to be reasonable prices. And computer power is widely available. Forecasting is a highly computational and reiterative process for which a manual system is wholly unsuited.

The steps in preparing a forecast include the following:

1. Collect and analyze available data.

2. Select a forecasting method.

3. Generate the base forecast.

4. Make adjustments and overrides.

Collect and Analyze Available Data

Starting with your demand history files you will need to clean up your data. You usually will have software tools to help you. Cleaning up requires purging data which is outside normal limits, correcting data entry errors, and reconstructing missing data.

Some seemingly ongoing products will come up with missing data because they carry new model codes and have lost the linkage to prior demand history. However, your software should have procedures for mapping these relationships and for synthesizing the appropriate demand history. Some of your products will have missing data simply because they are too new. In these instances there are methods for linking to another product's history on the assumption it applies. This provides an otherwise similar, but new, product with the necessary history on which to base a projection.

Also, be sure to capture your customers' original requested due dates, not just your promises. Even if you hit your promises, forecasting on this could perpetuate dissatisfaction among your customers, if you frequently promise a later date than they request.

Select a Forecasting Method

Here's where the software starts to really pay off. Because of the speed and power of most computers, the easiest way to identify the best forecasting method is to run it over and over and choose the one that would have been the most accurate. It is possible to do this in the past, so to speak, by using past history and generating a forecast that can be compared to actual results that are already in the data base.

Many forecasting software products will decompose your demand history into its seasonal, trend, and random components. Again, this is a computer application. Three years of history usually are required to establish the indices for random, seasonality and trend. Computing these indices for every item and for every month is simply too daunting to be processed manually, even if you use a simple technique.

Generate the Base Forecast

Generating the base forecast now becomes a fairly routine process after having made the previous selection and having cleaned up all the baseline data by purging the outliers, by correcting erroneous and missing data, and by linking new products to appropriate existing data.

Make Adjustments and Overrides

Who makes these adjustments and why they are made is well described later on. Instead, I want to describe the use of "pyramids of aggregation" which is how the software accommodates revisions and overrides. Here's an example.

Assume the company develops the usual forecast first in detail by stockkeeping unit, then by product, next by product group, finally rolled up to a grand total. Figure V.1 shows the Forecast Aggregation Pyramid.

Figure V.1 Forecast Aggregation Pyramid

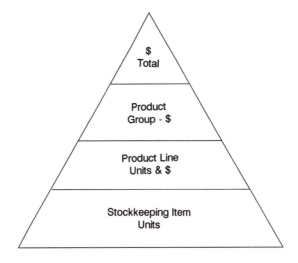

The software behind this pyramid will allow management to enter, say, a 5 percent across the board increase and it will be rolled down and reflected in all other levels. Meanwhile, a manager can adjust a particular product line and modify only that portion of the forecast and have those changes, too, reflected in the overall forecast again at all levels.

Most commercial forecasting software products accommodate two or more pyramids simultaneously which allows for another one constructed from the same basic data but by geographical region so that special modifications can be reflected for certain locations. Note, also, the software handles the conversion from units to dollars at the appropriate level.

This process of overriding is called "forcing" and it allows for forcing in either direction, up or down the pyramid.

WHAT YOU SHOULD FORECAST

Rule: Forecast all independent demand; do not forecast any dependent demand.

Even though you clearly know what products you sell, it is not always obvious what your company should be forecasting. A make-to-stock manufacturer will not forecast the same way a make-to-order manufacturer will forecast. A make-to-stock manufacturer will want to forecast finished goods sales. But, it will be more appropriate for an assemble-to-order manufacturer to forecast the major sub-assemblies and a make-to-order company will focus more on the forecasting of critical resources. To all these forecasts must be added the demand for service and repair parts. In summary, then:

If:	Forecast
Make to stock,	Finished Goods and Service Parts
Assemble to order,	Sub-Assemblies and Common Parts
Make to order,	Resource Usage and Raw Materials

APPROACHES TO FORECASTING

There are four general approaches to forecasting:

1. Qualitative—subjective estimates of new products' sales and trends

2. Mathematical—projections based on actual, historical sales data

3. Correlative—using outside data as a basis for projections

4. Integrated/Proactive—a process which integrates sales, marketing and operations efforts

Each of the above approaches is capable of making a distinct contribution to the corporate process of planning resources and facilities, and estimating customer demand for products and services. Which approach to use and when to use it is best determined by considering the purpose of the forecast and the life cycle phase of the product or service being forecasted. How to select the proper forecasting technique is discussed in more detail later on in this section of the appendix.

Within each of the four approaches to forecasting there are specific techniques and variations:

Qualitative

Delphi
Market research/Consumer survey
Management estimate/Judgmental
Historical analogy

Mathematical

Averages
Exponential smoothing
Seasonality and trend
Curve fitting

Correlative

Econometric models
External indices

Integrated/Proactive

FORECASTING TECHNIQUES DEFINED

Qualitative

• *Delphi.* The Delphi approach to forecasting is a variation on a panel of experts. The experts, kept apart, go through several assessment rounds. There are several ways to implement this approach, but most commonly they follow a similar scenario. A neutral facilitator reviews the iterations, questions the extreme projections and, later, shares the results with all participants. Then the participants alter their projections if they want to. The process repeats until there are no more changes. This technique is the most appropriate for long range projections of innovative new products and services. It is not useful for anything involving high volume.

• *Market Research/Consumer Survey.* I include all forms of inquiry under this category. That is, sales force estimates, consumer panels, mail and telemarketing questionnaires, test marketing and opinion surveys.

• *Management Estimate.* This is the simplest approach to forecasting. It relies on some person to provide a forecast based on their experience and knowledge of markets and products. More commonly, it pertains to management's estimate of, say, next year's sales volume compared to this year's based on management's view of the economy and the competitive situation.

• *Judgmental.* I call this a straightforward management decision. An executive with the authority to do so steps in and directs what future action to take. If this is done during the initial phase of a product's life cycle. The decision is usually whether to commit or withhold resources to the new product. During the final phase, the decision can be whether to enhance the product and thereby extend its life, whether to invoke some other end of life strategy, or to simply terminate the product.

• *Historical Analogy.* Historical analogy is normally used in one of two ways. One way is to base a new product's forecast on the actual sales history of a similar product. A variation of this is to use indices of previous sales experience to predict current trends. For example, a catalog sales company may know from past experience that the orders received in the first three weeks represent 18 percent of expected annual sales.

Mathematical [1]

Mathematics-based forecasting methods usually work with three years of your data. They analyze the past and attempt to predict the future from it. There are many techniques, going from quite simple to very complex. There are a number of good commercial software products available which will use several techniques at once, and pick the best fit to use for your forecast.

The most common mathematics-based forecasting methods, from simple to complex, are:

■ Simple Moving Average

---

[1] Much of this material on mathematical forecasting is adapted from literature provided by Walonick Associates, Minneapolis, MN.

- Single Exponential Smoothing

- Double Exponential Smoothing

- Holt's Two-Parameter Smoothing

- Harrison's Harmonic Smoothing

- Brown's Quadratic Exponential Smoothing

- Winter's Seasonal Smoothing

- Robust Decomposition

- Census X-11 Decomposition

- Regression Trend Analysis

- Multiple Regression Analysis

- Generalized Adaptive Filtering

- Box-Jenkins Analysis

• *Simple Moving Average.* The simple moving average is a good method to use with non-seasonal data; when the data are relatively stationary and unchanging. With this technique, a historical average is calculated and used to project the future. The simple moving average is easy to use and understand. It is best suited for short and intermediate term forecasts when the data has high randomness.

• *Single Exponential Smoothing.* This is a popular technique when the data are nonseasonal and the average level of the data remains steady over a long period of time; stationary data or data with slow growth or decline. As the name implies, forecasts for the next period are based on exponentially decreasing weighted past values. That is, past values are less important than the most recent values in calculating a forecast. This method will smooth the data in a decreasing exponential manner, through the use of a smoothing constant (α). The smoothing constant governs how heavy the weight should be from the most recent past vs from the distant past. The larger the smoothing constant the heavier the weight is for recent periods.

The formula for using exponential smoothing is:
New forecast = $(1-\alpha)$ * Old forecast + (α * Actual demand),
where α, the smoothing constant, is a value between .1 and .9.

For example: If   Old forecast = 500
                         Actual sales = 575
                         α   = .5

       Then   New forecast = (1-.5) * 500 + (.5 * 575)
                                       = .5 * 500 + 287.50
                                       = 250 + 287.50
                                       = 53

This formula will tell you how broad a moving average is for a given smoothing constant:

$$\alpha = \frac{2}{N+1}$$

A three-month moving average is the rough equivalent of a smoothing constant of .5 and .1 is the equivalent of a moving average of nineteen months. The larger the alpha factor the greater the impact of the most recent demand on the new forecast.

- *Double Exponential Smoothing.* The double exponential smoothing technique is appropriate for nonseasonal data when the average level of the data increases or decreases linearly with time, especially when the data exhibits significant and rapid linear trend. The only difference from single exponential smoothing is that it introduces an additional formula that estimates trend. Double exponential smoothing is the same as single exponential smoothing done twice, first on the raw data then again on the smoothed data. The technique can provide excellent short and intermediate term forecasts.

- *Holt's Two-Parameter Smoothing.* Two-parameter smoothing is similar to double exponential smoothing except that it smooths the trend values directly using two smoothing constants. One of the smoothing constants is used to smooth the trend component and the other is used to minimize randomness. By applying two separate smoothing constants, it is possible to produce more accurate forecasts than if only one were used. Like double exponential smoothing, it is appropriate for nonseasonal data that contains a linear trend.

- *Harrison's Harmonic Smoothing.* This technique is useful for data that has a linear trend and an additional seasonal component: seasonality superimposed on trend. This technique represents seasonality by combinations of sine and cosine trigonometric functions.

● *Brown's Quadratic Exponential Smoothing.* Quadratic or triple exponential smoothing, is used for nonseasonal data that has an underlying quadratic trend pattern. Quadratic exponential smoothing is based on the same principle as single and double exponential smoothing, except that the formula for a parabola is introduced into the equations. This makes it possible for quadratic smoothing to accurately forecast turning points in your data.

● *Winter's Additive and Multiplicative Seasonal Smoothing.* Some exponential forecasting methods do not work well when your data shows seasonal patterns. Winter's seasonal smoothing may be used when your data contains seasonality. The basic technique involves the use of three smoothing constants, for randomness, seasonality, and trend. Traditionally, Winter's technique has been difficult to use because of the large number of possible combinations for the three smoothing constants. However, since computer power has become abundant and cheap, this technique now is feasible in many applications.

● *Robust Decomposition.* This technique is used to decompose raw data into trend, seasonal, and random components. The method itself uses robust (resistant) smoothing techniques. The Bell Laboratories (SABL) method of decomposition makes use of a resistant filter so the smoothing operation will not be unduly affected by a small number of outliers. The robust decomposition technique allows different magnitudes of smoothing and a variety of data transformations. It may be used with monthly or quarterly data with additive or multiplicative seasonality.

● *Census X-11 Decomposition.* This decomposition method may be used with monthly or quarterly data containing multiplicative seasonality. It involves a combination of averaging procedures to reduce the effect of outliers. The main objective, like robust decomposition, is to separate the data into trend, seasonal, and random components.

● *Regression Trend Analysis.* This method is simply an ordinary least-squares regression using time as the independent variable. There are several formulas that can be used to find the best linear or nonlinear fit for your data. You can even smooth the data before applying the transformation. Outliers can be filtered out in order to avoid warping the results. Regression analysis is used for medium and long term forecasting of nonseasonal or seasonally adjusted data.

● *Multiple Regression Analysis.* Multiple regression analysis may be used to determine the importance of several independent variables, such as leading indicators, to predict the value of a dependent variable. Running a multiple regression will result in an equation that then may be used to predict the future values of the dependent variable. This multivariate technique is best used for intermediate and long term forecasts.

● *Generalized Adaptive Filtering.* This method uses a linear filtering technique to produce excellent short term forecasts for a large range of seasonal and trend time series. This method falls into a class of techniques called "Autoregressive Integrated Moving Averages" (ARIMA). The basic technique involves the continual refinement of the forecasts until all the forecast errors have been reduced to randomness. This is one of the most flexible forecasting techniques because an appropriate model can be fitted to almost any set of data.

● *Box-Jenkins Analysis.* This method is one of the best immediate and short term forecasting techniques. Like generalized adaptive filtering, it provides a wide range of possible models and a strategy for selecting an appropriate one. Its method is also similar to generalized adaptive filtering except that it provides tighter mathematical models capable of establishing confidence limits for the forecasts.

Moving averages and simple exponential smoothing can often be done with spreadsheet software on a personal computer. The more complex techniques will require special computer software. There are a number of good commercial products on the market to help you with your forecasting.

The better commercial products will provide tools to help you clean up your data. But more important, these products usually contain a wide range of forecasting methods and apply all of them to your data. Then the software automatically selects the one that best fits your specific data and uses it to make your forecast. This process is repeated with each forecasting cycle.

So if your environment changes, you would automatically be switched over to a better formula.

Correlative

● *Econometric Models.* Most of these models are quite complex involving at times a hundred or more equations which describe the interrelationships of the market-competitive-economic environment. This approach is usually employed only in large governmental or economic research agencies.

● *External Indices.* Published data such as the leading economic indicators, new housing starts, consumer confidence, employment, machine tool orders, etc. can sometimes be correlated to your product forecasts. An obvious example is to use new housing starts to project sales of appliances, furniture, and building supplies. The National Bureau of Economic Research publishes some of the best leading and lagging indicators monthly in its *Survey of Current Business.*

Integrated/Proactive

This technique differs from the others in that it is more of an integrated functional process whose primary goal is to insure that you achieve your forecasts, and that all areas of the corporation can communicate their activities and work together. That means, for example, that if the sales of your type 77 Widget are forecasted to be 12,000 units during the coming year, then everyone having anything to do with the sales, marketing, promotion, development, and production of these widgets, including upper management, gears up to make certain those sales do occur.

What's so special about that? Isn't that what these departments are supposed to do? Well, yes, but often a sales department will make specific product forecasts at the beginning of the year and then become distracted with other matters and not follow through. Maybe one or two sales reps leave during the year and coverage lapses. Or a particular sales region may have no assigned representative from the start. These gaps almost certainly mean that the expected sales will not occur as planned in the affected sales territories. It is left to manufacturing to track the deviations and to adjust production accordingly up or down as the numbers dictate.

The integrated, proactive process requires that manufacturing not be left to go it alone; that all functions in the company which influence product sales begin each year with all the resources in place or planned to be in place on the dates required. For instance:

- *Sales.* Every territory must be staffed with capable personnel whose commission structure supports the overall sales plan. A sales plan to sell one item and commissions which encourage the sale of a different item must be brought into agreement.

- *Marketing and Promotion.* The literature, trade shows, and special promotions must all support the sales plan. Feature changes and price changes which can have a big impact on sales outcomes must likewise be coordinated with the rest of the company's goals. Often companies forecast sales of one product while marketing develops plans to promote another.

- *Product Development.* Planned releases of new products must occur on schedule. Strong and disciplined project management is required to ensure schedule adherence.

- *Production.* Must have the skilled employees, equipment, and other resources that are necessary to meet the production plan. Master scheduling and materials planning systems must be in place to respond quickly to the day by day deviations in demand.

- *Administration.* The order entry process must be customer-focused and able to provide reliable promise dates, able to confirm and accept orders quickly and effortlessly, and able to update records immediately so that any of the related functions have the information they need in order to respond appropriately.

I call this approach *Forecasting II* to connote the inclusion of an integrated feedback loop within this process. Figure V.2 shows an Integrated Feedback Loop. The ability to feed back all changes as they occur and to react to them quickly is the essence of this technique.

HOW TO SELECT THE RIGHT FORECASTING TECHNIQUE

The selection of an appropriate forecasting technique depends upon two factors:

1. The purpose of the forecast

2. Which phase of the product life cycle is being forecasted

Figure V.2 Integrated Feedback Loop

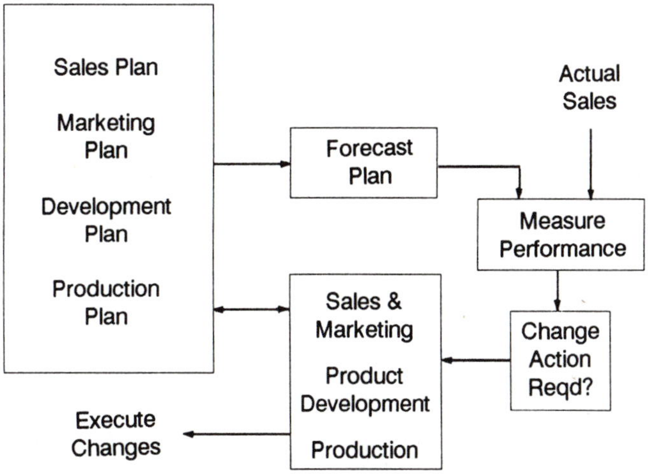

Purpose of the Forecast

Forecasts are used for many purposes, ranging from long to short range. You need a forecast to help you plan:

- New product sales
- Service parts requirements
- Aggregate sales and inventory planning
- Production materials planning
- Production capacity management
- Plant and equipment expansion planning
- And many others

Figure V.3 relates forecasting techniques to purposes and time frames.

Corporate Planning

In the long range time frame you are looking for aggregate sales estimates from which to derive resource requirements. Any need which would demand additional facilities would have to be anticipated far enough in advance to properly carry out site selection, building design, obtain capital expenditure financing, to specify and order major items of production equipment, and to plan and select personnel to meet organizational needs.

Figure V.3 Selecting a Technique Based on Purpose

Purpose:	Corporate Planning	New Product Marketing	Operations
Time Frame	Long: 3-5 yrs by qtrs of yrs	Medium: 2 yrs by mo or qtrs	Short: 1 yr by wk or mo
Technique	Qualitative Correlation	Qualitative	Mathematical Proactive
Source	Externally Published Data	Market Research	Demand History

Corporate plans will show sales in dollars by division or major product line. Critical equipment resources and total work force requirements will be stated in hours. The data on which these plans are made come from very high level sources. The primary source is the strategic corporate plan which specifies the direction the company is pursuing. This is modified by economic projections derived from external agencies such as the National Conference Board, the views of certain preferred economists, trade associations and their predictions of trends within the particular industry which they serve, consultants, competitive data regarding other companies in the same market, and the status of research projects within the company. The Delphi method is well suited to projections of long range trends.

Such information will be used to estimate the total market in units and dollars, the company's market share and any factors which will effect a change in that share percentage, and projections of the rate the market is increasing. And while much of this is in the form of numbers and percentages, the overall approach is generally qualitative and rests to a large degree upon opinion and experienced judgment.

New Product Marketing

The medium time frame is devoted to new product planning and development. I am not including here the basic research and development time where scientists seek out new technologies, but rather the time to design and bring reasonably defined products to market. Here the facilities, equipment, and personnel must be identified as in place, or planned and approved, so that sales will not be constrained by a lack of resources.

The data supporting these plans is derived from a combination of known technological feasibility and perceived customer needs as identified by market research. This is both a costly process and a high risk activity. A right decision on product strategy can bring great rewards and a wrong one could result in large losses. Where the products are new but within existing product lines historical analogy can be utilized effectively to forecast future sales.

Operations

Within the time frame dictated by operations and materials planning the forecasting techniques are nearly always mathematical with some modification by sales management where they have specific knowledge of an event that will directly affect customer demands. Such an event could be a promotion, the loss of an important customer, or a general override to the forecast due to a new market trend. Proactive measures come into play in order to make the forecast happen as planned. Regardless, the operations forecast will be specific; it will be stated in monthly and weekly requirements, and it will be the production plan.

PRODUCT LIFE CYCLE

Beyond the research and development phase, all products experience three additional phases during their normal life cycle in the marketplace. These three phases are start-up, stable demand, and decline. Figure V.4 shows a typical product life cycle. Knowing which phase a product is in, is an important first step toward the selection of an appropriate forecasting technique. Figure V.5 relates a forecasting technique for each phase.

● *Initial Start-up.* During the initial start-up period the big problem is the lack of any history on which to base projections. This situation usually means someone must venture an estimate based on their "feel" which may be augmented by market studies and customer surveys. Often a new product can be seen to resemble closely another product in terms of customer profile and sales expectations. In this case, the demand history for the other product can be used as a basis for forecasting, a practice known as historical analogy.

● *Stable Demand.* When the product has reached some level of sales stability, mathematical approaches can come into play and computer software can be employed to analyze and project sales into the future. Mathematical approaches are particularly appropriate when there are numerous items to forecast which are high volume but low impact and, therefore, cannot justify individual attention.

Figure V.4 Typical Product Life Cycle

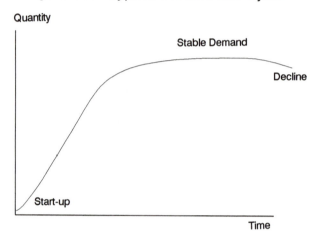

Figure V.5 Suggested Forecasting Techniques

Life Cycle Phase	Initial Start-up	Stable Demand	Decline
Technique	Qualitative-Historical Analogy	Mathematical	Qualitative-Judgmental

If, however, a significant number of changes are planned for the product then the forecast will require some modification based upon the judgement of the product managers.

One important aspect of this approach is to track the cumulative forecast error as well as the forecast itself.

● *Decline.* When the product is in decline, the forecasters are once again on their own judgment as they were in the earlier growth phase.

SERVICE PARTS

Any organization that desires to establish a repair or service operation must forecast the demand for repair parts. Considerably more information is available than for the typical new product startup. First of all, there is usually an identifiable installed base of potential customers. Next, out of that data base the age of each piece of equipment can be determined. From that a relationship between the equipment to be serviced and the required service parts can be derived.

A first step, in addition to the information described above, is to acquire the following information:

● *Component Parts List.* You can use your records of field tests, actual failure experience, or engineering estimates of expected mean time between failure (MTBF) to develop the service component parts list. Figure V.6 shows how the service life cycle lags behind the product life cycle.

In order to forecast repair parts needs more accurately it would be desirable to know the actual rate of usage of each piece of equipment in the data base. A reliable estimate of customer usage rates can be obtained by inquiring of each customer or by asking your own service engineers or sales account representatives to provide an estimate.

Figure V.6 Service Life Cycle

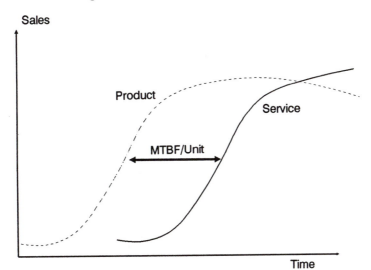

FORECAST ACCURACY

Experienced forecasters understand that all forecasts are more or less inaccurate. This means you should monitor your forecast accuracy to maintain its integrity and credibility. Forecasting accuracy can be improved through the use of various measures of forecast error and, especially, demand filters and tracking signals.

Measures of Forecast Error

In order to understand some of the statistical concepts behind the measurement of forecast error an understanding of the "normal distribution curve" is appropriate. I'll start by describing what is so normal about the normal distribution curve.

The Normal Distribution Curve

The concept of the normal distribution curve is this: Even the best, well maintained process does not produce the same output time after time. A machining process will vary due to differences in materials, cutting tools, wear, speed, power, temperature, etc. Similarly, in forecasting sales, the rate of customer demand varies. Statistical theory provides a mathematical basis for analyzing the dispersion of the data. Figure V.7 shows a typical Normal Distribution Curve.

Figure V.7 The Normal Distribution Curve

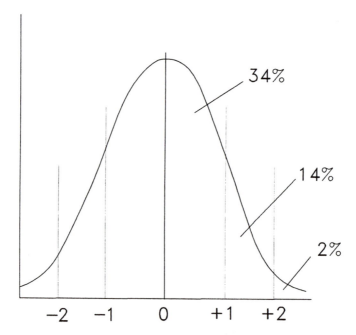

The vertical lines divide the normal curve into sections referred to as "standard deviations", or sigma(s), where one standard deviation takes in 34 percent of the data under the curve and two standard deviations takes in 48 percent. Plus or minus two standard. deviations, therefore, account for 96 percent of all the data.

Think of the forecast as the average drawn through the center of the curve and the curve itself as enclosing a plot of actual sales.

Measures of Forecast Error:

Cumulative Sum of Errors

$$\sum (F - A)$$

Bias

$$\frac{\sum (F - A)}{N}$$

Mean Absolute Deviation

$$\frac{\sum |F - A|}{N}$$

Standard Deviation

$$\sqrt{\frac{\sum (F - A)^2}{N}}$$

Where: F is the forecast for each period
A is the actual demand for each period
N is the number of periods

A few words about these measures: Bias indicates the average cumulative error or general tendency of the forecast. A persistent bias is remedied by a judgmental change in the forecast. Mean absolute deviation is a shortcut method of measuring data dispersion and is simpler to calculate than the standard deviation in that it avoids the square root computation. But the standard deviation is more precise and is preferred for such applications as the computation of safety stock. The two can be roughly related by multiplying the MAD by 1.25.

Demand Filters

Demand filters refer to any steps taken to purge erroneous and extraordinary data from the demand history. Some of the data that is flagged is not erroneous but is sufficiently extraordinary to be excluded for the purpose of future forecasts. For example, it is best to exclude a large one-time order that is not expected to recur. Initial forecast parameters should be set to flag data which exceeds three standard deviations. This will allow you to identify most of the errors which reside in the demand history data base.

Tracking Signals

Error tracking signals are established to indicate when the forecasting technique should be re-evaluated in light of the accumulated error history.

The most common error tracking signal is the ratio between the cumulative error and the mean absolute deviation. Generally any ratio greater than 4 indicates the method of forecasting needs to be reviewed. Figure V.8 shows an analysis of a tracking signal.

After ten periods, the forecast is tracking well within the limit of ±4.

CONCLUSION

- In modern manufacturing, independent demand items need to be forecast, whereas planning dependent demand items long since has been taken over by MRP II-based techniques.

- To implement a new forecasting system, you must first collect and clean up your historical demand data. Modern forecasting techniques analyze your demand history and project into the future based on the analysis.

- Most techniques require three years of data to work well, although some commercial software products will estimate missing data.

- After you have captured and corrected your data you will select a forecasting method to use.

Figure V.8 Analysis of Tracking Signal

Period	Forecast	Sales	Deviation	Absolute Deviation
1	1000	900	+100	100
2	1000	1000	0	0
3	1000	1100	-100	100
4	1000	800	+200	200
5	1000	700	+300	300
6	1000	900	+100	100
7	1000	1200	-200	200
8	1000	1400	-400	400
9	1000	1200	-200	200
10	1000	1000	0	0
Totals	10,000	10,200	-200	1600

Cumulative sum of error: -200
Mean Absolute Deviation: 1600 ÷ 10 = 160
Tracking Signal: -200/160 = -1.25

● Methods such as asking opinions from salespersons, customers, and managers can be useful for long-range planning and capital investment.

● Correlating your business to outside factors such as housing starts or family formations also serve for strategic planning. However when you need specific sales forecasts for end items or narrow families of end items, you probably will want to use one or more of the mathematics-based procedures.

● Simple and smoothed moving averages can work if you don't have pronounced seasonality. You could develop these forecasts on a personal computer spreadsheet. However, if your data contain trend and seasonality as well as random variations, you will be better served by using one of the more exotic forecasting models. There are a wide variety of them available. But they are much too complicated to be done by hand or by spreadsheet.

• To take advantage of these advanced techniques, you will need to select commercial software. Many of them are available at attractive prices. The better ones will analyze your data using several techniques and select the best one to use.

INDEX